PIRANESI AND THE MODERN AGE

THE MIT PRESS
Cambridge, Massachusetts / London, England

Piranesi and the Modern Age

Victor Plahte Tschudi

To Stephan
for the conversations we could have had

PRELUDE

In the late 1940s Anton Koolhaas and his wife returned home from vacation in Rome bringing with them Piranesi's etching of the Forum of Nerva (*see pages 278–279*). In remembering this precise moment—and exact etching—sixty years later, their son Rem joins a long history of Piranesi recollections. It was an "amazing image," Rem Koolhaas says, recalling being struck in particular by its vision of a classical colonnade sunk into the ground.[1]

Two hundred years earlier Johann Wolfgang von Goethe had also evoked the prints acquired by his parents, remembering how as a boy he would stand in the hallway looking at engraved views of Rome made by "one of the predecessors of Piranesi ... [t]hese objects impressed themselves on my memory."[2] Over time, Goethe would add several Piranesi engravings to his own private print collection, which would become one of the largest in Germany.[3]

For more than two centuries, the etchings of the Italian printmaker, architect, and antiquarian Giovanni Battista Piranesi (1720–1778) have maintained a firm grip on the Western imagination. Once seen, Piranesi's prints of architecture seem to draw the spectator into a world they can never completely escape. The majority of the compositions conjure the ancient world. But, as this book aims to show, Piranesi's crumbling ruins, complex geometries, and infinite views have also triggered attempts to inscribe within them a world that is very modern.

PIRANESIAN MODERN

Piranesi and the Modern Age charts the complex appropriation of Piranesi in literature, photography, art, film, architecture in the period after 1900. For more than one hundred years interpretations of Piranesi have served to legitimize forms, theories, technologies, and movements that are in fact quite new. And what has driven Piranesi's modern comeback—or series of comebacks—is not the unearthing of new prints, but rather the discovery of new dimensions that seem to reside within them. One field after the other has fallen under the spell of the eminent etcher, as if his oeuvre were a slowly turning kaleidoscope reflecting our own rapidly changing realities. For all the modern age's calculated and insistent efforts to formulate the new, the impossible, the limitless, and the contradictory—to cross into novel forms of expression—it always seems as if Piranesi got there first. Therefore, to claim that the modern age rediscovered Piranesi is only partly true, since Piranesi also helped to formulate that age precisely as modern.

Although Piranesi has no doubt inspired authors, artists, and architects in the recent past, he has been equally important for historians and curators who have (re)constructed that past in books and exhibitions. For example, in 1936 the

Museum of Modern Art in New York (MOMA) mounted two groundbreaking exhibitions in which prints by Piranesi were placed adjacent to cubist and surrealist works, producing a double effect; the prints anchored a new art form in history (even if it is unlikely that Piranesi actually inspired the works on display), while cubist art in turn made Piranesi's works seem proto-modernist. The radical update transformed him from an eighteenth-century printmaker into a twentieth-century avant-garde artist—a role he never really has lost. Consequently, this book is conceived not just as a history of Piranesi's influence, but as a history of that history, shedding light on the idea of influence as such and the conditions that enable notions of influence to form.

This study is long overdue and yet it is easy to understand why it has not been written before, as it necessitates excursions into vastly different fields, ignoring the limitations scholars prudently and rightly impose on their research in the knowledge that each of these disciplines requires a lifetime of learning and insight. Only a charlatan would embark on this project without the deepest humility. Yet the diversity of topics in a certain sense reflects the multiple roles of Piranesi himself. He was a student of stage design, an archaeologist of Roman antiquity, and the author of texts on architectural theory and history. He was the etcher who signed his plates "*architetto*," and the architect who constructed buildings as if they were etched; his renovation of the church of Santa Maria del Priorato on the Aventine hill in Rome (1764–1766) is a case in point.[4] Inversely, Piranesi's volumes of prints were themselves architectonic projects. As Marcia Reeds observes: "For him, a book was a building type, whose pages opened up like rooms along a paper corridor."[5] As an entrepreneur and marketer he was "modern" in his own right, energetically orchestrating the production and distribution of his volumes of prints.[6]

On another level, the modern interest in Piranesi derives from ambiguities perceived within the representations themselves—ambiguities between ruin and wholeness, light and shadow, confinement and endlessness, homogeneous and disjointed space, figurative and abstract forms. These and other conflicting elements recognized in the prints have helped pioneers—from Kahn to Koolhaas, from De Quincey to Disney—to formulate a language of instability, disruption, alteration, and transgression and to voice ideas ranging from existential anxiety to social liberation. References to Piranesi, whether implicit or explicit, unequivocally relay the suggestion that the reality we perceive contains a shadowy counterpart, or that it is in its entirety a projection of our own psyche. The blurring of distinctions between the inner and the outer worlds, and the disorientation that results from that blurring, capture the Piranesian modern in its essence.

The meaning of "modern" is potentially open to endless debate, and a single definition of the notion is in any case perhaps chimeric, especially in a cross-disciplinary study like this one. This investigation, therefore, is not based on preconceived definitions of what "modern" might be. Rather, it lets Piranesi's art function as a sieve through which such definitions might be filtered, allowing new or nuanced meanings of the notion to form.

But one denominator can be established. Insisting on an age being "modern" implies that it is forged in opposition to one that is perceived as "old." A rejection of what came before has arguably been an impetus shared by artists across disciplines for the last hundred years, and Piranesi was invoked precisely in the attempts to disengage the new from the old. As photography, painting, film, and architecture united as "modern" in their effort to break with the past, these disciplines, paradoxically, found a precursor for such a break with Piranesi. His architectural experiments always overstepped the past and, in the eyes of the moderns, displayed an eternal present; they became the historical source for an age that pretended it had no historical sources. Piranesi's art foreshadows qualities that made the modern "new" and as such questions its very newness, complicating the notion of its origin.

The modern period, as I have chosen to see it, largely coincides with modernism, the movement pervading art and architecture between 1920 and 1960. It is no surprise, then, that modernist pioneers like Le Corbusier and Picasso figure in the discussion alongside historians of modernist art, architecture, and literature. But acknowledging Piranesi's importance also means allowing established categories to corrode. Following in his trail soon leads to a terrain of reactions *against* modernism and to contradictions and counterforces within modernism itself. Piranesi is never stuck in one place for long, but slips between different roles, and prevails as a perpetually subversive force, summoned to advance disruption *per se*. Historicism, modernism, postmodernism, conceptualism—isms born as reactions to one other—all evoke Piranesi as if his prints herald *change* no matter what. "Piranesi" reinterpreted points to a history of discontinuity and instability which starts in the nineteenth century and continues to this day. The reintroduction of Piranesi in the modern age, then, also means the introduction of an alternative modern, on which this book aims to shed light.

Ultimately, the book is about time and the notion of it that allowed Piranesi to be included among the moderns. The temporal loops and dialectical history which underscore the exhibitions, films, and literature under discussion challenge conventional chronology. Piranesi's work figures in presentations that defy linear history and the idea of progress cultivated since the Enlightenment. Indeed, pioneers of modernism unite in the effort to establish the "eternal" validity of the movement by lifting it out of time, to exempt it from being anything that "moves" at all, and make it timeless. Arguably, a timeless modern embraces all of history; it permits prefigurations in the past and also invites Piranesi to inhabit the present. Put differently, the kind of modern that allowed Piranesi to be inscribed into its narrative understood itself as non-temporal, as an extended present—a hyper-now of sorts. Within the lofty superstructure of timelessness, Piranesi was as much at home in the twentieth century as in the eighteenth.

HISTORIES OF PIRANESI AND THE MODERN AGE

The chapters proceed in a thematic order from literature, photography, and art to film, architecture, and urbanism. This order, however, also follows a chronology that corresponds to when, roughly, Piranesi's impact on each of these areas peaked. In other words, the interest in his art did not affect all disciplines simultaneously, but infiltrated one after the other, manifesting a historiographically interesting succession that suggests how the weight of media somehow shifts throughout the twentieth and twenty-first centuries.

Chapter one asks how Piranesi's series of disturbing prison interiors, the *Carceri*, managed to became metaphors of the mind in genres ranging from poetry to psychoanalysis. Tracing the genesis for that translation to the English nineteenth-century author Thomas De Quincey, it shows how the literary appropriation of Piranesi provided analogies for new poetic sensibilities, letting architecture coincide with anxiety. Thus, a conception of the mind that is particularly modern seemed to nestle within Piranesi's ambiguous interiors.[7] The inner world is not a modern discovery, of course, but the intense and systematic charting of it arguably is. Of that intangible domain—whether identified as the nineteenth-century "soul" or the twentieth-century "unconscious"—Piranesi became the architect.

From around 1900 Piranesi's art was interpreted through a new medium, namely photography. Judged through the lens of an art of which he himself had no knowledge, the verdict was far from favorable, as chapter two shows. Authors at the time found Piranesi's compositions marred by excessive contrasts, as if he had miscalculated the exposure. Nonetheless, photography depended on Piranesi, and not only for the vantage points on Rome broadcast in his panoramas. The technique and effects of etching paradoxically helped photographers attain a singularity of expression and autonomy for their art. Ultimately, Piranesi's virtuoso handling of graphic techniques promoted etching as a mode of cognition with repercussions in the histories of print, architecture, and, indeed, history itself.

No study so far has attempted to dissect systematically the associations Piranesi often evokes in modern art. Chapter three explores the notion of Piranesi's alleged abstraction, tracing the origin of that idea to two pivotal exhibitions in New York in 1936, curated by Alfred H. Barr. Remarkably, the difference between cubism and surrealism came to hinge on the contrasting editions of one and the same *Carceri* plate. The chapter also traces the popularization, or parody even, of cubist Piranesi in the late 1940s. Piranesi as Picasso was a trope that infiltrated scholarship and introduced "ambiguity" as one of the main characteristics of the Venetian's art.

The idea of *montage* is central in Piranesi's relevance to modern cinema. Chapter four delves into the theory and application of montage in the writings and films of Russian filmmaker Sergei Eisenstein and investigates how he reinvented Piranesi as a progenitor for his own innovative film language. The chapter also sheds light on the role of Piranesi in the effort to profile film as an art with esteemed antecedents, so as to provide it with a history matching the other visual arts. One might even say that cinematography historicized its own technology by inventing a cinematic Piranesi.

Chapter five adopts an explicit historiographic perspective and traces Piranesi as a subversive force in the retelling of modernist architecture. Reconsidering the historiography of modern architecture from the 1920s to the 1970s, it becomes clear how Piranesi's art infused the very structuring of that history. Le Corbusier was able to celebrate the supremacy of simple forms only by first "removing" the historicist veneer that seemingly obscured them—a strategy also apparent in his ambiguous relation to Piranesi's prints. In turn the histories of modern architecture advanced by Henry-Russell Hitchcock and Sigfried Giedion were countered by Vincent Scully, who proposed Piranesi as point of origin for that architecture, thereby admitting contradiction as a force inherent in modernism itself.

Chapter six brings the discussion up to our own times. Here I ask how and why a single image—Piranesi's plan of Rome from *Campo Marzio*—infiltrated the discourse on architecture after modernism to the extent that it did. More precisely, I argue that the revival of the plan triggered, and in fact partly caused, a rift between postmodernism, which looked to the past for motifs, and a new formalism, which discerned in the plan a design methodology. In other words, the chapter traces the shift of focus from the plan's archaeology to its geometry. The chapter is long, but interviews I have conducted with central architects, including Peter Eisenman, Bernard Tschumi, Steven Holl, and Rem Koolhaas, provide important testimonials and establish the instrumentality of the plan in a strand of conceptual architecture.

The coda returns to the Piranesian *descent* introduced in chapter one, but recaptures it in an updated manifestation. Despite the ostentatious modernity of the modern metro system, with its tracks, lifts, and escalators, literature repeatedly measures the subway against the subterranean labyrinths conceived by the Venetian. A refocus on this underground world as fundamentally Piranesian also redefines its inhabitants, or its commuters, as seemingly confined in the light of his visions to an architecture of endless halls.

The themes in this book can also be presented differently. As much as it is true that the rediscovery of Piranesi happened in a sequence, it also happened in clusters—in sudden cross-disciplinary bursts of interest—which points to the wider political and cultural context for the revival of his work. For example, between 1910 and 1918 texts on Piranesi were published in London (Arthur Samuel), Turin (Federico Hermanin), Leipzig (Albert Giesecke), Paris (Henri Focillon), and New York (William M. Ivins) all embarking on the mission to redeem a neglected artist. The emancipation of Piranesi—the etcher—from the cobweb of Romantic projections corresponds to a general modernist approach. The "purity" identified in his work, even in widely complex compositions such as the *Carceri*, shows the attempt to usher Piranesi into the modern age.

The 1930s emphasized the "transgressive" Piranesi evident in Henri Focillon's *The Life of Forms in Art* (*Vie des formes*) (1934); in the two MOMA exhibitions figuring Piranesi (1936–1937), and in Rudolf Wittkower's reappraisal of Piranesi as an architectural theorist (1938).[8] These works helped to recreate Piranesi as a figure who transcended any specific period, preparing him for a role as a perpetual contemporary, as it were.

The late 1940s marked an extraordinarily rich revival of "dystopian" Piranesi across continents and disciplines—in film, fiction, and art. Essays by Sergei Eisenstein (1946–1947) and Aldous Huxley (1949) both evoked a sense of violence and fragmentation in the *Carceri* series.[9] The vast, desolate underworlds of Piranesi echoed in other works in these years too, from Jorge Luis Borges's short story "The Immortal" (1947) to Carol Reed's noir, *The Third Man*, set in the sewers of Vienna (1949). I argue that, on the one hand, the reason for the late 1940s resurgence is that Piranesi's fragmented and disconcerting prison series no longer seemed imagined, but real, capturing the devastation of World War II in images expressing turmoil and upheaval. On the other hand, a sophisticated concept plays out in the examples mentioned above, namely that special kind of entrapment that only the infinite suggests. A seemingly endless expanse frozen in a maze of subterranean vaults and gangways helped authors and artists formulate an existential anguish, allegorized in different ways.

The late 1950s aimed to chart and integrate a "contradictory" Piranesi in various disciplines. A standpoint in psychology and psychoanalysis unites attempts to establish connections either between Piranesi's mind and his art, as in Marguerite Yourcenar's celebrated essay, *The Dark Brain of Piranesi* (*Le cerveau noir de Piranèse*) (1959–1961), or between the mind of the beholder and Piranesi, as in Ernst Gombrich's *Art and Illusion* (1960). Ulya Vogt-Göknil, in her study on Piranesi's *Carceri* (1958), unveiled structural contradictions in the *Carceri* series. These had always been sensed, of course, but they were previously expressed mostly in poetic terms.[10] Now, Vogt-Göknil's meticulous diagrams unmasked with unequivocal clarity a deliberately impossible architecture, laying bare the "deconstructivist" tendencies in the old Venetian. The triumph of "contradictory" Piranesi led Vincent Scully to place the origin for a dynamic modern architecture in the *Carceri*; Piranesi's non-functional and psychologically charged architecture obviously represented an antithesis to a rational and monolithic modernism. Guy Debord and the Situationists proposed a way forward with reference to the same prints.[11]

In the 1970s debate about the future of architecture, opposing factions claimed Piranesi as an ally. Whereas architects such as Aldo Rossi and Leon Krier valued Piranesi as a historical source and included his works in collages that can be called postmodern, a "conceptual" Piranesi appealed to Peter Eisenman, Stanley Allen, and Rem Koolhaas, who took an interest in the discrepancy—the fruitful non-relation—between Roman antiquity and Piranesi's inventive representations of it. In a post-1968 climate, the battle over Piranesi as antiquarian or avant-garde was in reality a battle over the idea of history as such, evidenced by the heated discussion between Italian historian Manfredo Tafuri and his contemporaries.

The years between 2005 and 2015 saw the publication of multiple monographs, anthologies, and exhibition catalogues on Piranesi, for example by Lola Kantor-Kazovsky (2006), Joseph Connors (2011), John Pinto (2012), and Heather Hyde Minor (2015).[12] These have recovered the historical figure of Piranesi, his activities and milieu. In parallel, however, Piranesi has emerged as a prophet of a new urbanism, inspiring meditations on the modern city addressed in texts and projects by Rem Koolhaas, Pier Vittorio Aureli (2011–2012), and Gijs Wallis de Vries (2014).[13]

Finally, in the run-up to Piranesi's tercentenary, the materiality of his legacy has come into focus. In reconsidering the copper, the paper, the books, scholars are presenting history in its most tangible form. I like to think that Piranesi's renown, too, can be broken down into concrete components and treated almost as tangibles. To the extent that a material turn in history can also embrace ideas, this book contributes to such a history.

The history unfolding in the succeeding chapters also ties to specific prints. Over the years, Piranesi's more than a thousand etchings have been classified in multiple catalogues raisonnés, which have placed his drawings and prints in chronological sequences.[14] This book places them in an altogether different order. From the perspective of the modern age, and over the course of a hundred years or so, it seems as if a torchlight has passed over the oeuvre and lit up one portion—even one composition—at a time, as orientations have shifted and sensibilities changed.

Admittedly, not all of Piranesi's prints have spoken to posterity with equal immediacy. In the early twentieth century, writers caught in the afterglow of the Grand Tour cherished Piranesi's views of Rome—squares, streets, palaces, ruins—published in volumes such as *Vedute di Roma* (late 1740s onwards), *Le antichità romane* (1756), and *Della magnificenza ed architettura de' romani* (1761). Although Piranesi often exaggerated the effect of buildings in these views by the means he had at his disposal as an etcher, they nonetheless showed recognizable sites and anchored him in a tradition of *vedutisti*. The views of Rome, then, define Piranesi's role as a sophisticated historian, but not as an avant-garde artist.

There is a world of difference between buildings that are merely exaggerated and ones that are wholly invented. Piranesi's images of structures that were neither real nor even possible belong to an interpretative domain to which progressive moderns could connect without fear of being backward. It would be pointless to conceal the fact that the modern fascination with Piranesi centers on two hallucinatory works: the series of imagined prisons, the *Carceri* (1749–1750 and 1761), presented in chapter one, and the great plan of Rome from *Il Campo Marzio dell'antica Roma* (1762), presented in chapter six.[15] Although Roman architecture always is a point of departure, these works escape the specifics of time and place. In them, Piranesi drew up a willfully uncertain realm positioned somewhere between a vanished past and an unbuilt future. A modern age that insistently sought to break new ground recognized in these designs the very images of transgression.

In contrast to Piranesi's views of Rome, the *Carceri* do not portray anywhere real, but, on the contrary, they came to symbolize a disintegration of reality as such—outer as well as inner. Their experimental form and unsettling content arguably entwined with two main accomplishments of the modern age—abstract art and psychoanalysis—prefiguring both in a powerful amalgamation. Interestingly, it was less the series as such than the fact that it came in two very unlike editions that sparked the modern interest in the *Carceri*.[16] The awareness that different editions of the *Carceri* existed at all was voiced surprisingly late and originates with the tight liaison between scholars and collectors around 1900. More precisely, the discovery connects to the monograph on Piranesi authored by

Arthur Samuel and published in 1910 with the London firm of B. T. Batsford. While preparing the book for publication, Herbert Batsford himself discovered a set of the rare first edition of the *Carceri*, which revealed to him the difference between this and the darker and denser second edition (just in time for Samuel to include illustrations from both editions in his book). It was a discovery print historian Arthur Hind immediately endorsed and a difference modern pioneers would repeatedly invoke to highlight opposing qualities at work in modernist histories of prints, art, and film, as we shall see.[17]

On an even more minute level, we shall encounter a modern history hinged not only on a shift of interest from one *Carceri* edition to the next but also on a shift from one specific print to another. For example, whereas publications and exhibitions in the 1930s preferred the tightly composed *The Drawbridge* (plate VII), the preference after World War II changed to the more dramatic and fragmented *The Gothic Arch* (plate XIV), which arguably spoke more directly to a civilization traumatized by war, as we shall see in chapters three and four.[18]

In summation, prints of architecture, editions of those prints, and even single plates of those editions emerge as precise graphic constituents that underscore the movements and concepts of the modern age.

MULTI-DIMENSIONAL SPACES

Piranesi and the Modern Age does not present Piranesi in the context of his own time and adds little to what we already know about his biography and catalogue of works. The book treats his oeuvre in a far from systematic fashion and excludes large portions of it from consideration, including most of his drawings, texts, and designs for chimneypieces, candelabra, furniture, and other objects. Moreover, only a fraction of Piranesi's prints—his richest legacy—figure in the chapters that follow. In short, rather than a study of a historical figure, this is a book about an ahistorical Piranesi—a character reinvented in the modern age to legitimize that age precisely as modern.

The succession of chapters reveal how Piranesi helped formulate modern notions like "the unconscious" in literature (chapter one), "contrast" in photography (chapter two), "abstraction" in painting (chapter three), and "montage" in cinema (chapter four)—qualities in part projected onto Piranesi's vision and to some extent inconceivable without him.

The book also points to other and less distinct notions that reveal the deep level on which Piranesi operated throughout the twentieth and twenty-first centuries. For example, beholders of the *Carceri*, across disciplines and periods, have noted the paradox that an architecture of enclosed walls nonetheless seems to extend without limits. This unsettling mix of freedom and confinement arguably captures a modern existential condition. It suggests a self-imposed imprisonment—an imprisonment of the mind—more than one imposed by the surroundings. Piranesian "prisons of infinity" reverberate in texts and projects that range from Freud to Foucault, from Kafka to Koolhaas. "[E]ven where the enclosure is more or less complete," Aldous Huxley wrote in 1949 with reference to the *Carceri*, "this colossal pointlessness goes on indefinitely, and is co-extensive with the universe."[19] Twenty years later Manfredo Tafuri would sum up his discussion of Piranesi's *Carceri* on a similar note, writing that "the prison, precisely because infinite, coincides with the space of human existence."[20] The point that these two authors make is unequivocal: in spite of Piranesi's many apparent exits there is simply no way out. The architecture extends in time and space to the point of embracing the observer no matter where or *when* they exist. Boundlessness and timelessness are thus the true building blocks in Piranesi's airy prisons.

Another notion is the one I have chosen to call the "Piranesi Pivot," which I identify as a trope that structures narratives in literature and film, with examples ranging from Théophile Gautier's travel account *Voyage en Espagne* (*Travels in Spain*) (1845) to Denis Villeneuve's film *Blade Runner 2049* (2017). The Piranesi Pivot often takes the form of a descent or the image of a stairway. The occurrence is symbolic. Happening about midway through a story, it marks a turning point when the protagonist, triggered by a sudden memory or insight, abandons their outer quest only to embark on an internal one and the search for a true self, a lost identity, or the like.

In covering a variety of fields, this book draws on correspondingly extensive material, including interviews, letters, exhibition catalogues, novels, diaries, poems, travel accounts, histories of art, architecture, and literature, besides paintings, photographs, installations, drawings, plans, models, and buildings. However, the book can never (nor does it aim to) offer a complete inventory of Piranesi references after 1900. Inevitably, therefore, it is bound to come across as a catalogue of missed opportunities. Readers will lament the inexplicable exclusion of this or that author, artist, architect, historian, or composer—some of which I am aware of and several, surely, of which I am not. One example that would have merited attention is the experimental music of Brian Ferneyhough, the composer of a suite of works from the 1980s, *Carceri d'invenzione*, inspired by the interlocking of incompatible fields in Piranesi's compositions.[21] Or, again, Piranesi and Russia offers a history of the modern age all by itself, represented by key figures ranging from the post-revolutionary architect Ivan Fomin to the paper architecture of

Alexander Brodsky and Ilya Utkin in the 1980s and 1990s.[22] Nor is Piranesi's impact on Italian rationalists and futurists in any way accounted for, given the omission of the works of Alessandro Limongelli or Antonio Sant'Elia, for instance. However, the book is not a survey, but is structured around case studies that connect to what I consider to be turning points in the retelling of twentieth- and twenty-first-century history. The chapters and subchapters center on certain junctures at which Piranesi's works helped to formulate the modern with a particular force and potency. These junctures often take the form of explicit reactions against prevailing aesthetics, conventions, and opinions. Thus, the book extricates a series of contrapositions from the history of the recent past, such as the ones between pictorial and straight photography, figurative and abstract art, dialectic and linear narrative structures in film, and postmodernism and conceptualism in architecture. The references I have chosen to include represent encounters between the moderns and the Venetian that somehow came to redefine both. The reciprocal reinvention of the two—of our age and of Piranesi—forms an intermediate *third*, which is this book's true, albeit elusive, subject.

The ideas and notions presented in this book point to the domain in which Piranesi's art truly exists, namely the domain of interpretation. In the way they are discussed here, the prints belong neither entirely to Piranesi, nor to the moderns looking at them—nor to us, for that matter. In this sense, the book conforms to Roland Barthes's observation that all texts eventually eschew whatever intention their authors might have had and persevere as an accumulation of interpretations. A text—or an etching—exists as a "multi-dimensional space" in which all the things that come before or after the genesis of the work blend and clash.[23] An original meaning simply does not exist, according to Barthes. In this sense, Piranesi's compositions remain open-ended; they continually engender mutations that allow new expressions to take form. It is precisely what one does *not* see in these prints that inspires posterity. As Harold Bloom has shown, influence rarely takes the form of a direct imitation of an admired original. Influence, rather, reveals itself in operations that distract from the original through strategies that bypass, distort, improve, or ignore it. Poetic history, says Bloom, is a history of poets misreading one another "so as to clear imaginative space for themselves."[24] The pictorial nature of Piranesi's art leaves it all the more susceptible to creative misinterpretation. The visual components are obviously unchanging but the narratives in which these components make sense are constantly reinvented.

THE DE

QUINCEY EFFECT

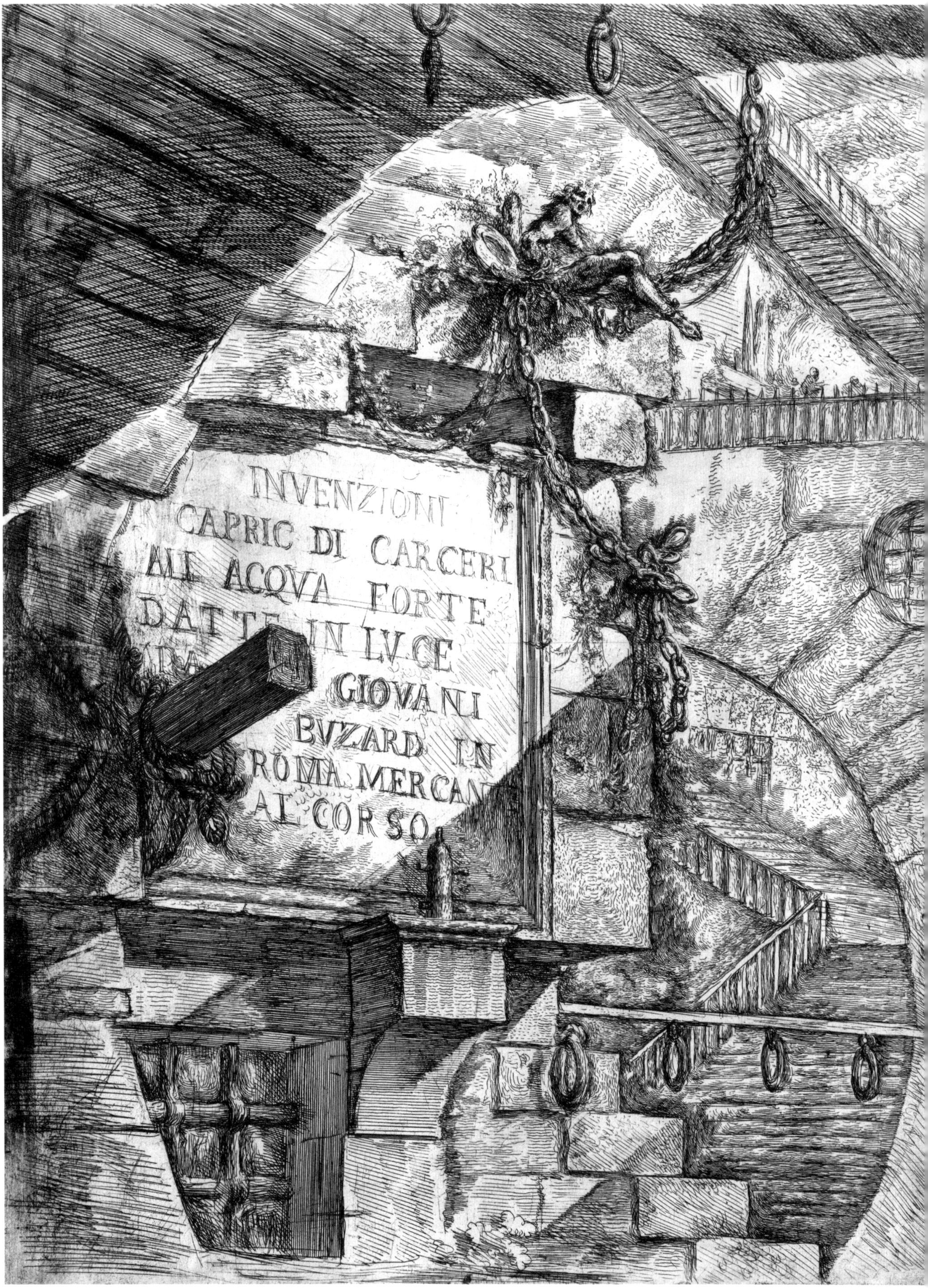
INVENZIONI
CAPRIC DI CARCERI
ALL ACQVA FORTE
DATTE IN LVCE
DA
GIOVANI
BVZARD IN
ROMA MERCAN
AL CORSO

Piranesi, as a reference, has spread contagiously from one field to another from the nineteenth century to the present day. However, his fame is grounded less in his actual prints, and more in the literary interpretation of them. For example, late-nineteenth-century surveys of prints and printmaking, including Adam Bartsch's *Le peintre-graveur*, do not even mention Piranesi, whereas authors of poetry and fiction, including Horace Walpole, Victor Hugo, Charles Baudelaire, Herman Melville, and Marcel Proust, molded psychological and emotional truths on the idea of his art. It was in literature—in fact *as* literature—that writers re-established Piranesi as a universal reference. Tracing the impact of this poetically transformed Piranesi on modern culture, the present chapter suggests that this version of him helped to make that culture modern in the first place.

The idea of a literary Piranesi rests in particular with the series of imagined prisons, published in 1749–50 under the title *Invenzioni capric di carceri* (*see opposite*), and then again in 1761 in a much reworked edition renamed *Carceri d'invenzione*, in which two new plates were added to the fourteen original ones (*see following*).[1] The rococo lightness of the first edition, capturing the atmospherically dissolved forms of Piranesi's native Venice, evaporates in the second edition with the impact of the heavy masonry and ancient substructures of Rome, the city in which he had in the meantime settled. The expansive blanks of the first edition are compressed into defined luminous fields and the loosely incised surfaces coagulate into shadows seemingly so solid as to assume ontological status. Whether the focus is on the rash and impetuous Piranesi of 1749, or on the artist drenching the world in blacks twelve years later, more often than not the etchings are seen as reflections of the maker's own mind, a myth that trails back to early reports on Piranesi's difficult temper and "turbulent character."[2]

The difference between the editions became a significant point in twentieth-century attempts to frame modernist expressions in print (Arthur Hind), in art (Alfred H. Barr), and in cinema (Sergei Eisenstein), as we shall see. But regardless of this difference, the *Carceri* series remains enigmatic because of the deliberately staged contradictions in which Piranesi indulged. Although Roman architecture is a clear reference, the series does not show anywhere real, and although the masonry seems solid, spatially it cannot exist; stairways shift position midair and arches cross where they cannot go. The architectural elements constantly seem to defy the world of tangibles, pushing towards abstraction—a domain that strictly speaking did not invade art before the twentieth century. Spatial complexities aside, the *Carceri*'s evocation of prisons, complete with inmates strapped to instruments of torture, invites meditations on incarceration and penitence, physical as well as existential, themes Michel Foucault or Manfredo

Giovanni Battista Piranesi, title plate from *Invenzioni capric di carceri*, first edition, ca. 1749–1750.

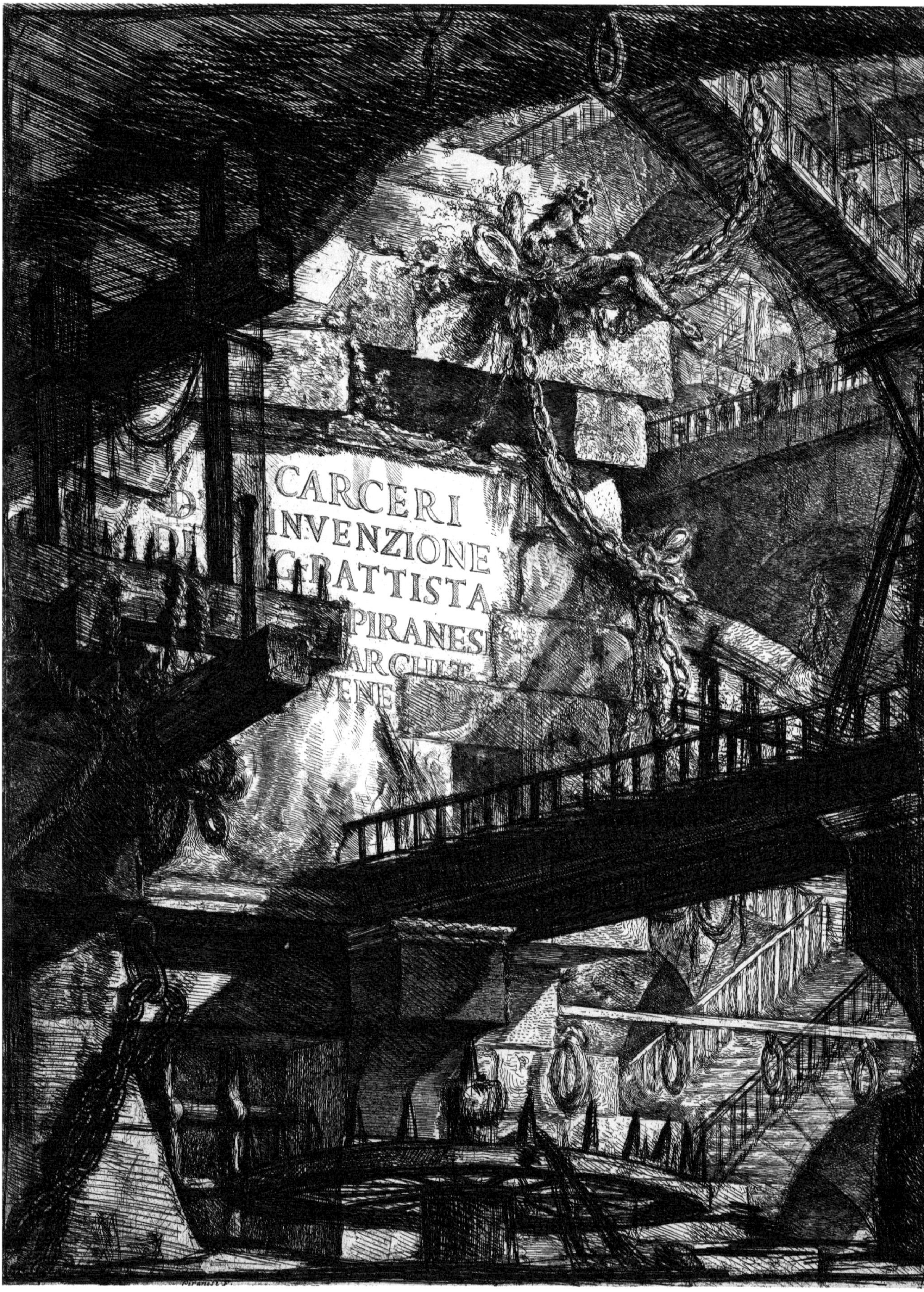
CARCERI
D'
INVENZIONE
DI
G. BATTISTA
PIRANESI
ARCHIT.
VENE

Tafuri were to reflect on. However, the attempt to identify with the figures populating the scenes splinters into contradictions too, since some appear to contemplate the view, or quietly converse, oblivious to the torment of others (*see below*). No less destabilizing, then, than the disjointed formal space is the disjointed psychological one. The deconstructed forms frame a deconstructed human collectivity in which people occupying the same space act as if they were in different worlds. In short, the compositions pull the beholder into a labyrinth from which there is no escape—a space that became identified with the modern mind and its imagined chasms and entrapments.

Already in 1915, William M. Ivins admits that the *Carceri* "are known not so much in fact as through certain wonderful pages written about them by several great masters of English prose style."[3] Ivins, as I shall return to, set out to resurrect the pictorial value of a series that literature had transformed into poetry. This poetic transformation, I argue, originates with the Romantic essayist Thomas De Quincey and his arresting paragraph on Piranesi published in *Confessions of an English Opium-Eater* (1821). De Quincey's fanciful description, cited below, unlocked the *Carceri* as displays of an inner world and inaugurated a tradition that annexed these prints and converted them into topoi that engendered dizzying

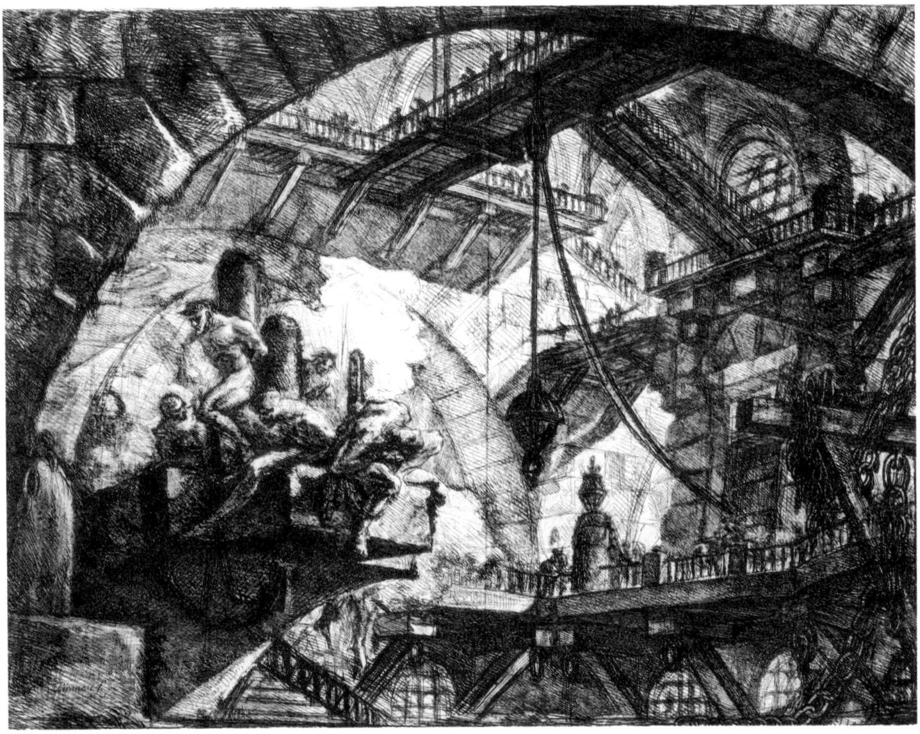

Giovanni Battista Piranesi, plate X, *Prisoners on a Projecting Platform*, from *Carceri d'invenzione*, second edition, 1761.

facing Giovanni Battista Piranesi, title plate from *Carceri d'invenzione*, second edition, 1761.

feats of soul-searching across the arts. In other words, De Quincey's influential but largely reinvented Piranesi pushed the limits of architecture, or, rather, extended its range to include also metaphorical realms; Piranesi emerged as the architect of an entirely new *conceptual* landscape that spanned hallucinations, dreams, and memories. As we shall see, the disconcerting prisons, recreated as captivating prose, enriched the fields of psychoanalysis, philosophy, poetry, and literary criticism as well as the history of art and architecture. The *Carceri*, on De Quincey's cue, came to occupy a domain beyond the finite and the rational and provide a scenery—a mental stage set—in a vast and varied literature of introspection from Joyce to Jung, from Baudelaire to Borges. The modern self, it seems, emerged from within these compositions.

This chapter has a different focus than Erika Naginski's "Romanticism's Piranesi" (2002), which analyzed the veneration of Piranesi in Romantic literature, also recognizing in it remnants of a nineteenth-century medical, sociological, and philosophical discourse.[4] Whereas Naginski uncovered the realities on which the literary fascination with Piranesi rested, my concern is to identify the *unrealities* that made the prints literary in the first place. De Quincey's passage on Piranesi contains interpretations that distort the reality of the prints, but for that precise reason it secured their success as references in the formulation of a frail and disoriented modern existence. Piranesi became responsible for a realm he strictly speaking had not authored, with writers attempting to pin elusive sensations on his armature of dangling bridges, airy landings, and narrow stairs.

THOMAS DE QUINCEY'S PIRANESI

Oscar Wilde refers to Piranesi only once and the comment is telling: "And who does not feel that the chief glory of Piranesi's book on Vases is that it gave Keats the suggestion for his 'Ode on a Grecian Urn'? Art, and art only, can make archaeology beautiful."[5] In Wilde's opinion, the true value of Piranesi's visual oeuvre is the one that poetry finds in it; its importance is the *words* it inspires. The quote, published in *Intentions* from 1891, sums up a century that had subjected Piranesi's art to literature and transformed his visions into tropes, or at least into themes, to which writers repeatedly turned.

By the time of Wilde, English writers had long sought to capture in eloquent prose Piranesi's grand and implausible architecture, which seemed to embody notions of the sublime and the infinite defined in contemporary philosophy and aesthetics by Edmund Burke, Archibald Alison, and others.[6] Recognizing the magnificently impossible nature of these architectural visions, Horace Walpole writes in 1771 that Piranesi "has imagined scenes that would startle geometry, and exhaust the Indies to realize. He piles palaces on bridges, and temples on palaces, and scales heaven with mountains of edifices."[7] Others projected Piranesi's dizzying heights and bottomless pits onto nature, among them William Beckford, who had a near out-of-body experience on a journey to Bonn:

> I kept gazing at the azure irregular mountains which bounded the view, and in thought was already transported to their summits. Vast and wild were the prospects I surveyed from this imaginary exaltation, and innumerable the chimeras which trotted in my brain. Mounted on these fantastic quadrupeds, I shot swiftly from rock to rock, and built castles in the style of Piranesi, upon most of their pinnacles.[8]

For Walpole and Beckford alike, Piranesi is associated with an architecture that is mountainously majestic but also only a spectacle—a tableau—best appreciated from a comfortable distance. Beckford's phrase, "in the style of Piranesi," suggests a connoisseur able to maintain a certain level of detachment and resist getting too closely involved.

This comfortable distance, however, collapsed with Thomas De Quincey. In a dramatic turnaround, De Quincey situates the beholder not outside Piranesi's dizzying architecture, but within it. Put differently, the architecture appears no longer founded in the outer world, but in an inner one. If Piranesi's tableaus inspired a thrilling sense of awe in Walpole and Beckford, it all turned interior with De Quincey. Now it was as if man stood at the precipice of his own inner self, gazing into the abyss of the unknown. Though associated with English Romanticism, De Quincey's works plough deep and exceed mere polished expressions of nostalgia and yearning, revealing a meticulous observer of the mind and its mechanics. In his autobiographical writings De Quincey subjected his "proto-modernist anxiety," as Elizabeth Fay puts it, to intense scrutiny and dissected his own mental states—his compulsive thinking and an acute

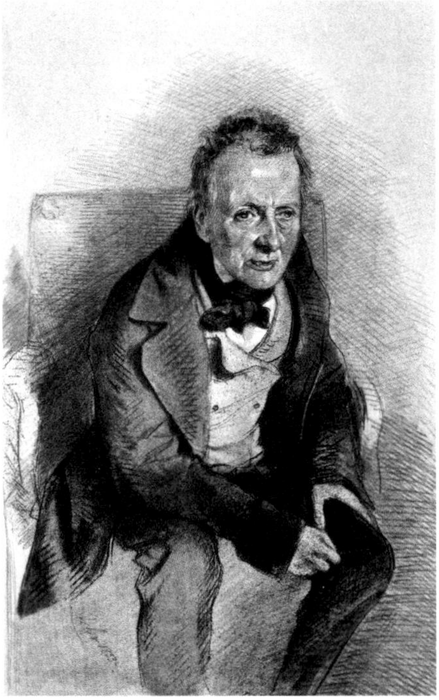

Portrait of Thomas De Quincey by James Archer.

sense of meaninglessness—with a persistence and indeed understanding that foreshadow a psychoanalytical approach.[9] With a single passage from *Confessions*, De Quincey managed to relocate Piranesi and his influence from the visual arts to literature, with lasting consequences. This passage's few convenient "misinterpretations," as we shall see, allowed posterity to reimagine Piranesi as a continually updated reference in psychology, literary criticism, fiction, and poetry.

> Many years ago, when I was looking over Piranesi's "Antiquities of Rome," Coleridge, then standing by, described to me a set of plates from that artist, called his "Dreams," and which record the scenery of his own visions during the delirium of a fever. Some of these (I describe only from memory of Coleridge's account) represented vast Gothic halls; on the floor of which stood mighty engines and machinery, wheels, cables, catapults, &c., expressive of enormous power put forth, or resistance overcome. Creeping along the sides of the walls, you perceived a staircase; and upon this, groping his way upwards, was Piranesi himself. Follow the stairs a little farther, and you perceive them reaching an abrupt termination, without any balustrade, and allowing no step onwards to him who should reach the extremity, except into the depths below. Whatever is to become of poor Piranesi, at least you suppose that his labours must now in some way terminate. But raise your eyes, and behold a second flight of stairs still higher, on which again Piranesi is perceived, by this time standing on the very brink of the abyss. Once again elevate your eye, and a still more aerial flight of stairs is descried; and there, again, is the delirious Piranesi, busy on his aspiring labours: and so on, until the unfinished stairs and the hopeless Piranesi both are lost in the upper gloom of the hall.[10]

Tracing this passage's extraordinary afterlife of citations, mistranslations, and elaborations across fields and genres reveals that it is not so much the prints themselves, as De Quincey's interpretation of them, that secured Piranesi a place in modern culture. No monograph or substantial article on Piranesi fails to quote the passage above in whole or in part. In the early twentieth-century efforts to establish the biography of Piranesi, De Quincey's artful ekphrasis constituted a fundament as shaky as those on which Piranesi's own towering edifices were founded. When, for example, the standard reference *Bryan's Dictionary of Painters and Engravers*, in its 1904 edition, claims that the prison etchings record the artist's "visions during the delirium of a fever," the assumption rests less on reality than on an identically worded claim in De Quincey's *Confessions*.[11]

I am not suggesting that De Quincey was the only agent through which Piranesi triumphed as prose. A number of nineteenth- and twentieth-century authors elaborated on Piranesi's art independently, among them Edgar Allan Poe, Ralph Waldo Emerson, and Herman Melville.[12] However, De Quincey's free reinterpretation gave the series of prints a new existence not only *as* prose but as an analogy of human existence. Closer scrutiny reveals that his apparent reverie is a remarkably controlled rhetorical exercise. By means of a series of calculated moves, the writer subtly disassociates himself from the actual etched motifs, a distance that allows him to "misinterpret" the content and reimagine it on terms that forged a connection between his own mind and that of Piranesi. In fact, the passage quoted above functions as a prelude to an account of the hallucinations De Quincey himself once experienced. No sooner has he referred to Piranesi than he goes on to say: "[w]ith the same power of endless growth and self-reproduction did my architecture proceed in dreams." De Quincey invokes his own interior world of proliferating structures, remembering "he beheld such pomp of cities and palaces as never was beheld by the waking eye, unless in the clouds."[13] The words bring to mind the description in the Book of Revelation (Rev. 21.2) of a new holy city coming down from heaven, only here they record the vision, not of a prophet, but of a poet lost in opium reveries.[14]

De Quincey presumably had one or several prints from the *Carceri* series in mind, but he does not convey a direct and immediate impression of them.[15] On the contrary, the imprecise, erroneous nature of the reading only confirms what De Quincey freely admitted: that he had never even seen the prints and was simply relating what he remembered his friend Samuel Taylor Coleridge had told him about them. The slightly cynical view would be that these layers of evocations gave De Quincey the opportunity to reinvent Piranesi's prints almost as he pleased. The filtering through a double set of recollections absolved him of the obligation to render the prints faithfully. By letting the Piranesian architecture "sink" into memory, and thus into the deep strata of the mind, he also grounded the prints in the realm of fiction, in a psychologically driven plot. One could say, therefore, that through a series of artful distortions, the prints were reborn as literature. The De Quincey tradition did not subtract anything from the interpretation of Piranesi but, if anything, added layers that constituted a tradition on its own, to the point where the reality of the etchings themselves became superfluous. It is a tradition that has turned Piranesi and his art into a narration of our deepest fantasies, fears, and urges, casting a spell over generations of biographers, poets, novelists, diarists, and psychologists.

A reader of Victor Hugo's early poems may be deceived, for while the author conjures the name and world of Piranesi, he had probably not seen the etchings.[16] Hugo exemplifies a group of French authors associated with the Romantic movement who emulated De Quincey's passage on Piranesi in their attempt to capture aspects of the human condition in poems, essays, and autobiographies. Importantly, however, they never simply copied the text but targeted elusive psychological truths by means of De Quincey's arresting terms and metaphors.

In the history of Piranesi and the French it is of course significant that Piranesi's sons, Francesco and Pietro, transferred his copper plates to Paris in 1798, twenty years after his death. In the French capital, new editions of the etchings were printed, first by the two Piranesi brothers, later by others, culminating in the editions of the *Carceri* published by Firmin Didot in the 1830s. The acquisition of the plates undoubtedly had an effect on French culture, boosting enthusiasm for the artist. Among others, Piranesi's early biographer, Jacques Guillaume Legrand, took obvious pride in their inclusion in the Louvre.[17]

However, it is also true that French authors at this time were under the spell of De Quincey's *Confessions*, which was first published in French in the journal *La pandore* in September 1827, and then appeared in a new translation, or, rather, free adaptation in October 1828 by a very young Alfred de Musset, who would revisit and reinterpret the work in a second adaptation in 1853, just a few years before his death.[18] Charles Baudelaire, too, translated *Confessions* in 1860, but left out the Piranesi epiphany.[19] The omission does not indicate that De Quincey's Piranesi passage failed to interest French authors; on the contrary. Luzius Keller and Georges Poulet have both traced the impact of this particular passage on French nineteenth-century authors and identified its recurrence in the works of Charles Nodier, Victor Hugo, Théophile Gautier, and Charles Baudelaire, to mention only a few.[20] An imagery of spiral stairs, infinite labyrinths, and towering interiors, plundered and expanded from De Quincey's passage, constitutes what Keller identifies as a "Piranesian universe" in French literature; it defines a group of writers that Poulet even terms "*poètes piranésiens*."[21] In short, through translations, adaptations, and elaborations, French authors propagated a Piranesi that originated not in the actual prints but in De Quincey's interpretation of them.

However, in French hands, De Quincey's passage underwent significant changes. The "Piranesi" that emerged in their adaptations was more charged, more existential (to use an anachronism) than the one De Quincey had fashioned. Just as elements in the actual etchings faded from view, so elements in De

Giovanni Battista Piranesi, plate III, *The Round Tower*, from *Carceri d'invenzione*, second edition, 1761.

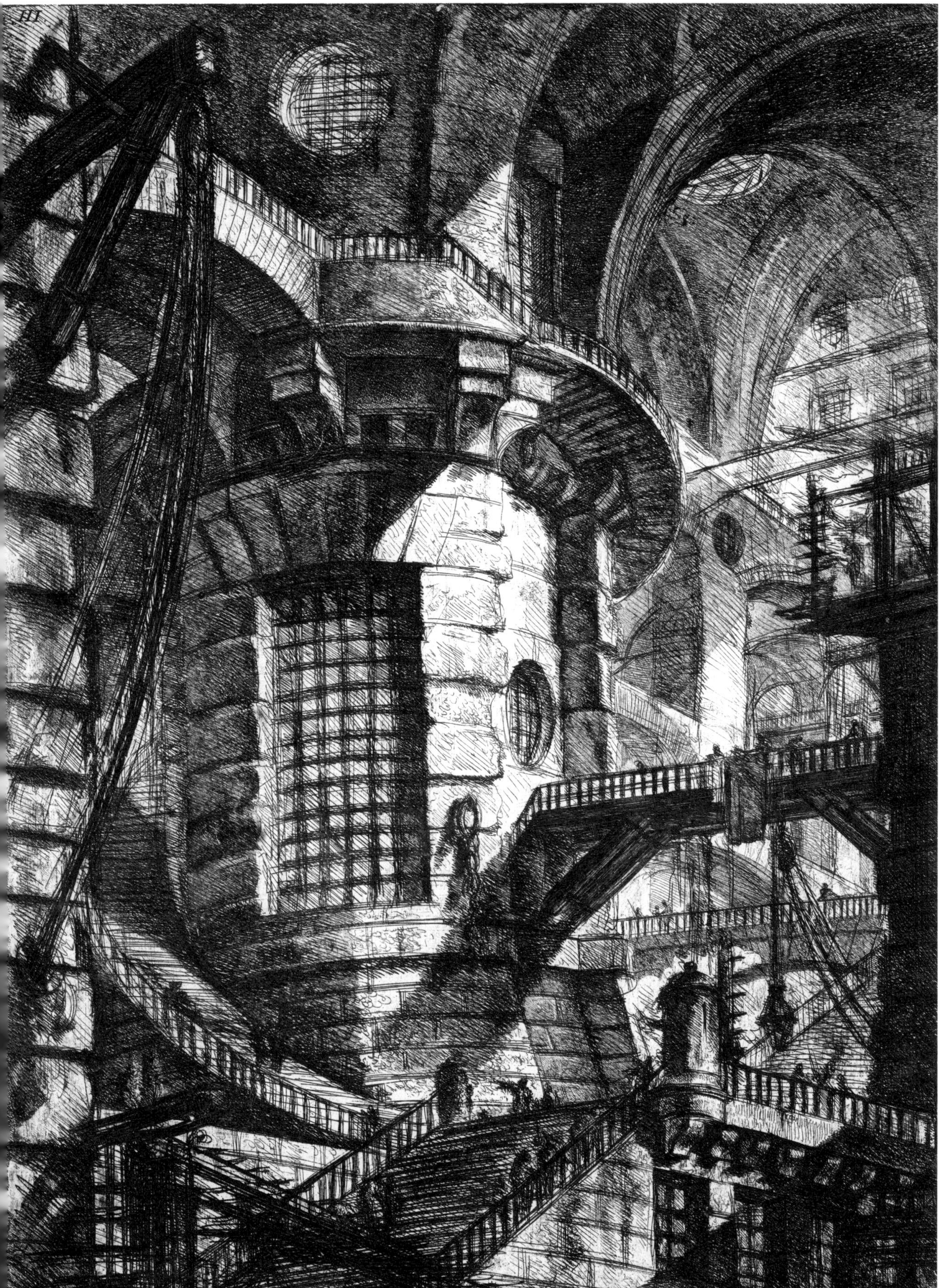
III

Quincey's description were misinterpreted or even omitted and replaced. For instance, while the "spiral stair" became a literary motif *par excellence*, it is mentioned nowhere in De Quincey's text and appears in just one prison etching (*The Drawbridge*), or, with a bit of good will, two at most. Moreover, elements in De Quincey's architecture were transported to new realms, or, alternatively, authors transported their projected selves into the architecture. Bridges and towers of Babel, ladders and labyrinths, served as a framework, however shaky, for various kinds of internal experiences expounded in diaries, poems, and novels. As if it were a psychological pop-up architecture, De Quincey's Piranesian fantasy was re-erected as a backdrop to the inner life of hyper-sensitive cosmopolitan moderns.

In the Piranesi passage in *Confessions*, De Quincey never entirely identifies with the scene he conjures; instead, he compares Piranesi's "dreams" with his own. By comparing, he places himself at a certain distance to the vision of stairs and landings. French authors, by contrast, allowed those stairs and landings to invade the mind, as it were, and constitute its very structure. From representing a construction, the prisons come to represent a condition. Charles Nodier performs such a maneuver in a remarkable text, dated 1832, in which he elaborates on De Quincey's suggestion of a ceaselessly climbing Piranesi.[22] For Nodier, the never-ending ascent illustrates a condition he terms "*monomanie reflective*"—reflective monomania. Extracting a particular scene from De Quincey's recollection, he recasts it as a universal *exemplum* of someone who "is always bound to climb, always bound to move on, always bound to arrive."[23]

Of course, if the stairs were truly infinite one would never reach either the top or the bottom but would always find oneself somewhere in between. The existential vertigo of that in-betweenness is voiced by Théophile Gautier in the semi-autobiographical *The Club of Assassins* (*Le club des hachichins*) (1846). Reportedly recording his own hallucination during an opium session, Gautier nevertheless possessed enough reasoning to fashion it on the passage in *Confessions*. He, too, emphasizes the architecture's infinite expanse, but unlike De Quincey or Nodier, who viewed the Piranesian construction somewhat from the outside, Gautier places himself in its midst. Now *he* is the climbing Piranesi. Stumbling onto the landing of a half-lit staircase, he recalls how "it assumed in my dreamlike state, cyclopean and gigantic proportions," before continuing with the familiar invocations of endlessness and abysses.

> Its ends were drowned in gloom and seemed to penetrate the gulfs of heaven and hell; looking up I could barely see, in frightening perspective, an endless succession of landings and flights to be ascended as if

to reach the summit of the tower of Lylacq; looking down, I saw abysses of stairs, whirlpools of spirals, fainting-fits of circumvolutions.[24]

With Victor Hugo's adaptation of De Quincey, the Piranesian scenography assumes a new and existential importance. In an entirely novel take, Hugo rebuilds his own poetic self around Piranesi's gloomy hollows. In other words, instead of picturing someone going up or down an endless flight of stairs, those stairs descend into the abyss of his own being. Hugo's originality was to place the prison inside man—an idea that was to retain its hold on French thought, as we shall see in chapter six.[25] All considered, the mind itself as an infinitely extending entrapment is perhaps Piranesi's most lasting legacy as an architect. Hugo's poem, *La pente de la rêverie* (1830), for example, pictures a spiral descent that "goes from the real world to the invisible sphere" at the bottom of which fatal enigmas linger. Again, in *Puits de l'Inde!* (1839), the author pales as in his mind he peers into depths that compare to the "frightening Babels dreamed by Piranesi."[26] Georges Poulet identifies a particularly Hugolian Piranesi—a Piranesi appearing no longer as a person but as a concept—when he points out that apart from Piranesi the artist, and apart from Piranesi the tragic explorer of depths, there exists a Piranesi that is identical to those depths themselves—a Piranesi-abyss that sinks into its own mystery and entwines with the very fabric of our soul.[27]

In Hugo's oeuvre, the De Quincey model is not always obvious; it fuses with the French author's own powerful imagination.[28] Moreover, by the late 1830s, Hugo shows every sign of having seen the actual prints, evidenced by references to Piranesi that have become increasingly rich and complex:

The dark brain of Piranesi
is a gaping furnace
where the ark and the sky blend,
the staircase, the tower, the column;
where the immeasurable Babel
grows, rises, swells, and boils![29]

Here, and with abundant imagery, the French poet leads the reader through the blistering interior of a feverish mind. The brain of Piranesi is moreover dark; it contains a staircase, a tower, a column. In short, his mind is like a *Carceri* print and not merely a reflection of De Quincey's fictionalization of one.

However, in the works of Nodier, Gautier, and Hugo the terror remains theatrical—a horror to enjoy, and which these authors are ultimately able to step away from, as if they had an emergency exit behind their backs. Baudelaire, by contrast, goes further. To him a Piranesian-De Quinceyan universe does not simply supply architectural elements; it reframes the entire inner self as a descent. When Baudelaire in his own translation of the *Confessions* strikingly omits the passage of Piranesi's "dreams," it is possibly because the vision of the little figure re-emerging at successive flights of stairs appears too concrete, almost comical. It externalizes the climb. To Baudelaire, the spiraling stair is more than a mere spectacle to behold as it embodies our very moral constitution. In contrast to Hugo, Baudelaire's descent entwines with our character and spirals down through lust and desires, licentiousness and depravity, and ultimately perhaps through remorse. "I feel a gaping abyss broadening in my being; this abyss is my heart," he has Hippolyta exclaim to her lesbian lover in one of the poems expunged from *Les fleurs du mal* (1857).[30] The Piranesian theme assumes a moral significance.[31]

De Quincey's "unfinished stairs" become important in the French articulation of the modern soul. But no less important is the repositioning and transformation undergone by these stairs. It is telling how the viewpoint shifts from De Quincey, who somehow stands at the foot of the staircase, looking up, to Hugo and Baudelaire, who stand on top, peering down into the chambers of the soul. In this shift, one observes the gradual internalization of architecture and its reconstitution as a construct within the minds of the authors. While perhaps remaining as insubstantial as any paper fantasy, this internal architecture was infinitely more elastic, its form constantly adapting to new psychological experiences. As we have seen, the endless stair (and its tireless climber) enabled authors to formulate compulsion (Nodier), hallucination (Gautier), terror (Hugo), and degeneration (Baudelaire). In short, De Quincey's passage did more than simply provide a model in literature; it allowed the formation of a distinct notion of the self—a self that one might call Piranesian.

The *Carceri*, or at least the idea of them, engendered a Piranesi resurgence among French authors. De Quincey's contribution was to enable these authors to frame a distinct "I" within the *Carceri*'s airy constructs—a subject restlessly on the move through their spaces, tumbling through dark pits or groping towards the daylit world above. One could argue that the embedding of a *subject* in this universe constitutes a particularly French tradition which permeates the modern age. "I write to tell of the prison I am writing from," Pierre Seghers wrote in the collection of poems titled *Piranèse* (1960). Seghers filtered his wartime experience in Nazi-occupied France by placing his poetic alter ego at the bottom of prisons "where the dungeons go so deep that endless stairs are sensed within the walls, winding into blackest black, as if to the heart of silence."[32]

To conclude, it was the writing of De Quincey, rather than the physical transfer of Piranesi's plates to Paris, that had the greatest impact on French literary culture. At least, it is fair to say that phrases and themes migrating from one literary passage to another manifest a more demonstrable relation than the one existing between visual impressions and words. With texts layered upon texts—from De Quincey to Musset, from Musset to Nodier and Gautier—printed motifs distilled into metaphors. By the end of the nineteenth century, then, and certainly by the beginning of the twentieth, Piranesi had come to represent a category of motifs that alone or in combination with others signaled an inner state, regardless of whether or not he had actually depicted them. Piranesi became responsible for a realm that he had not authored. A transition of meaning from "Piranesi," as a maker of etchings, to "Piranesian," as an adjective referring somewhat vaguely to a bundle of concepts—awe, terror, alienation, endlessness, complexity—is an affirmation of an oeuvre that became ingrained in modern culture on a deep, and one is tempted to say, subconscious level. As Huxley insightfully noted, the *Carceri* spoke to De Quincey and Coleridge "and they speak no less eloquently to the condition of twentieth-century men and women brought up on the literature, imaginative or descriptive of, deep psychology."[33]

THE ARCHITECT OF THE UNCONSCIOUS

The French assimilation of De Quincey was fundamental in the diffusion, not simply of Piranesi's art in modern culture, but of a poetically transformed version of it. Now, as we return to De Quincey's passage, we shall see that its impact on modern culture is based on what we may distinguish as three separate interpretations of the *Carceri*, each of which invites its own course of investigation. The first departs from his interpretation of these prints as "dreams"; the second from his suggestion that the prison paradoxically extends infinitely, and the third from the associations with memory and the act of recollecting evoked by these prints. In the remainder of this chapter, I intend to show how these three De Quinceyan interpretations have become entwined with modern culture.

A number of distortions make their way into De Quincey's Piranesi recollections. The most significant misinterpretation, however, is his characterization of the *Carceri* as "dreams." By calling them "dreams," a title Piranesi never used, he ingeniously relocated the enigmatic realm they pictured to the psyche and extended their influence far beyond the visual arts. As "dreams," they suddenly seemed to represent the chambers of the mind rather than the ones of Roman architecture. Whatever basis Piranesi's thick masonry and deep vaults may have had in reality, it corroded as De Quincey's interpretation reconstituted them as the setting for nightly visions.

Even today, it requires considerable effort to look through the veil De Quincey cast over these prints and *not* see them as expressions of the deeper layers of our mental constitution. The characterization of the compositions as dreams demonstrates the extent to which twentieth-century scholarship on Piranesi has become entangled in a literary interpretation born with De Quincey. If early, influential Piranesi scholars like Arthur Samuel or Arthur Hind simply called them "dreams," as De Quincey had done, others, like Aldous Huxley or Ernst Gombrich, elaborated on the darker quality of dreams and called them "nightmares."[34] But whether perceived as dreams or nightmares, the *Carceri* seemed to transport their beholders to a place that was highly emotional or "intensely private," to quote John Wilton-Ely, a domain that was less architectural than psychological.[35]

The significance we attach to dreams, however, has become more pronounced since the days of Thomas De Quincey, and this in turn has heightened the significance of the *Carceri*. How Marguerite Yourcenar writes about the series is telling: "No connoisseur of oneiric matters will hesitate a moment in the presence of these drawings evincing all the chief characteristics of the dream state: negation of time, incoherence of space, suggested levitation."[36] She goes on to enumerate several other characteristics, as if the enigma of dreams could be solved by subjecting them to cataloguing. Clearly, the language available to describe Piranesi's visions had changed since the days of De Quincey. The invocation of the *Carceri* as dreams in a poetic sense had turned into a classification of those dreams in terms of analytical psychology. Piranesi's prison interiors had gone from being metaphors of the mind to become illustrations of its actual mechanics.

Reinterpreted as "dreams," the *Carceri* delineated the scenography of our inner world and, accordingly, the elements in that scenography assumed a symbolic meaning. In literature, spiral stairs and endless galleries seemed to connect to a deeper and, in psychoanalytical terms, unconscious, stratum of the psyche. On the one hand, the temptation was always there to see Piranesi's *own* unconscious reflected in these prints. Though nothing from Piranesi's life suggests that the images were self-portraits, De Quincey's (and/or Coleridge's) surprising identification of "poor Piranesi" as a figure climbing his own labyrinthine structures relaunched the series as a mental autobiography. The etchings came to offer a panorama not merely of the unconscious but of the specific incarnation of it that belonged to their author. They show the "subterranean workings of a tormented soul," Aldous Huxley wrote in 1949, convinced that Piranesi poured his own despair into these spatial configurations.[37] In his 1952 article on Piranesi and British Romantic authors, Jørgen Andersen claimed there were "links between Piranesi's archaeological research and those underground vaults of his subconscious

Giovanni Battista Piranesi, plate V, *The Lion Bas-Reliefs*, from *Carceri d'invenzione*, second edition, 1761.

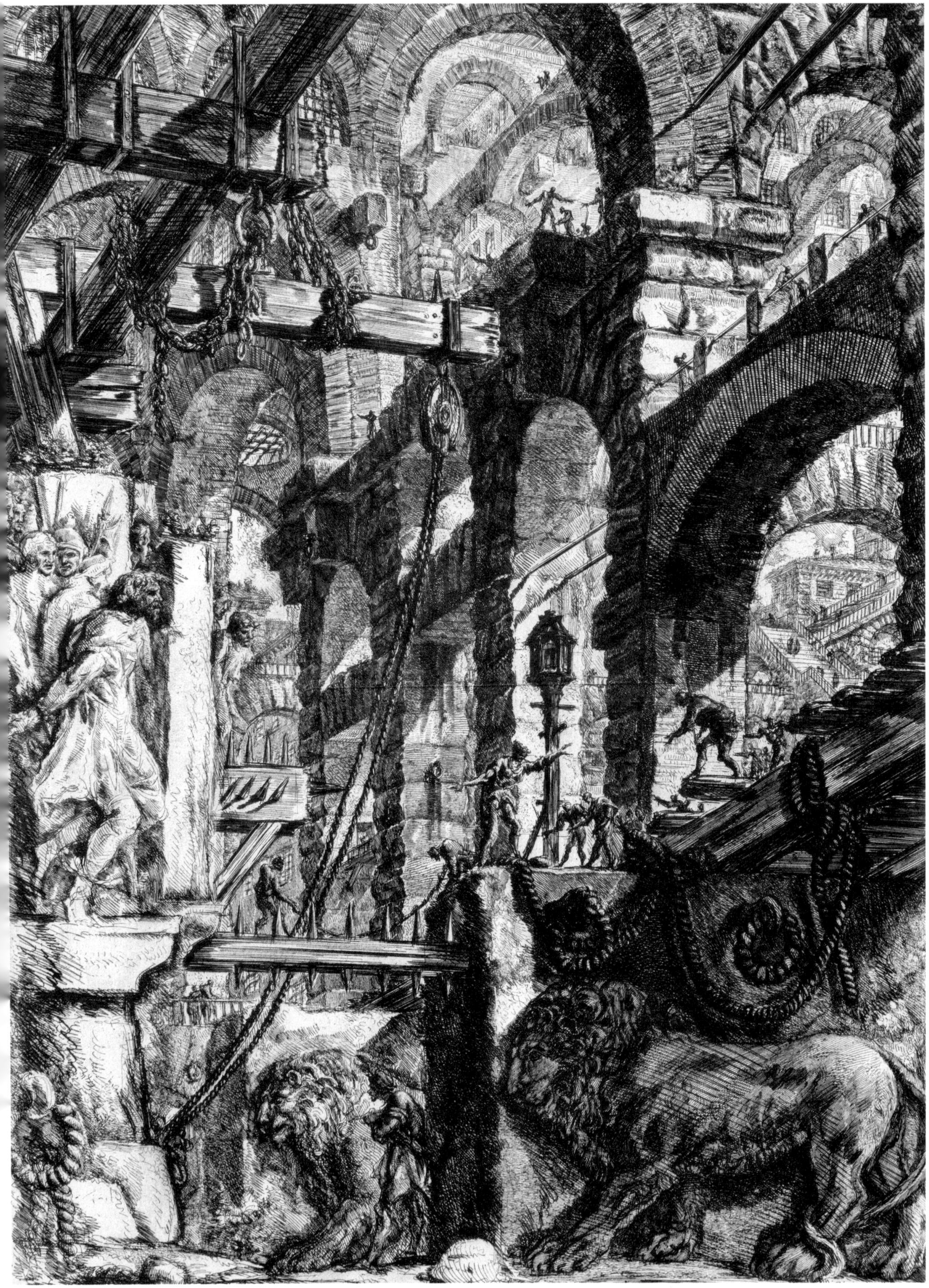

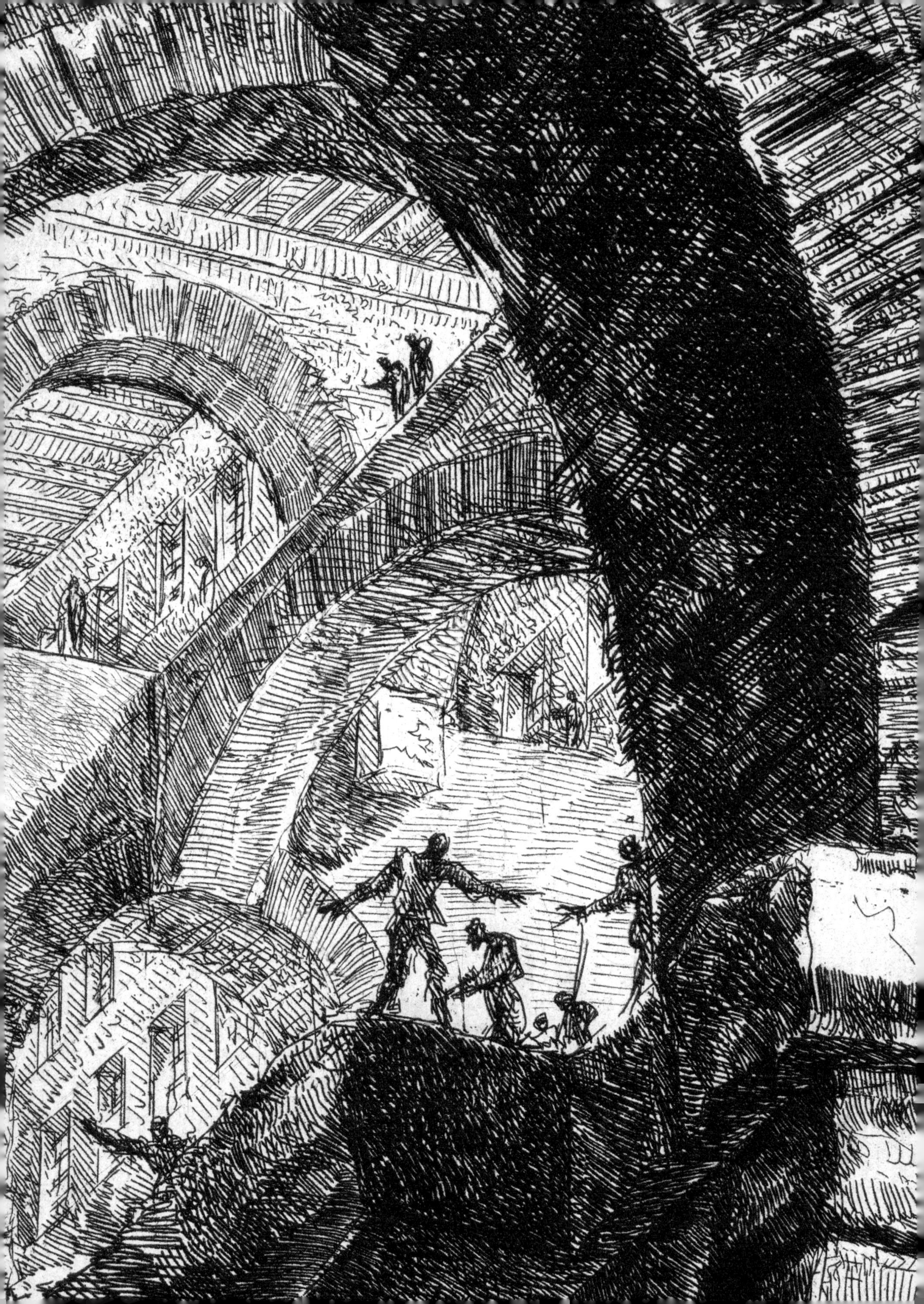

in the *Carceri* scenes, which look like dramatizations of his own Self."[38] The phrase "underground vaults of the subconscious" perhaps says more about the impact of psychoanalysis on Andersen than it does about the actual structure of Piranesi's mind. However, the myth of the *Carceri* as a self-portrait of the artist's soul has proved long-lived. As late as 2010, Grégoire Dupond and Factum Arte promised the audience for their animation of the *Carceri* an experience "literally like entering Piranesi's mind," an extraordinary claim of course, but one that has become a commonplace two centuries after De Quincey.[39]

On the other hand, it was but a short step from the idea that these prints represent the mind of Piranesi to the conclusion that they represent the mind of everyone—of you and me—manifesting the caverns, recesses, passages, and descents of a fundamentally spatially conceived self. A variety of writers, across disciplines and genres, turned to Piranesi's unstable structures to illustrate an elusive inner life. Since the routes traced by these structures were mostly looping, or led nowhere, they aptly visualized the situation of anyone who felt that their search for an origin, a fundament, an exit—in every sense of these words—was going in circles. In short, just as psychoanalysis "animated" the endless halls and narrow stairs in Piranesi's compositions, these elements in turn offered psychoanalysis a set of architectural metaphors to support its effort to organize, or in fact construct, the modern soul. Piranesi became the architect of the unconscious.

However, at this point a distinction needs to be made, for there is not a single or universal definition of the interior space suggested by the unconscious. Above all, opinions differ over where precisely that interior space resides. Is it a space unique to each of us, molded by individual traumas and repressions, or is it a space which on a deep level is shared by us all? The difference broadly corresponds to the diverging models of the unconscious developed by Sigmund Freud and Carl Gustav Jung respectively, the two founding fathers of modern psychoanalysis.

It is interesting that De Quincey was the first to use the term "subconscious," at least in print, in an essay published in 1834, and then on several occasions, in an effort to pin down the operations of the mind.[40] And a similarity of thought exists between De Quincey and Freud, as Charles L. Proudfit and others have pointed out. Both entertained the idea that dreams reflect the unconscious, or, in De Quincey's terms, that they "throw dark reflections from eternities below all life upon the mirrors of the sleeping mind."[41]

Freud did not resort to the analogy of mirrors to explain the psyche but, famously, he resorted to the idea of Rome. The city's unique process of accumulation, in which one layer of the past rests on top of another, suggested a model of the mind "in which nothing that has once come into existence will have passed

Detail of *The Lion Bas-Reliefs.*

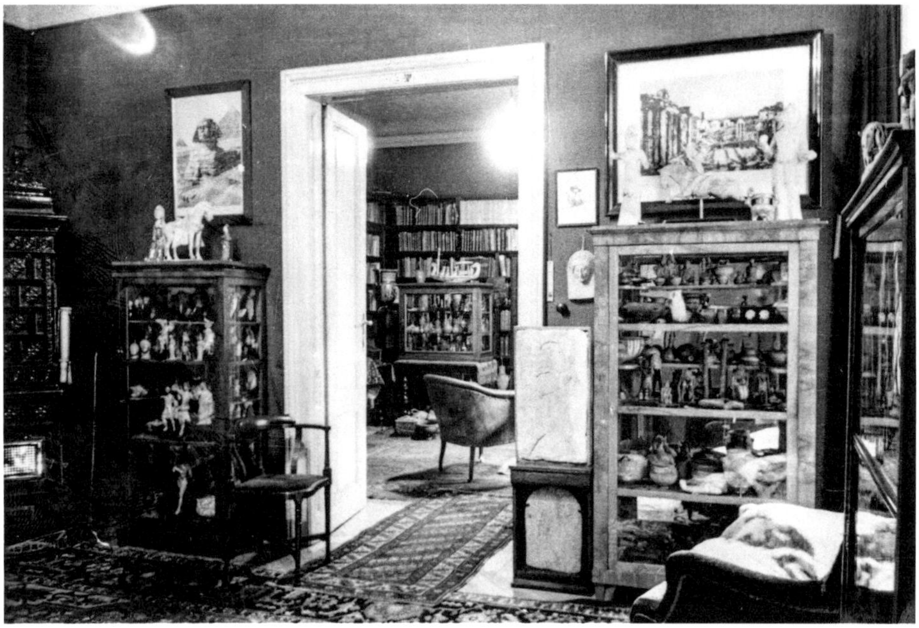

away and all the earlier phases of development continue to exist alongside the latest one."[42] Freud took no apparent interest in Piranesi and never subjected him to retrospective analysis, as he did for example with Leonardo and Michelangelo, although Piranesi would doubtless have proved a rewarding case, considering Freud's claim that "staircases, ladders, and flights of stairs, or climbing on these, either upwards or downwards, are symbolic representations of the sexual act."[43] With Rome as an image of the soul, we are on Piranesian ground anyhow, and in more than one sense. A framed etching of the Forum Romanum decorated the wall of Freud's consulting room in Vienna, executed not by Piranesi, but by one of his heirs, Luigi Kasimir.[44] But Freud had probably also seen Piranesi's prints. The enduring connection between the Venetian's compositions and the realm of dreams is given a twist in a story Freud tells about himself in *The Interpretation of Dreams* (1900). Freud dreamt that he was looking out a train window at the Tiber and the Ponte Sant'Angelo in Rome. But since he had never been to Rome, it occurred to him that the view he saw "was taken from a well-known engraving which I had caught sight of in the sitting room of one of my patients."[45] As Tarnya Cooper argues, it is likely that the print he saw was by Piranesi, published in *Vedute di Roma* (*see opposite*).[46] In any event, now imprinted on his memory, the engraving sinks into the depths of his mind to found a new reality. Rather than recognizing his own dreams in Piranesi's prints, as De Quincey did, Freud sees a Piranesi print in his own dream.

Freud's consulting room in Berggasse 19 in Vienna with Luigi Kasimir's etching of the Forum Romanum on the wall. Photograph from before 1936.

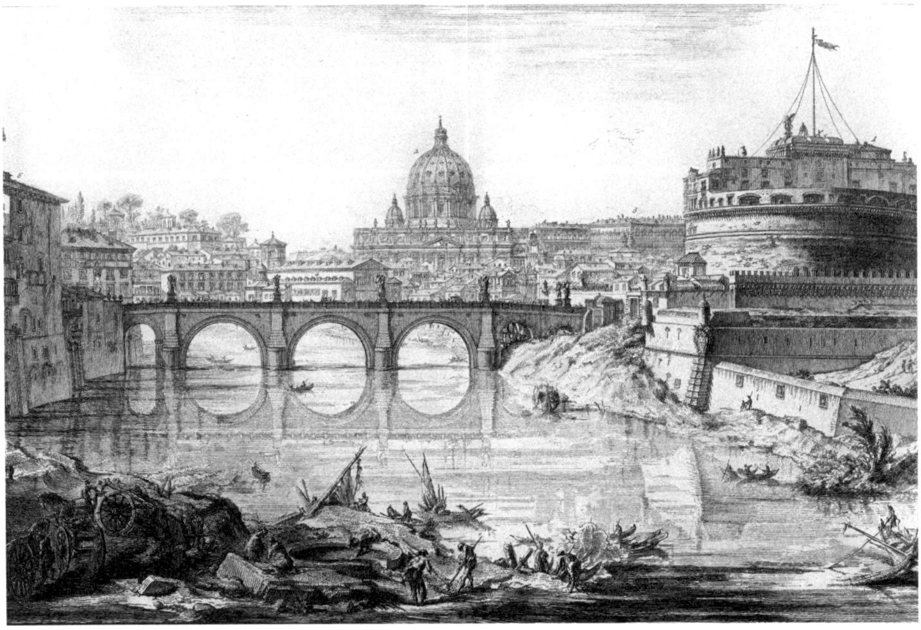

In the shadow of Freud, Piranesi's art seems to make sense in a new way. Occasionally, his compositions can be seen as closer illustrations of psychological truths than archaeological ones. In *Campo Marzio* (1762), for example, Piranesi renders ancient monuments neither in their actual rebuilt form, nor as reconstructions. Instead, he imagines how these monuments would have looked if they had been allowed quietly to decay; he bestows on them a fictive history of deterioration. The view of Castel Sant'Angelo exemplifies one such non-existent ruin. It uncovers the monument's "true" self, as it were, by removing its later additions but without restituting the original form (*see following*). The result is strangely ahistorical.[47] We find ourselves in a time between times, one might say, in a purely analytical realm. The building expresses several of its existences at once in the same way Freud argued that in the mind all layers of the past continue to exist simultaneously.

To judge from recent literature, the psychoanalysis of buildings seems to be a branch Piranesi himself introduced. Ulrike Brunotte, for example, writes of the Venetian etcher:

> In his manic reconstruction of Etruscan-Roman Antiquity, which had been suppressed by Classicism, Piranesi seems to have been following the same psychoanalytical rule: everything is significant, particularly the incidental, the fragmentary, the ignoble and ugly.[48]

Giovanni Battista Piranesi, *View of the Bridge and Castel Sant'Angelo*, from *Vedute di Roma*, 1754.

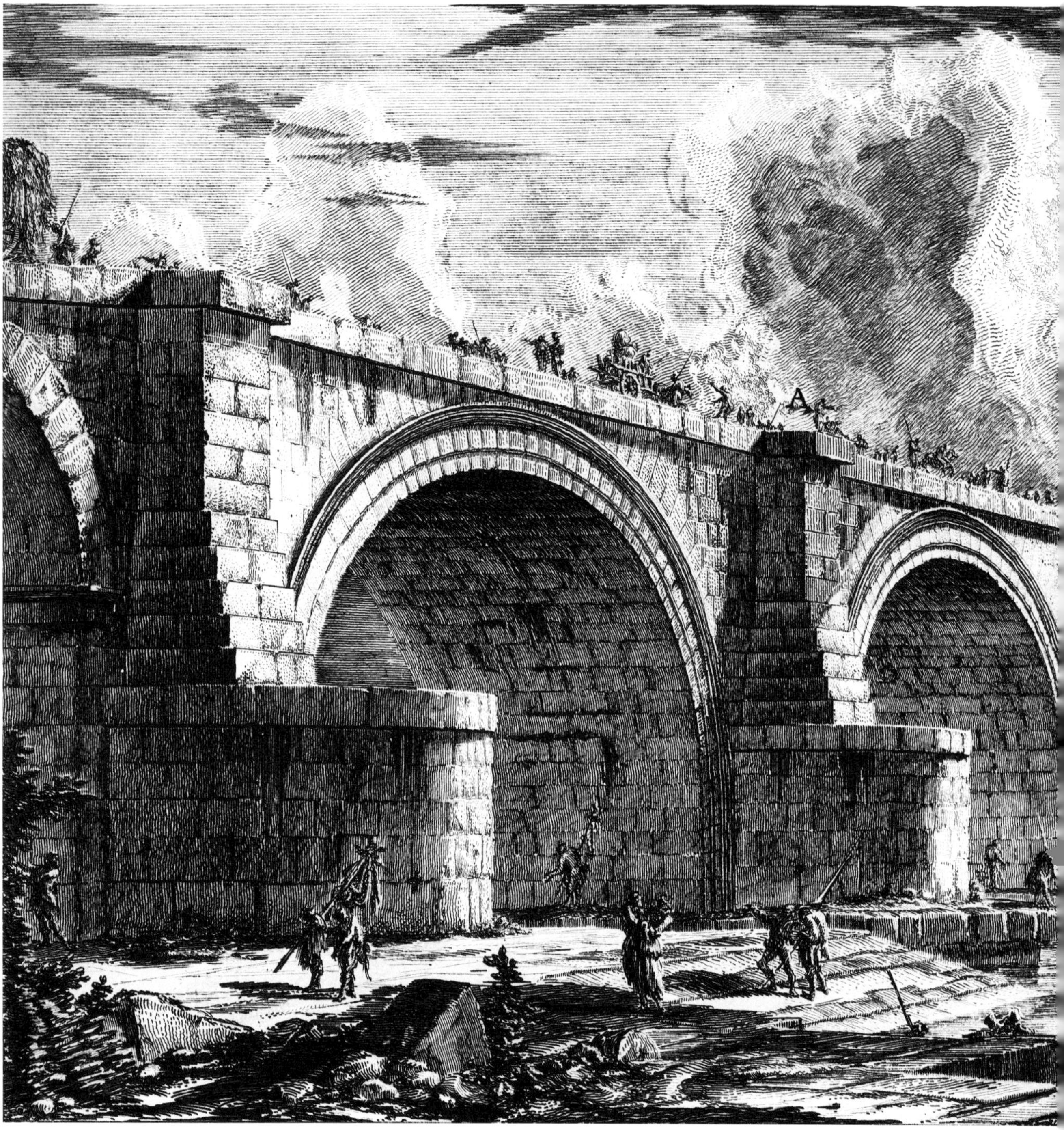

Giovanni Battista Piranesi, *The Aelius Bridge and the Mausoleum of Hadrian*, from *Il Campo Marzio dell'antica Roma*, 1762.

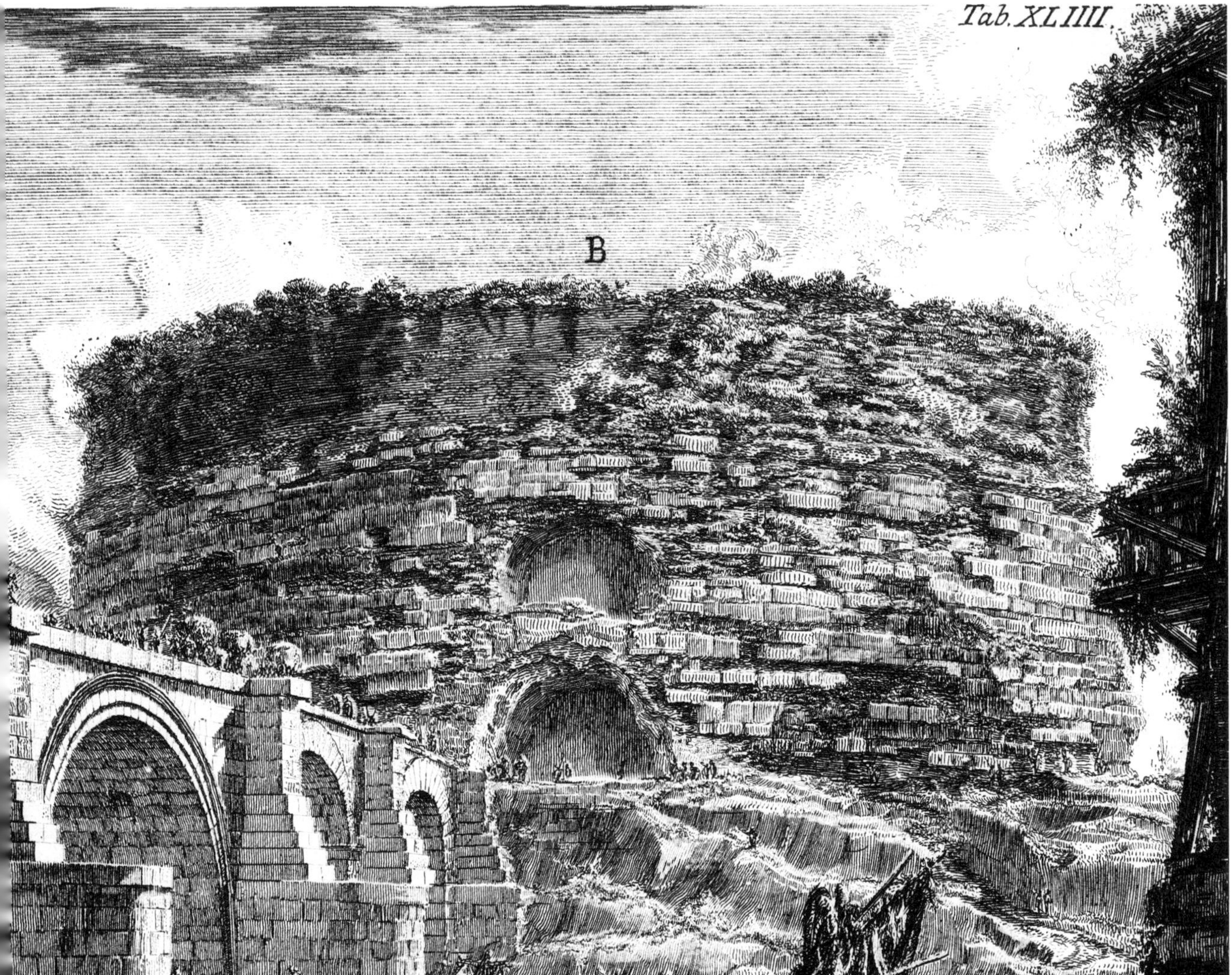
Tab. XLIIII.
B

With one period "suppressed" by another, as Brunotte puts it, the monuments themselves take to the couch, with Piranesi acting as their proto-psychoanalyst.

Whereas Freud's model has served to unlock the enigmatic content of the prints, the prints in turn have helped illuminate Freudian concepts, pinning elusive conditions on an architecture of dangling bridges, airy landings, and labyrinthine passages. And in this transaction, De Quincey has acted as negotiator in quite explicit terms. In *Crimes of Writing* (1994), Susan Stewart redefines Freudian anxiety against a background partly of Piranesi's *Carceri* and partly of De Quincey' description of them, which she quotes in full. In Freud's view, anxiety arises from needs and cravings that are never fulfilled—a continuous search for something that can replace a basic but lost gratification. Stewart finds a visual correspondence to that search in Piranesi's labyrinthine interiors and their effect of constantly "returning us to the same structure under modified terms."[49] Stewart is not the only one to advance a Freudian Piranesi. In *The Architectural Uncanny* (1992), Anthony Vidler reconsiders Freud's concept of the uncanny—the *unheimlich*—and connects it to architecture. The uncanny, according to Freud, is the unease, even terror, provoked when something familiar suddenly appears inexplicable or unrecognizable. One aspect of the uncanny, says Freud, is "the constant recurrence of the same thing," whether of a number or a name or a face.[50] Vidler sees Freud's definition manifested not so much in Piranesi's etchings as in De Quincey's artful reading of them (also quoted in full by Vidler). De Quincey was the first to express a "spatial uncanny," Vidler argues, with the image he created of "Piranesi" climbing the stairs of a structure that seemed never to end. Where De Quincey had formulated the Piranesian self-multiplication, and Nodier developed it, Vidler now *diagnoses* it with backing in Freud.

In the same way that Piranesi's dizzying interiors had served the Romantics, the Romantic distortions of Piranesi served modern psychoanalytical readings—at least in the reinterpretations of anxiety and uncanniness.[51] De Quincey had opened up a (mis)understanding of these prints as dreams, but through these "dreams" states and conditions that were otherwise hard to grasp suddenly gained an aspect that seemed concrete and comprehensible.

REARRANGING THE COLLECTIVE REALM

Whereas Freud confined the unconscious to a private sphere, anchoring it in individual fears and repressions, Jung coined the term "the collective unconscious," claiming there is a common psychic substrate of a suprapersonal nature.[52] In other words, at some deep level, and apart from our personal psyche, there exists a "second system" connecting all of us, according to Jung.[53] The unconscious is simply a container, a mental reservoir consisting of certain motifs—"pre-existent forms"—implanted in humankind from time immemorial. Jung famously named these forms "archetypes" and much of his effort as a scholar was directed at charting their manifestation in myths, religion, esoteric teaching, and dreams. Dreams, then—as the vocabulary of the unconscious—reemerged with particular significance also for Jung. And for Jungians studying Piranesi, the interiors that Piranesi's "dreams" constituted turned symbolic, inviting decoding, as if the hidden forces that shape our character lay encrypted in the designs.

Occasionally, Jung himself described the unconscious with spatial analogies referring to it as a "region" or as a building—a kind of museum even—calling it a "treasure-house of eternal images."[54] In any event, the unconscious emerged as a realm that "contains" its potent objects—its archetypes—among which Jung included architectural elements like stairs and ladders.[55] He never referred to this realm, however, as an interior of the kind Piranesi envisioned, which says as much about Jung's conservative art-view as it does about Piranesi's preemptive membership of the avant-garde.

To be precise, Jung's approach to art was generally ambivalent, or, more correctly, it was divided. His ideal unconscious, if one may put it like that, consisted of a vast depository of motifs like a gallery or a museum filled with objects and images drawn from myth, religion, alchemy, and cultural history, ranging from ancient Egypt to the Renaissance. But this generous view on the mind's hidden artworks was in sharp contrast to his fierce rejection of "modern art," by which he meant cubism and other contemporary movements of "non-objective" representations. Only in the last minute did Jung spare himself the embarrassment of diagnosing Picasso with schizophrenia: in an article first published in 1932, he made Picasso the scapegoat for an art characterized by its "paradoxical, unfeeling,

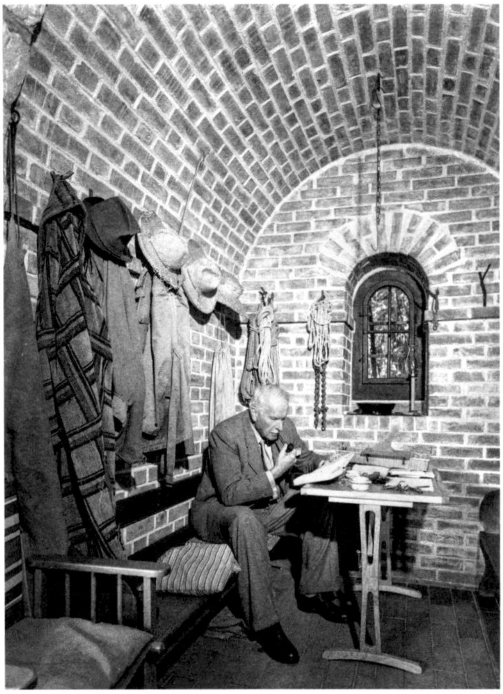

Carl Gustav Jung reading in the Tower at Bollingen, ca. 1960.

and grotesque unconcern for the beholder."[56] Picasso's art testified to Luciferian forces, "veiling the bright world of day with the mists of Hades, infecting it with discarded remnants, debris, shreds, and disorganized units." In short, "Picasso conjures up crude, earthy shapes, grotesque and primitive, and resurrects the soullessness of ancient Pompeii in a cold, glittering light." To Jung, Picasso invoked a chaotic world that did not lend itself to interpretation and therefore occupied a different dimension from an enigmatic but basically "figurative" unconscious. What is interesting is that Piranesi's prints, at the very time Jung wrote the essay, were being cast as "proto-cubist," as we shall see in chapter three. Abstraction and non-objectivity were themes extracted from his art at the time. If, for the sake of it, one equates Piranesi with Picasso, it is not an architecture of the soul that Piranesi conveys, but precisely the opposite, the image of soullessness.

In a letter dated 1932 Jung held "unswervingly to the view that modern art is much more correctly judged from the psychological rather than from the artistic standpoint"[57] and in another letter, written the same year, he claimed that modern art had "invaded the realm of the mind," where it tried on its own to decipher the unconscious.[58] As I see it, Jung's interpretation of dreams depended on a model of the unconscious as a realm of recognizable objects and events—of iconographical elements. Non-figurative art, by contrast, devoid of narrative, threatened to replace or confound that realm, not fill it, and thereby overthrow the entire construction Jung had devoted his métier to building up. Abstract art simply illustrated a competing system, a shadowy "other," to the unconscious. If Jung ever pondered over the *Carceri*, he may have thought of the disjointed, fragmented spaces as a corrosion of the unconscious and its world of symbols—a rival order to the neat mental archive he spent a lifetime charting—which is perhaps why he made no mention of these works.

If Jung himself displayed no interest in Piranesi, historians inspired by him have eagerly approached the stairways and drawbridges in the Venetian's art as symbols pointing to a deeply situated substratum connecting humanity. The prisons are landscapes not only of the mind but of the *collective* mind of Piranesi, Coleridge, and De Quincey, writes Paul Jamieson in 1956.[59] The mind understood in this way emerges as a universal storehouse, a container of "items" which historians may retrieve and organize according to their respective histories. For example, when Luzius Keller in *Piranèse et les romantiques français* (1966) traces Piranesi's spiral stair as a motif in literature from Victor Hugo to Stéphane Mallarmé, it is with explicit backing in Jung.[60] From this literature he collects examples that enable him to present a history in which the stair goes from being an allegory of the soul to become its very scaffolding, locking the inner self into an inevitable and terrifying descent.[61] It is Jung's model of the unconscious, not Freud's, that allows historians to identify, gather, and bestow meaning on Piranesian elements in broad cross-temporal sweeps. The approach rests on the notion that all expressions, regardless of medium, resurface from a shared inner space. In contrast to the privatized unconscious of Freud, then, the collective one of Jung suggests a timeless interior in which things and concepts—Piranesi and poetry—seemingly combine.

Reinterpreted as a collective space, Piranesi's *Carceri* have served modern culture on a profound level. But as J. Hillis Miller reminds us, consciousness as "a homogenous inner realm" is a fabrication informed less by the actual structure of the psyche than by the literary historian trying to sort his material.[62] The idea that the mind is a domain one might enter is but a convenient illusion. In fact, that this domain should be in any way architectural, built on vaults and arches, is an analogy that I think trails back to Piranesi, occasionally without authors themselves being aware of the connection. For example, after having discussed the *Carceri*, the art historian Henri Focillon seems unaware that the architecture the prints represent also influences his conception of how the mind "looks" in general: "The life within the artist's mind develops on many planes, all of which are nevertheless connected by various bridges, corridors, and stairways. These are thronged with all that inhabits his mind: travelers, so to speak, coming and going, ascending and descending, laden with most extraordinary burdens."[63] Focillon presents the internal structure in which our creative forces operate essentially as a Piranesian structure. In other words, Piranesi not only profited from twentieth-century spatial analogies but was also in large part responsible for creating them.

The history of the *Carceri* as psychology is not exclusively tied to the field of psychoanalysis but also extends to the psychology of perception. When Ernst Gombrich in *Art and Illusion* (1960) calls the *Carceri* prints "nightmares," he is referring more to a convention than to a genuine belief in them as reflections of the unconscious. In a shrewd balancing act that acknowledges their history but prepares the reader for a fresh interpretation, Gombrich claims Piranesi's prison series "hovers on the fringe of the dream world." He thus flirts with the De Quinceyan tradition whilst remaining detached from it. For what interests Gombrich is the constitution not of the unconscious but of *perception*. With this agenda in mind, his question simply is: "Is the perspective in Piranesi's print correct or false?"[64]

Rather than manifesting the depths of the unconscious, the *Carceri* to Gombrich manifest a trick of the eye. In *Art and Illusion*'s history of world art, Piranesi's disturbing dungeons and caverns resurface as what they truly are,

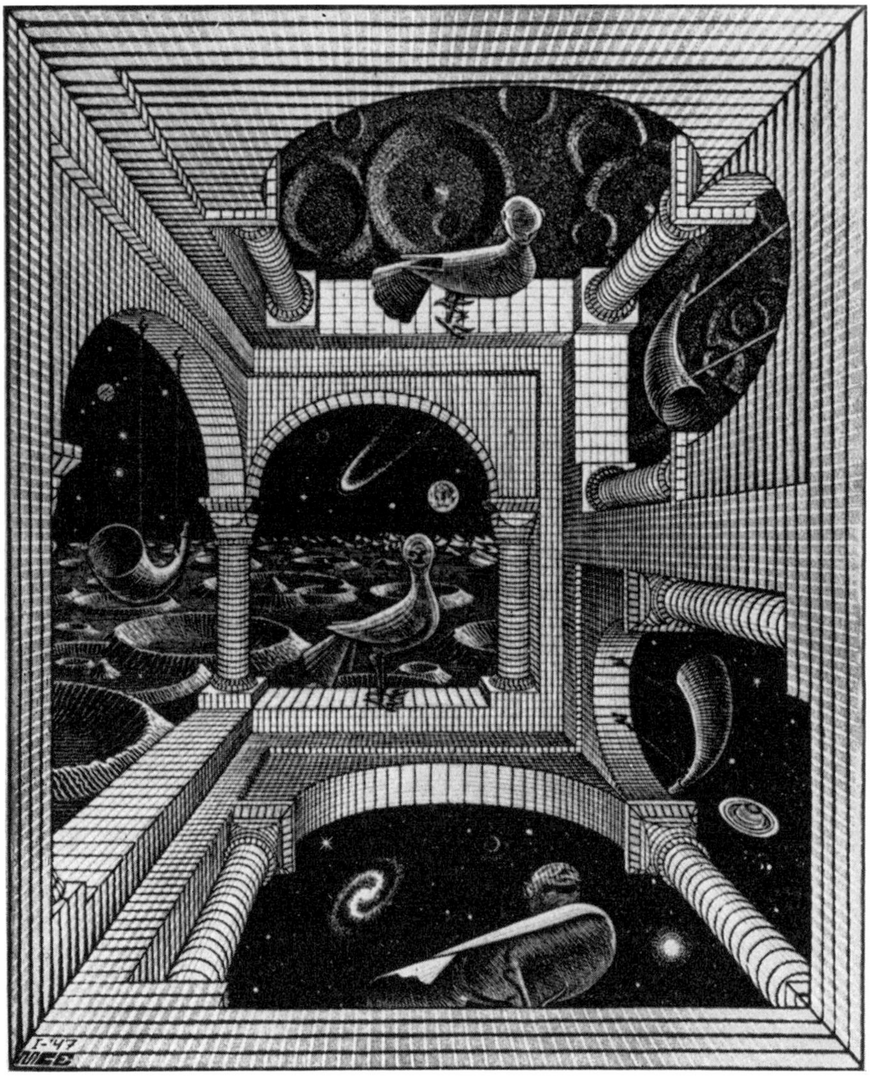

namely imagery—as if psychological literature itself has awoken from a nightmare and the rays of reason have rendered the prints harmless, revealing that they are, after all, only illusions. Reproducing *The Drawbridge* from the *Carceri* alongside a work by Austrian artist M. C. Escher in a spectacular double spread, Gombrich wants to display what he sees as the ambiguity in Piranesi's work and the artist's deliberate effort to engage the viewer in an optical game.[65] Colliding perspectives form part of this game, writes Gombrich. So, too, do the patches of smoke that drift by, which partly obscure the construction, making the viewer involuntarily imagine an architecture that is not there.

Escher and Piranesi (figures 207 & 208) in Ernst Gombrich, *Art and Illusion: A Study in the Psychology of Pictorial Representation*, 1960. These pages recreate the layout from the 1972 edition onward.

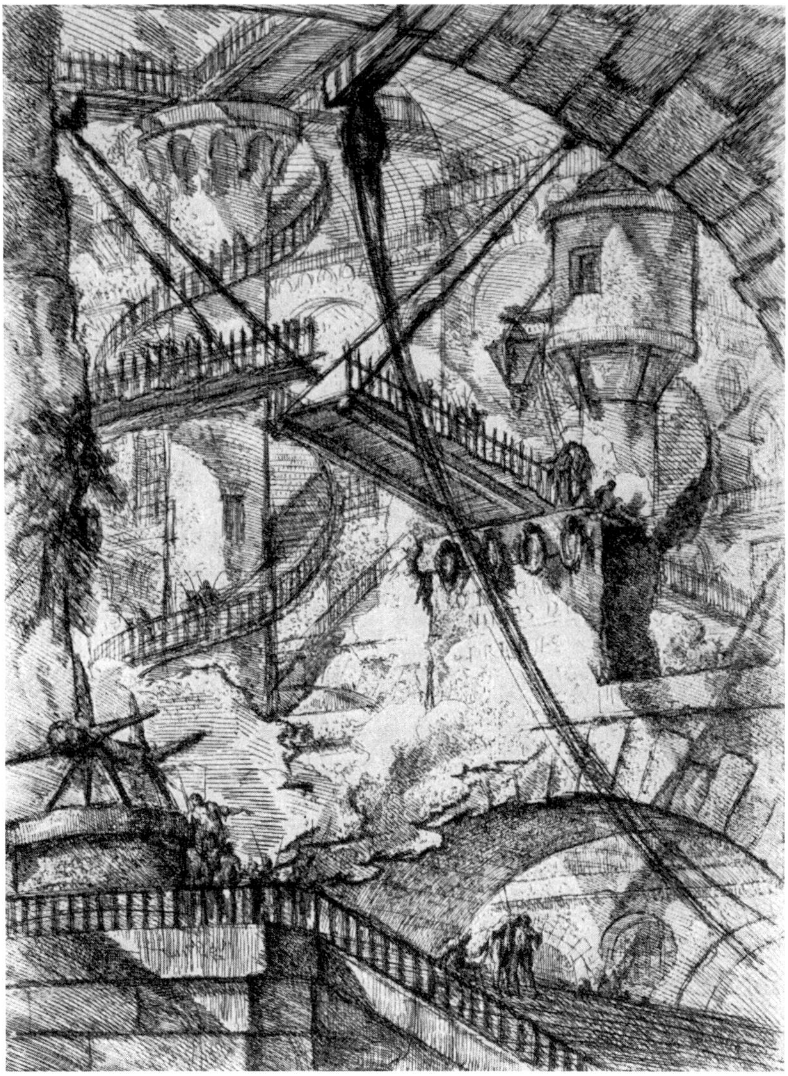

Gombrich's analysis of Piranesi's prints replaces an uncertainty as to who we are with an uncertainty as to what we see. Now manifesting ambiguities, rather than neuroses, the troubling dimension in the *Carceri* is relegated from the soul to our senses. With this, Gombrich seems to redeem Piranesi from a long history of literary interpretations. But then again, that is also the history on which he relies. Just like the Romantics, Gombrich is saying that we cannot trust our mind, that it tricks us into believing we see things that do not exist. So, even if the uncertainty produced does not stem from hallucinations and dreams, as was the case in *Confessions*, perception can be equally deceptive.

Returning to the passage from *Confessions* quoted at the beginning of this chapter, and to the second of De Quincey's consequential (mis)interpretations, my concern now is his evocation of an architecture that appears to extend indefinitely. That "Piranesi" fails to find his way out is only one part of the picture, as De Quincey's description also suggests an interior that has no end. The stairs multiply until both they and the "hopeless Piranesi" disappear from view, "lost in the upper gloom of the hall." The implications of this are quite complex. As the boundless space suggested by De Quincey is, paradoxically, still a prison, it is the endlessness of the architecture—its apparent pullulation right in front of our eyes—that holds us captive. A prison that gives the illusion of freedom is more frightening than one that keeps us locked up, in that it produces a perpetual uncertainty, a sense of existential entrapment.

In *The Disappearance of God: Five Nineteenth-Century Writers* (1963), literary historian J. Hillis Miller takes a cue from De Quincey's passage on Piranesi, coining the term "the Piranesi effect" to describe the process of endlessly replaying events in dreams and nightmares. "It is the power which the mind has to sink into its own infinite abyss, not by emptying itself out, but by becoming trapped in some form of thought or mental experience which is repeated forever."[66] To De Quincey, Miller observes, the content of dreams had one horrible quality, the propensity of inexhaustible self-reproduction. Whether the content is majestic buildings, a multitude of faces, the ocean, or a jungle, the mind involuntarily recreates them in unending and inescapable patterns of repetition, illustrated by De Quincey's description of the little figure, Piranesi, who is destined to keep on climbing without getting anywhere. So far, we have considered the psychological implications of the soul(s) seemingly lost within Piranesi's architecture, but the description also invokes an architecture without end. It manifests transgression as such—the continuous redoubling of our environs. In contrast to an architecture that is finite, De Quincey's description suggests an architecture about to form: its stairs are "unfinished" and the number of landings lost in an "upper gloom"—characterizations that help to erase any perceptible boundary. To speculate further, an architecture that never ends is also one that is still under construction. It unfolds, in other words, in a dimension that is in fact acutely contemporaneous. Although originating in an eighteenth-century printmaker's studio, a world that continually self-multiplies extends beyond time and place to a point where it ultimately also embraces the spectator.

The phenomenon Miller termed the Piranesi effect has proved to be useful in the understanding of modern literature. I do not claim of course to speak for twentieth-century fiction at large, nor for the almost equally extensive historiography of that fiction. But a few examples may indicate how the reference to Piranesi is the decisive point where literature and the history of that literature often diverge. Historians turn to De Quincey's *Carceri* adaptation to define texts that themselves contain references to neither De Quincey nor Piranesi. In other words, Piranesi—in De Quincey's rewriting—constitutes a theoretical model with sufficient authority to promote the innovative modern quality in authors such as Franz Kafka or James Joyce. The stories of Kafka's *The Trial* (1914–1915) and *The Castle* (1926) unfold within a reality that is decidedly architectural and that also cements an existence without exits, whether physical or psychological. In *The Castle*, for example, the protagonist named K can neither gain entrance to the castle nor escape his obsession with it. While Kafka himself never disclosed the possible sources for this castle, the literary historian Patrick Bridgwater calls it a "Piranesi-like aerial prison-edifice" and thus connects Kafka to Piranesi's *Carceri.* [67] It is a just comparison, of course, given the acute sense of anxiety that these architectural visions have seemed to illustrate ever since the days of De Quincey. A psychologically conditioned architecture—that is, an architecture in which physical and mental spaces interweave—recharges both Kafka and Piranesi through the connecting plug of De Quincey's *Confessions.*

Interpretations of James Joyce's authorship have also benefitted from the prison labyrinths mediated by De Quincey. A recurrent theme in this book is the *Carceri*'s disconcerting effect of locating the spectator in the midst of an architecture that seems to extend infinitely in all directions. Joyce also used the compositional device of the apparent maze that keeps the logic of the structure hidden. *Finnegans Wake* (1939) is an architecture in itself, according to Jennifer Bloomer: "The text is less a narrative to be apprehended than an object to be entered, less narrated than constructed."[68] Yet Joyce's textual structure is far from sound and unified. Intersected by "colliding geometries," it is still in the making, fraught with ambiguities, requiring the reader to complete it in their imagination. Bloomer sees in Piranesi's *Carceri*, and a few other prints, a similar "strategic operation of making."[69] But for Bloomer, it is De Quincey's "edifice" of distortions that draws the most precise comparisons with *Finnegans Wake*. More precisely, she finds in Joyce's text a perpetually repeated version, not of the same architectural form, but of the same person. She points to a character in the novel who reappears in the continually changing guise of "the fallen one," from Adam to Napoleon, "much as Piranesi's, or De Quincey's, or, rather, Coleridge's stairs."[70] In her analysis,

Bloomer personifies the theme of never-ending occurrences codified in *Confessions* and perpetuated, as we have seen, in literature from Nodier onward.

In an overall perspective, and exemplified by Bridgwater and Bloomer, De Quincey's famous passage constitutes a theoretical model deployed by the historian, not by the author, in order to capture manifestations of alienation and anxiety, disconnectedness and repetition. In other words, Piranesi in his literary transformation becomes an aid in critics' attempts to formulate ideas of modern fiction precisely as modern.

However, De Quincey's infinity architecture also permeates fiction itself, especially descriptions of imagined cities in fantastic literature. The idea of self-perpetuating urban clusters is developed in the evocations in Italo Calvino's *Invisible Cities* (*Le città invisibili*) (1972) of the cities of Leonia and Olinda. Surreally, these cities renew themselves and continuously expand, but in different ways. Olinda grows in concentric circles: "the old walls expand bearing the old quarters with them, enlarged, but maintain their proportions on a broader horizon at the edges of the city."[71] By contrast, the center of Leonia is completely regenerated every day, the old fabric pushed to the perimeter, where it accumulates in ever-greater heaps. "A fortress of indestructible leftovers surrounds Leonia, dominating it on every side, like a chain of mountains"—much like the piles of fragments in Piranesi's visions of Rome.[72]

The idea of a city that is self-generating and therefore beyond control is an urban dystopia that comes with an explicit reference to Piranesi in the Swede Sam Lundwall's Gothic science-fiction novel, *The Prison City* (*Fängelsestaden*) (1978). The book's true protagonist is a vast metropolis inhabited by millions of people: "And all the time it grew this gigantic organism of stone and flesh. Tentacles of stone reached tryingly from the almost homogenous body of the city, tossed away grass, soil and trees, cut the mountains into new building materials."[73] In an explanatory note, the author informs the reader that the *Carceri* prints "have provided the basis and the source of inspiration for the novel." To emphasize the point, reproductions of the complete suite of sixteen prints from the second edition appear at intervals throughout the publication, as if they constituted different perspectives on the same city, "the prison city." Lundwall, it seems, takes up an imagined standpoint within Piranesi's prison etchings, profiting from their ever-widening expanse of halls and galleries in the manner proposed by De Quincey.

One could argue that fiction of the 1960s and 1970s, from Calvino to Lundwall, used Piranesi as an analogy of urban development schemes gone off the rails. In these texts the "endless growth and self-reproduction" perceived by De Quincey is reconstituted as a critique of urban expansion. Indeed, the paradoxical effort to structure endlessness, as it were, governed not only the fantastic cities imagined by authors, but also the utopias envisioned by architects at the time, exemplified by Superstudio's *Continuous Monument* (1969), Archizoom's *No-Stop City*, and Rem Koolhaas's *Exodus, or the Voluntary Prisoners of Architecture* (1972), discussed in chapter six. With twentieth-century urban growth, the never-ending multiplication of forms that De Quincey connected to Piranesi arguably became at once a reality and a theme in fiction and urban experiments allegorizing that growth.

De Quincey's description, while it offers only a hazy and obscure image of Piranesi's edifices, advances an architecture that is in its own way new—one that derives its existence from concepts, not construction. By necessity inner edifices and endless spaces remain abstractions, and therefore timeless and universal. The *Carceri* etchings, in De Quincey's interpretation, re-emerge as their own emblems, seeming to hide more than they reveal. They disclose an architecture forever slipping beyond perception and, indeed, comprehension.

BORGES AND THE LABYRINTHS OF TIME

William Beckford's short story *Vathek* (1787), according to Jorge Luis Borges, contains the first description in literature of a truly atrocious hell. Beckford wrote of an underground world of endless halls and galleries crowded with people who "each wandered at random unheedful of the rest."[74] Among the works that influenced Beckford, Borges continues, was Piranesi's *Carceri,* "depicting mighty palaces which are also inextricable labyrinths."[75]

"Mighty palaces," however, form an ensemble grounded less in Piranesi's prints than in Thomas De Quincey's interpretation of them. In recollecting the *Carceri*, or more precisely Coleridge's description of the print(s), De Quincey was reminded of the "pomp of cities and palaces" that he himself had seen in the splendors of his dreams; remember, too, that William Beckford imagined "palaces in the style of Piranesi." With the reference to the *Carceri* architecture as palaces—and not prisons—Borges, who was a student of English Romantic literature, inscribes himself into a tradition of literary emulations of Piranesi's images.

"I met Piranesi through Thomas de Quincey," Borges admitted in an interview a few years before he died.[76] And although he also came to know the etcher through his prints, it was De Quincey's visionary retelling of them as dreams that arguably secured Piranesi's influence on Borges. However, what interested Borges in general was not so much the content of dreams as the dream itself, as a kind of framework for a new and heightened existence. The thinking and storylines in Borges's poems, short stories, and essays are structured by dreams enveloping

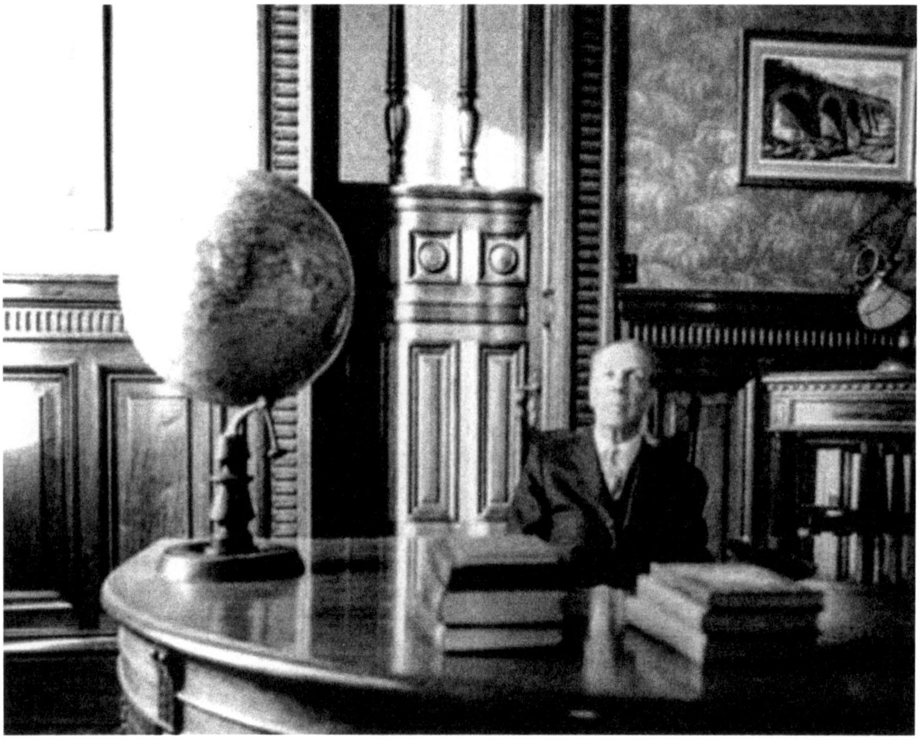

dreams, to the point where new realities are produced. And Piranesi—through De Quincey—is a progenitor of the compositional structures perfected by the Argentinian author.

Borges, however, extracts a new and what may ultimately be called a modern dimension from the compositions. In 1947 he published a short story, "The Immortal," which evokes an ominous setting. The Palace of the Immortals in Borges's tale is a terrifying place, built by and for human beings doomed to live forever. After entering the palace, traversing its caverns, descending a ladder, and making his way "through a chaos of squalid galleries" the protagonist concludes: "I am not certain how many galleries there were; my misery and anxiety multiplied them."[77] The emotional basis underpinning and generating such a structure derives from Piranesi, mediated through De Quincey, as Cristina Grau points out.[78] Borges, however, adds a dimension that is crucial in the history of Piranesi in the modern age, and that Grau never addresses: in Borges's interpretation, Piranesi's labyrinths of stairs and passages indicate not only a space but also a *time* prolonged with no end in sight. An architecture unfolding according to no coherent plan corresponds to a life that simply goes on and consequently has lost all meaning. To the infinite spatial sequence, which the *Carceri* seemed to codify, Borges adds an infinite temporal one.

Jorge Luis Borges in his office in the Biblioteca Nacional, Buenos Aires, with an etching by Piranesi on the wall behind him. Undated photograph.

The added dimension entails a subtle shift of architectural typology as well. Even more devious than a building that has no exits, like a prison, is a building with exits that lead nowhere, like a labyrinth. In Borges's world, the Piranesian edifice becomes an analogy of life itself.

In *Chronicles of Bustos Domecq* (1967), Borges and his co-author Adolfo Bioy-Casares created the character of Bustos Domecq, the fictional writer of a series of essays that aim to capsize accepted truths. The ironic dedication, "To those three forgotten greats—Picasso, Joyce, Le Corbusier," invites the reader to imagine a world in which these icons of modernism exerted no influence at all. On that cue, the book draws up alternative routes through the twentieth century, including its architectural history.

In the essay "The Flowering of an Art" Bustos Domecq acts as mouthpiece for Borges's dislike of modernist architecture and of Le Corbusier in particular. Borges never took to modernism. "The cubes of Le Corbusier never interested me," he admitted on one occasion; on another, he lamented the atrocities committed by Le Corbusier and Frank Lloyd Wright.[79] Although he was quick to exonerate Wright (recalling his own visit to the Guggenheim Museum in New York), no pardon was in store for Le Corbusier.[80] On the contrary, the essence of Le Corbusier's philosophy, the house as a machine for living, is the target in "The Flowering of an Art," which celebrates a non-habitable architecture, in a parodic inversion of functionalist discourse. We are introduced to "Adam Quincey," the fictitious author of a "short and badly printed" 1937 study, *Towards an Uncompromising Architecture*. The title paraphrases Le Corbusier's classic manifesto from 1923 but a couple of "quotes" from Quincey's "book" outline the somewhat opposite ideal of an architecture "not subject to the demands of inhabitability": "Le Corbusier speaks of the house as a machine for living—a definition which seems less applicable to Taj Mahal than to an oak tree or to a fish."[81] The name Adam Quincey, too, is a calculated part of the rhetoric. "Adam," as Ricardo Romera Rozas observes, alludes to Piranesi's English patron and friend, Robert Adam, whereas "Quincey" of course refers to Borges's muse, the inexhaustible dream-monger among the British Romantics.[82] It is impossible to envision a greater contrast than the one that exists between Le Corbusier's housing machines and De Quincey's imagined palaces. From within the reality of a modernist architecture, Borges unwinds an opposite reality, drawing on modernism's apparatus, references, terminology—a Trojan horse of dreams unleashed in the midst of functionalist facts.

In the second example of inhabitable architecture, Piranesi himself makes an entry, guised as a modernist, although a subversive one. In Borges's and

overleaf Giovanni Battista Piranesi, *Remains of the Temple of the God Canopus in Hadrian's Villa in Tivoli*, from *Vedute di Roma*, 1768. The print decorated Borges's apartment in Buenos Aires.

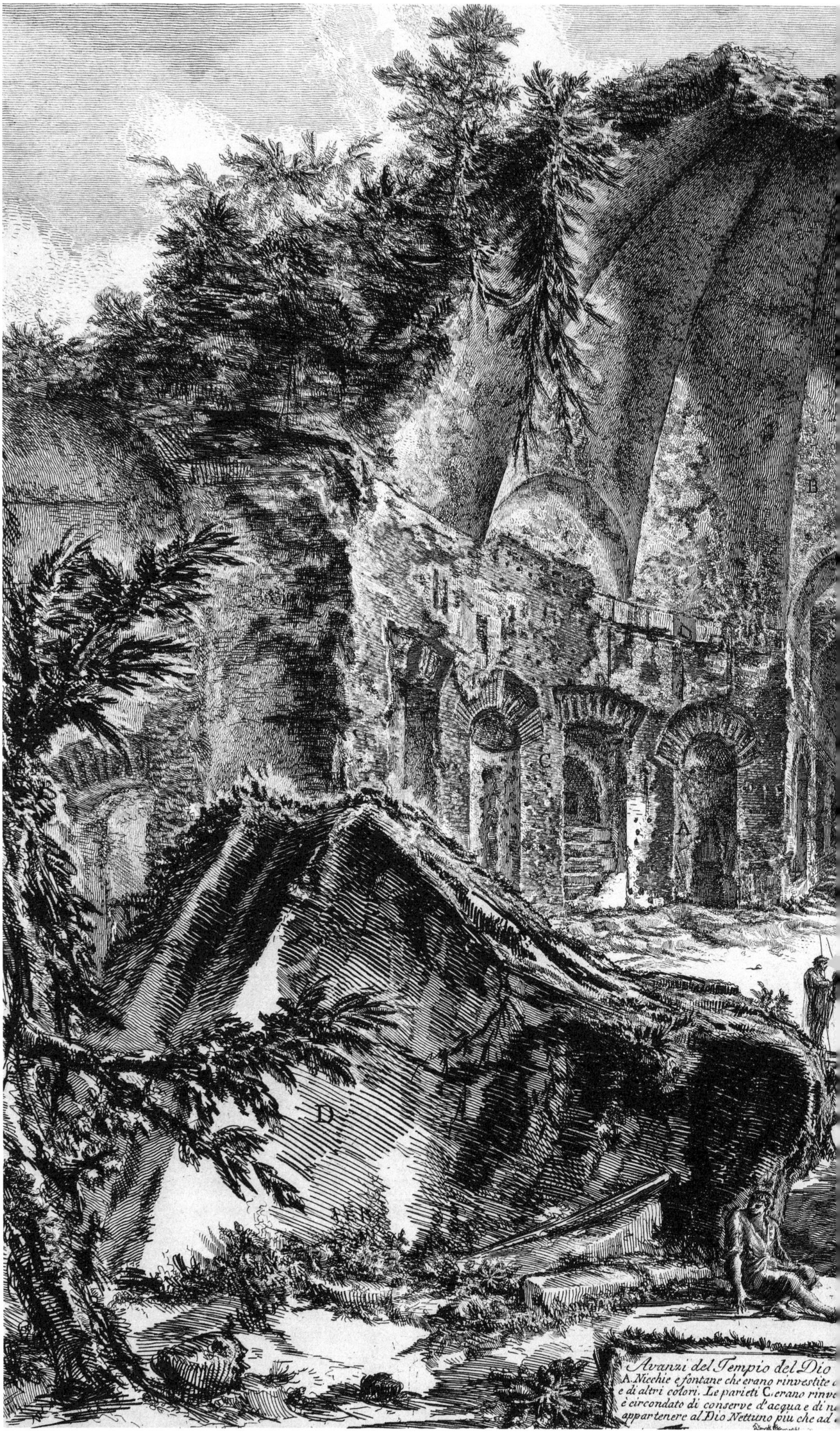

Avanzi del Tempio del Dio
A. Nicchie e fontane che erano rinvestite
e di altri colori. Le parieti C. erano
è circondato di conserve d'acqua e di
appartenere al Dio Nettuno piu che ad

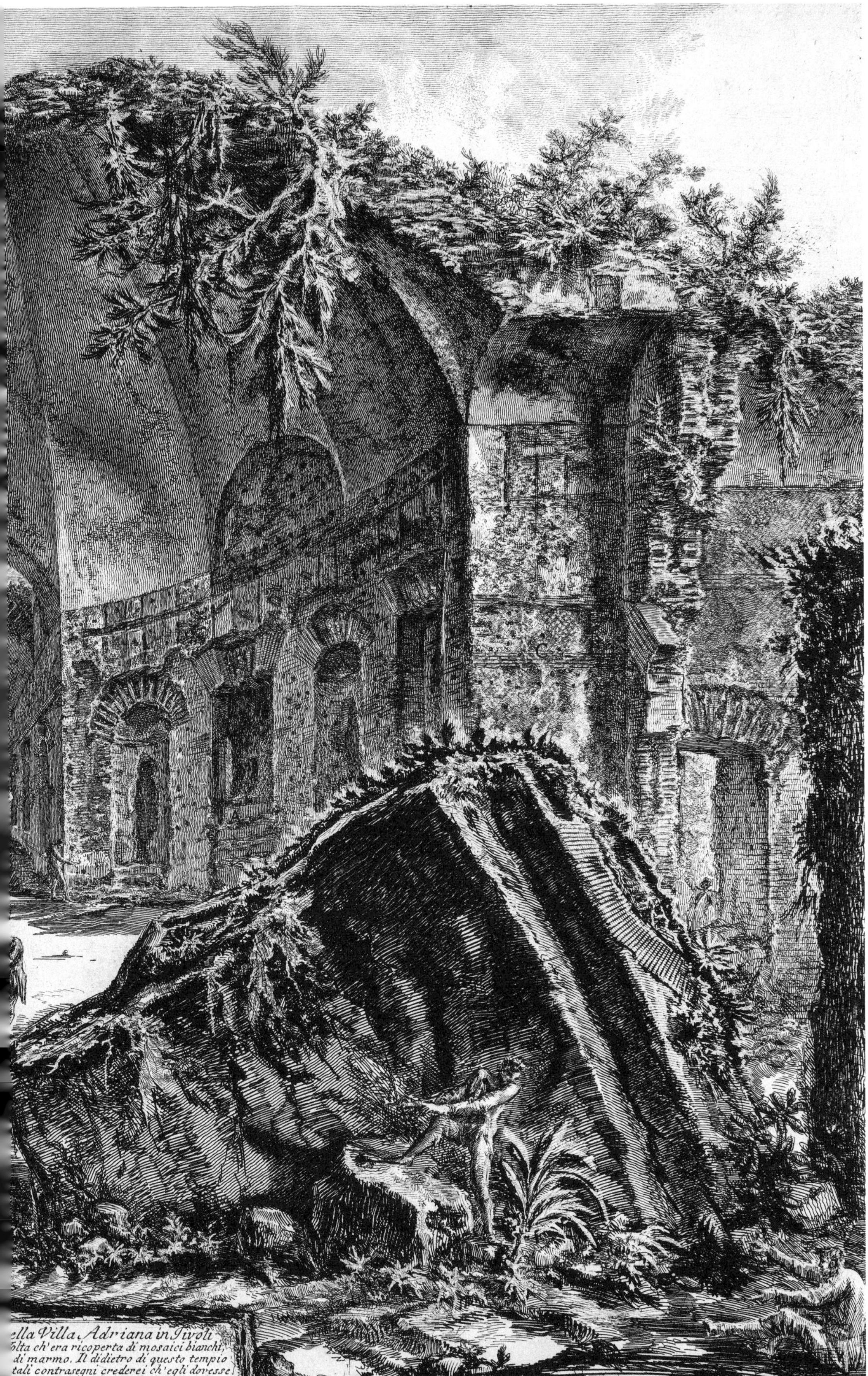
ella Villa Adriana in Tivoli
olta ch'era ricoperta di mosaici bianchi,
di marmo. Il didietro di questo tempio
tali contrasegni crederei ch'egli dovesse
. Due gran macigni caduti dalla Volta

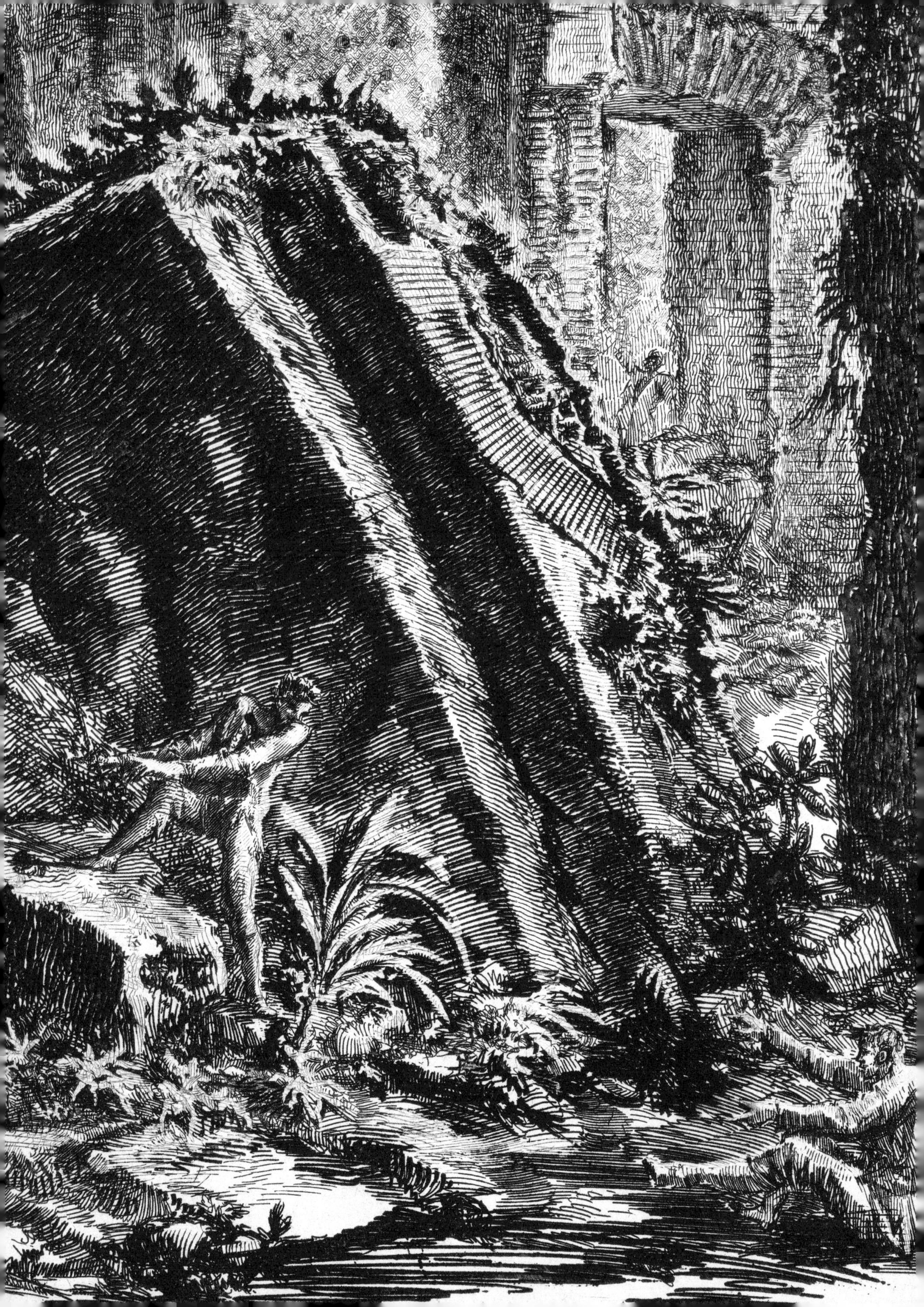

Bioy-Casares's inverted history of the modern age, Bustos Domecq now evokes "Alessandro Piranesi," architect of the so-called "Great Chaotic of Rome" erected in the late 1930s:

> This noble edifice [...] consisted essentially of truncated bridges, of spiral stairways that gave access to impenetrable walls, of balconies to which entrance was impossible, and of doors that opened either into pits or into high, narrow rooms from whose ceilings soft armchairs and comfortable double beds hung upside down.[83]

It requires little imagination to see how the Great Chaotic expands on the *Carceri*, as if the architecture conveyed by the prints was the only rational solution to the needs of the 1930s. Parodying the sensationalist tone of modernist discourse, the (fictive) journal *Architectural Forum* proclaims the edifice "the first concrete example of the new architectonic conscience."

In the persona of a fictive twentieth-century architect, then, the eighteenth-century engraver reappears as a figurehead in Borges's crusade against modernism. The ironic pairing of Le Corbusier and Piranesi is interesting because it reflects an identical pairing in architectural theory at the time, prompted by a similar revolt against modernism. In *Complexity and Contradiction in Architecture* (1966), issued the year before Borges's *Chronicles of Bustos Domecq*, American architect Robert Venturi undermines the stern functionality associated with the Swiss architect by describing the Villa Savoye with the exact same phrase that he reserves for one of Piranesi's impossible structures, a point to which I will return in chapter five.

The Argentinian author drew inspiration from De Quincey's Piranesi visions but I believe he also drew inspiration from Piranesi's prints themselves. In the short story, "The Circular Ruins" (1941), Borges describes a derelict temple in which humans may dream up tangible realities, including other humans. At the end of the story, the narrator discovers that he too is a mirage conjured by an earlier dream-monger: "With relief, with humiliation, with terror, he understood that he too was a mere appearance, dreamt by another."[84] The buildings that enable this dreaming are described as "broken," circular temples—temples "long ago devoured by fire, which the malarial jungle had profaned and whose god no longer received the homage of men."[85] On the wall of the living room of Borges's apartment in Buenos Aires was an impression of Piranesi's rendering of the temple of the god Canopus at Hadrian's Villa (now believed to have been a nymphaeum) from *Vedute di Roma* (*see preceding*), which depicts half of a circular structure, a giant, ruined hall, with its remaining half a gaping void.[86] We will never know if Borges had this structure in mind when he conceived of the short

Detail of *Remains of the Temple of the God Canopus in Hadrian's Villa in Tivoli.*

story's "dream-factory," but it is likely. In any event, an architecture of "dreams" that allows for a surreal duplication of the self seems taken out of De Quincey's recasting of Piranesi's universe as dreamlike and highlights the uncertain states of existence that Borges's characters share in. "Not to be a man, to be the projection of another man's dream, what a feeling of humiliation, of vertigo!"—Borges's main character exclaims.[87] Borges, the observer of details, may even have noticed the enigmatic figure in the corner of Piranesi's print who may be seen to "create" the entire scene—buildings and people included (*see preceding*).

THE PIRANESI PIVOT

De Quincey's passage on Piranesi's "dreams" holds yet another interpretation unraveling a dimension of the mind. In *Confessions*, De Quincey admits that he never saw the print(s) he describes but only relates what his friend Coleridge had told him about it "years ago." In other words, the true object of his description is not a print but a recollection. In a strand of literature, from Théophile Gautier to W. G. Sebald, Piranesi and memory form a particularly interesting relation.

The connection between print and memory has always been close, as seen by the confluence of terms, and indeed concepts, in printmaking and remembering. We refer to "impressions" being formed, as if they were folios of prints, and to events being "imprinted"—or "*gedrückt*" as Goethe called it—on memory. A difference between "states" applies to changes made on the copper plate as well as in our inner life.[88] In short, we speak of images impressed or imprinted on the mind with such conviction that prints seem to provide more than a metaphor, pointing also to the mechanism of the elusive act of remembrance itself.

In Marcel Proust's *In Search of Lost Time* (*À la recherche du temps perdu*) (1913–1927), the effort to capture a precise memory of people, things, events pervades the several thousand pages of the entire novel. A particularly important but slippery image for the protagonist to retain in his mind is the church in Combray, the village where he spent his childhood summers. Just as one medium envelops another in De Quincey's Piranesi tale, the past doubles as layers upon layers for Proust. In one particular passage in the novel's first part, Proust describes how the jumbled roofs of Paris, seen from a certain window, make up "a first, a second, and even a third layer"—as if the view had been re-engraved several times.[89] Across this view, Proust remarks, the dome of the church of St. Augustine shows a spectrum of hues "sometimes ruddy, sometimes too, in the finest 'prints' which the atmosphere makes of it, of an ashy solution of black," before he adds, "and which imparts to this view of Paris the character of some of the Piranesi views of Rome."

The introduction of the name Piranesi triggers a contemplation on remembering, as if the mere mentioning of the name cast a magic spell, for in the second part of the passage Proust turns to the medium of graphic reproduction as a model with which to grasp the very mechanics of recollecting. More precisely, and now explicitly calling the imprints on the atmosphere "engravings," he writes that in whatever fashion his memory may have executed the Parisian skyline, "these little engravings" do not have the same substance as his recollection of the steeple of Combray seen from the street behind the church.[90]

The connection that Proust makes between print and remembrance is more complex than the one demonstrated by Goethe and Koolhaas in the opening paragraph of this book. The transition from an outer to an inner view—from a view Proust's protagonist can see to one he recalls—passes through "layers" of imprints incised with equal subtlety by the atmosphere and by memory. Proust, moreover, describes the "engravings" in terms of etchings, which interestingly suggests that for Proust the very process of covering the plate with wax, then allowing acid to burn the engraved lines into the metal, in some way corresponds to the technique of memorizing. If the minds of Koolhaas and Goethe seem to contain a gallery of printed images, for Proust Piranesi informs the process of remembering itself. In the example from *In Search of Lost Time*, the mentioning of Piranesi marks a pivot point in the protagonist's quest—the point at which his search for worldly connections turns introspective and becomes instead a search in his own memory. It is a shift I shall call "the Piranesi Pivot."

Piranesi as a narrative hinge between an outer and an inner quest, between seeing and remembering, is a trope I believe Proust found elsewhere. Théophile Gautier referred to Piranesi repeatedly in his works, but only once in his artful diary, *Travels in Spain* (*Voyage en Espagne*), published in 1843. Gautier evokes Piranesi about midway through the book, at a moment in his journey when imagination and reality are becoming confused. More specifically, Gautier, touring Toledo, recollects a visit to the ruined fortress of Alcazar, which he describes as if he was entering a *Carceri* print. He relates how he was "led through a labyrinth of small lanes" to the ruins, which "might be one of those remarkable visions which Piranesi sought and realized in his magnificent etchings." He particularly recalls a great staircase leading to a door that opened onto an abyss and that produced "a strange and threatening effect." At this point, for the only time during his Spanish travels, Gautier is struck by existential doubt:

> I fell into a deep meditation in the presence of all these shapes which I saw and probably would never again see. I began to doubt my identity;

> I felt so far away from myself, carried to such a distance outside my usual sphere that it all seemed to me a hallucination, a strange dream of which I should start awake to the sharp, trembling strains of some vaudeville music as I sat in the theater box.[91]

The Piranesian architecture with stairs leading to nothing induced a sudden sense of alienation, which in turn trigged a crisis of identity. Gautier was outside himself, and for a moment reality seemed like a dream.

Proust was an admirer of Gautier, and of his *Voyage en Espagne* in particular. In this travel account, according to Proust, each sentence "accentuates and pursues the graceful and cheerful traits of his [Gautier's] personality."[92] From this book too, I argue, Proust learned to use Piranesi as a literary device, as a key to shift the focus from an outer realm to an inner one, from a firm grasp of the world to a fleeting sense of one's own self. In short, he learned the use of the Piranesi Pivot.

The century-long tradition in French and English literature of imagining the chambers of the soul decorated à la *Carceri* made Piranesi a gatekeeper in modern-day odysseys of the self. The evocation of Piranesi's name signaled a deepening of the plot or an altered course in the telling of a story.

A fine example of the Piranesi Pivot in modern literature occurs in W. G. Sebald's novel *Austerlitz* (2001). The book is structured as a series of conversations between the narrator and the character named Jacques Austerlitz. In the first part of the book, Austerlitz relates his life from childhood to manhood while both he and the reader are aware that his origin is clouded in mystery. The turning point comes in the middle of Sebald's novel, when Austerlitz unexpectedly finds himself in an abandoned part of London's Liverpool Street Station and experiences an architectural epiphany. He lifts his head and looks into the interior space above him:

> From time to time, and just for a split second, I saw huge halls open up, with rows of pillars and colonnades leading far into the distance, with vaults and brickwork arches bearing on them many-storeyed structures, with flights of stone steps, wooden stairways and ladders, all leading the eye on and on. I saw viaducts and footbridges crossing deep chasms thronged with tiny figures who looked to me, said Austerlitz, like prisoners in search of some escape from their dungeon, and the longer I stared upwards with my head wrenched painfully back, the more I felt as if the room where I stood were expanding, going on for ever and ever in an improbably foreshortened perspective, at the same time turning back into itself in a way possible only in such a deranged universe.[93]

Sebald never mentions Piranesi, but one or several of his *Carceri* prints undoubtedly constitute the architectural framework of the account.[94] More precisely, the framework derives from De Quincey's description of Piranesi's "dreams" in *Confessions* in an almost element-to-element literary takeover: a gaze gradually moving upwards, trying to take in a never-ending space of arches and stairways, structures both accounts. Figures appearing like prisoners searching for an escape is also a motif that both texts share. What is significant, however, is that this passage not only occurs at the center of Sebald's book, but marks a turning point in the narration—the juncture at which Austerlitz's day-to day existence turns into a quest for his true identity. The Piranesi epiphany marks the exact moment in the novel when the protagonist, who up till now has forgotten his childhood, starts to remember, when he experiences "scraps of memory beginning to drift through the outlying regions of my mind." As the reader will learn, it was at Liverpool Street Station that Austerlitz arrived as a child refugee, brought to safety from a Nazi-occupied Europe. Finding himself underneath the station's huge vaults decades later, memories keep flooding back: "and for the first time in as far back as I can remember I recollected myself as a small child."[95]

Piranesi's "dreams" represent a vision of architecture that expands at the moment of beholding, inwards as well as outwards. In other words, the Piranesi-De Quinceyan architecture opens chasms in the mind through which one sees oneself as a child—by which one remembers. The "knowing" child constructed by Goethe finds a counterpoint in the forgotten boy remembered by Austerlitz. And Piranesi triggers the memory of both.

The Piranesi Pivot is above all a literary device employed to denote a change—to define the experience of a familiar world suddenly "turning back into itself," as Austerlitz in Sebald's novel puts it. Years of translations, interpretations, and adaptations, across periods and genres, put the *Carceri* in command of an extraordinary double realm—a psychological one, derived from the inner landscape they allegedly invoked, and an architectural one. Conflating an exterior and an interior space, reconciling the outer and the inner world, they constitute a scenic backdrop for any narrative in need of a game-changer, not only in literature but also in film, as we shall see. Inextricably linked to dreams and dreaming, these spaces were always also a vestibule to the soul, as this chapter has intended to show. Continuing in a tradition from the early nineteenth century and the Romantic movement, modern psychology merely had to reinvent and relabel the interiority they represented, just as Piranesi's representations in turn facilitated modern conceptualization of the mind in poetry, fiction, and literary criticism.

THE

ETCHER EXPOSED

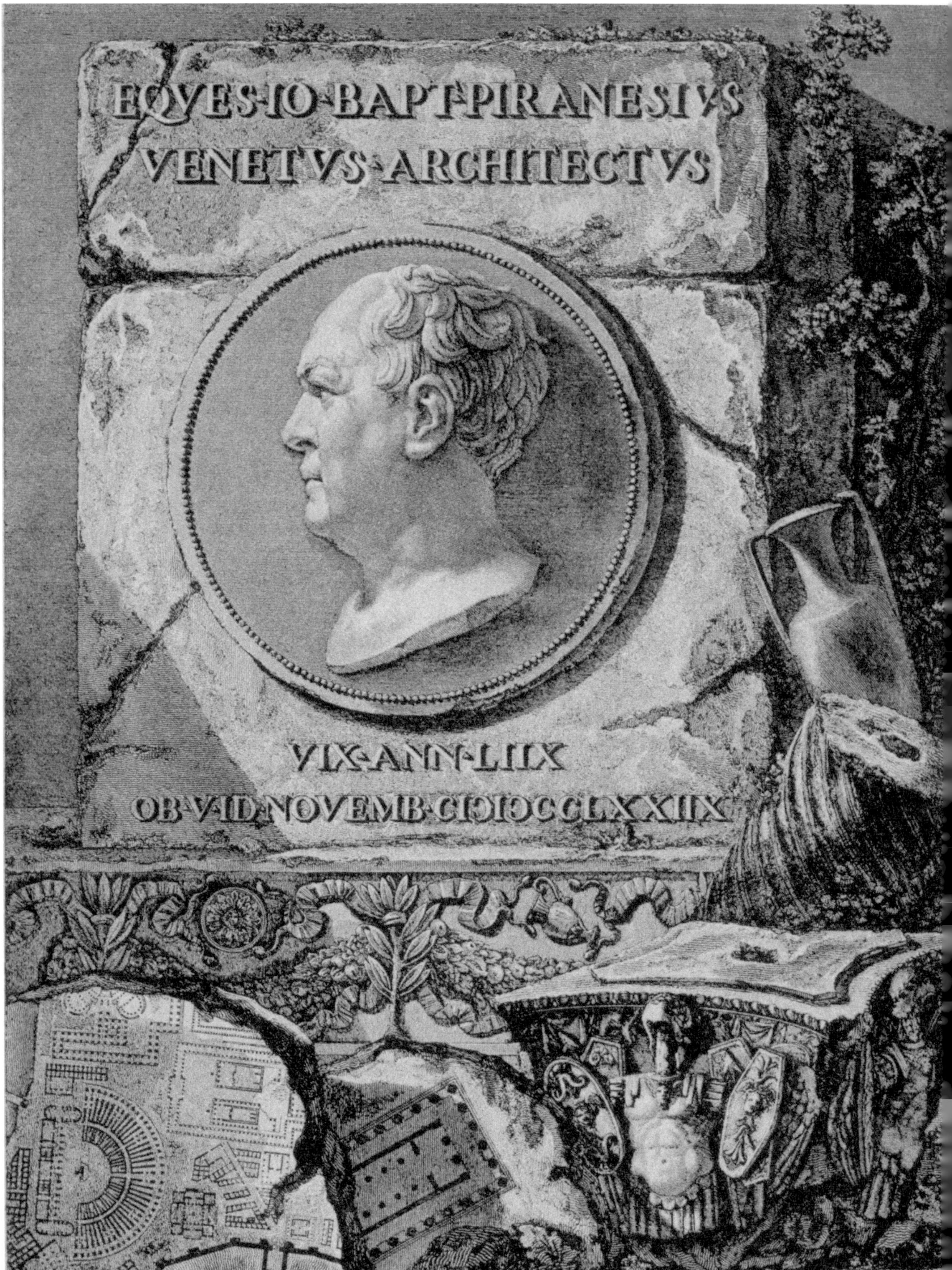
EQVES·IO·BAPT·PIRANESIVS
VENETVS·ARCHITECTVS
VIX·ANN·LIIX
OB·V·ID·NOVEMB·CIƆIƆCCLXXIIX

"Giovanni Battista Piranesi, the etcher of the views which hung in Sir Walter Scott's dining parlour, was born at Venice on 4 October 1720." Thus begins Arthur Samuel's book on Piranesi published in 1910. It is an interesting introduction, because the most urgent thing for Samuel to tell his readers about the artist, even more urgent than when and where he was born, is the fact that his views decorated the dining room of the novelist Walter Scott.

The connection to the famous author was crucial. It helped promote Piranesi's etchings as collectibles at a time when his prints were not in favor. The text addresses the ideal collector, who Samuel imagines is sitting comfortably at home, pondering the next acquisition, eager to fill free wall space, but unknowledgeable, even suspicious of the Venetian etcher.

Around 1900, Piranesi's art was, if not entirely unknown, at least vastly underrated. Disillusioned travelers had discovered that Roman architecture was not at all as magnificent as Piranesi had portrayed it.[1] He also failed to impress as an etcher. His name did not even appear in important surveys like Bartsch's *Le peintre-graveur* (1803–1821), Hamerton's *Etching and Etchers* (1868), and De Vesme's *Le peintre-graveur italien* (1906). When he was acknowledged, it would be for his originality and imagination, but, as Joseph Pennell in *Etchers and Etching* (1919) flatly observed, "he is not a great etcher by any means."[2] On the whole, the Victorians did not take kindly to Piranesi. He was seen as somehow irrational, unpredictable, even slightly "possessed"—an image that owed much to De Quincey. Standard biographies even took the poet's flights of fancy as facts. For example, the idea that the prison etchings recorded the artist's "visions during the delirium of a fever" was restated almost verbatim in the 1904 edition of *Bryan's Dictionary of Painters and Engravers*, which declared that the *Carceri* were "said to consist of prison-interiors seen by Piranesi during the delirium of a fever."[3] As discussed in the previous chapter, for a long time, novelists and scholars paid more attention to Piranesi's inner state, to his "dark brain," than to his art.

THE FAILED PHOTOGRAPHER

If it is possible to speak of a rediscovery of Piranesi just after 1900, it is because the perspective changes. In the first decade of the twentieth century a small but significant number of books and articles on Piranesi were published. Authors such as Russell Sturgis, W. J. Woodworth, Arthur Samuel, and Arthur Hind seemed to detect a new quality in the etchings. This fresh view, I argue, was prompted by a general reorientation in art and aesthetics at the time. In short, what these authors saw when they looked at Piranesi was no longer a delirious Romantic, but a modernist at work.

Francesco Piranesi's portrait of his father from 1779, illustrating the title page to Arthur Samuel, *Piranesi*, 1910.

Before 1900, the taste had been for prints with a soft tonality and gentle gradation, of the kind produced by celebrity printmakers such as Christian Friedrich Müller, Auguste Boucher Desnoyers, and, indeed, Raphael Morghen, whose reproduction of Leonardo's *Last Supper* was hailed as a triumph of etching. Copies of Morghen's Leonardo adorned countless homes of the growing middle class, who found in it that irresistible, self-improving Victorian blend of Christian morality and the celebration of "genius."[4]

With Piranesi's art, by contrast, the question was whether it would fit into a decent home at all. Not only were the etchings seen as disturbing, even brutal, they were also sizable: "His big etchings [...] are too big for collectors to enjoy heartily," Russell Sturgis writes in the first modern monograph of Piranesi, published in 1900. He adds, "Nobody's house is large enough, at least in the cities, to contain Piranesi's work with any satisfaction or comfort."[5] Sturgis makes it sound as if the Venetian's prints are as big and unmanageable as dining tables.

Size was also a problem for W. J. Woodworth, who writes in the journal *Brush and Pencil* in 1902: "These marvellous plates by Piranesi have small charm for the collector. They are too big and bold; they lack the daintiness and delicacy that the collector prizes; they are for the gallery, and not for the home." He ends with a sigh: "One would wish that the plates were of less generous proportions. They might perhaps lose in dignity and importance, but they would be more in keeping with present-day decorative requirements."[6]

Arthur Samuel, in his 1910 monograph of the artist, tackles the potentially overwhelming effect of Piranesi's art on otherwise tranquil domestic settings by suggesting a precise number of prints for each room. "[U]nless the wall space be very extensive, half a dozen Piranesi etchings are about as many as one room will accommodate." At the same time, Samuel is at pains to insist that the number should also not be too low, because, as he points out with a wonderful analogy:

> An etching or two will no more show the irresistible force of this man than will the bazaar-born glass paper-weight with a photograph of Niagara reconstitute the appalling spectacle of the Falls at flood-time.[7]

A paperweight with a cascade trapped inside was the metaphor Samuel hoped would stir the print-collector, immersed in his or her library, into action. A collector of Piranesi around 1900 was obviously not considered avant-garde: Frederick Wedmore, writing in 1911, thinks the prints are too large: "But framed, and hung together in a moderate-sized hall, they imply, albeit a little monotonously, that we find ourselves in the dwelling of a cultivated person of the older type."[8]

Overall, Piranesi's reintroduction into the modern world was a battle against taste. The artist strove to gain access, literally, to homes governed by the ideals of nineteenth-century historicism. Even the eminent Arthur Hind, who was perhaps the first true print historian, feels he has to negotiate a place for Piranesi's dramatic expression in late Victorian interiors. Having carefully weighed the pros and cons of the *Carceri* series, he cautiously concludes that "they will bear hanging on one's walls [...] without inducing the obsession of a nightmare."[9]

The rediscovery of Piranesi around 1900, then, went anything but smoothly and stumbled at the outset on the issue of interior decoration. On a closer reading, the resistance to Piranesi boils down to an objection to his technique. This went beyond the disturbing effect of having too many Piranesi prints on the wall. Rather, within each single composition, a striking imbalance was observed. Compared to the even expression in the prints of Raphael Morghen and other contemporary engravers, Piranesi was seen to have exaggerated the contrast between black and white.

Russell Sturgis, in 1900, is quite explicit in his criticism: "The fault of his work as an engraver is in the extreme contrasts of dark and light. He had a natural tendency towards blackness. There can be no mistake about that."[10] *Bryan's Dictionary*, in its 1904 edition, strikes a slightly more forgiving tone: "Despite his weakness for the blackest of blacks and the whitest of white, the artist's own proofs are full of fine touches, and one *can* peer into their shadows." Whereas Samuel, in 1910, remarks critically that "with the extreme contrasts of light and shade, the sight is often baffled, and there is nothing left but for the eye to grope for what is intended." In those prints, he adds, "the limit is overstepped and the balance ruined."[11] Even Arthur Hind "regrets the blackness" in the second, 1761 edition of the *Carceri*.[12] In fact, all early twentieth-century writers on Piranesi react to what they perceive as extreme contrasts between light and dark, marring the etcher's entire production.

Neither De Quincey nor any of his early nineteenth-century contemporaries seem to have observed any such disparity within the compositions. It is an observation born around 1900. In fact, the perception of exaggerated contrasts between light and dark, between black and white, originated not in etching at all, but in the spectrum of hues and subtle gradations introduced by photography. When Woodworth writes that in Piranesi's etchings we find "the sunlight as intense as electric flash, and the shadows of midday absolutely stygian," it is the reality of the camera that informs his understanding.[13] Because of Piranesi's love of contrasts, Woodworth specifies: "details which photography would have recorded are subordinated to strong lights and equally intense shadows."[14] In other words, by

overleaf Plate XI from the first edition of Piranesi's *Carceri* reproduced in Arthur Samuel, *Piranesi*, 1910.

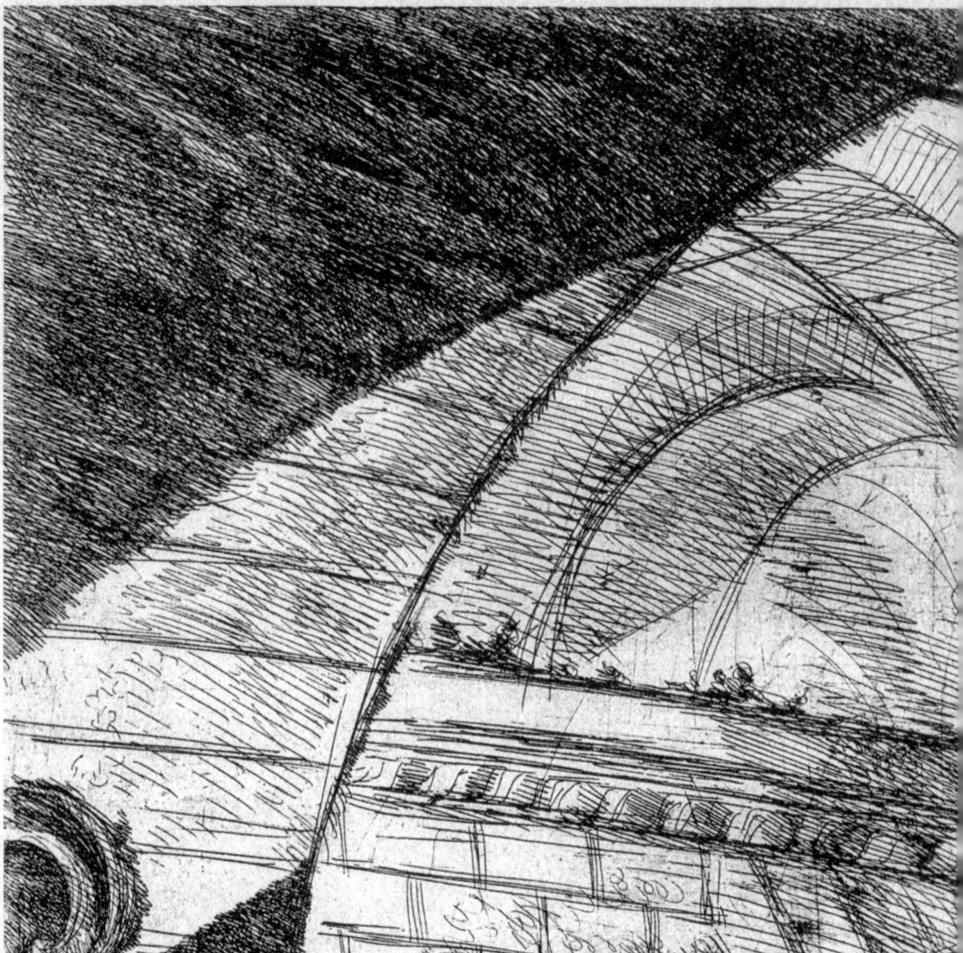

INTERIOR OF A PRISON, FROM "CAR

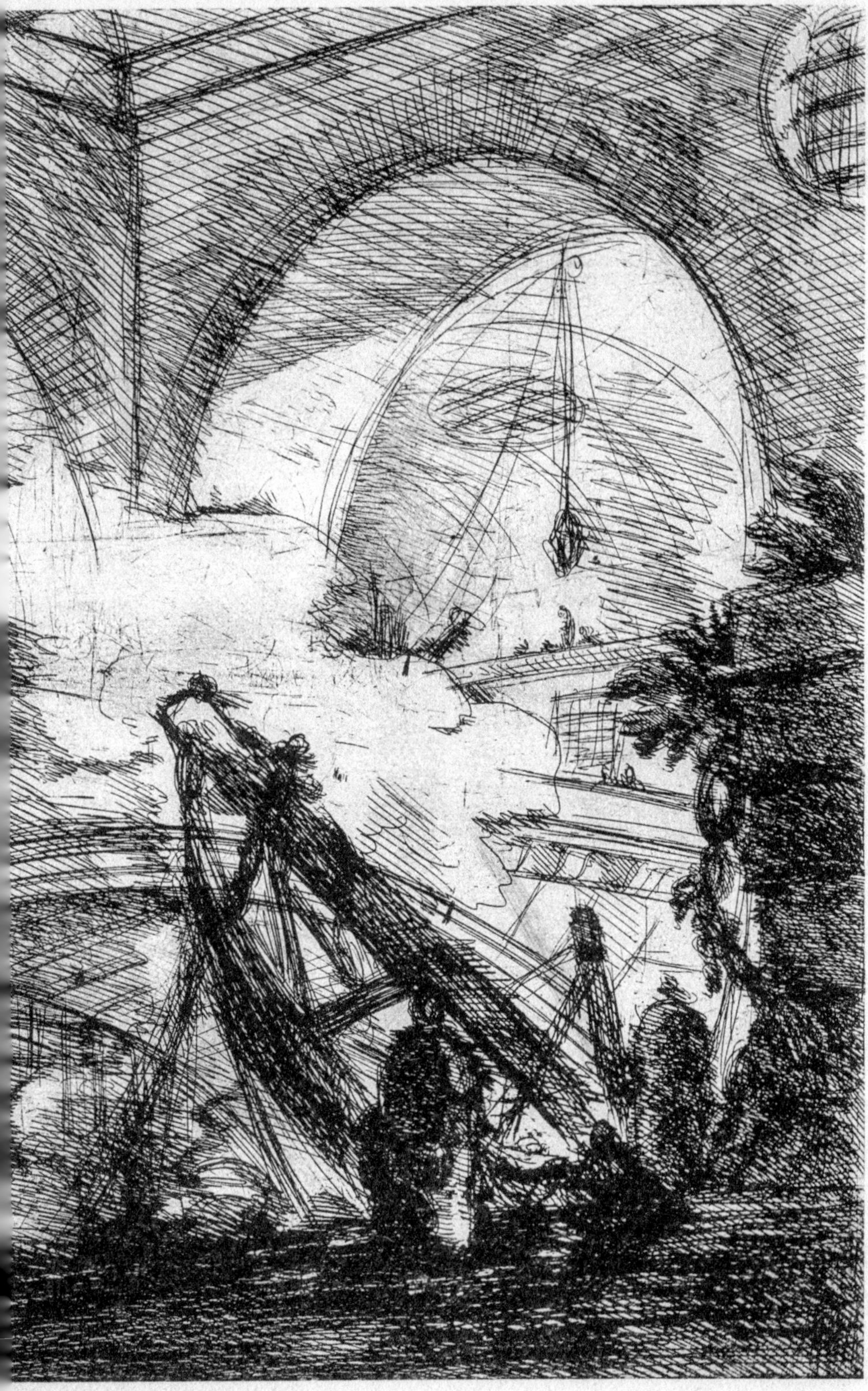

INVENZIONE," FIRST STATE, 1750

1900, photography had established the ideal of an evenly lit, high-resolution representation of reality. As a result, the art of the past fell, unfairly, under the spell of the new technology.

In the light of photography Piranesi therefore seemed to have failed, because the dramatically lighted images appeared badly exposed or, as Russell Sturgis puts it, "over-charged."[15] The acute awareness of contrasts in his prints, not to mention the impression of these contrasts as too high, was informed less by the eighteenth-century plates than by a modern sensitivity to the incorrect handling of aperture and shutter speed. In short, at the core of Piranesi's comeback in the twentieth century was the rediscovery, not of a good etcher, but of a bad photographer.

Not all of his etchings, however, suffered from high contrasts. Looking at Piranesi's representation of the French Academy on the Corso, presently known as the Palazzo Salviati, Sturgis in 1900 writes that there is "no excess of blackness here, and the effect of sunshine has been seized" (*see following*). He continues:

> If the photographic process print, the heliogravure, the heliotype, the Lichtdruck and the photogravure had not come to reconstitute the whole business of rendering architecture, one might point to this plate and bid the engraver of the present day try to imitate its merits.[16]

When Sturgis declares the French Academy to be a successful print, I think it is fair to add that it is photography, and its extremely fine-grained rendering, that makes him see it as such in the first place.

Overall, caught under the spell of light-sensitive photographic prints, Piranesi's art seemed composed of nothing but "light, shadow, and stone," to quote Albert Giesecke's book on the artist from 1911.[17] Each plate was judged a success or failure by criteria used to evaluate photography. The dark brain of Piranesi turns out to be a brain functioning more precisely as a darkroom—in the way Yourcenar sees in Piranesi's prints inverted images of Roman architecture "reflected in the darkroom of his visionary mind."[18]

Only with Henri Focillon's two-volume study published in 1918 did scholarship seem prepared to view Piranesi's prints for what they were, namely etchings. It was Focillon who disentangled Piranesi's art from a black-and-white dichotomy and saw his prints instead as part of a development. The intensity of his expression was no longer judged as failed photography but as the sign of an etcher who had gradually learned to exploit the possibility of his technique. "The chiaroscuro that flames in the *Carceri* is due to the acid, to the depth of the bites, to the audacity of a technician sure of his mastery, using the resources of a palette filled with brilliant and deep blacks," Focillon writes.[19] The idea of "brilliant blacks" reveals an observer no longer distracted by the sharp contrasts between light and shade but sensitive to the luminous hue that even shadows might hold.

To conclude, the rediscovery of Piranesi in the twentieth century interacts with the formulation of new visual paradigms across several fields, as we shall see in the following. Piranesi might have been perceived as erring, but he erred in a manner that made him seem modern. In other words, the obsession with contrasts, aroused more in response to the avant-garde than to any actual quality in his etchings, amounted to a discourse that launched him as a contemporary.

PHOTOGRAPHY AFTER PIRANESI

Since the invention of photography, professionals and tourists in Rome have taken up the vantage points and adopted the perspective of Piranesi's views. Piranesi and other *vedutisti* of his day established a visual paradigm with which photography has had to compete ever since. Photographers from Giacchino Altobelli, in the nineteenth century, to Gabriele Basilico, Randolph Langenbach, and Gianluca Baronchelli in the twenty-first have gone to the length of confronting Piranesi's legacy head on in projects that deliberately imitate prints in *Vedute di Roma.*[20] Piranesi's art, and not the views they picture, is the true subject in these projects. However, the carefully staged imitations also serve to demask Piranesi's *vedute* as engineered representations of reality; they reveal the artful manipulations of scale and perspective that exaggerated Rome's grandeur to the point of placing the city itself in their shadow.

The examples mentioned above are explicit homages to Piranesi, quarrying his work for appealing urban tableaus. They qualify as pictorial investigations of his art and only indirectly—or perhaps too directly—reflect his impact on modern culture. In photography's effort to reinvent itself as an independent art, however, Piranesi's oeuvre came to have a deeper impact. As we shift focus to the early twentieth century, photography "in itself" was intensely debated and explored as a unique visual expression, separate from the conventions imposed by centuries of painting as well as from the sea of mere illustrations flooding all aspects of culture.

In *Painting, Photography, Film* (1925), the Hungarian artist László Moholy-Nagy answered those who still doubted photography was an art. "Only now and then does one find really 'good' photographs among the millions which appear in illustrated papers and books," he wrote, continuing to define the parameters that distinguished photography as an art.

overleaf Giovanni Battista Piranesi, *View Along the Via del Corso of the Palazzo dell'Accademia* [also known as the French Academy], from *Vedute di Roma*, 1757–1758.

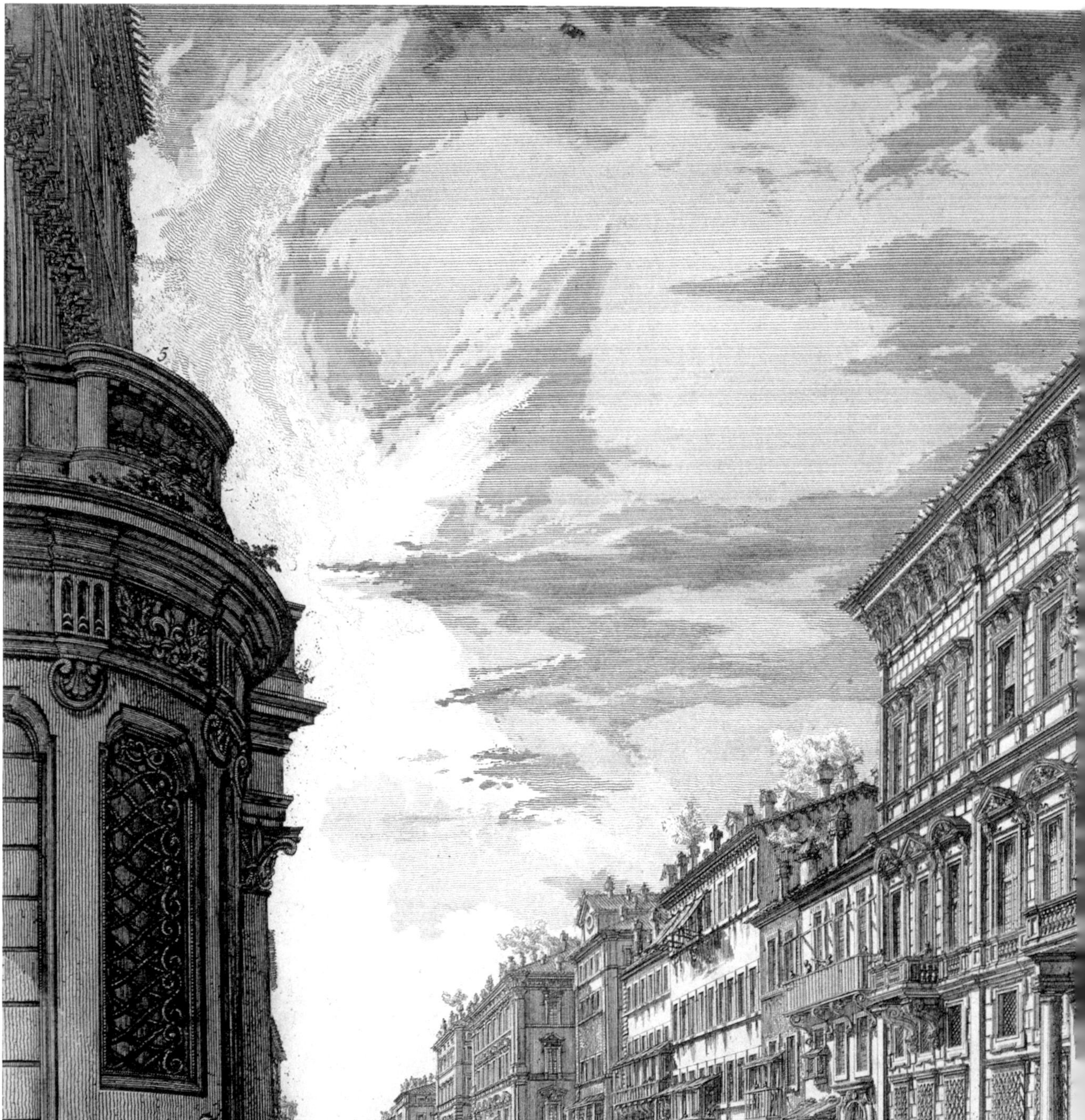

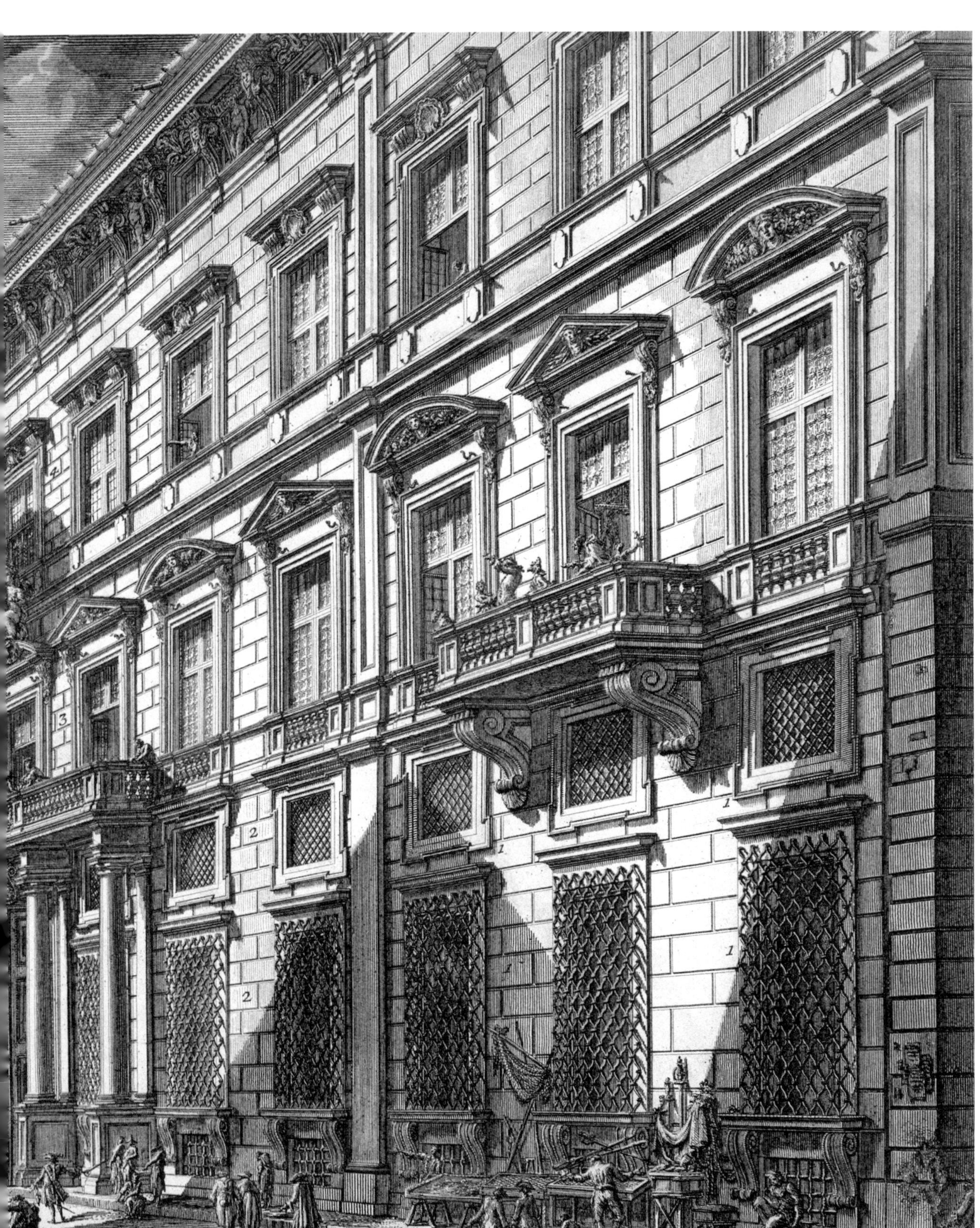

3
2
2
1
1
1
1
6

> We have gained a new feeling for the quality of chiaroscuro, shining white, transitions from black to grey imbued with fluid light, the precise magic of the finest texture: in the framework of steel buildings just as much as in the foam of sea—and all fixed in a hundredth of thousandth fraction of a second.[21]

In light of Moholy-Nagy's photographic ideal, the qualities that had made Piranesi's prints seem like "bad" photographs twenty years earlier were the same as those that now made them appear as "good" ones—the chiaroscuro, the shining white, and the stark architecture. Obviously, much had changed since Sturgis and Woodworth published. In the intervening years, photography had developed a range of expressions and established a visual discourse that enhanced its uniqueness—its novelty. When dissected element by element, however, much of that novelty resonates with the methods Piranesi used and the effects he achieved. Although the name of Piranesi seldom enters the discourse on photography, his compositions and even his technique suggest a gradual transition between the arts and, at times, even an overlap.

This is not the place to relate the history of photography nor to give an exhaustive account of photographic techniques.[22] I shall focus on a stage in the art's development which pioneer photographers themselves defined as modern although they did not always agree what "modern" meant. But one thing stood fast: photography was never simply about "snapshotting." All agreed that it consisted of series of deliberations and interventions, from the mixture in the emulsion and the choice of paper to exposure time and processing. From the late nineteenth century, photographers sympathetic to so-called "pictorialism" crusaded against the idea of the camera as a mere recorder of reality and manually intervened to perfect an expression that was seen as particular to photography. Such interventions, which included retouching and blurring, resulted in prints that some would deny were photographs at all. But, as the French photographer Robert Demachy emphasized in 1907, all photographs were at some point modified; the question was only where in the process the image was manipulated—whether one meddled with the negative or with the developed print.[23]

The British-American photographer Alvin Langdon Coburn explicitly identified the result of manual treatment as "a hybrid of graphic and photographic art," emphasizing the blurred distinction between etching and photography.[24] The process of applying layers of varnish to the print, often multiple times, gave his photographs a "remarkable force, solidity, and richness of color," according to Coburn's friend and supporter George Bernard Shaw.[25] The procedure corresponds to Piranesi, who repeatedly waxed, incised, and immersed in acid one and the same plate in order to enhance the visual texture of the representation. The motifs Coburn sought, and not the least the effect he cultivated, are decidedly Piranesian too. The low, close-up view in photographs such as *The Bridge, Ipswich* (1903) and *The Tiber, Rome* (1905) recalls the viewpoint Piranesi chose in the series of etchings depicting the massive vaulted bridges spanning the Tiber (*see following*). Like his predecessor, Coburn also exaggerated the contrasts. *The Bridge, Ipswich* is a photogravure, a technique that brought Coburn close to Piranesi as it implied adding ink to a photo-engraved plate, and also close to what critics perceived as an excessive blackness: the view of the bridge did not correspond to how it would appear in reality. One critic of Coburn complained: "Surely some quiver of light would interrupt the blackness of the shadow on the water, some hint that the arch was not the entrance to a dungeon, but was open on the other side."[26] The critic, clearly, is put off by the same "stygian" shadows that characterized Piranesi's dark hollows in the contemporaneous verdict of W. J. Woodworth, as we recall.

In another image from the same period, *St. Paul's and Other Spires* (1908), Coburn allowed luminous patches of smoke to waft, abstractedly, across the composition, obscuring the view. The effect is Piranesian and evokes the swirling smoke and drifting clouds that sometimes relieve the Venetian's architectural build-ups from an excessive formalism, as in *The Smoking Fire* from the *Carceri* series (*see pages 82–83*).

In contrast to pictorial photography, so-called straight photography triumphed as "modern" in the sense that it implied a more direct and immediate take on reality, capturing scenes from urban life and the sharp-edged geometries of industrial architecture and cityscapes. "Photography is the experimental science of Form," Marius de Zayas declared in 1913, and American photographers like Alfred Stieglitz, Paul Strand, and Charles Sheeler caught modernity on camera in images composed of crisscrossing elements, sharply divided fields of light and shadow, and contrasts of scale—large monuments versus miniscule men—in short, images that emulated the schemata established by Piranesi (*see pages 86–87*).[27]

Through the lenses of these photographers, a Piranesian imagination is aligned with the aesthetics of modern industrial architecture. The "untamed" forms proliferating in the *Carceri* had of course always escaped the neat types and styles codified in architectural history (*see page 88*). Giving photography its due share, they now emerged as precedents for the non-architecture of factories, power plants, and glass structures—an architecture that Henry-Russell Hitchcock would call the "New Tradition" and that Vincent Scully would trace back to Piranesi himself in his revised history of modern architecture, discussed in chapter five.

overleaf Alvin Langdon Coburn, *The Bridge—Ipswich*, 1903. Photogravure. Giovanni Battista Piranesi, *View of the Ponte Molle*, from *Vedute di Roma*, 1762.

following spread Alvin Langdon Coburn, *St. Paul's and Other Spires*, 1908. Photogravure. Giovanni Battista Piranesi, plate VI, *The Smoking Fire*, from *Carceri d'invenzione*, second edition, 1761.

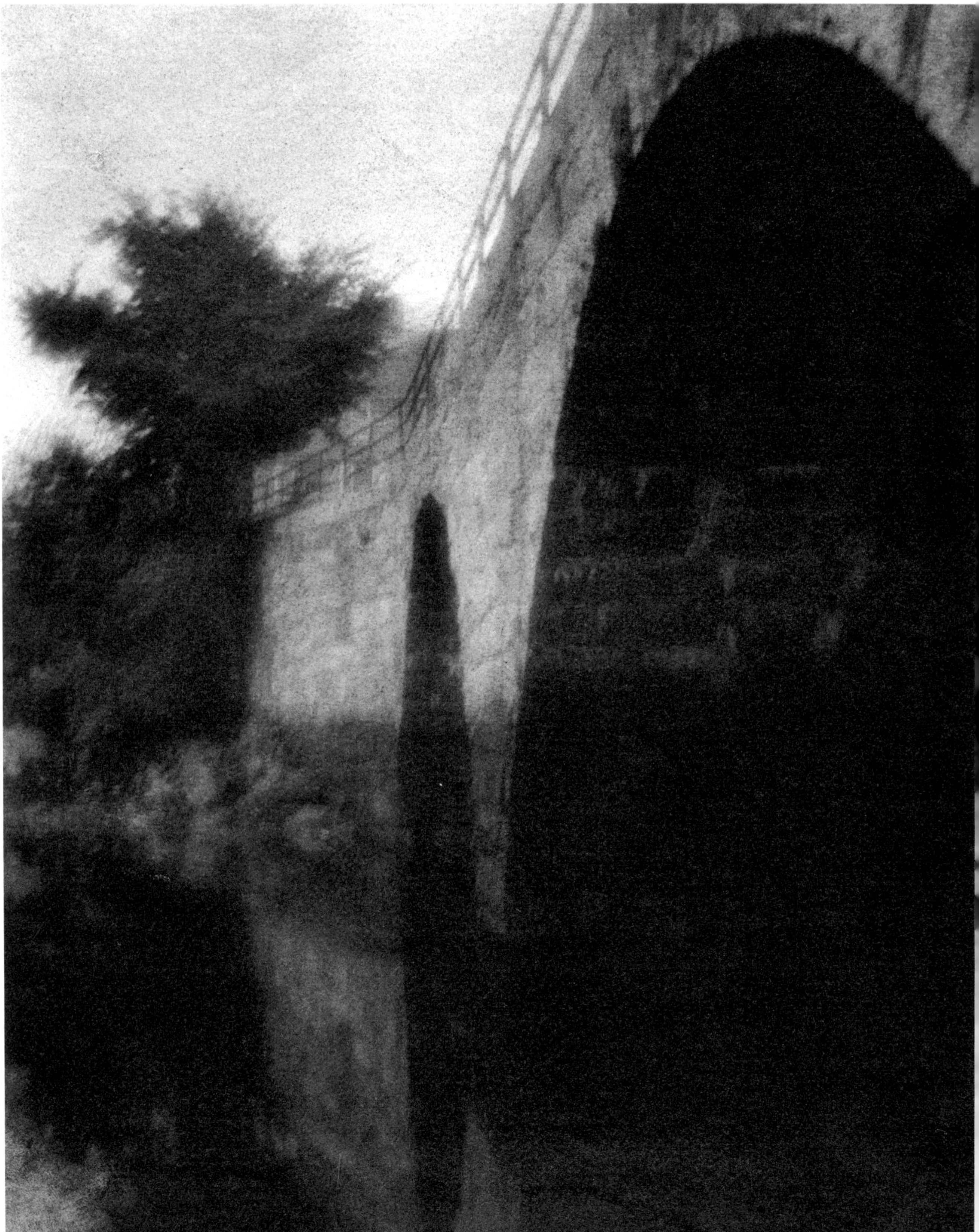

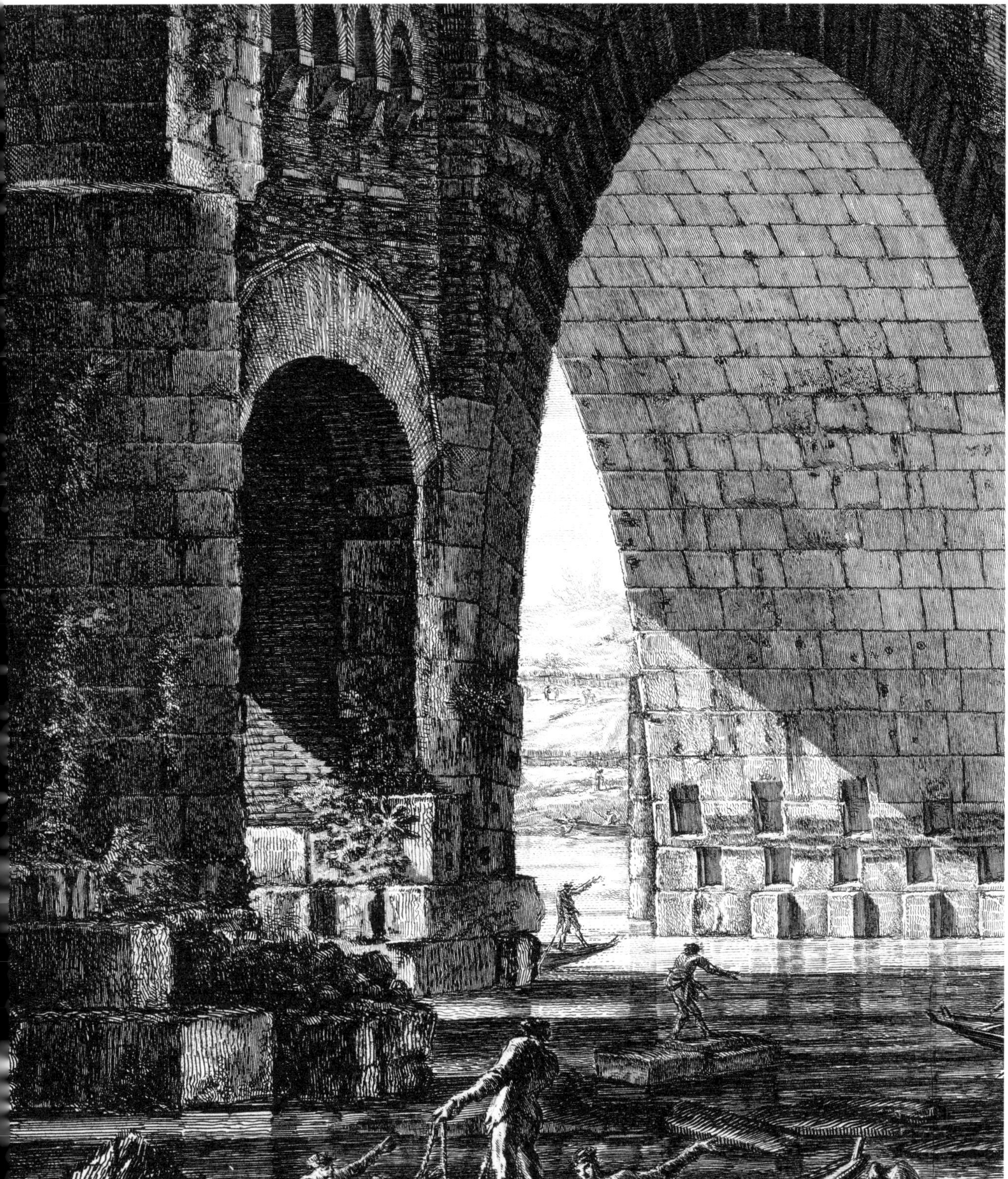

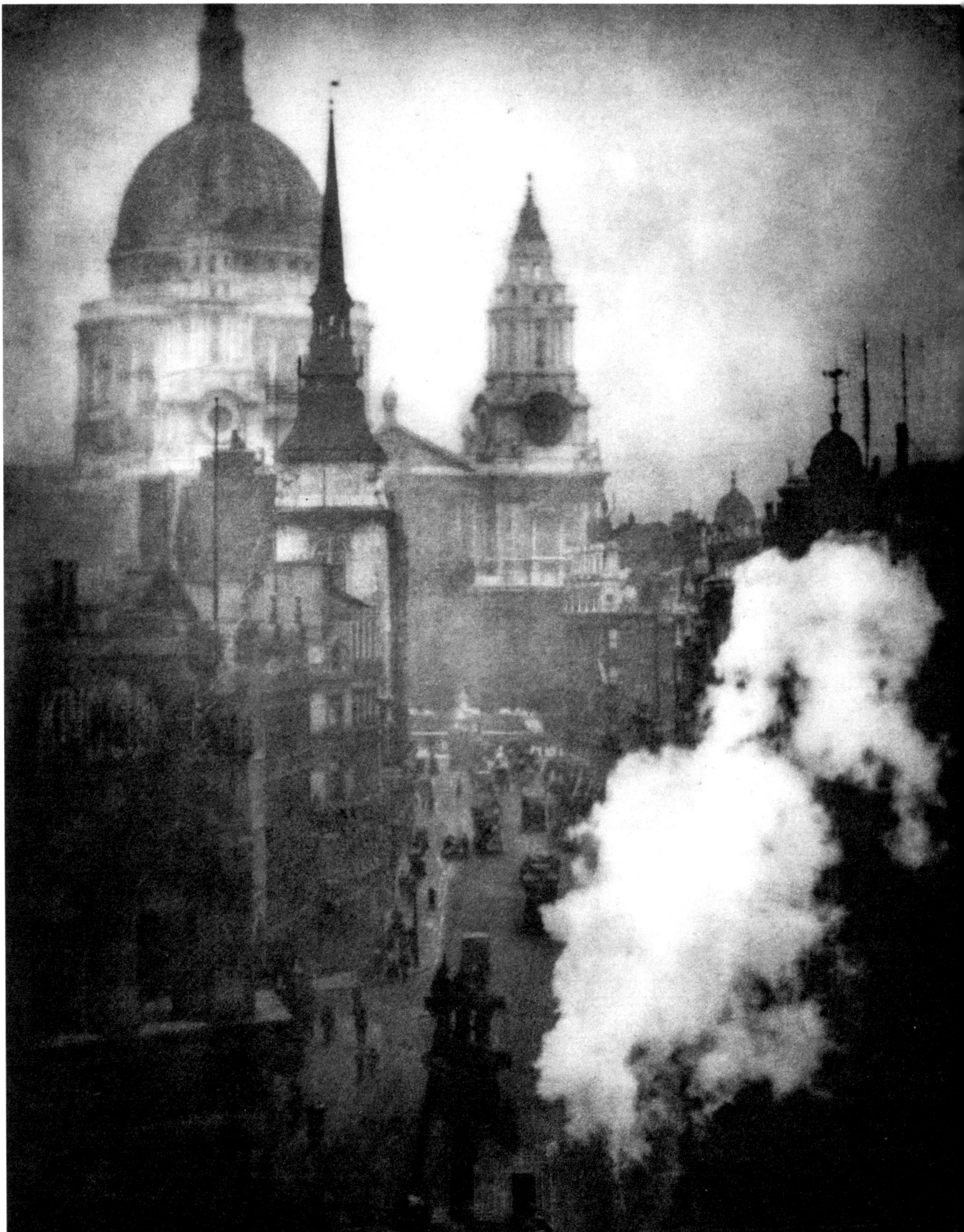

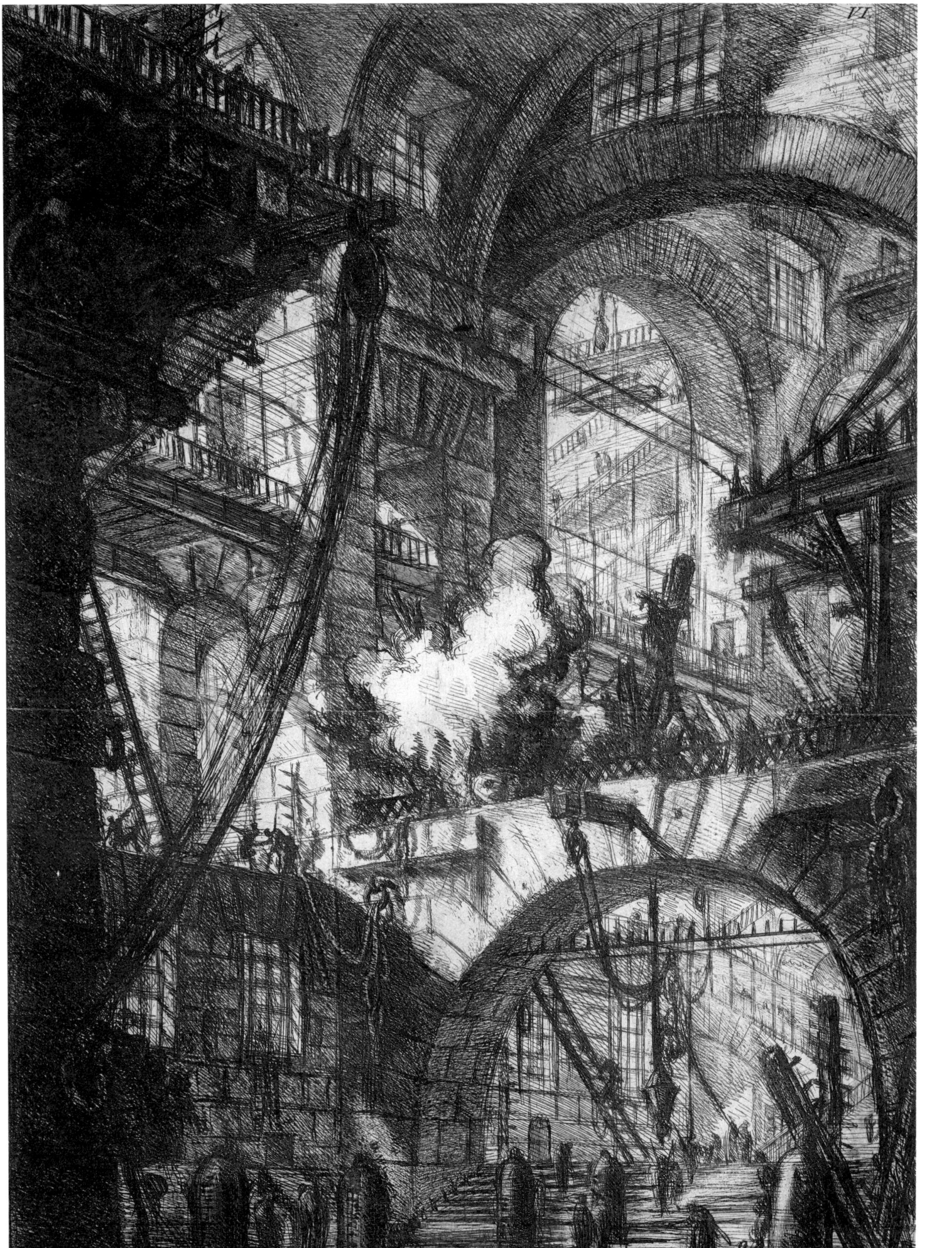
VI

Straight photography, sometimes called pure photography, evolved in many ways from cubism and especially from Picasso's art.[28] Alfred Stieglitz, who was the first to exhibit Picasso in New York in 1911, took a photograph from his gallery titled *From the Back Window—291* (1915). According to Stieglitz himself, the platinum print is "intensely honest," and yet it is as if the composition exploits, exaggerates even, the points for which Piranesi was criticized by Woodworth, Sturgis, and Samuel.[29] The photograph shows a pile of edifices delicately penciled by the snow covering the rooftops. The architecture emerges from the shadows as if "built" by contrasting blacks and whites, by light and darkness (*see opposite*). Arguably, it is Piranesi's dramatically illuminated etchings, not the purity of the medium, which informs the modernity of Stieglitz's nightly vision. Whilst Piranesi's prints were judged as if they were photographs by Sturgis and Woodworth, photography from Coburn to Stieglitz broke new ground because of Piranesi.

The interweaving of Piranesi and photography invites a broader investigation than this discussion allows, and while I have limited the focus to British-American photography around 1910, pioneering work produced elsewhere also resonates with Piranesi's art, even that connected to the Bauhaus, the fiercely avant-garde school and community founded by Walter Gropius in Weimar in 1919. László Moholy-Nagy, an active force in building up the Bauhaus, published *The New Vision* in 1928. In this book, carefully selected photographs conveyed his attempts to formulate new concepts of space. Alongside painting, sculpture, and music, he considered "space creation" a special form of human expression, which he found manifest in stage design and motion pictures.[30] One example is the photograph *Staircase in a Film Studio* representing an unidentified film set at the Emelka Studios outside Munich (*see page 90*). Regardless of whether it is the vantage point of the photographer or the chosen set that creates the resemblance, this image suggests that the new "space creation" in film was not so new at all, but was in fact wrenched from the complex *Carceri* designs, and, in this particular instance, from *The Staircase with Trophies* of the second edition (*see page 91*). The vertical shafts of light and dark, intersected by beams and stairways, define a novel space, according to Moholy-Nagy, realized by the new medium of film, but with an obvious forerunner in Piranesi's theatrical designs.

Although avant-garde photographers hardly mentioned Piranesi, it is not difficult to see how they isolated and explored the various components of his prints—the motifs, the elements of abstraction, his conceptions of space, and contrasts of light and shadow. If one were to "locate" Piranesi around 1900, the realm in which he was first recognized and categorized as a visual artist is

Alfred Stieglitz, *From the Back Window – 291*, 1915. Platinum print.

following spread Paul Strand, *Wall Street*, 1915. Platinum print.

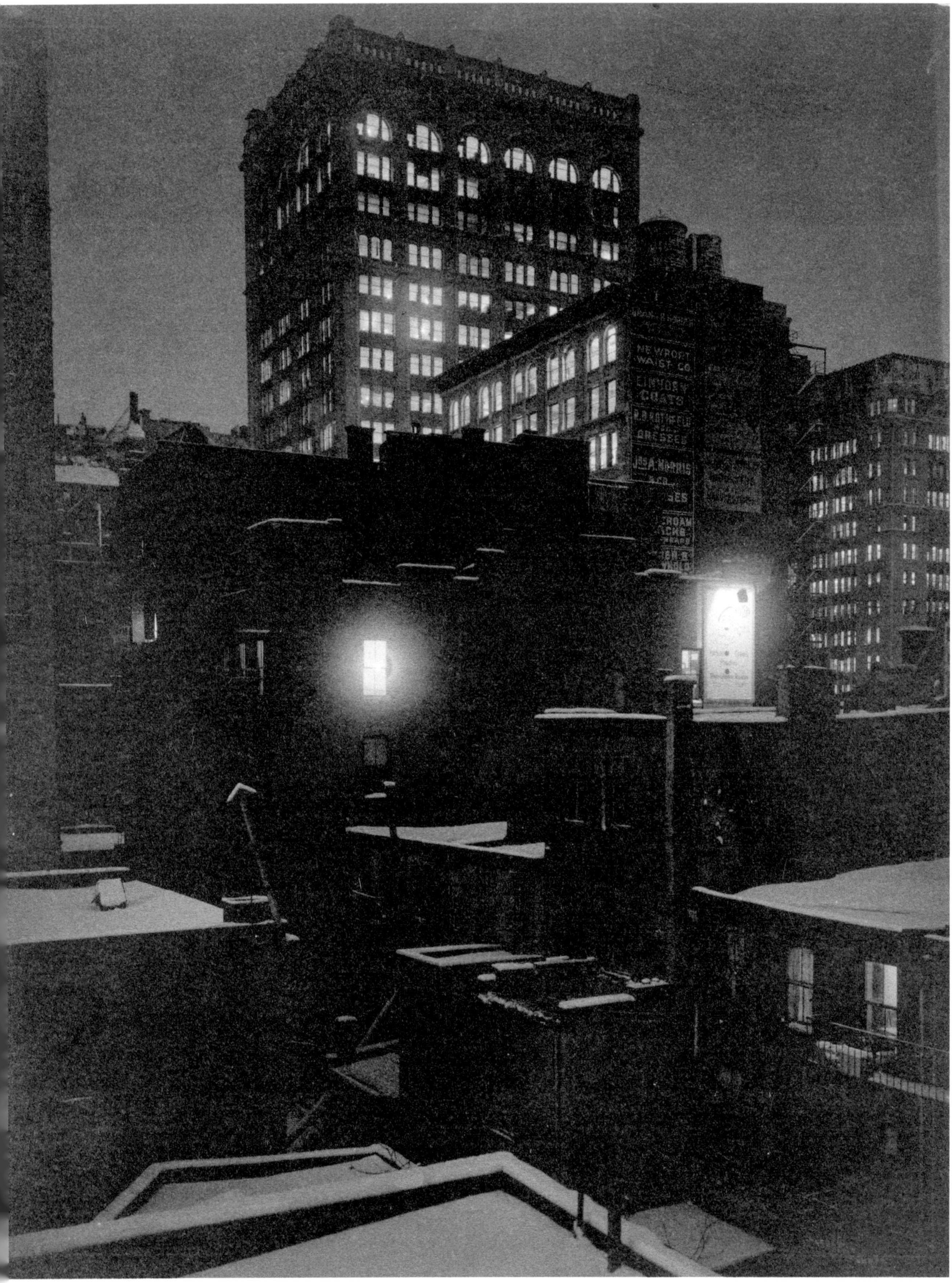
WAIST CO.
COATS

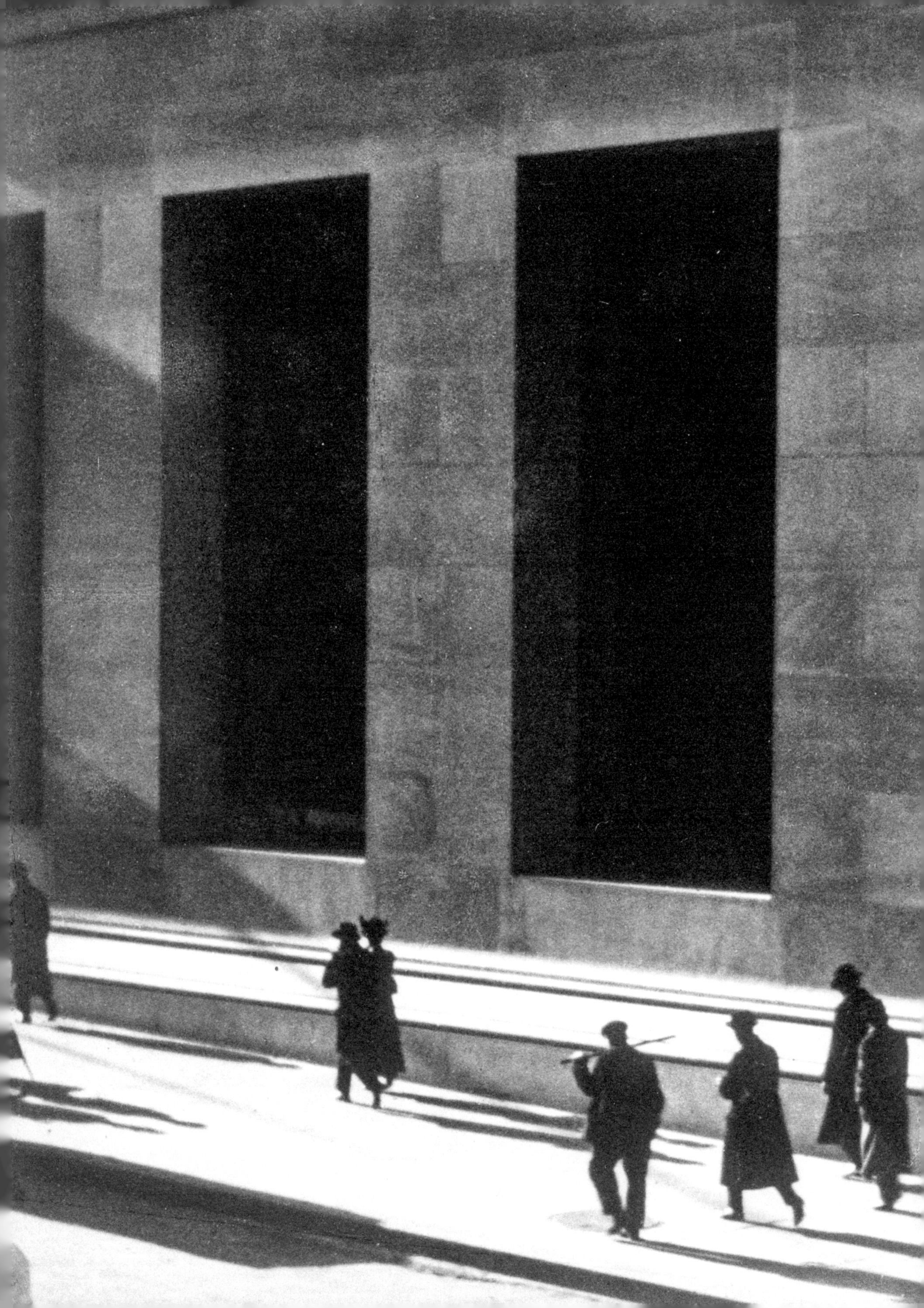

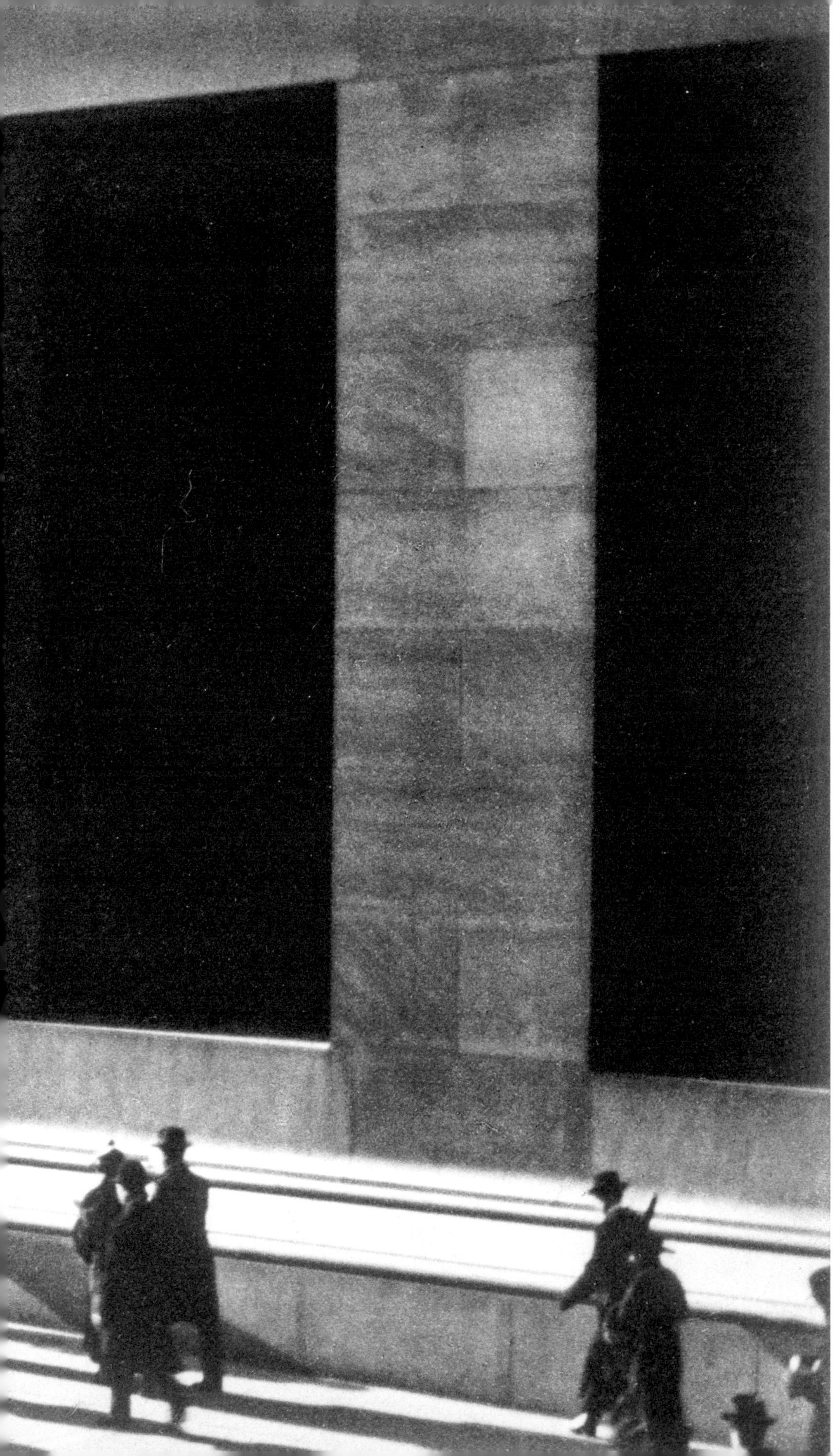

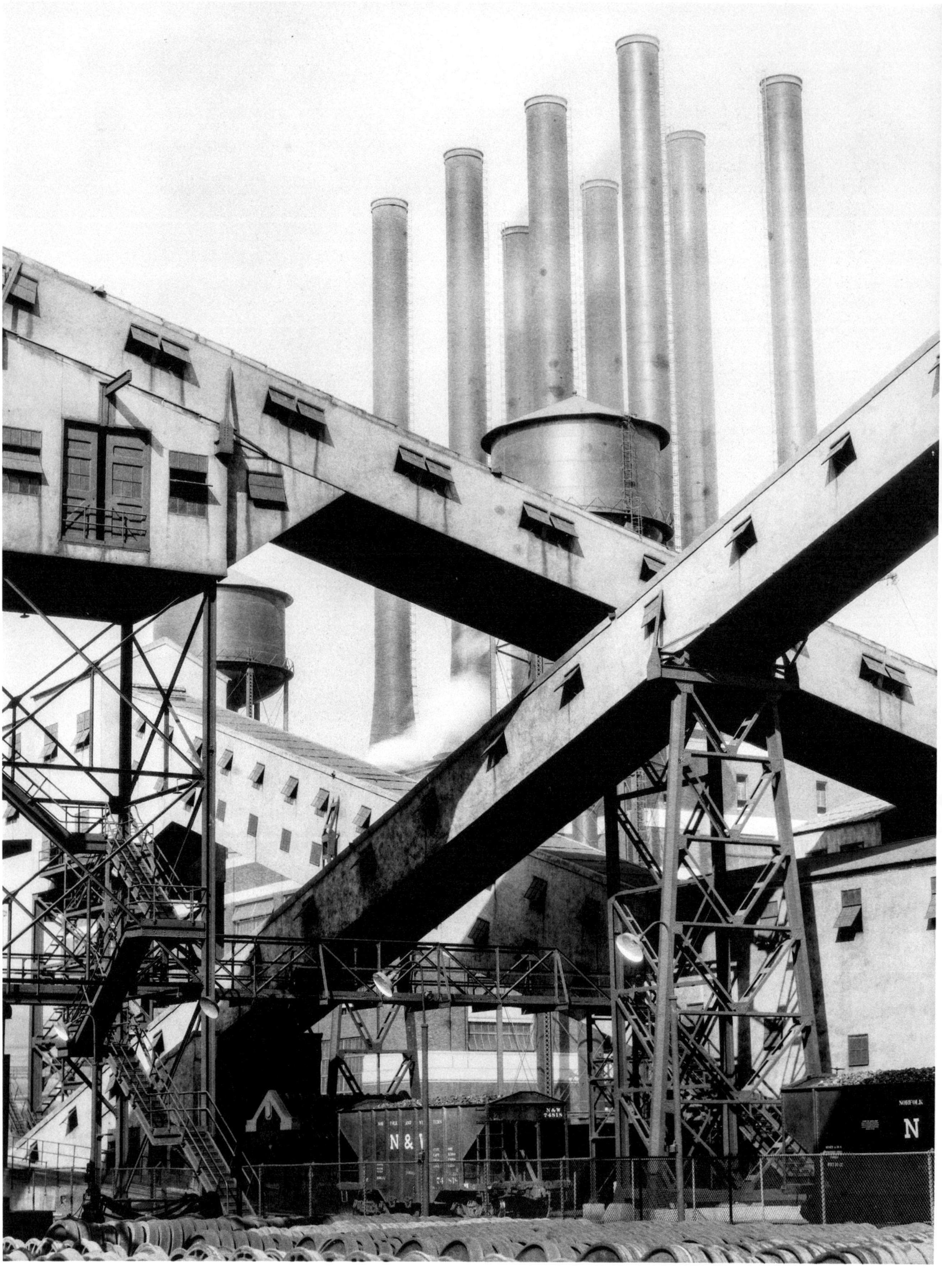
N & W
N&W
74818
NORFOLK
N

photography. In almost every way, his etchings prefigured the new art's experimental black-and-white aesthetics. In short, photography re-actualized Piranesi in the same move as it reinvented itself as modern.

THE REMBRANDT OF ARCHITECTURE

"PIRANESI, Giambattista, etcher and architect, the so-called 'Rembrandt of Architecture,' was born at Venice in 1720." Thus begins the enlarged and revised entry on Piranesi in *Bryan's Dictionary of Painters and Engravers* from 1904, published some six years before the Arthur Samuel quote that appears at the beginning of this chapter. In this case, however, it is Rembrandt van Rijn, not Walter Scott, who acts as Piranesi's guarantor. The sobriquet "Rembrandt of Architecture" evokes of course Piranesi's preeminence as etcher. It compares him to the Dutch master, but, subtly derogatory, it also subjugates the branch of expertise in which he excelled, namely architectural prints, to Rembrandt's overall supremacy.

The analogy originates in Giovanni Ludovico Bianconi's eulogy of Piranesi printed the year after the artist's death. Bianconi wrote that Piranesi gave to his prints "a sort of magic" that made him the "Rembrandt of the ancient ruins."[31] When late-nineteenth-century dictionaries and magazines picked up the epithet, it was in the effort to boost the reputation of Piranesi, who at the time lingered in the shadow of the more famous and popular Rembrandt.[32] Scholars, too, fell for the analogy. W. J. Woodworth even made it the title of his 1902 article, "Piranesi, the Rembrandt of Architecture." Arthur Samuel, in his 1910 monograph, called Piranesi "The Rembrandt of Etchers," a complete misunderstanding further compounded by his attribution of the term to De Quincey/Coleridge, who never wrote such a thing.[33] Arthur Hind, in the following year, carefully weighed the comparison against his own judgment, concluding that the *Carceri* made Piranesi wholly deserving of the title "the Rembrandt of Architecture."[34]

The Rembrandt analogy served to reconsecrate Piranesi as an etcher, and tracing its reappearances in literature can help us see how the modern age gradually harnessed the characteristics that distinguished him in the field. Even as Piranesi's virtuosity in the graphic art was increasingly acknowledged, even celebrated, writers did not tire of the worn analogy. On the contrary, they deepened and expanded its validity. The comparison with Rembrandt, for better and for worse, was the prelude to meditations on the very essence of etching—its ontology, as it were. As we shall see, modern age observers formulated with increasing eloquence a correspondence, even a complete melding, between Piranesi's technique and the ruinous architecture he depicted.

Charles Sheeler, *Criss-Crossed Conveyors, River Rouge Plant, Ford Motor Company*, 1927. Gelatin silver print.

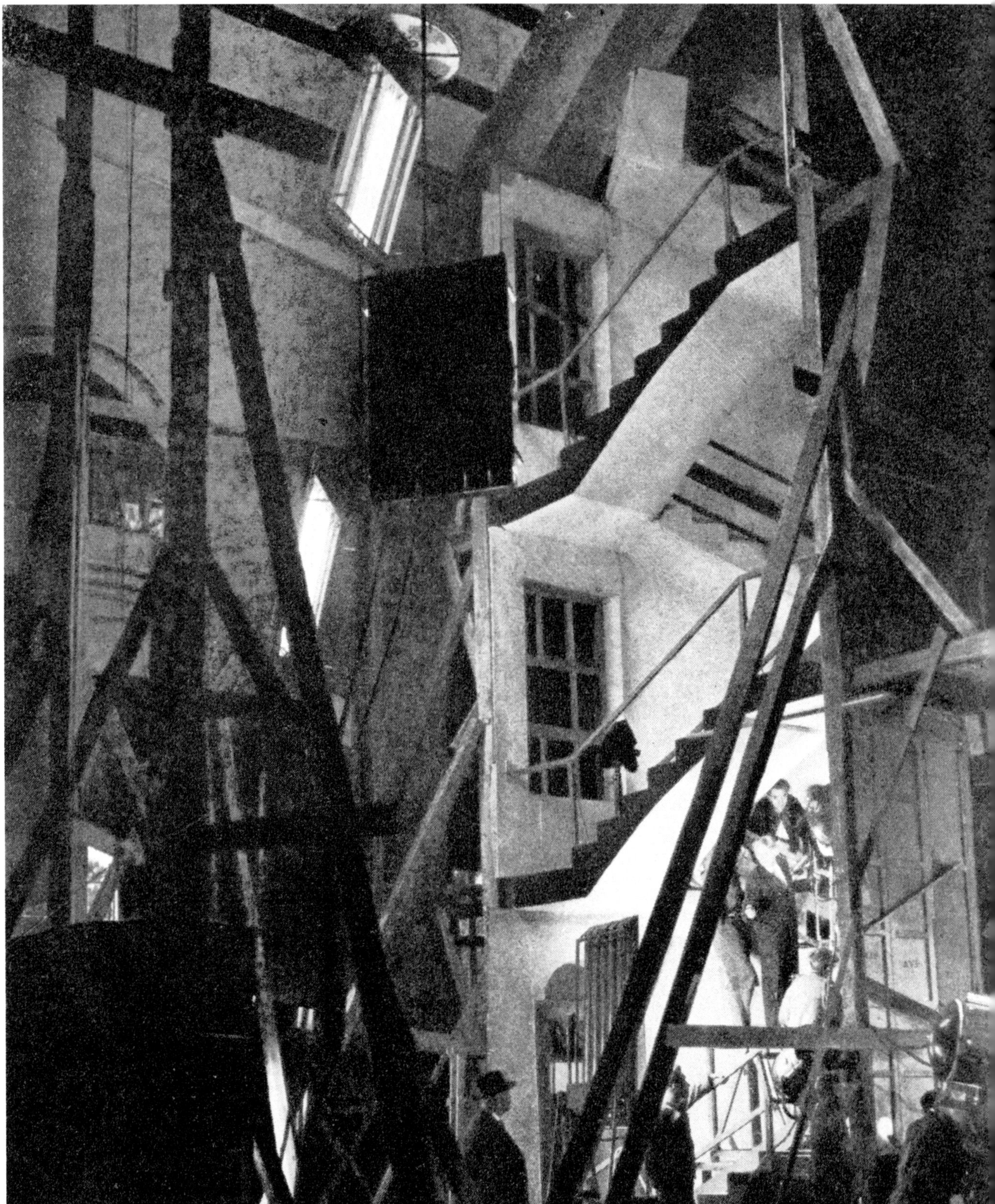

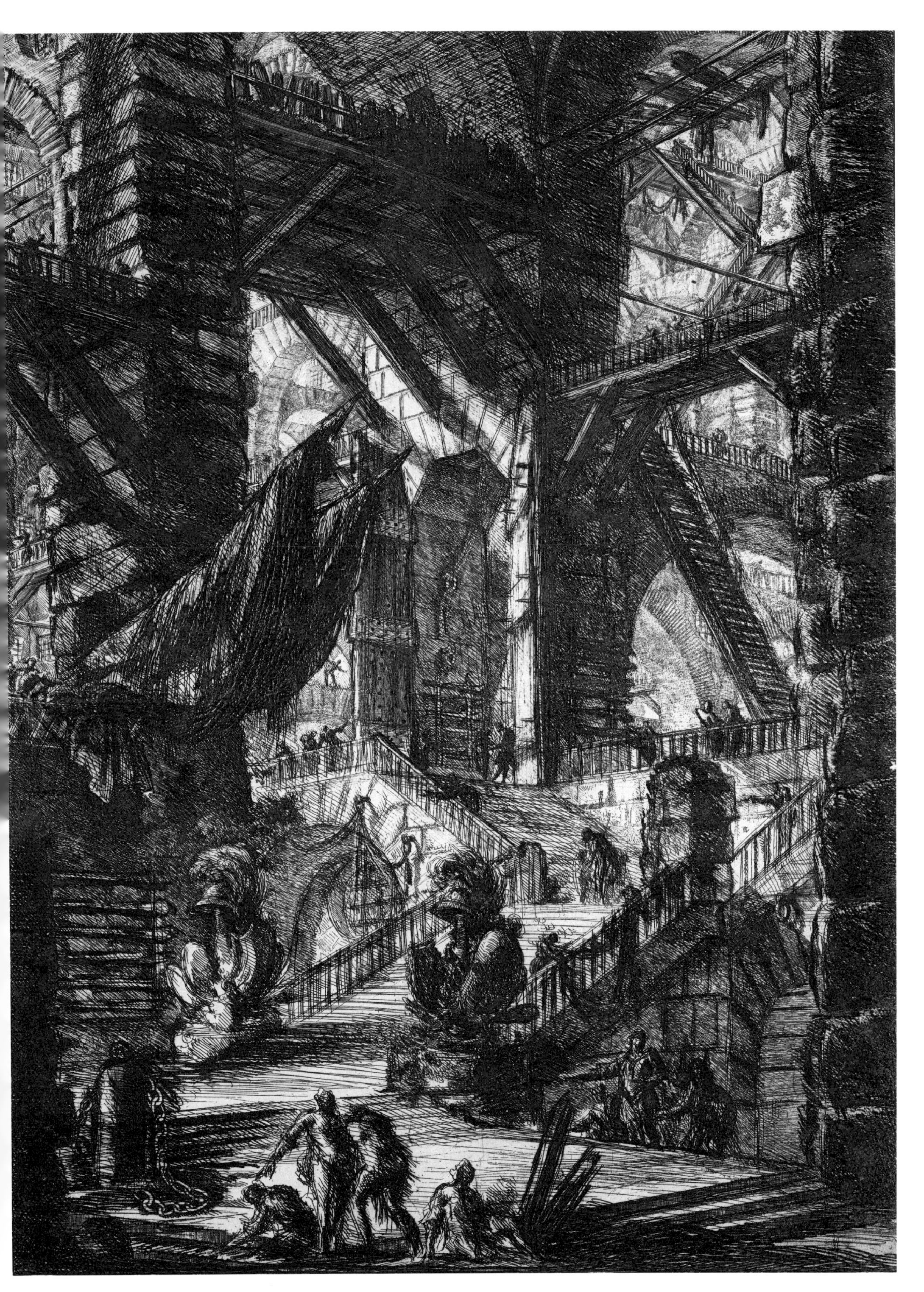

Above all, it was the French art historian Henri Focillon, in *Giovanni-Battista Piranesi* (1918), who extricated from his prints their value precisely as etchings and in the process revealed a sensitivity to the versatility and originality of Piranesi's technique, which had been obscured by a century-long tradition of literary interpretations. In Focillon's analysis, etching took on an almost material quality, a substance of its own. Whereas the first edition of the *Carceri*, in Focillon's opinion, was monotonous and weak, the reworked second edition displayed the depth and audacity of a masterpiece: "Never has the poetry of etching, produced out of candor and even violence, obtained such singular effects."[35] Focillon reminds his readers that Piranesi always had etching in mind, almost in a literal sense: "Etching is the material in which his imagination naturally takes its form." Etching, then, lingers at some deep level of his being.

The Rembrandt analogy is shallow, in Focillon's view, and he aims to deliver its deathblow. Calling Piranesi "the Rembrandt of ruins," he writes, is both inaccurate and rash since the two artists differ in mindset, goals, and technical procedures. Moreover, Rembrandt's subtle technique, developed to register the finest facial expressions, would only appear limp and lifeless if applied on surfaces of the dimensions used by Piranesi. The art of Piranesi, on the other hand, surpassed drawing and painting, attaining a "power of expression, superior to ordinary sight impressions":

> Rome, a hundred times the subject of studies by painters and engravers, appears here for the first time majestic and true. On the gray and dilapidated walls, the burning sun of etching makes a ray radiate more beautifully than that from the sun of each day; it illuminates them with so much force that it restores to them their relief and their prestige.[36]

Among the historians writing on Piranesi as an etcher, Arthur Hind, as opposed to Focillon, represents a modernist turn. Perhaps we can see in this relation a shift comparable to the one between pictorialist and pure photography. "The purity of etching" is a recurring phrase in Hind's 1922 monograph on Piranesi, and, according to Hind, Piranesi used etching most purely in his earliest work. Therefore, the first edition of the *Carceri*, which Focillon had dismissed as monotonous, is to Hind superior, whereas the second edition collapses in a dense and overworked pictorialism.[37] In the first edition, as well as in Piranesi's early views of Rome, we can admire the autonomy of the incision, undistracted by the later addition of shading and detailing, Hind writes in words informed by the ideals of modernism. In the same years that Hind promoted the "purity of etching," Le Corbusier championed a new purity in architecture in a series of

overleaf Staircase in a Film Studio by unknown photographer. Illustration in László Moholy-Nagy, *The New Vision: Fundamentals of Design, Painting, Sculpture, Architecture*, 1938. Giovanni Battista Piranesi, plate VI, *The Staircase with Trophies*, from *Carceri d'invenzione*, second edition, 1761.

essays in *L'Esprit Nouveau*, published from 1921 onwards, and Robert Demachy and Marius de Zayas coined that phrase, "pure photography." However, Hind seems at loss to classify the dash and exuberance that he also observes in the *Carceri*. A bit feebly, he retracts to the conclusion that these are qualities that give Piranesi "every title to be called the Rembrandt of Architecture."[38] The sobriquet emerged as a category in which to file an expressiveness at odds with modernist clarity and simplicity.

A modernist view on etching celebrated the technique in its "true" form, as an entity almost abstracted from the planes and volumes it served to define. Etching, then, as Piranesi appeared to use it, more than merely represented things; it acquired a life of its own, seeking out forms that enhanced its very own nature. Ruins existed in states—frail, deteriorating, overgrown—which etching was most adapted to convey convincingly. The burnishing, the angularity of cross-hatching, the quivering lines produced by the needle gliding through wax were the true components of a Piranesian architecture. However, Focillon and Hind generated two separate strands of interpretation of Piranesi's technique as an etcher. In the tradition of Focillon and what we may call the ontology of etching, David Rosand, for instance, recognizes motifs apparently unrelated to the depicted landscapes and interiors. Rosand observes curious configurations that seem to hover on a separate plane, such as the spiral motif visible in one of Piranesi's *Grotteschi* from 1747–1749 (*see following*). Appearing "dissociated from the illusion of representation, it declares itself an independent linear construct."[39] Objects that curl and curve with no apparent figurative or narrative function are in this way born from the process of etching itself: "It is the swing of the etching needle that seems to determine form," Rosand writes with reference to the *Carceri* series.[40]

In the tradition of Hind, by contrast, Andrew Robison observes a Piranesi who subordinated technique to architecture with an aim to clarify form. With the architectural fantasies as a case in point, Robison charts a development of technique that goes from young Piranesi's mastery of etching to the mature artist's inclusion of a range of other effects as well—sulfur tint, open bite, drypoint, burnishing, and all of them at times used in combination. The innovation of technique, Robison argues, was simply a means to arrive at increasingly powerful and concentrated expressions of mass. For instance, the broad hatching, which in itself might seem abstracted, or the scratching with zigzag strokes, both allowed Piranesi to build up forms rapidly (*see page 95*). While it is too simple to label Robison's vision modernist, he tends to see a simplicity behind the fuzzy detailing and is inclined to regard Piranesi's technique as a progression towards a clearer and more effective manifestation of "the general patterns of large forms and spaces."[41]

In the late twentieth century, the Rembrandt analogy made a comeback. However, this time the comparison did not rest on a clichéd *paragone* between the two artists but on an actual analysis of their respective techniques. As Robison observes, Piranesi adopted a method, also used by Rembrandt, of dabbing ink directly onto the plate with a rag or with his fingers to enhance the effect of shadow and mass.[42] The question is, as Myra Nan Rosenfeld speculates, whether Piranesi learned this method from studying actual prints by Rembrandt, or whether he reinvented it unaware of the Dutch master.[43] With this last possibility in mind, Piranesi, the Rembrandt of Architecture, emerges instead as the architect of Rembrandtesque techniques.

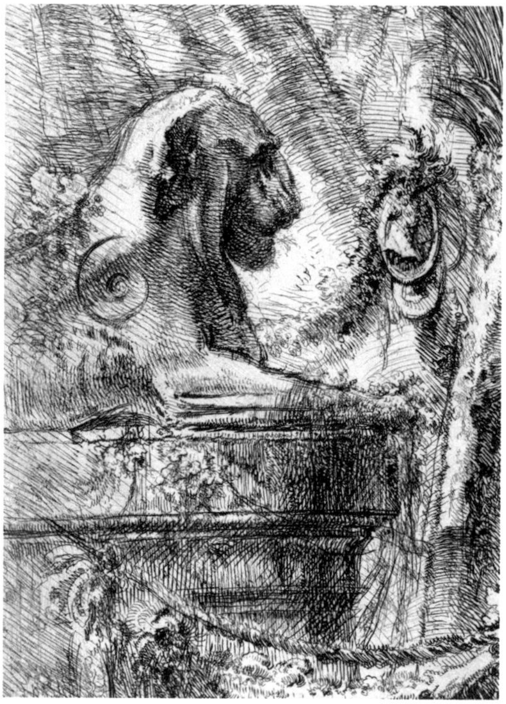

ETCHING AND EROSION

The "Rembrandt of the ancient ruins," as Bianconi put it, suggests another interpretation too. Rembrandt was renowned for etchings that conveyed his sitters' feelings (including his own). Just as the Dutch artist conveyed the depths of the human soul, so Piranesi, from a similar standpoint, captured the psychology of ruins. Whereas previous *vedutisti* had shown what monuments looked like, Piranesi also showed how they *felt*. "The ruins of Piranesi want to crumble. They groan, they scream," Charles Nodier wrote in 1833.[44] Piranesi animated architecture with surfaces that "appear like tender flesh," as Gijs Wallis de Vries noted, and with forms expressing "spiritual confusion," according to Huxley. By means of his technique alone, it seems, the Venetian etcher penetrated the inner states of buildings.[45]

Piranesi's technical command "activated" his architecture in several different ways, which invite comparisons to the processes of the psyche, to processes of nature, and to the processes of history itself, challenging the model of progression

Giovanni Battista Piranesi, detail of *The Triumphal Arch*, from *Grotteschi*, ca. 1748.

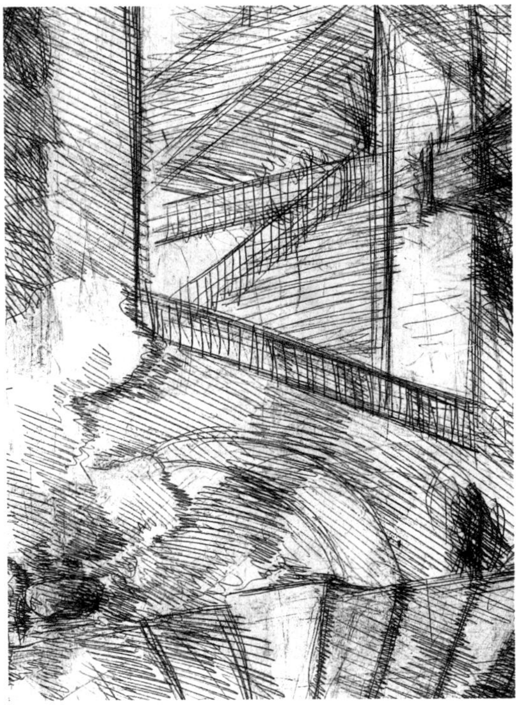

reigning since the Enlightenment. Considering these three shades of the idea of process brings us first deeper into the thinking of Henri Focillon. In Focillon's *Vie des formes* (1934), published in English as *The Life of Forms in Art*, etching is no longer a mere technique but a vital force in the creation of art. In this book, Focillon takes a more radical view on the autonomy of etching than in his 1918 monograph on Piranesi. With the concept of *form*, he explains how technical skill sinks into the deepest layer of the human psyche, as if it is the craft that molds the inner self, the innermost resource on which art depends. It is not easy to grasp the precise meaning of form in Focillon's sense. More tangible than an idea, and yet eerier than matter, form is a compulsion to execute born from the very materiality of a medium, be it music, painting, or sculpture. It is not an abstraction, but "the tones, the modeling and the touch" stirring the artist; it is the outcome of the "hand that is in his mind," restlessly at work creating "the concrete within the abstract, and weight within the imponderable."[46]

Etching constitutes a form on its own. Its vibrant line, warmth of tone, and luminous blanks fashion a unique, self-contained universe. Focillon is especially fascinated by the translucent qualities achieved by etching's use of acid. Rembrandt, he writes, realized etching as form in his own particular way when he carved from copper a world seemingly lit by a torch light. In Piranesi's work, Focillon's second example, etching found its expression in the moonlight he let shimmer over the ruins. The two artists compare on a level where their techniques remain only superficially the same but have sunk into their innermost beings and melded with their creative energy. A medium is not a choice, then, but an existential necessity.

In *The Life of Forms in Art* Focillon returned to the *Carceri* and deepened his argument for the supremacy of the second edition. As etchings, the lighter first edition "still stay at the surface of the copper." The point of the needle whirls about without biting into the material and penetrating it. On taking these plates

Giovanni Battista Piranesi, detail of plate VI, *The Smoking Fire*, from *Invenzioni capric di carceri*, first edition, ca. 1749–1750.

up again several years later, Piranesi had matured, according to Focillon. Now "he poured into them shadow after shadow," excavating their astonishing darkness not from brazen plates "but from the living rock of some subterranean world."[47]

The force of Piranesi's art, which so impressed Focillon, subjects the ruins and monuments to processes that transcend the aim of verisimilitude, a point that posterity has expanded on: "[I]n Piranesi's etchings, there is a rhetoric of *enargeia* at work that causes the illusion of presence, but very little sense of mimetic fidelity to reality," Caroline van Eck observes.[48] In spite of an extreme exactitude in the rendering of details—or perhaps because of it—familiar buildings seem curiously displaced. Piranesi's hyper-representations hijack monuments and re-present them in a realm that is not real, but etched. A purely visual history unfolds, independent of any theoretical schemes, shaping the flow of time in sequences of mute images. As George Kubler remarks, it is only the "outer surface" of the historical past that we can know.[49]

The temptation to locate Piranesi's architecture in processes of nature rather than in a history of building also stems from his technique, or more precisely from the metaphors his technique seems to evoke. Focillon's impression of an architecture "carved from a rock" brings the world of building close to the point where it becomes geology, while reminding us that the graphic art also carves its motifs, albeit from copper. In Focillon's interpretation of Piranesi, the incision seeps through the representation to a certain extent, coagulating as a motif. The motif helps illustrate the method, not vice versa. No one prior to Focillon had quite so eloquently formulated the perception of Piranesi's architecture as not permanent but corruptible. The slow process of decay becomes a characteristic of the architecture itself and indeed one of its principal virtues. In the continuation of Focillon, Marguerite Yourcenar, looking at an obelisk in the image of Palazzo Barberini, notices how materials in Piranesi's hand exist in a gray zone between the manmade and the natural (*see following*):

> The ruin leans against the new palace like a dead log against living trees; the half-collapsed dome seems to be a mound scaled by a troop of bushes; buildings assume the aspect of lava, of sponge, having reached the degree of undifferentiated matter where we no longer know if this pebble picked up on the beach has once been carved by the hand of man or was fashioned thus by the tides.[50]

As buildings are on the verge of dissolving, they also betray more clearly their character as etched. The "undifferentiated matter" is the borderland in which the artist's virtuosity as an etcher impinges on the reality of the things shown. It is the purest expression of *form*, Focillon might have argued. Unsure of where the etching ends and the architecture begins, the abstract patterns in the *Carceri* are like "ink blots," Hyatt Mayor observes, suggesting that these blots might be what Piranesi in fact wished to represent.[51]

The corrosion that characterizes both Roman antiques and the process with which to show them leads Richard Wendort to see in Piranesi's prints a "double ruin." He compares an architecture ruined by the tooth of time to the copper plates bitten by the acid. In this sense "the process of physical deterioration we witness in his ruins is analogous to the etching process itself." Representing ancient Rome in etching was thus "not merely an antidote to loss, but a reenactment of loss."[52]

In a final instance, etching associates not only to deteriorating buildings but to deterioration as a philosophy of history. In the way Piranesi's decaying architecture emblematized process, in contrast to progress, it held the kernel to a revision of history itself. The cycles of nature, which Focillon and Yourcenar saw at play in Piranesi's visions, point to a processual movement adhering to no ideals, no program, no goal. Such a rearticulation of the idea of history served in particular a post-World War II Europe in which the relentless force of progress had only led to fascism and devastation. Arguably, Piranesi helped formulate a history that was refracted, discontinuous, and heterogeneous. As Andreas Huyssen sees it, Piranesi's "refusal of wholeness" and insistence on the incomplete connect to Theodor W. Adorno's anti-totalitarian ideal of the fragmentary work (although Adorno never refers to Piranesi).[53]

In a climate of totalitarian regimes, Piranesi's own theory of history began to attract attention, starting with Rudolf Wittkower's pioneering study on Piranesi and the Greco-Roman controversy published in 1938.[54] In several publications of the 1760s, Piranesi engaged in a polemic with French contemporaries, among them Pierre-Jean Mariette and Julien-David Le Roy, on the relative value of Greek and Roman architecture.[55] Furiously objecting to the French idealization of classical Greece, Piranesi championed the supremacy of Roman architecture, or, rather, he championed a Roman architecture that was in a continuous state of transformation, first formed by influences from Egypt and Etruria and then *de*-formed by its various stages of corrosion. In short, historical process took two forms, as Lola Kantor-Kazovsky sums up, namely "accumulation and decay."[56]

In contrast to the "*belle et noble simplicité*" of the Greeks, to quote Mariette, Piranesi's accumulation of motifs pointed to an opposite ideal, to an obsessive recombination, a "will to formlessness."[57] A return to the origin of architecture was simply a return to the creative force of the architect, paving the way for an alluring, open-ended history.[58] Manfredo Tafuri grasped the theoretical significance of this development, likening Piranesi's never-ending accumulation of elements to Foucault's notion of "heterotopia." Whereas utopia manifests an ideal wholeness, a heterotopia is a wholeness consisting of parts—a pile of fragments defying unity and coherence.[59] Indeed, the urge actively to decompose, to deconstruct, made Piranesi a prophet of anti-modernist architecture, as discussed in chapter six. But the piles and heaps also helped conceptualize the idea of the collapse of history as such in the same visual terms as Walter Benjamin's description of history as "one single catastrophe which keeps piling wreckage upon wreckage."[60] With Piranesi, disintegration became a constructive principle.

Accumulation and decay are processes that etching in particular is able to capture—processes that etching in fact visually conditions, as suggested by Focillon, Yourcenar, and Wendort. The trembling line of the needle, the burnishing of layers of copper, the manual intervention of dabbing, all correspond to an architectural history of instability and erosion. Limited by such material conditions, any grand idea of progress falters and collapses in subjective expressions. The organicity, ambivalences, and traces of wear—the very pastness of the past—thwarted any attempt to subordinate Piranesi's architecture to historical determinism and utopian wholes and cast him instead as an advocate of forces that ran counter to modern progress. From this viewpoint, the quality of his technique assumes a significance which is not about the history of etching but about the etching of history.

Giovanni Battista Piranesi, detail of *View of the Palazzo Barberini*, from *Vedute di Roma*, 1758–1759.

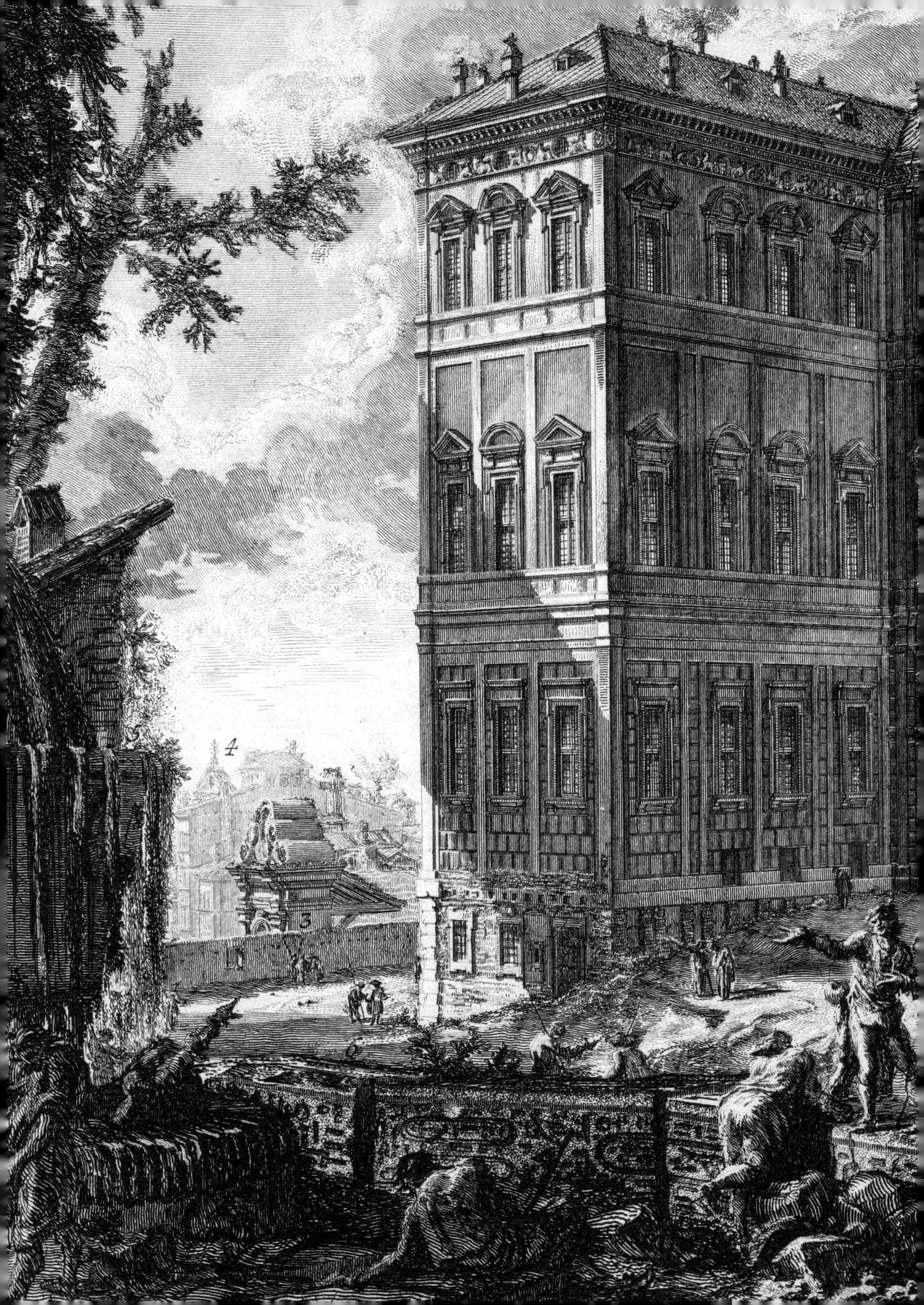

PIR

ANESI AT MOMA

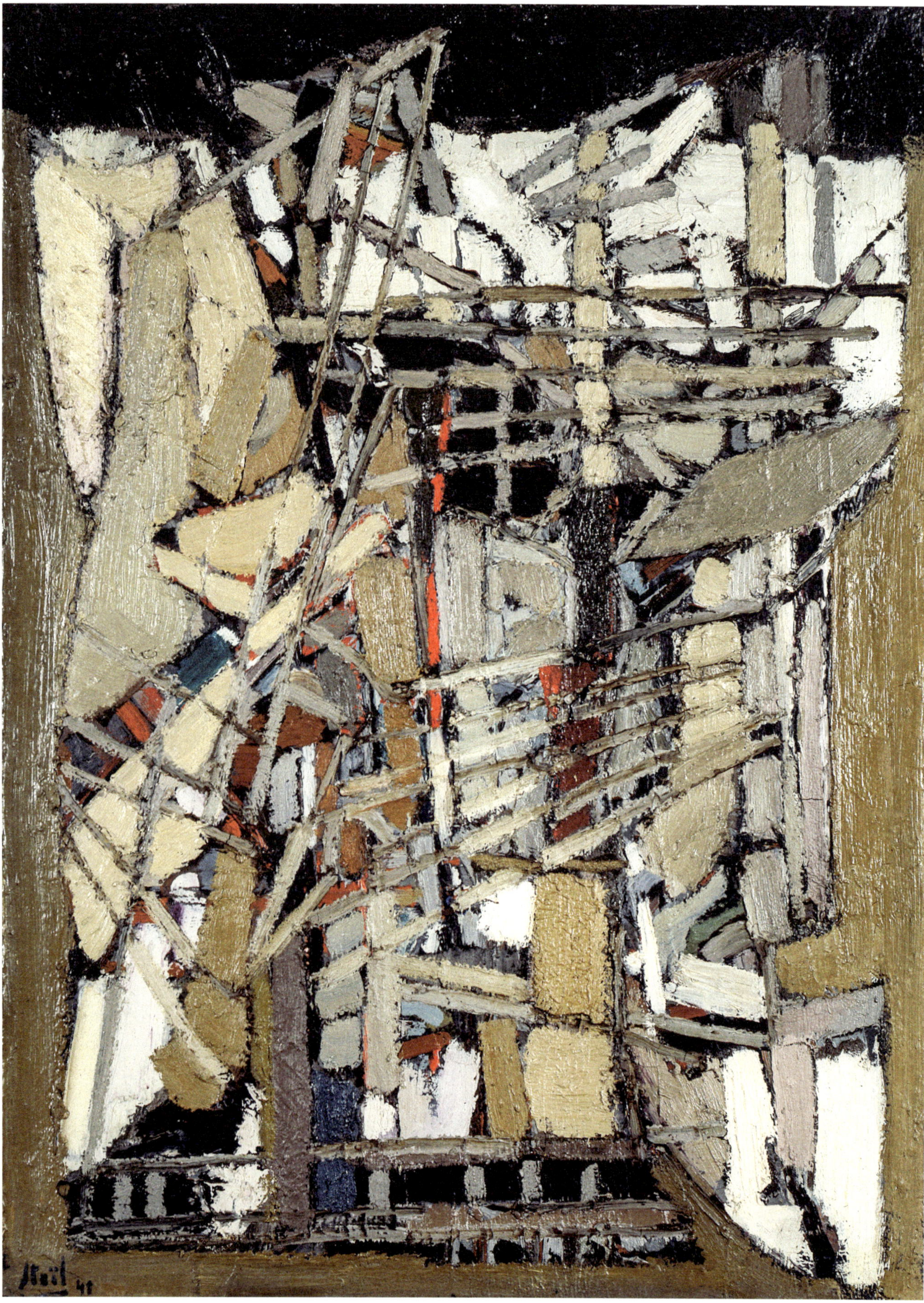

From the 1930s onwards a shift of perception allowed a new dimension to Piranesi's art to come into view. Images that since the eighteenth century had been seen as spatial representations, however dark and troubled, now appeared as configurations of planes and volumes. Artists and historians of art eyed an abstract quality in Piranesi's compositions that earlier times had been oblivious to. Among others, Nicolas de Staël seemed to bring the *Carceri*'s formal and psychological disorder to a heightened form of expressive non-figuration in *Hommage à Piranèse* (*see opposite*).

Even though explicit references and points of connection are difficult to identify, Piranesi's influence on modern art seems unquestionable. Late twentieth-century artists mentioned in association with Piranesi include Kurt Schwitters, Roberto Matta, Jackson Pollock, Frank Stella, Andy Warhol, Bruce Nauman, Richard Serra, and Anselm Kiefer. As Norman Rosenthal sums up, "there are no end of artists at the highest level that one might summon to see in terms of both Piranesi's ruins and prisons."[1] However, influence is an elusive category. Pointing out resemblances between Piranesi's compositions and modern art does not really tell us why the Venetian was important, nor who would benefit from his inclusion in the canon of modern art, nor, indeed, how his art helped shape the idea of the modern.

Already in 1915, William M. Ivins, curator of the print department at the Metropolitan Museum of Art in New York, recognized in the *Carceri* formal qualities that to him betrayed a modern, even modernist, point of view. The series "must stand or fall on its own intrinsic merit," Ivins wrote. They tell no tale, he continued, but amount to a "pure and unadulterated work of art in which manual felicity and 'human interest' play no part."[2] Ivins removed the "subject" from the *Carceri*, dismissing the prints as mirrors of the soul, an idea that had governed their perception since the days of De Quincey. What Ivins's essay also indicates is that abstract Piranesi was very much an American discovery, confined to a Manhattan milieu of curators, gallerists, and collectors.

CUBISM AND ABSTRACT ART

Reflecting on the *Carceri* in 1947, filmmaker Sergei Eisenstein wrote: "A stone is no longer a stone, but a system of intersecting angles and planes in whose play the geometrical basis of its form explodes." Placing Piranesi in a history of art that ran from Cézanne to Picasso, unperturbed by the twists of chronology implied by such a trajectory, he even designated Picasso's stirring *Guernica* as the *Carceri*'s "third" edition.[3] Aldous Huxley, in 1949, made a similar connection: "because the

Nicolas de Staël, *Hommage à Piranèse*, 1948. Oil on canvas.

Prisons are images of confusion, because their essence is pointlessness," they are "designs which resemble the abstractions of the Cubists."[4] Manfredo Tafuri, twenty years later, also linked Piranesi and Picasso: the plan of *Campo Marzio* and Picasso's *Femme au violon* (1911) combine in their "profoundly critical elaboration of form," each targeting a stagnant bourgeoisie.[5] In an extraordinary turn of events, then, Piranesi seemed to make as much sense in a twentieth-century development as in an eighteenth-century one.

This chapter asks when and why Piranesi's art first tied to notions of abstraction, addressing a quality in his prints that at times was explicitly advanced and at others remained implicit. Adopting a historiographic approach, it traces the origin of "abstract Piranesi" to three exhibitions at MoMA: the two groundbreaking exhibitions in 1936 curated by the museum's first director, Alfred H. Barr, and a third show in 1948, picking up the thread from Barr, but curated by René d'Harnoncourt. At MoMA, the *Carceri* were presented in a context entirely detached from Rome and, indeed, from any reference to an external reality. In the museum's relaunch, Piranesi's architectural views were no longer views, nor in fact were they architectural. Their value was as configurations of planes, lines, and volumes.

Based on unpublished archival material, catalogues, and photographs, the chapter offers the first thorough attempt to situate Piranesi within a cubist and surrealist discourse in what we must call the modernist revival of the artist. I shall investigate the formal, ideological, and historical reasons for including etchings from the *Carceri* in the three shows and draw out some of the consequences of the radical updating of the eighteenth-century Venetian. In other words, the chapter not only places Piranesi within a history of modern art but also points to the trajectories modern art took with the help of Piranesi.

No early cubist painters professed, as far as I know, a reliance on Piranesi; nor did any early authors on cubism. Manifestos such as André Salmon's *La jeune peinture française* (1912), Albert Gleizes's and Jean Metzinger's *Du "Cubisme"* (1912), and Guillaume Apollinaire's *Les peintres cubistes: Méditations esthétiques* (1913) celebrated Picasso and Braque's revolution in art, but were silent on the Venetian etcher.[6] For these authors to declare a dependence on past art would seem irrelevant, even counterproductive, as it would undermine cubism's claim to represent a new beginning; Cézanne was about as far back as any of them was willing to go when establishing an origin for the movement.[7]

It is true that some, less canonical, texts attempted to connect the works of Braque and Picasso to older art. Ardengo Soffici, publishing in Florence in 1913, and unable to sever the ties to history completely, wrote: "The one who wishes famous names of forerunners to cubism, even without going back to our

Cover of the exhibition catalogue *Cubism and Abstract Art*, MoMA, 1936.

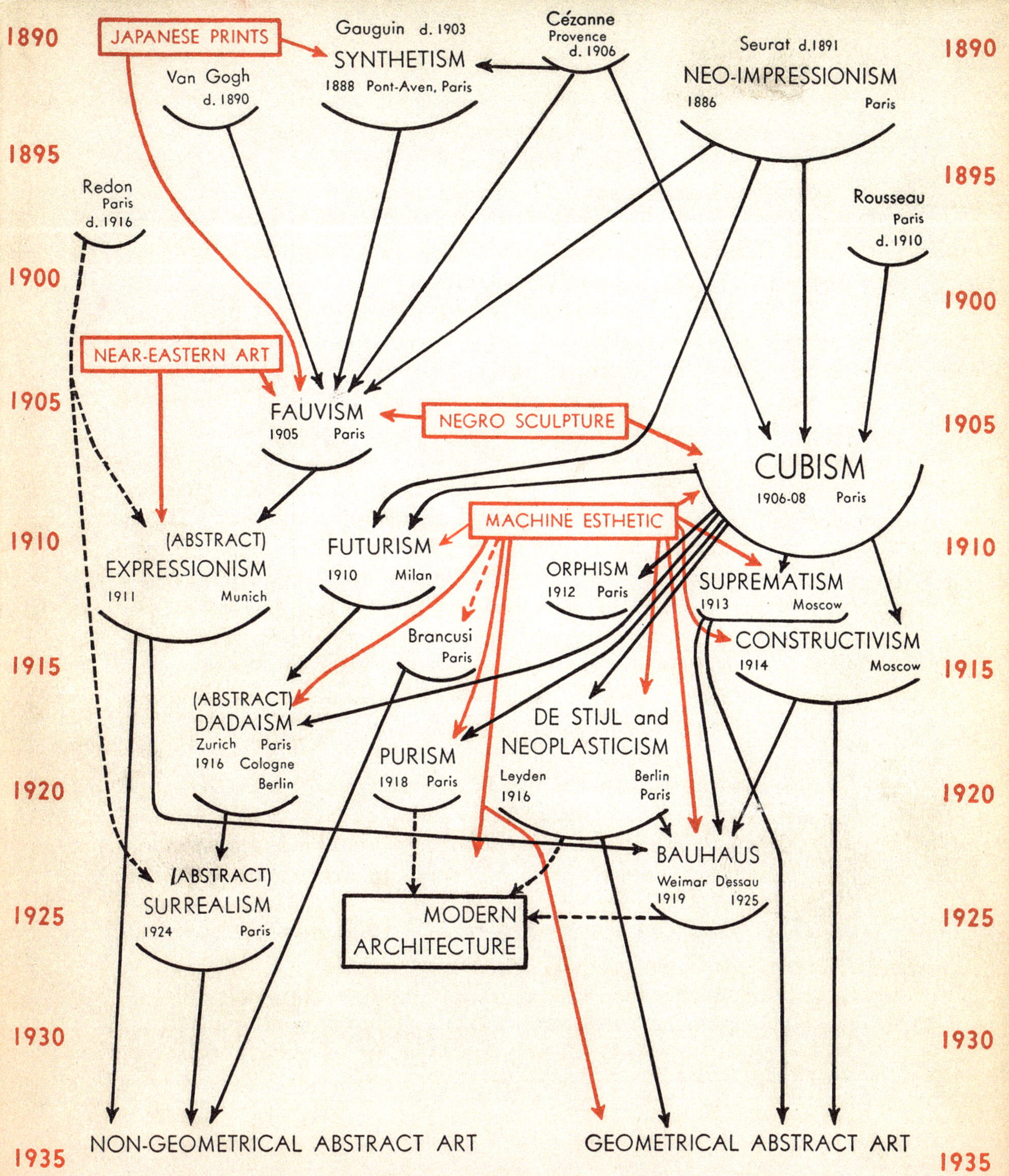

CUBISM AND ABSTRACT ART

primitives, to the Byzantines, to the Egyptians, to the Africans, may cite the names of Masaccio, El Greco, Rembrandt, Tintoretto."[8] Piranesi, however, was not on Soffici's list. Willard Huntington Wright, publishing in 1915, in New York, was even more eager to recognize precursors to the cubists. A torrent of names from history sprang to Wright's mind, including Michelangelo and Rembrandt, and among Picasso's kindred spirits in particular he mentioned Raphael, Goya, and El Greco.[9] But not Piranesi.

The exhibition *Cubism and Abstract Art* ran from March 2 to April 19, 1936 and included exhibits by over two hundred artists, but only one of them was born in the eighteenth century, namely Giovanni Battista Piranesi. In the catalogue to the exhibition, the curator Alfred H. Barr calls his art "proto-cubist" and includes as evidence a print from the *Carceri* series. Subjugating Piranesi to a modernist vision was a radical move, reflecting Barr's ambitious scheme to unify the arts across time and space in a single system. His *Cubism and Abstract Art* not only displayed the history of modern art but also for a large part invented that history. The flowchart on the catalogue's dust jacket has influenced the thinking of modern art ever since(*see preceding*). As famous now as many of the artworks in the show, it pinpoints Barr's mission to sort the plethora of modern "isms" into clear developments. In Barr's rich metaphorical language, these developments materialize less as a history and more as a marshland of brooks and rivers. Abstract art, according to Barr, follows two "main currents."[10] One has a source in Cézanne and Seurat. It then "passes through the widening stream of Cubism and finds its delta in the various geometrical and Constructivist movements." The second current, with a source in Gauguin and his circle, "flows" through fauvism and abstract expressionism, then keeps "running under ground for a few years" until it resurfaces in the art of surrealism. Although Barr admits that the currents may intersect, the polarity between the "intellectual, structural, architectonic, geometrical" and the "mystical, the spontaneous and the irrational"—in short between cubism and surrealism—ran deep in his vision of art and dictated the two contrasting shows mounted at MOMA in 1936.

In the catalogue, Barr obligingly concedes that Piranesi primarily made etchings of Roman ruins, but is quick to add that Piranesi also "anticipated Cubist-Constructivist esthetics."[11] Labeling the *Carceri* "proto-Cubist," he chose plate VII, *The Drawbridge*, for display in a section of the exhibition that included works by Cézanne, Picasso, Gris, Delaunay, and others.[12] In what can only be called a sensational update for an old master, Piranesi was now an exponent of a movement that between 1906 and 1913 experimented with and produced "increasingly abstract compositions."[13] Abstraction, to Barr, distinguishes modern art from older representational art. Within the paradigm of abstraction, painting's mission is no longer to mirror the world but to display the elements that constitute painting itself—to place the "emphasis not upon the reality of the represented objects but upon the reality of the painted surface."[14] However, Barr also differentiates between degrees of abstraction. Drawing on a classification introduced by Daniel-Henry Kahnweiler, he assigns *The Drawbridge* to a section of the exhibition devoted to analytical cubism.[15] In contrast to synthetic cubism, this represented a mild form of abstraction, one that still clung to the world of recognizable objects even if these objects were at times hard to discern. Occasionally, no other clues to the subject matter existed than the title, such as "violin," "head"—or alternatively "prison," the title given to the Piranesi print on display. In short, "proto-cubist" Piranesi was classed as abstract, but not as non-figurative.

Thanks to an installation photograph, we can identify *The Drawbridge*'s precise location in the show (*see below*). It concluded a series of images, a lithograph and two ink drawings, produced by Robert Delaunay between 1909 and 1912. Although the Delaunay images evoke real places, namely the Church of Saint-Séverin and the Eiffel Tower, the sequence clearly manifests an increasing dissolution of architectural form. So did the Piranesi print, coming at the end, represent an ultimate stage of abstraction? To answer that question, we need to consider first the formal resemblance that Barr possibly perceived between the works by

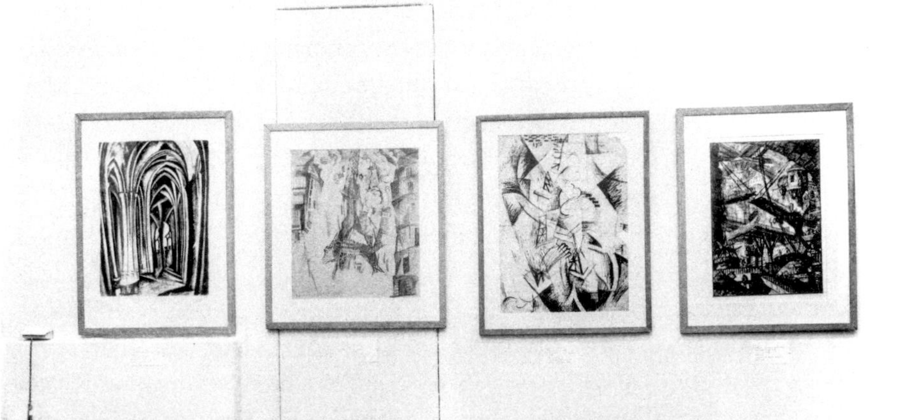

Installation photograph from the exhibition *Cubism and Abstract Art*, MOMA, March 2–April 19, 1936.

Piranesi and Delaunay, and then the conspicuous conflation of historically distinct periods that allowed them to form a meaningful assemblage.

Seeing Piranesi's composition as "abstract" was not entirely anachronistic. *The Drawbridge* abounds with ambiguities and contradictions. For example, the spiral stair encircling the massive column to the left passes impossibly on the outside of the bridge. On the level above, the drawbridge would never connect as both sections of it tilt outward.[16] The architecture's instability no doubt contributed to the perception of its cubist quality. That the print moreover occupied the spot immediately next to Delaunay's drawing of a fragmented Eiffel Tower, *The Tower and the Wheel* (1912–1913), enhanced the print's abstract qualities. The triangular shapes formed by lines in Delaunay resemble the geometry of ropes in Piranesi, while sharp contrasts between light and dark produce corresponding patterns.

The catalogue tied Piranesi and Delaunay even more firmly together in a striking double spread (*see opposite*). Compared to the double spread in Gombrich's *Art and Illusion*, which we remember included *The Drawbridge* too (see chapter one), Barr, significantly, chose the image in its second edition, not the first as Gombrich did. Whereas the first edition remains light and airy with patches of smoke obstructing parts of the construction, the second edition adds architectural elements and deep shadows in an image that better corresponds to Delaunay's *The Tower and the Wheel* (*see following*). Several components therefore—even the print's edition—were taken into account when Piranesi's print joined Delaunay in a juxtaposition meant to illustrate how cubist art connects across the ages.

The Drawbridge from the *Carceri* has become one of Piranesi's most iconic images and its breakthrough in the modern age trails back precisely to *Cubism and Abstract Art* (*see following*). The particular impression on show, however, did not belong to MOMA; archival material reveals that Barr borrowed it from the art dealer and print collector Carl Zigrosser, who ran the Weyhe Gallery in nearby Lexington Avenue.[17] Nor was the print valued very highly. An insurance list was put up prior to the opening. Whereas, for example, Picasso's painting "Dancer" was valued at four thousand dollars and Louis Marcoussis' etching "Music" at two hundred dollars, Piranesi's "prison" was insured for a mere fifty dollars, the lowest estimate of any artwork in the show. But its role in Barr's presentation of history was invaluable, far surpassing its function as a mere companion piece to Delaunay's drawing.[18] The print's inclusion in *Cubism and Abstract Art*, as we shall see, served to portray the modern period as exempt from any periodization at all.

While a full consideration of Barr's conception of modern art is beyond the scope of this discussion, the sources and ideas that allowed Piranesi to fit into that conception need to be reviewed.[19] Barr's encounter with Sergei Eisenstein and

Delaunay and Piranesi (figures 38 and 39) in the exhibition catalogue *Cubism and Abstract Art*, MOMA, 1936.

overleaf Robert Delaunay, *The Tower and the Wheel*, ca. 1912–1913. Ink on paper.
Giovanni Battista Piranesi, plate VII, *The Drawbridge*, from *Carceri d'invenzione*, second edition, 1761.

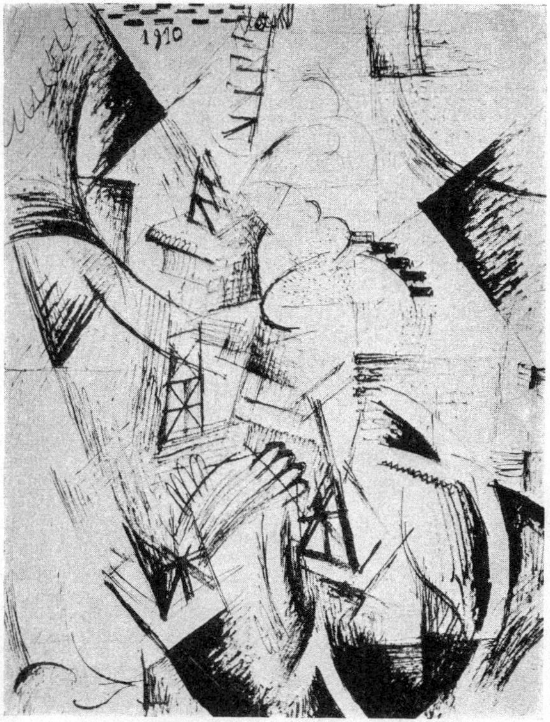

38 (43) Delaunay: Tower with a ferris wheel, 1909-10

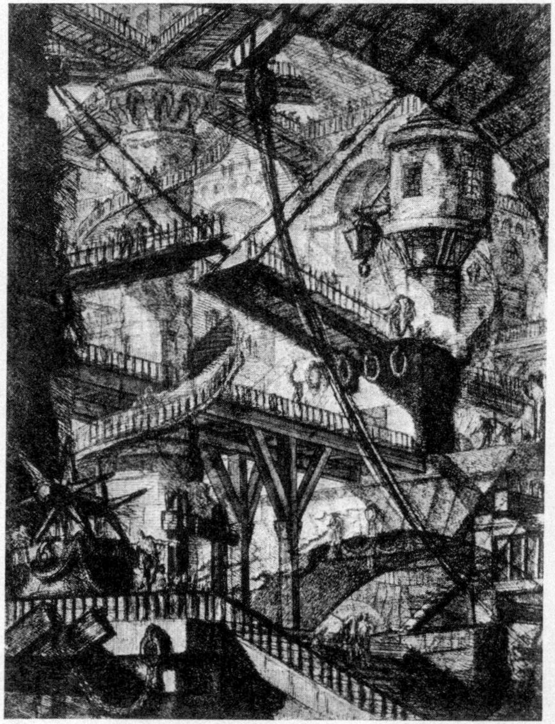

39 (232) Piranesi: Prison, *c.* 1745

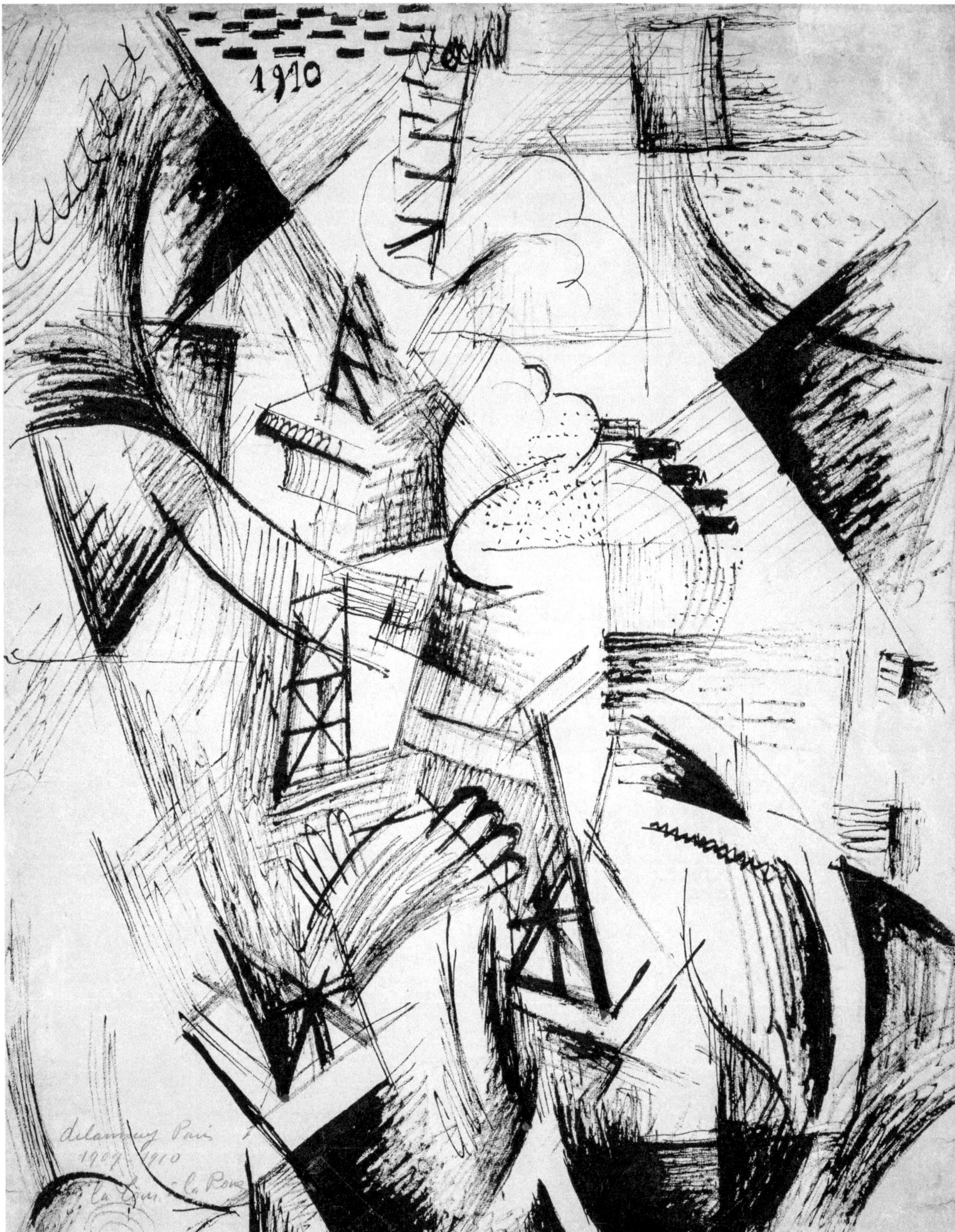
1910

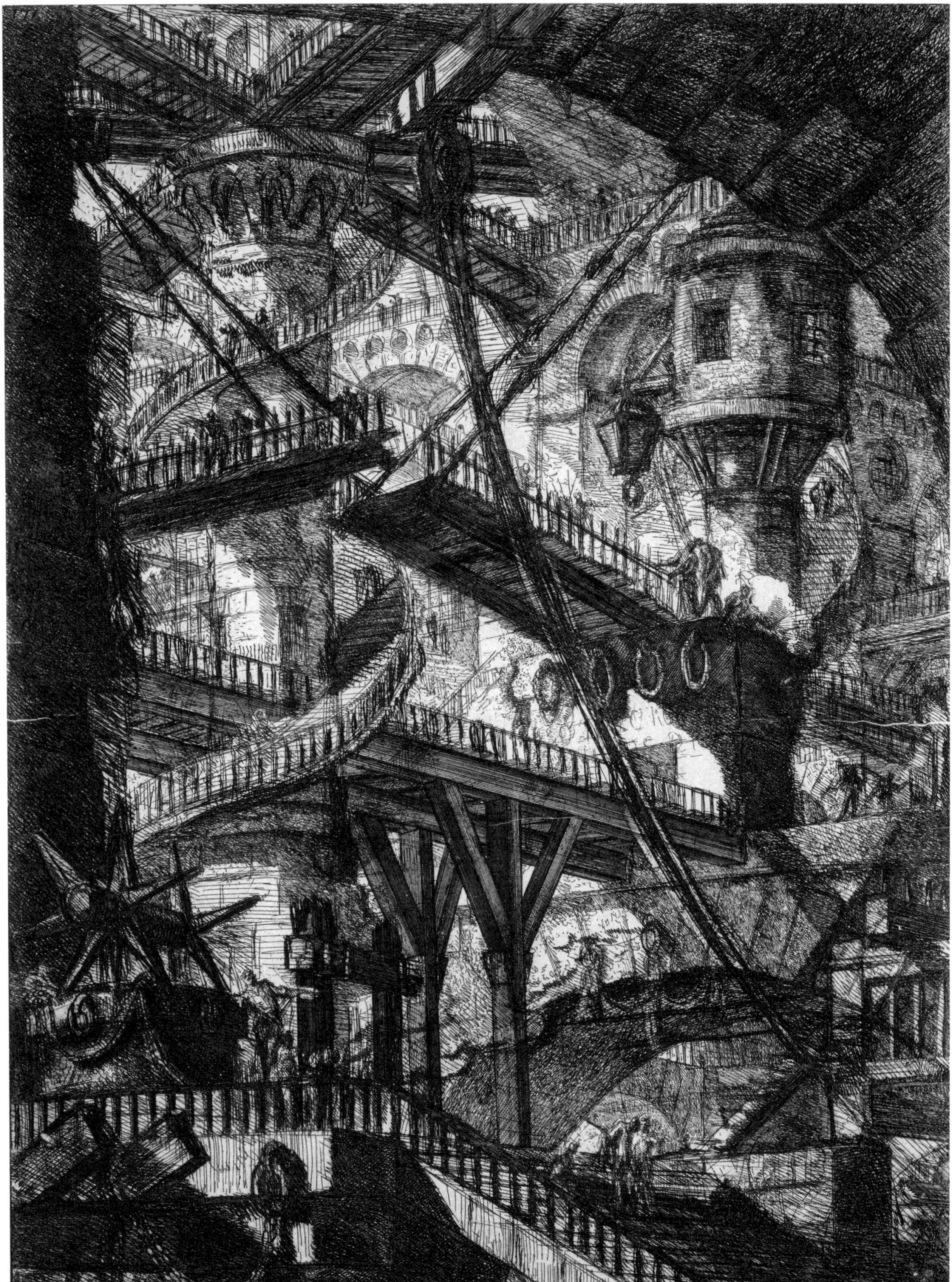

his expressed admiration for the filmmaker's montage technique is a factor I will consider in the next chapter. A more immediate influence connects to the historiography of modern art available by the 1930s. In 1925 El Lissitzky and Hans Arp published *Die Kunstismen: 1914–1924*, a pioneering attempt to catalogue the isms in art that had emerged over the previous decade. Sybil Gordon Kantor refers to the importance of this publication for Barr's effort to systematize art in *Cubism and Abstract Art*. But in my opinion, László Moholy-Nagy was an equally important source. Barr first met Moholy-Nagy in 1927 during his visit to the Bauhaus, where the Hungarian was a professor at the time. Several works by Moholy-Nagy were included in the 1936 show and he and Barr also corresponded.[20] Like Lissitzky and Arp, Moholy-Nagy approached the issue of isms, but by a more profound route, addressing the question of how to legitimize the profusion of art movements—a question that Barr also addressed, but not Lissitzky and Arp. To the extent that modern art hinged on isms, the principle behind those isms was crucial to define. Moholy-Nagy found such a principle, or "common denominator," in what he recognized as laws governing both the movements of art and human nature. Grasping this correspondence, "the art forms and art 'isms,' which at first appeared complicated, will order themselves in organic relationships," Moholy-Nagy claimed in *Neues Sehen* (1928).[21] *The New Vision,* an English translation printed in New York in 1930, figures in the bibliography of the catalogue to *Cubism and Abstract Art*. Arguably, the exhibition as such was in part a response to Moholy-Nagy's call to uncover the fundament on which the movements were based, and not merely list them, as Lissitzky and Arp had done. The "organic relationships" suggested by Moholy-Nagy would appeal to Barr, who was passionate about botany and zoology and who was inclined in any case to think metaphorically about the developments in modern art. However, whereas Moholy-Nagy found the "common denominator" in inner laws, Barr, as we have seen, found it in a recurring dichotomy between logic and intuition, rationality and feeling—indeed between Apollo and Dionysus, the Greek deities Barr conjured to illustrate the opposites in human nature—a dichotomy that ultimately resulted in the separation of cubism and surrealism into two major strands.[22]

Exhibiting *The Drawbridge* in *Cubism and Abstract Art* therefore served a wider agenda than merely showing a "modern" Piranesi. To return to Barr's analogy of a landscape, the "stream" that flowed from Cézanne through cubism, only to end in the delta of constructivism, obviously also engulfed Piranesi. But where exactly Barr imagined Piranesi stood in that stream—at the source or at its outlet—is unclear and perhaps also irrelevant. For in the staging of art as modern, history might also flow backwards. The arresting juxtaposition of Piranesi with

Delaunay proclaimed a defiance of chronological history. In this perspective, the print by Piranesi represented, not a time that had passed, but the modern as timeless. Its crucial function was to confirm that abstraction was no fleeting phenomenon, but a constant, intrinsic to all times, although brought to maturity with the modern age. To Barr, formal qualities alone were sufficient to validate connections across time and movements. The geometries of planes and angles constituted a sovereign pictorial reality that lifted the work of art above history and also above the psychological and social influences on its making.

The analogy between Piranesi and cubism, therefore, was strictly curatorial, conceived within the circuits of the museum, if not within the mind of the curator himself. Beyond merely naming Piranesi a proto-cubist, a truly bold stroke on Barr's part would have been to backdate cubism itself to the eighteenth century, since abstract art was exempt from time. In any case, the inclusion in the exhibition of Piranesi's *Carceri* shows that Barr already glimpsed an origin in a period earlier than Cézanne. Apart from endorsing specific works like Delaunay's, Piranesi's mission was to illustrate the continuity of history, indeed to emphasize its "flow"—to demonstrate not that historical art was abstract, but that abstraction, as such, was ahistorical.

FANTASTIC ART, DADA, SURREALISM

In an extraordinary double act, the Piranesi print from *Cubism and Abstract Art* reappeared in MOMA's next show, used on this occasion to exemplify the exact opposite tendency in modern art, namely surrealism. The etching was the same, on extended loan from Zigrosser, but the modern movement it endorsed had changed.

If *Cubism and Abstract Art* had been a sensation, *Fantastic Art, Dada, Surrealism*, running from December 7, 1936 to January 17, 1937, was little short of a scandal (*see following*). MOMA's neighbors even took action to try "to suppress the Dada Movement on 53rd Street," fearing it would have "an adverse effect upon the Artistic Instinct of our Neighbourhood."[23] In the catalogue, counting nearly seven hundred exhibits, Barr wrote that *Cubism and Abstract Art* was "diametrically opposed in both spirit and esthetic principles to the present exhibition."[24] Whereas the first show had focused on the formal aspects of art, the new show presented an art that went beyond, or beneath, mere form and explored the obscure depths of the self. Georges Hugnet, in his contribution to the catalogue, put it bluntly: "What a work of art expresses formally is of no importance—only its hidden content counts."[25] The two exhibitions, mounted less than eight months apart, were in every way antithetical. A rare point of connection, it seems, was Piranesi's *The Drawbridge*.

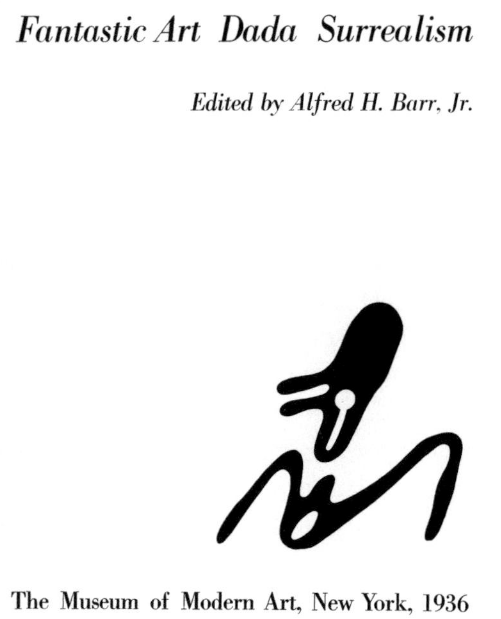
Fantastic Art Dada Surrealism

Edited by Alfred H. Barr, Jr.

The Museum of Modern Art, New York, 1936

The fact that the same print could illustrate two contrary developments testifies to the rich history of interpretation that by the 1930s attached to the *Carceri*, and the range of associations the prints induced. Different meanings were unveiled for different purposes, and for different exhibitions. With Barr taking up a reversed curatorial standpoint, "the mind of the artist" was now the touchstone that justified the inclusion of past art in the show. In the juxtaposition of works from different periods, a likeness of forms gave way to a correspondence of souls. However, Barr offered a clear warning: "Genuine analogies may exist but they must be kept tentative until our knowledge of the states of mind of, say, Bosch or Bracelli has been increased by systematic research and comparison."[26]

Barr's promotion of psychology as a tool to penetrate the mind of the artist—living or dead—paved the way for the uncovering of a layer in Piranesi's art latent since the days of De Quincey, and discussed in chapter one. When Barr wrote that the exhibition responded to "the deep-seated and persistent interest which human beings have in the fantastic, the irrational, the spontaneous, the marvelous, the enigmatic, and the dreamlike," he was describing the impact of psychoanalysis on art.[27] But these same terms had, over the course of a century, also become the vocabulary of Piranesi's prison etchings. In order to evaluate how exactly Piranesi fitted into this new show, we need to establish its context.

Fantastic Art, Dada, Surrealism explored movements that delved deeper into the conditions for artistic creation than the cubist tradition's mere reassembly of forms. The Dada movement's cultivation of the accidental, spontaneous, and meaningless—in poetry and paintings—ridiculed both the society that had plunged the world into war and the art that had complacently served that society, Barr observed.[28] The presentation at MOMA of Dadaist works by Hans Arp, Max

Title page of the exhibition catalogue *Fantastic Art, Dada, Surrealism*, MOMA, 1936.

Ernst, Marcel Duchamp, Francis Picabia, and others, was a landmark event, "virtually defining a new field," as Anne Umland among others has noted.[29]

Outrageous, playful, and deliberately provocative, Dada differed from the surrealist movement and the latter's more systematic and serious investigation of the mechanisms of the psyche. Surrealism sought ways to short-circuit reason and unlock the deeper strata of the self. In the *Surrealist Manifesto* (1924), the movement's founder, André Breton, declared his explicit allegiance to Freud. It was thanks to Freud, he wrote, that an ignored part of our mental world had been brought back to light. The artist's mission was to recuperate that part and give it expression in images and objects: "I believe in the future resolution of these two states, dream and reality, which are seemingly so contradictory, into a kind of absolute reality, a *surreality*."[30] Images surfacing from dreams and memory constituted a new pictorial language explored by Max Ernst, Paul Klee, Joan Miró, Man Ray, René Magritte, and Salvador Dalí, to name but a few. And Barr exhibited them all.

By 1936, Dada and surrealism were acknowledged labels on defined artistic movements. The exhibition's less precise "*fantastic*," by contrast, denoted a category Barr devised to embrace historic art. Although Breton and Hugnet objected to the term, Barr insisted, and under this heading the show came to include a large number of prints and paintings predating Dada and surrealism proper. Works by Hieronymus Bosch, William Blake, Francisco Goya, and Odilon Redon, among others, were labeled "fantastic" and distributed in sections ranging from the fifteenth century to World War I.

However, as so often, the Piranesi etchings on show slipped through historical categories, introducing into modern art distinctions that nuanced the very idea of the modern as such.

The Drawbridge on loan from Zigrosser was presumably included in the section of the exhibition called "Fantastic art: 17th and 18th centuries," although in this instance there is no installation photo to locate it with absolute certainty. To judge from the catalogue, however, the etching that had been sensationally juxtaposed with Delaunay a few months previously was now placed in a correct chronological sequence between the printmakers Nicolas de Larmessin and Philip Morghen (*see following*).

As a leftover from the previous exhibition, but reinterpreted from a psychological standpoint, *The Drawbridge* now heralded the ominous shadow worlds of De Chirico, Magritte, and Dalí, who were also represented in the show. Moving beneath the surface of cubism's fragmentation of objects, so to speak, these artists examined a deeper realm. In that landscape, the objects that cubism had

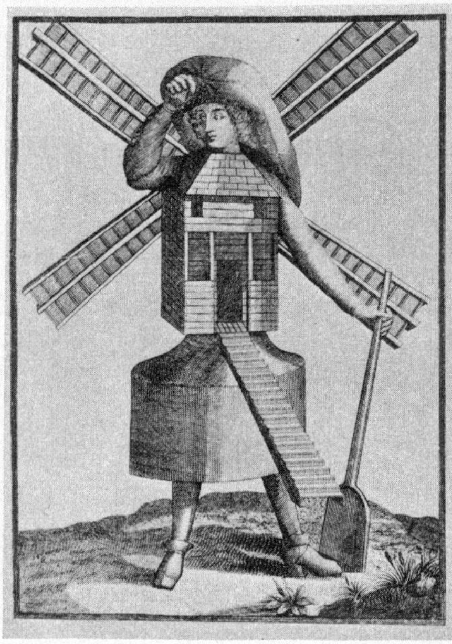

70 Larmessin: Miller's costume

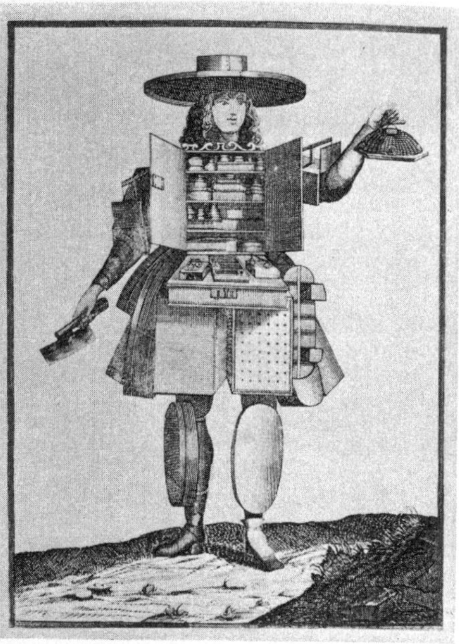

71 Larmessin: Box-maker's costume

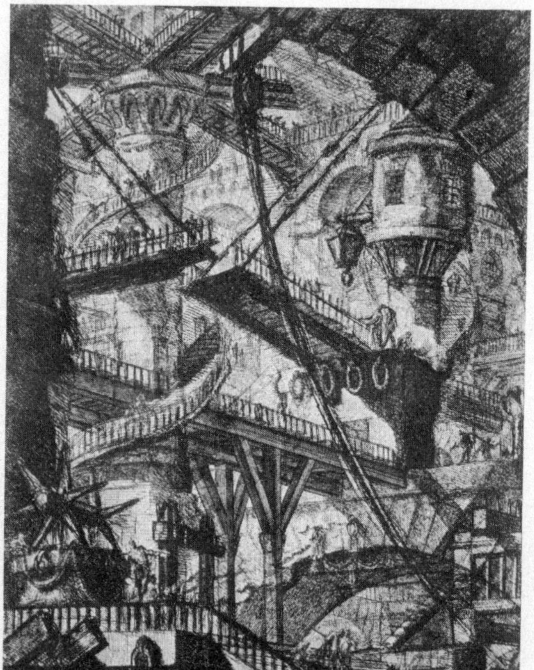

81a Piranesi: Prison interior, *c.* 1745

decomposed regained (or had not yet lost) their shape and familiarity. Train, clocks, and lighthouses are perfectly recognizable and yet the settings in which they appear are inexplicable, disquieting, dreamlike. Barr let Piranesi join these artists in that mysterious realm. The change to the wording of the catalogue caption, from "Prison" in *Cubism and Abstract Art* to "Prison interior," reflects the new show's emphasis on psychology and introspection; "interior" evokes a spatiality of *self*, as discussed in chapter one, adding depth of meaning to a mere architectural type.

However, Zigrosser's *The Drawbridge* was not the only Piranesi print on display. The Boston print collector and curator, W. G. Russell Allen, made available no less than four additional *Carceri* prints, along with graphic works by other artists ranging from Nicoletto da Modena to Odilon Redon. Unpublished correspondence in the MOMA archives reveals that Barr had Allen's collection of prints in mind from the early days of planning the exhibition. Supremely knowledgeable on modern art, but no great expert on old masters, Barr wrote from Germany on August 7, 1936, asking Allen to "give some suggestions" of prints to include in a show that would consist of the "foremost masters of the fantastic and marvellous."[31] He carefully avoided the terms Dada and surrealist, unsure of how Allen would react to contributing to a show that canonized these controversial movements. Hearing nothing from Allen, Barr wrote again on October 1, adding that he should be glad to come to Boston himself to go through the collection, feeling "sure that no one else in New England has more material which might be used in the exhibition."[32]

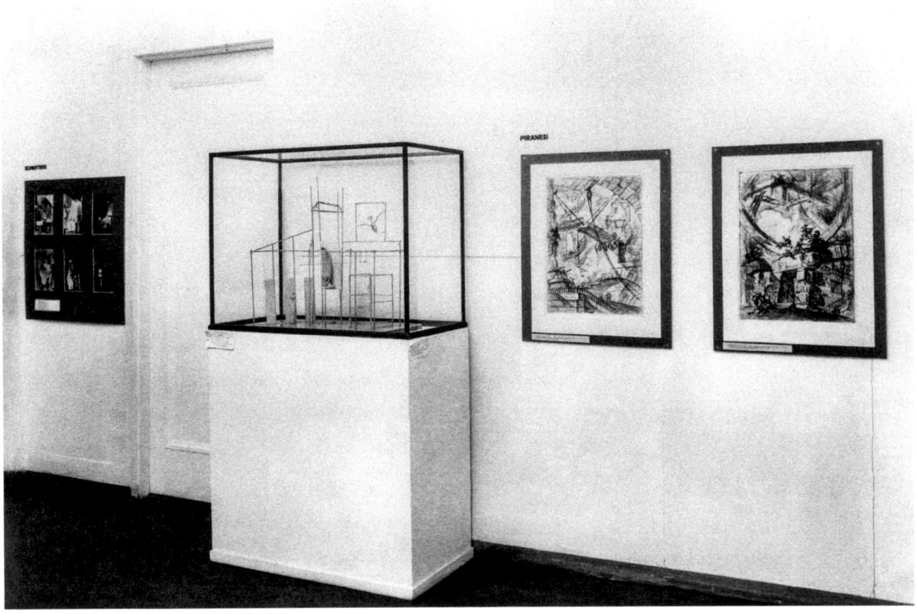

Installation photograph from the exhibition *Fantastic Art, Dada, Surrealism*, MOMA, December 7, 1936 – January 17, 1937.

facing Larmessin and Piranesi (figures 70, 71 & 81a) in the exhibition catalogue *Fantastic Art, Dada, Surrealism*, MOMA, 1936.

Allen, as it turned out, had nothing against contributing. In November 1936, he shipped no less than thirty-two prints to the museum. Whether he compiled the material alone, or in tandem with Barr, is unknown. Whatever the case, Barr quickly made a selection of just ten works, excluding two Piranesi prints from the *Carceri* series.[33] The prints he retained were *The Giant Wheel* and—extraordinarily—a second version of *The Drawbridge*, a print already represented in the exhibition by Zigrosser's loan.

Two impressions from the same Piranesi plate now infiltrated the surrealist pageant on 53rd Street. But this remarkable and apparent unnecessary redoubling was far from accidental, as will become clear. Allen's loan was hung on the wall next to Alberto Giacometti's sculpture *The Palace at 4 a.m.*, a recent piece, executed in 1932, and acquired by MOMA from the artist in 1936, just in time for the exhibition (*see preceding*). In other words, when the Giacometti arrived it had no "history," a temporal void that I believe Piranesi helped fill. That Piranesi's prints served to provide new works with a "past," especially works that belonged to MOMA, is already evident with Delaunay's *The Tower and the Wheel*, which had reached the collection in 1935, only a year prior to its premiere at *Cubism and Abstract Art*. But the Piranesi–Giacometti connection also appears more subtle than a mere historical alibi.

Composed of wood, glass, wire, and string, *The Palace at 4 a.m.* suggests the bare skeletal framework of a house in an extremely frail set-up (*see opposite*). In Giacometti's words, the structure relates to a love affair he once had with a woman and a "very fragile palace of matchsticks" that the lovers built during the night. In the middle, he writes, we see "the scaffolding of a tower which is perhaps unfinished, or perhaps the whole of its top has fallen in, been broken."[34]

At first glance, the juxtaposition at MOMA highlighted the difference between Giacometti's and Piranesi's works (*see opposite and following*). The three dimensions of the sculpture contradict the two dimensions of the picture. However, on a closer look, it is a difference that the juxtaposition also tries to counteract—or even out. Displayed next to each other, their rectangular frames neatly aligned, the one enhances the quality of the other: the sculpture makes the spectator grasp the eerie contraption "imprisoned" in Piranesi's print. Conversely, Piranesi's print, with its rough scratching, exposes the drawn character of the Giacometti sculpture. Indeed, on subsequent occasions, MOMA would characterize *The Palace at 4 a.m.* as "a vertical immaterial drawing in space."[35] The print, then, framed the conception of Giacometti's surrealist palace as "surreal" precisely by relocating it to the realm of dream, the realm that the *Carceri* had so successfully monopolized in art, accentuating the sculpture as unbuildable—as an "empty architecture."[36]

Giacometti's *The Palace at 4 a.m.* (fig. 379) in the exhibition catalogue *Fantastic Art, Dada, Surrealism*, MOMA, 1936.

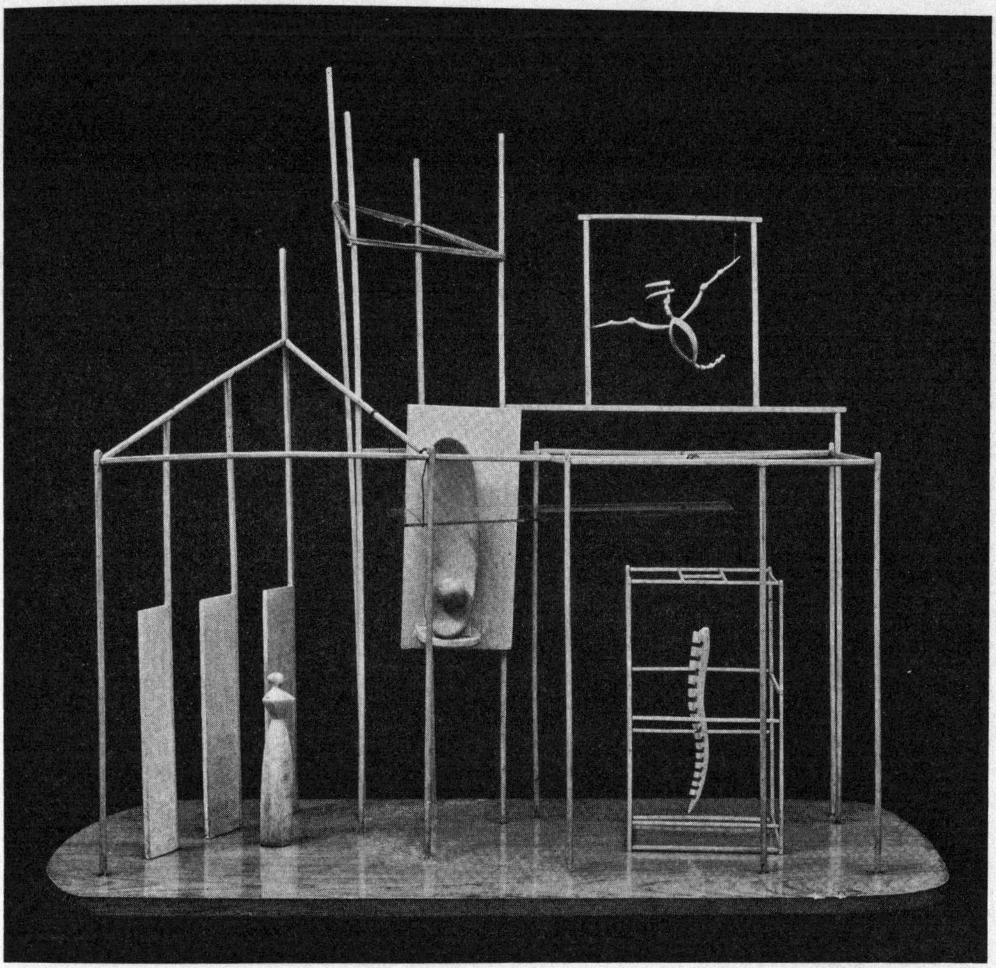

379 Giacometti: The palace at 4 a.m., 1933

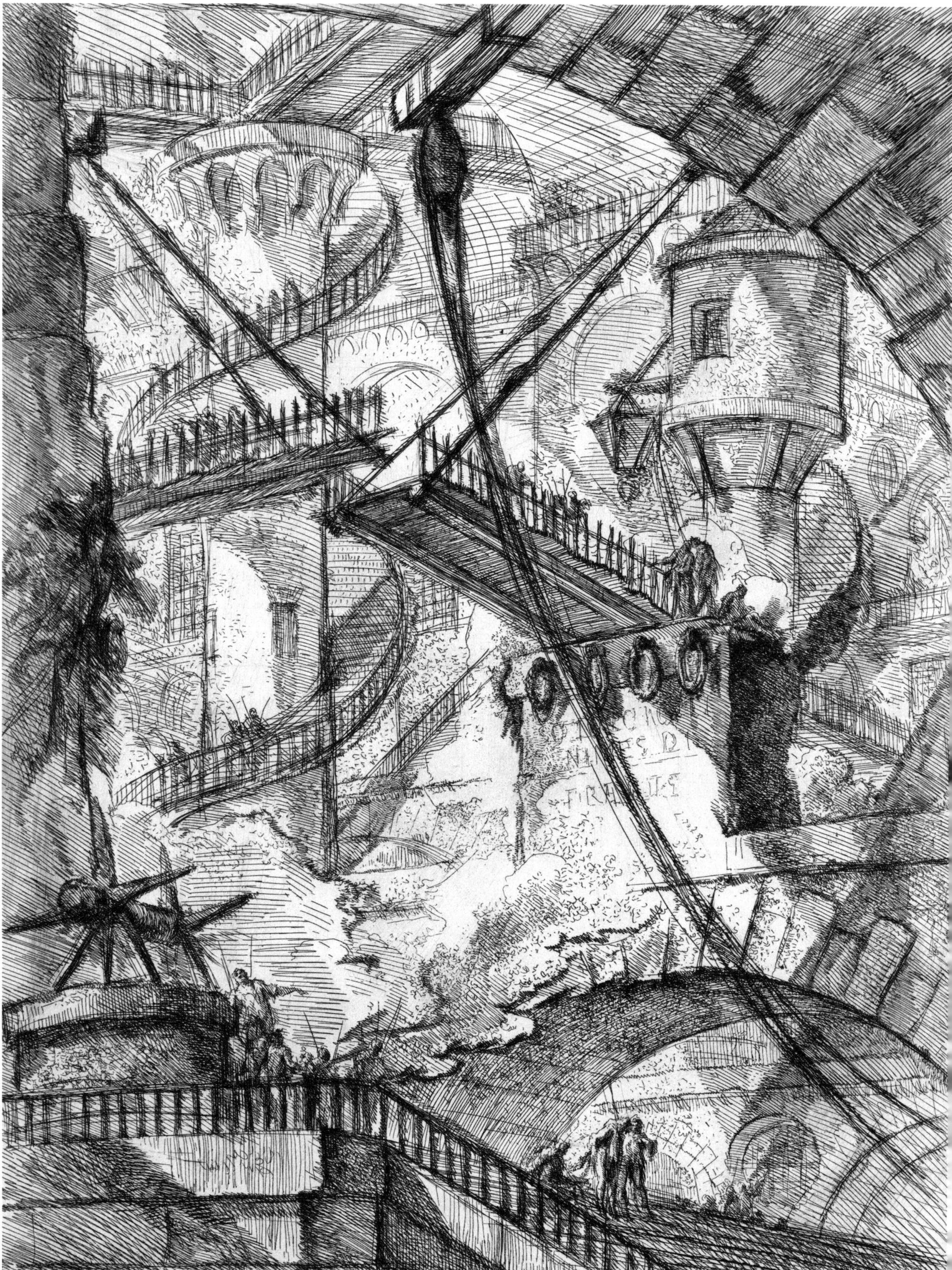

An obvious question remains. Since two impressions of *The Drawbridge* were on display, how do we know that the one adjacent to Giacometti was the loan from Allen and not the leftover from *Cubism and Abstract Art* on loan from Zigrosser? An expert eye will soon detect that Allen's loan derives from the first edition of the *Carceri* and Zigrosser's from the second. Old prints were anomalies in the show in any case, but now, surprisingly, their different editions also came to play an important role. Whereas the dense and architectural second edition invited comparison to Delaunay and cubism, the sketchier and lighter first edition invited comparison to a more delicate and mysterious Giacometti—and by implication to another movement. With the two exhibitions in 1936, Barr, unwittingly, ended up as a connoisseur of prints, promoting not only different Piranesi etchings but also the difference between the original and reworked plates. No big deal perhaps, save for the fact that two major developments in art, and in Barr's mind two opposite ones, hinged on that difference. Ultimately, and on a micro level, the cubist and the surrealist movements depended on the minutiae of eighteenth-century print production.

The third *Carceri* in the show was *The Giant Wheel*, hanging to the left of the Giacometti and *The Drawbridge*—this too a loan from Allen (*see following*). The dominant feature in the composition is a large wheel ambiguously tilting towards the spectator. We do not know why Barr chose to include the print, nor what hung to the right of it, but it did relate to other exhibits. In fact, in calling this wheel an "enormous oval eye" forty years later, Tafuri possibly evokes the association induced by the print in the context of the surrealist exhibition.[37] Also classed as "fantastic" in the 1936 MOMA show, and illustrated in the catalogue, was Odilon Redon's lithograph *The Eye Like a Strange Balloon Mounts Towards Infinity* from 1882, a symbolist work (*see following*). Magritte's *The False Mirror* (1929)—also on display—paraphrases seeing as well. Man Ray, who owned the Magritte until the museum bought it in 1936, described *The False Mirror* as a picture that "sees as much as it itself is seen."[38] Again, Piranesi may have been selected to guarantee a continuity for recent acquisitions and strengthen the legitimacy of the museum's own holdings.

Piranesi's *The Drawbridge* was one of the very few artworks figuring in the two "diametrically opposed" 1936 exhibitions, to quote Barr again.[39] Exemplifying abstracted form in the first show and a surreal content in the next, the composition was sufficiently powerful to signal multiple realities, which of course contradicted Barr's strictly separated isms. In short, as Piranesi came to Barr's assistance in the effort to stake out the trajectories of modern art, the Venetian etcher also revealed that "modern" was a fragile construction that at times depended on interpretations of one and the same image.

Giovanni Battista Piranesi, plate VII, *The Drawbridge*, from *Invenzioni capric di carceri*, first edition, ca. 1749–1750.

overleaf Giovanni Battista Piranesi, plate IX, *The Giant Wheel*, from *Invenzioni capric di carceri*, first edition, ca. 1749–1750. Odilon Redon, *The Eye Like a Strange Balloon Mounts Towards Infinity*, 1882. Lithograph on chine appliqué.

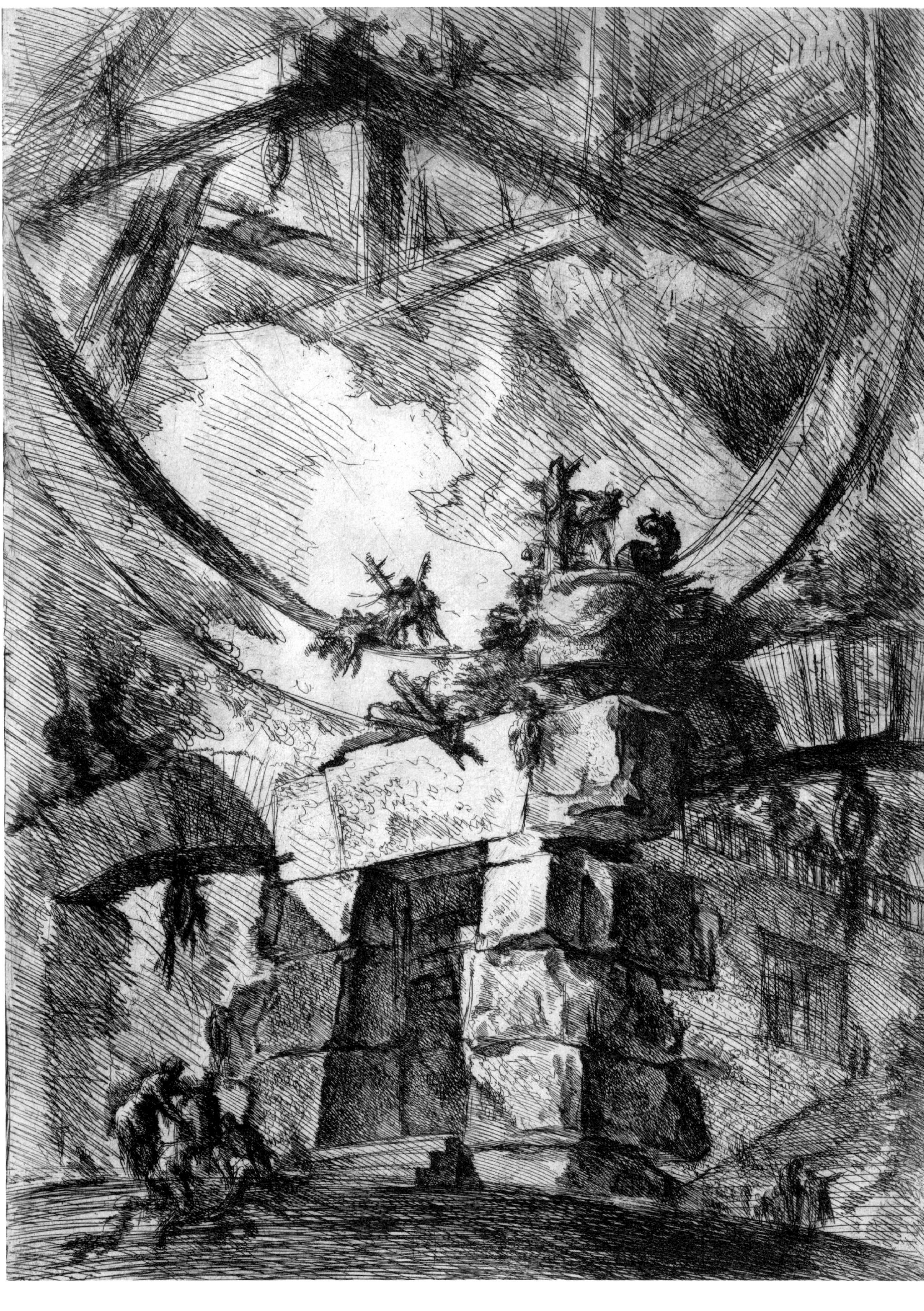

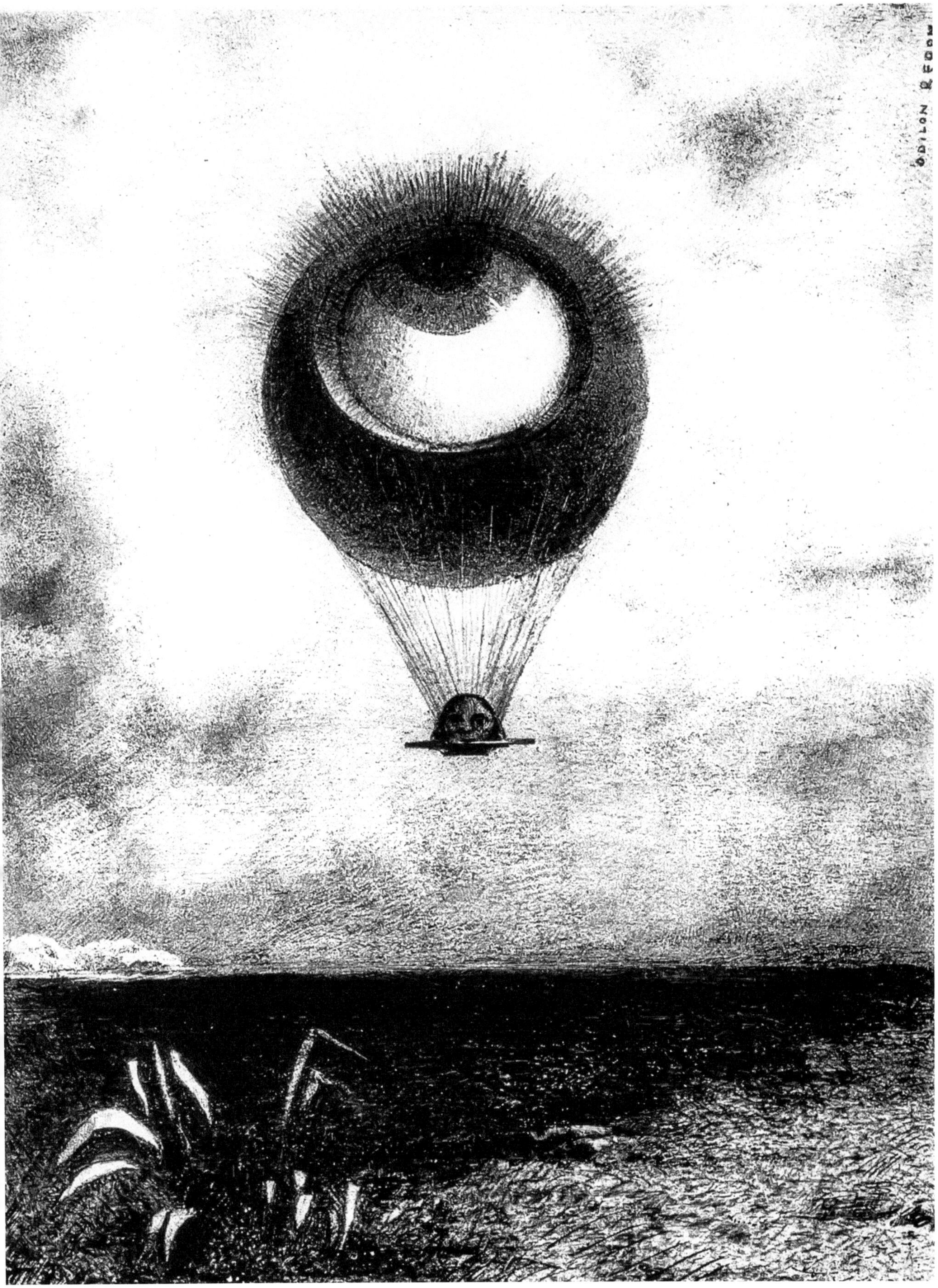
ODILON REDON

World War II was also a watershed in the preference for Piranesi prints. For a civilization that had endured the calamities of war, the fragmentation and disunity of the *Carceri* interiors no longer evoked dreams, but reality. "Piranesi's prisoners," Huxley wrote in 1949, "are the inhabitants of a hell, which [...] is completely credible and bears the stamp of an unquestionable authenticity." It is a chillingly sober verdict on the prison caprices. The *Carceri*, which up to then had visualized private infernos, were now elevated to emblems of a collective trauma—representing a world ravaged by war, not merely a mind plagued by inner demons.

The Drawbridge, although complex enough, did not quite capture the gravity and drama of the postwar period, but other prints did. Around the same time that Sergei Eisenstein was writing on the "explosive" forces that connected the *Carceri* to cubism, the art historian and curator René d'Harnoncourt, by all accounts unaware of the Russian director's 1946–1947 essay, was planning a show that illustrated precisely that connection. Eisenstein in Moscow and d'Harnoncourt at MOMA were not only looking to Piranesi at the same time, but were looking at the same etching.[40] As we shall see, *The Gothic Arch*, plate XIV from the *Carceri*, became a highpoint in MOMA's postwar tour of world art.

Timeless Aspects of Modern Art ran from November 16, 1948 to January 23, 1949. D'Harnoncourt, who succeeded Barr as director of the museum in 1949, had lived and worked in Mexico and showed a passion for primitive art in Latin America and elsewhere. The timeless aspects announced in the title were in fact matched by global ones in an exhibition whose itinerary wound its way from one civilization to the next (*see following*). D'Harnoncourt's point was to show that "modern" was a universal quality discernable everywhere and at all times. The carefully orchestrated comparisons with the past in Barr's 1936 shows had now ballooned to the point of caricature: rather than providing the modern with a "history," the museum turned that relation around and presented historic art as modern. "[A] walk through the galleries will show that modern art is not an isolated phenomenon in history but is, like the art of any period, an integral part of the art of all ages," the catalogue declared.[41] The exhibition therefore presented a history without history; d'Harnoncourt's lofty outlook, at once global and timeless, annulled any discussion of movements and concrete artistic influences. In the conciliatory spirit of the late 1940s, not only nations but art united in New York.

In a series of drafts, d'Harnoncourt revised and refined his proposal. At one point he wrote "This exhibition will answer the common accusation that modern art is created in a vacuum by showing that it is, in fact, part of the stream of history and uses many of the plastic means to express fundamental human concepts and emotions that were used by the arts of all ages."[42] The expression "the stream of history" of course harks back to Barr, who was still the museum's director at this point, but d'Harnoncourt's vision is considerably broader, aiming to link modern art to the development of civilizations across epochs and continents.

An equally important aim was to confront the accusation that modern art had "lost its human and social content."[43] This concern prompted a shift of focus. Rather than the rational basis in art governing *Cubism and Abstract Art,* or the subconscious one in *Fantastic Art, Dada, Surrealism*, it was the human form, in a very general sense, that seems to have been at the center of d'Harnoncourt's vision. The principle (or metaphor) that sanctioned a resemblance between artworks was no longer an invisible psychological connection but its opposite, so to speak, namely human physiognomy. "The problem of understanding the affinities between works of art is not unlike that of understanding affinities between people," d'Harnoncourt wrote.[44] But affinity is a slippery category, he admitted. It could "be based on likeness of features and body or on similarities in ways of thinking and acting." With regard to both people and artworks, a distinction had to be made between "superficial likeness" and "true affinity." Ultimately, it is as if the social bonds that link humankind, the ones Huxley deemed so lacking in Piranesi's *Carceri*, had crystallized into a curatorial principle.

Timeless Aspects covered a broad canvas. It was left to fifty-six exhibits to represent the entire world from prehistoric times to Alexander Calder, from a Chinese landscape to an Inuit mask. A world map put up on the wall, and reproduced in the catalogue, charted the places of origin of the exhibits, while a timeline that stretched from 75,000 BCE to 1948 noted when they were made (*see page 128*). It goes without saying that a timeline covering the last seven hundred and fifty centuries leaves little scope for detailing artistic highlights. Print enthusiasts must have rejoiced at the discovery that "Giovanni Piranesi" was one of only three individual artists named in a history that extended back to Paleolithic times. The others were Piero di Cosimo and Peter Paul Rubens. It is hard to imagine being chosen for a more exclusive list.

The Piranesi print on display had not previously been shown at MOMA. An extremely dense composition, *The Gothic Arch* from the *Carceri* is a conglomeration of arches that multiply at different levels and distances, creating a complex pattern deepened by sharp contrasts of light and shadow (*see page 129*). As in *The Drawbridge*, inconsistencies abound and the architectural space seems on the verge of turning into pictorial abstraction. The actual impression derived from

overleaf Itinerary of exhibition in the guide to *Timeless Aspects of Modern Art*, MOMA, November 16, 1948–January 23, 1949.

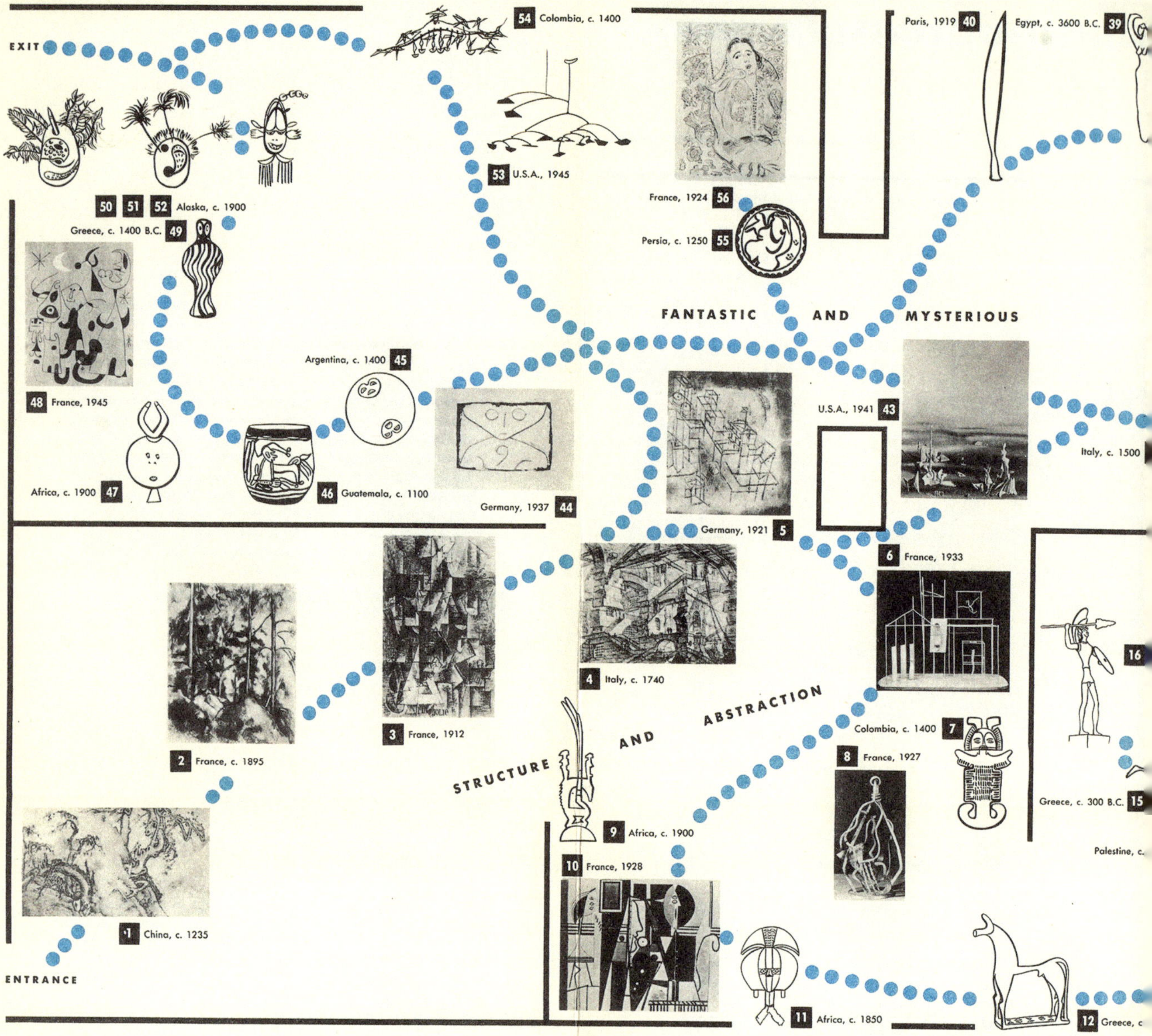

1. Sung Dynasty: *Dragons and Landscape*. Grisaille. Attributed to Ch'ên Jung. 1235-1255 A.D.
   Collection Metropolitan Museum of Art, New York
2. Paul Cézanne: *Pines and Rocks*. Oil, 1895-1900
   Collection Museum of Modern Art, New York
3. Pablo Picasso: "*Ma Jolie*" (*Woman with Guitar*). Oil, 1911-12
   Collection Museum of Modern Art, New York
4. Giovanni Piranesi: *Prison Interior*. Etching, c. 1740
   Collection Metropolitan Museum of Art, New York
5. Paul Klee: *Architecture*. Watercolor, 1921
   Collection Buchholz Gallery, New York
6. Alberto Giacometti: *The Palace at 4 A.M.* Construction in wood, 1932-1933
   Collection Museum of Modern Art, New York
7. Chimbayan Gold Figure. Colombia. c. 1400
   Collection University of Pennsylvania Museum, Philadelphia
8. Jacques Lipchitz: *Woman and Guitar*. Gilded bronze, 1927
   Collection Curt Valentin, New York
9. Sudanese Wooden Figure. Africa. Nineteenth century
   Private Collection, New York
10. Pablo Picasso: *The Painter and His Model*. Oil, 1928
    Collection Sidney Janis, New York
11. Gabun Funerary Figure. Wood covered with metal. Africa. Nineteenth century
    Collection University of Pennsylvania Museum, Philadelphia
12. Archaic Greek Horse. Bronze. c. 800 B.C.
    Collection Metropolitan Museum of Art, New York
13. Mary Callery: Horse. Bronze, 1942
    Collection Museum of Modern Art, New York
14. Canaanite Idol. Bronze. Palestine. c. 1000 B.C.
    Collection Walters Art Gallery, Baltimore
15. Hellenistic Runner. Bronze. Greece. c. 300 B.C.
    Collection Walter C. Baker, New York
16. Etruscan Warrior. Bronze. c. 600 B.C.
    Collection Walter C. Baker, New York
17. Wilhelm Lehmbruck: *Standing Youth*. Cast stone, 1913
    Collection Museum of Modern Art, New York
18. Pablo Picasso: Horse (Study for *Guernica*). Oil, 1937
    Collection Museum of Modern Art, New York
19. Mask Representing Deer. Barkcloth. Panama. Nineteenth century
    Collection Museum of the American Indian, Heye Foundation, New York
20. Edvard Munch: *The Cry*. Lithograph, 1895
    Rosenwald Collection, National Gallery of Art, Washington
21. Early Christian Head. Stone, c. 400-600 A.D.
    Collection Dr. Jacob Hirsch, New York
22. Georges Rouault: *Christ Mocked by Soldiers*. Oil, 1932
    Collection Museum of Modern Art, New York
23. Romanesque Crucifix. Wood. Spain. c. 1200 A.D.
    Collection Museum of Art, Rhode Island School of Design, Providence
24. Unknown American artist: *Henry Ward Beecher*. Wood, c. 1850
    Collection Museum of Modern Art, New York
25. Hyman Bloom: *The Synagogue*. Oil, c. 1940
    Collection Museum of Modern Art, New York
26. Coptic *Madonna and Child*. Ivory. Syria or Egypt. Ninth century A.D.
    Collection Walters Art Gallery, Baltimore
27. Christoffel Jegher after Rubens: *Hercules Fighting Envy and Deception*. Woodcut, c. 1600 A.D.
    Collection Metropolitan Museum of Art, New York
28. Jacques Lipchitz: *Prometheus*. Bronze, 1942
    Collection Buchholz Gallery, New York

Plan of the Exhibition

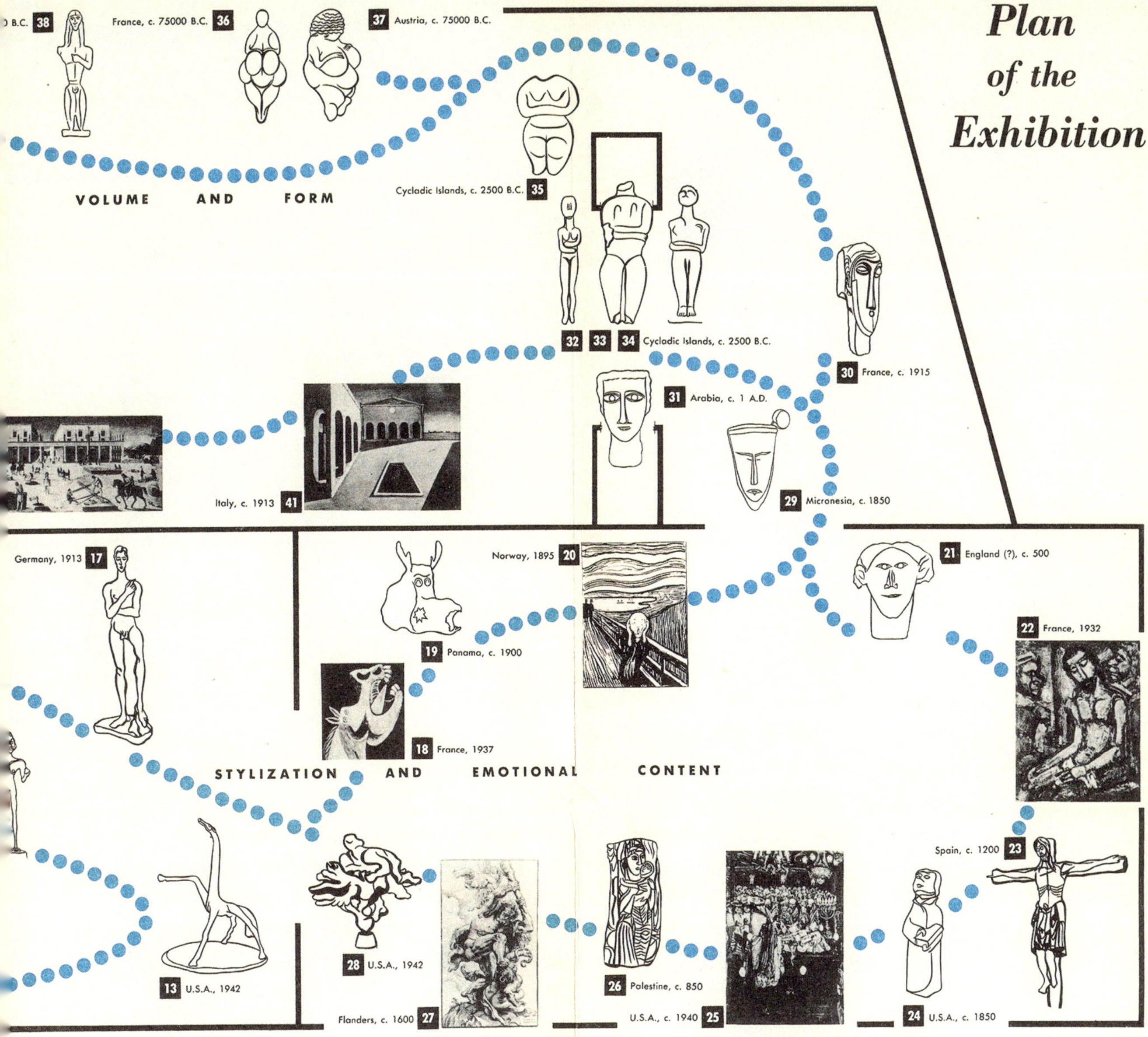

29. House Mask. Painted wood. Mortlock Island, Micronesia. Nineteenth century
Collection University of Pennsylvania Museum, Philadelphia
30. Amedeo Modigliani: *Head.* Stone, c. 1915
Collection Museum of Modern Art, New York
31. Sabaean Head. Alabaster. Saudi Arabia. c. 1 A.D.
Collection University of Pennsylvania Museum, Philadelphia
32. Cycladic Figurine. Alabaster. Third millennium
Collection Metropolitan Museum of Art, New York
33. Cycladic Figurine. Alabaster. Third millennium
Collection Brooklyn Museum, New York
34. Cycladic Figurine. Marble. Third millennium
Collection Walter C. Baker, New York
35. Cycladic Figurine. Marble. Third millennium
Collection Walter C. Baker, New York
36. Paleolithic Figure "*Venus of Lespugues.*" Reconstruction of original. c. 75,000 B.C.
Collection Dr. Harry L. Shapiro, New York
37. Paleolithic Figure "*Venus of Willendorf.*" Cast. c. 75,000 B.C.
Collection American Museum of Natural History, New York
38. Archaic Apollo. Bronze. Greece. c. 700 B.C.
Collection Boston Museum of Fine Arts, Boston
39. Egyptian Female Figurine. Clay. Predynastic, c. 3600 B.C.
Collection Brooklyn Museum, New York
40. Constantin Brancusi: *Bird in Space.* Bronze, 1919
Collection Museum of Modern Art, New York
41. Giorgio de Chirico: *Delights of the Poet.* Oil, c. 1913
Collection Museum of Modern Art, New York
42. Piero di Cosimo: *Building of a Palace.* Oil, c. 1500
Collection John and Mable Ringling Museum of Art, Sarasota, Florida
43. Yves Tanguy: *The Five Strangers.* Oil, 1941
Collection Wadsworth Atheneum, Hartford
44. Paul Klee: *Letter Ghost.* Gouache, 1937
Collection Museum of Modern Art, New York
45. Disk with Two Faces. Copper. Northern Argentina. Before 1500 A.D.
Collection Museum of the American Indian, Heye Foundation, New York
46. Maya Painted Bowl. Ceramic. Guatemala. Eleventh or twelfth century A.D.
Collection University of Pennsylvania Museum, Philadelphia
47. African Mask. Wood. Ivory Coast. Nineteenth century
Collection Brooklyn Museum, New York
48. Joan Miro: *Woman in the Night.* Gouache on canvas. 1945
Collection Mrs. Pierre Matisse, New York
49. Mycenaean *Figurine.* Clay. c. 1400 B.C.
Collection Metropolitan Museum of Art, New York
50. Eskimo Mask. Wood. Nineteenth century
Collection University of Pennsylvania Museum, Philadelphia
51. Eskimo Mask. Wood. Nineteenth century
Collection American Museum of Natural History, New York
52. Eskimo Mask. Wood. Nineteenth century
Collection Museum of the American Indian, Heye Foundation, New York
53. Alexander Calder: *Petals and Yellow Half-Moon.* Mobile. 1945
Private Collection, New York
54. Chibcha Gold Ornaments. Colombia. c. 1400 A.D.
Collection University of Pennsylvania Museum, Philadelphia
55. Persian Deep Plate. Rayy Ware. c. 1250 A.D.
Collection Walters Art Gallery, Baltimore
56. Henri Matisse: *Arabesque I.* Transfer lithograph, 1924
Collection Museum of Modern Art, New York

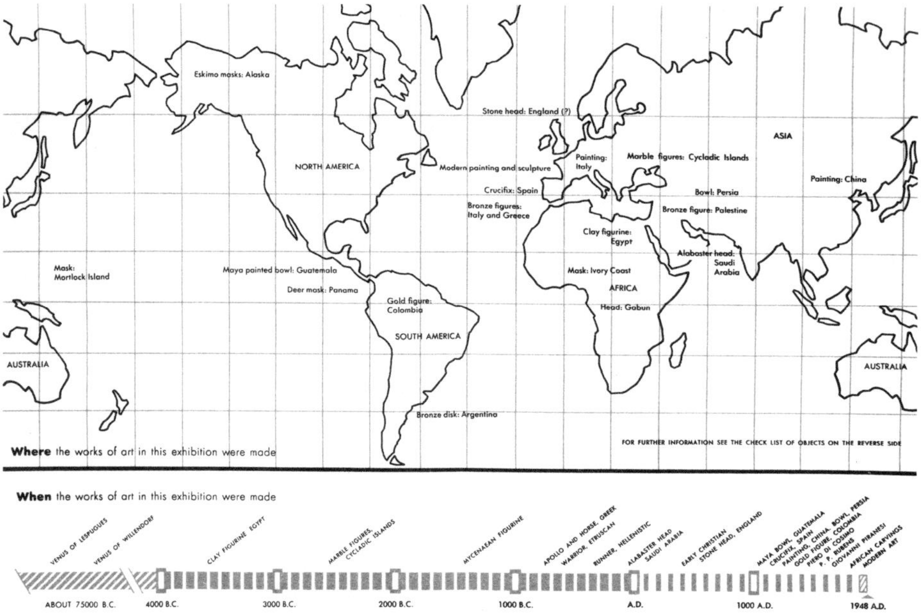

the first edition of the series printed in 1749–1750, which was lighter and less worked than the second edition. However, the museum's research on Piranesi had advanced little since 1936. On the contrary, the catalogue identifies the exhibit as "Giovanni Piranesi: *Prison Interior*. Etching, c. 1740." A part of his name is omitted, no distinction between editions is made, and the date is off the mark.

The print was a loan from the Metropolitan Museum of Art. In a letter dated October 27, 1948, d'Harnoncourt approached the museum's director, Francis Henry Taylor, with a wish list of six items that he hoped to borrow for the show, including a Greek bronze horse from 800 BCE, a Chinese ink drawing, and Piranesi's "Prison Interior."[45] Taylor shared d'Harnoncourt's passion for art history's truly *longue durée*; indeed, his own book, *Fifty Centuries of Art,* was just a few years away. D'Harnoncourt thanked "Dear Francis" for advice that he had already received from various department heads at the Metropolitan Museum of Art, among them Alpheus Hyatt Mayor, who ran the print department and would publish his monograph on Piranesi in 1952. The initiative to include the Piranesi print, then, may well have come from Mayor in a collaborative effort reminiscent of Barr's earlier reliance on W. G. Russell Allen. In any case, a week before the opening of the show, the six items were collected and brought to MOMA.[46] The insurance value on the Piranesi print (along with a seventeenth-century print by Christoffel Jegher) was seven hundred dollars, a considerable increase from the mere fifty dollar estimation twelve years back.[47]

World map with timeline in the exhibition brochure
for *Timeless Aspects of Modern Art*, MOMA, 1948.

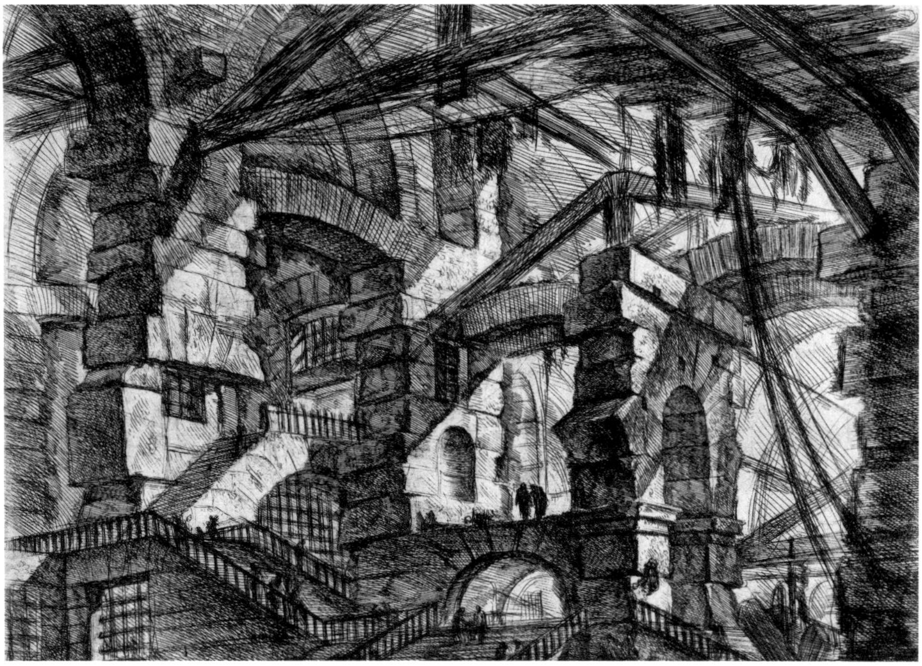

Timeless Aspects presented Piranesi's print as its fourth exhibit, displayed in the section titled "Structure and Abstraction." In d'Harnoncourt's itinerary the works that preceded it were a Chinese thirteenth-century landscape, Cézanne's *Pines and Rocks* (ca. 1897), and the painting *Ma Jolie* (1912) by Picasso (*see following*). "All these pictures are linked by emphasis on structure," the catalogue claimed. The first section, then, repeated somewhat unimaginatively the sensational Piranesi–cubism lineage established by Barr's presentation of analytical cubism in 1936. The Cézanne was even the same, whereas the Picasso belonged to the museum's collection. However, as visitors continued onward, past these paintings and past Piranesi's *The Gothic Arch*, the exhibition shifted focus and led them via a work by Paul Klee to Giacometti's *The Palace at 4 a.m.*, also re-exhibited here, so one might say that surrealism continued at one end of the show, while cubism led up to *Carceri* at the other. Piranesi's print, then, is presented as the pivotal point in the unfolding of two modern art movements, also linking the two exhibitions of 1936 in a continuous display. This first leg of d'Harnoncourt's itinerary through the ages might therefore be seen as a tribute to Barr, who was still an active presence at MOMA, and to the history famously charted by the museum. Rehearsing cubism and surrealism, however, was not d'Harnoncourt's main concern, and the abbreviated sequences of the movements in *Timeless Aspects*, including the exact same artworks, appear as "quotations" of earlier curatorial victories.

Giovanni Battista Piranesi, plate XIV, *The Gothic Arch*,
from *Invenzioni capric di carceri*, first edition, ca. 1749–1750.

overleaf Paul Cézanne, *Pines and Rocks*, ca. 1897. Oil on canvas.
Pablo Picasso, *Ma Jolie*, 1911–1912. Oil on canvas.

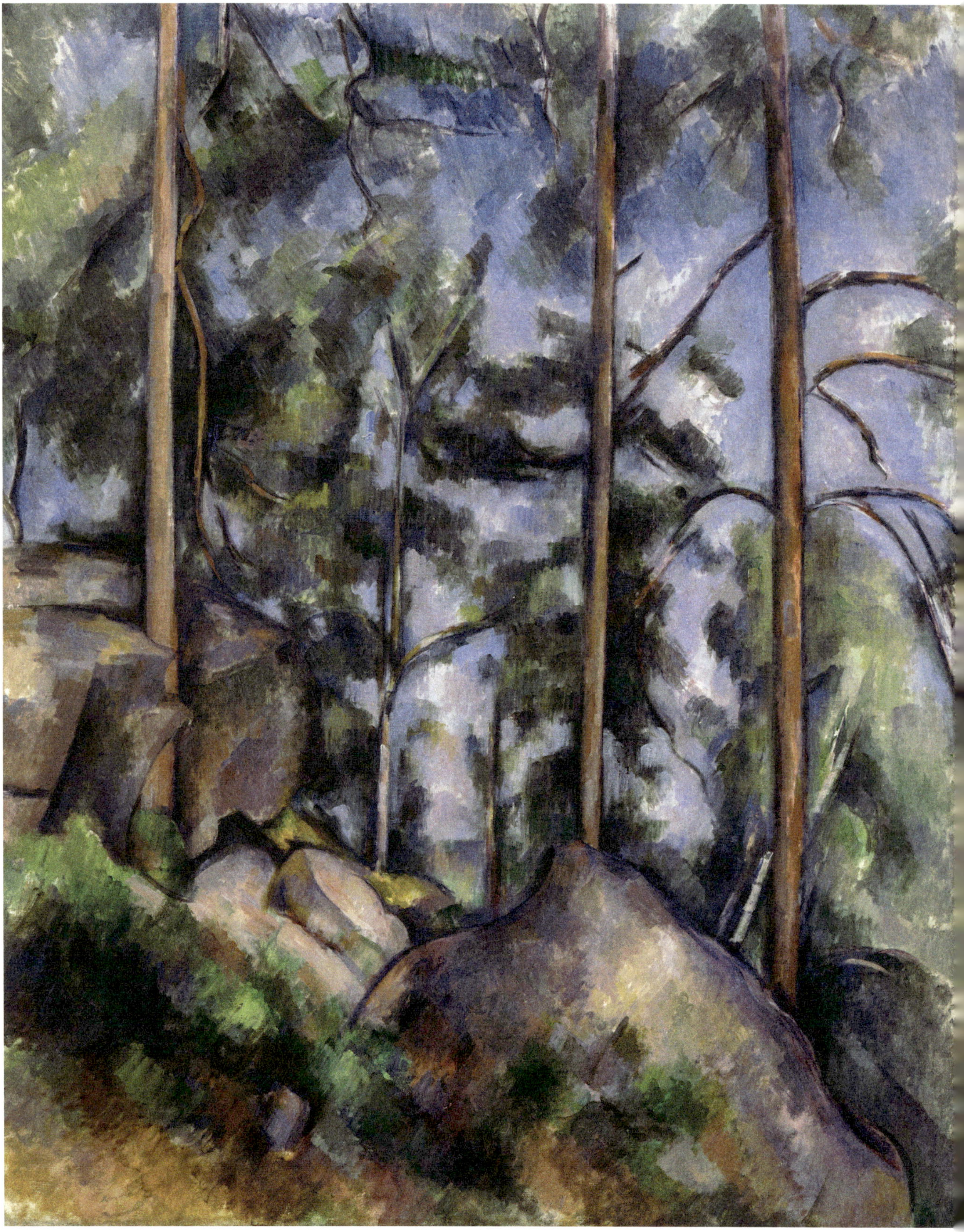

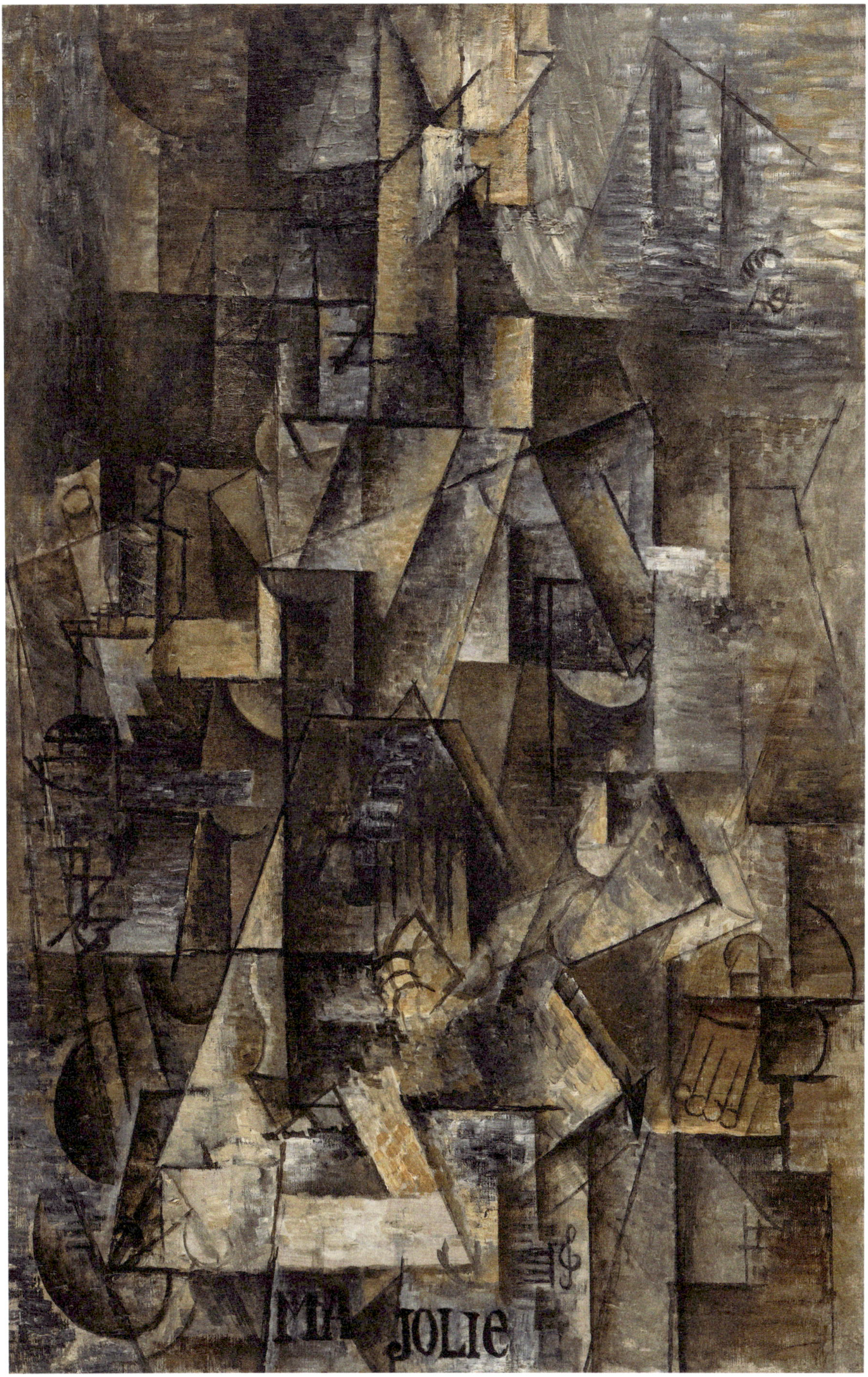
MA JOLIE

Yet on some points the display also marked a radical advance. It presented the progression Cézanne–Picasso–Piranesi in an anti-chronological sequence, an overt demonstration of timelessness. A sketch by d'Harnoncourt represents the exhibition plan in the form of a grid holding beautifully executed miniatures of some of the exhibits.[48] Neatly penciled, in identical rectangles, it includes representations of Cézanne's *Pines and Rocks*, Picasso's *Ma Jolie*, and Piranesi's *The Gothic Arch*.

The *Carceri* drawing is turned ninety degrees in order to fit the vertical format of the rectangles, but also in order to make the correspondence with the other two images more obvious. It is a subtle manipulation which emphasizes, even creates, a relationship between the works and reveals the structural essence that underscored modernism's universality in d'Harnoncourt's view. The vertical position of course enhanced the *Gothic Arch*'s abstract quality as well as strengthening its resemblance to the adjacent Picasso—a resemblance A. Hyatt Mayor endorsed when recalling a visit to *Timeless Aspects of Modern Art* in his book on Piranesi published three years later: referring to the Picasso–Piranesi juxtaposition, Mayor chose to see (or thought he remembered) the Picasso as a charcoal drawing, not as the actual oil, in a way that made the two works express an "identical sharp-edged bleakness."[49]

Overall, d'Harnoncourt's series of miniature sketches reveals the skeletal core he imagined existed within each carefully selected exhibit in the show—a structure that he pictured as shared. The progression from Piranesi's *Carceri* print, drawn in its bare contours, via Giacometti, to a Colombian gold figure from 1400 forms a sequence of increasingly simple configurations. The schematic renderings can be seen to draw out the inner "affinity" between different works, conforming to the vision proclaimed by d'Harnoncourt in the catalogue. An art history stripping works of art of their volume, weight, and color—qualities that tie them to respective cultures—testifies to the same ideal of purity, albeit on a grander scale, that the modernists de Zayas, Le Corbusier, and Hind imposed on their material. D'Harnoncourt's sketch codifies the meaning of modern in the sense that it records not only a series of timeless artworks but also, more interestingly, d'Harnoncourt's vision of the quality that made them modern. Reduced to a pictogram and turned on its vertical, Piranesi's *Carceri* prevailed as timeless, at least for a while.

In a letter dated January 27, 1949, the registrar at MoMA wrote to Mr. Fred Hahn "[P]lease have your truck pick up at the Museum of Modern Art on January 31st, the following paintings and sculptures for delivery." Alongside the Klee, the Picasso, and the Miró that Hahn picked up that day and unloaded at various locations in New York City, was "Piranesi, Prison Interior, etching (frame and glass)."[50]

Piranesi returned to storage, but not without having done his bit to redirect the "stream of time."

René d'Harnoncourt, sketch of the exhibition plan for *Timeless Aspects of Modern Art*, MoMA, ca. 1947–1948. Pencil on paper (including drawings of Cézanne, Picasso, and Piranesi).

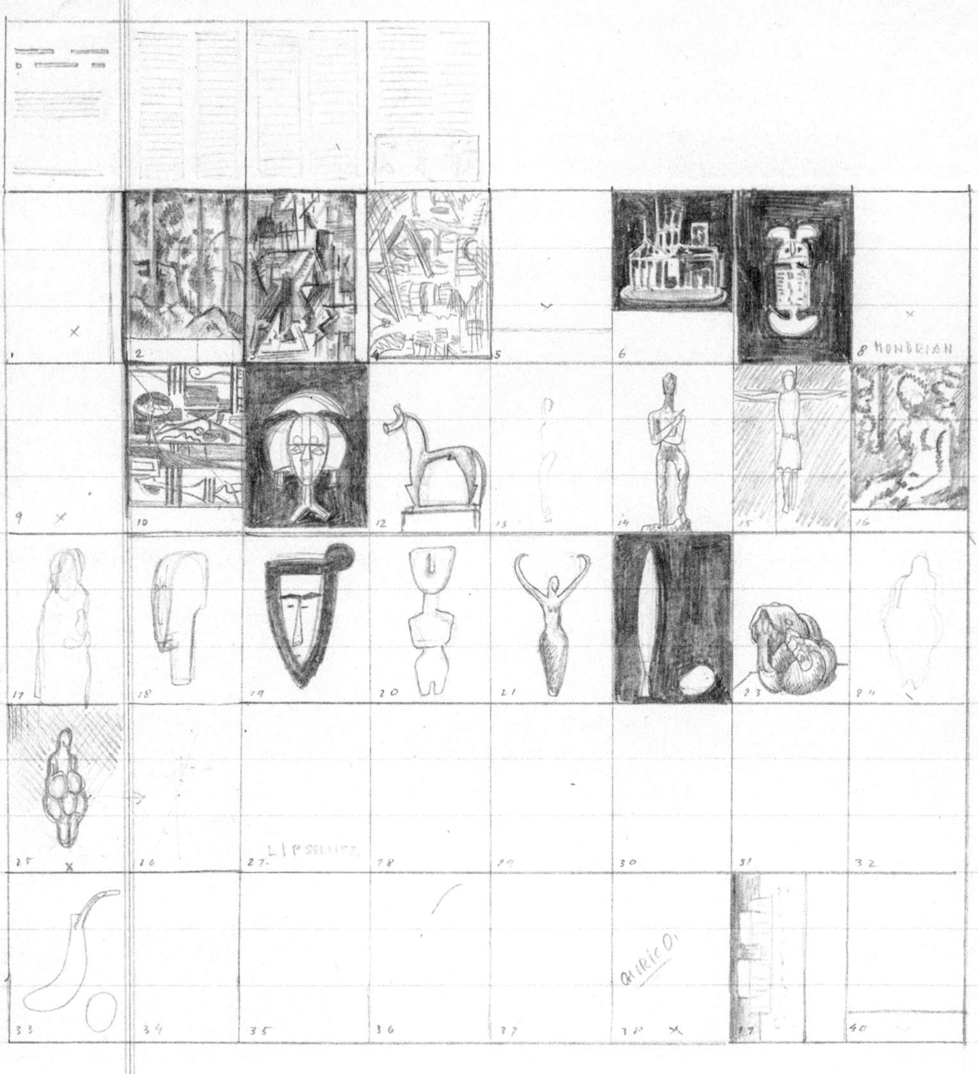

MONDRIAN

MOVING PRINTS

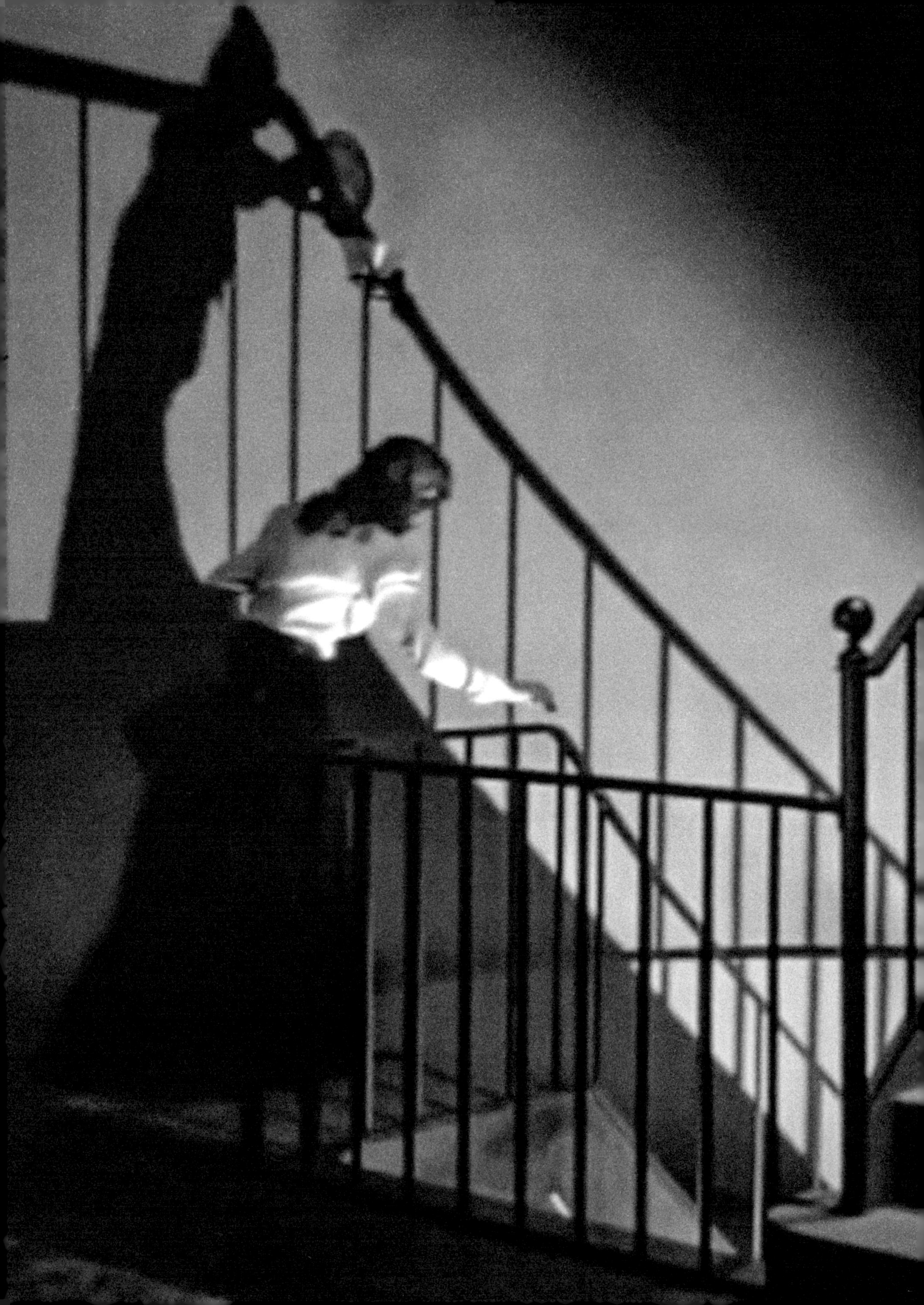

Of Piranesi's many modern designations, "proto-cinematic" is perhaps the most challenging, more so than the "proto-cubist" coined by Barr, because cinema entails a technology obviously at odds with eighteenth-century etchings. The prefix "proto" belongs of course to a posterity that is able to project a phenomenon onto the past in the knowledge that the real manifestation is yet to come. Many have yielded to the temptation to connect Piranesi to cinema in these retrospectively prophetic terms: Piranesi as a "precursor" of motion pictures and his prints as "prefigurations" are notions that recur in literature, alongside observations that his prints "evoke," "trigger," and "anticipate" modern filmmaking.[1]

However, proto-cinematic Piranesi also suggests a more profound approach, namely the idea that the "cinematographic" exists prior to and independent of the actual invention of cinema as technology. André Bazin in "The Myth of the Total Cinema" (1967) held cinema to be an ideal object dormant in humankind since time immemorial. "The concept men had of it existed so to speak fully armed in their minds, as if in some platonic heaven."[2] Twenty years earlier, Sergei Eisenstein had observed how "[a]ll arts appear to stretch across the ages towards cinema; and conversely, cinema in many ways helps us understand their method."[3] Thus, the triumph of the moving picture also redefines the past, as if all the arts, including eighteenth-century printmaking, "already carried within [themselves] the principle of cinema."[4] Cinema's *longue durée*, then, left ample opportunities for writers to consider Piranesi as a harbinger of cinematic scenery, effects, and preconditions.

Ultimately, the proto-cinematic history in which Piranesi is inscribed challenges the view on history itself. In the twentieth century's self-assessment, cinema does not merely fulfill the promise of previous art forms—painting, print, theater—it also makes those arts retroactively cinematic; the modern age lets its novelties and inventions irrigate the past, making us see, and indeed believe in, the role of Piranesi (and others, of course) as a precursor of media and movements that had yet to appear.

This chapter investigates how film owes an understanding of itself—of its own medium—to a reevaluation of Piranesi's etchings, their compositions, organizations, and editions. On the whole, we shall encounter a filmmaking that recognized and formulated the fundamentals of the art via reinterpretations of Piranesi. The films and texts of Eisenstein, especially, exemplify how the Russian filmmaker came to a gradual realization of cinematic motion and montage through studying the works of the Venetian master.

The Spiral Staircase, directed by Robert Siodmak, 1946.

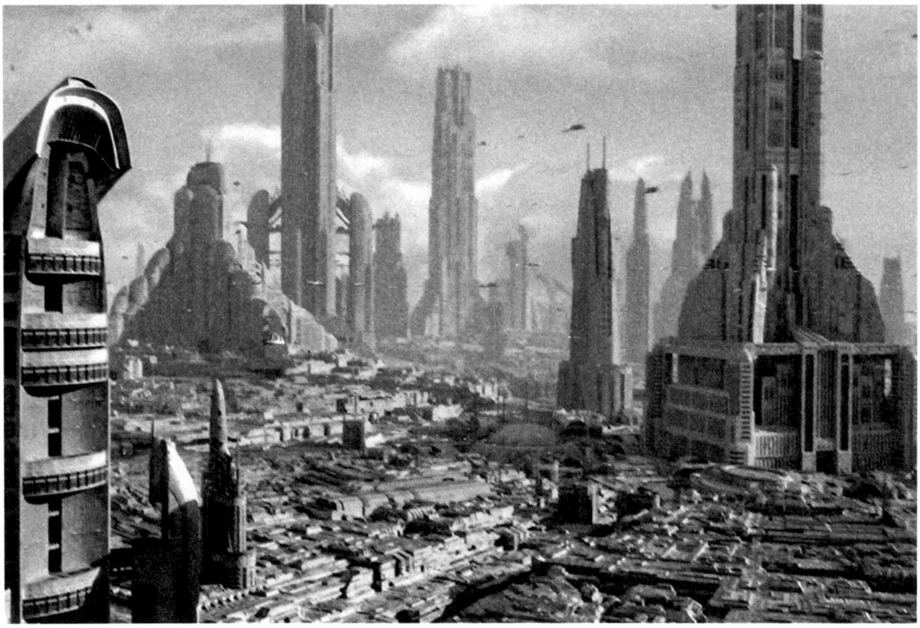

PIRANESI, SET DESIGNER

No discussion on Piranesi and moving pictures can avoid addressing the associations he evokes with film sets in general. Piranesi is perhaps the greatest set designer of all, conjuring the grandeur of ancient Rome for an audience of eighteenth-century armchair travelers. As an apprentice in Venice, he learned perspective theory from Carlo Zucchi, studied the construction of theatrical scenery in Ferdinando Bibiena's *L'architettura civile*, and worked with professional stage designers.[5] Had he lived in a later period, it is not unlikely that he would have ventured on a Hollywood career, producing set designs for epics like D. W. Griffith's *Intolerance* (1916) or William Wyler's *Ben-Hur* (1959). Like Piranesi's prints, these films evoke Rome and other ancient civilizations in arresting detail and majestic exaggerations.

Piranesi's art has without question also inspired actual film sets. A more comprehensive study than this one would surely reveal how imagined realities in film, from dreams and hallucinations to underworlds and fantastic cities, often draw on Piranesi's visionary archaeology, which has become embedded in visual culture. Science-fiction films, for example, frequently evoke the architecture of ancient Rome to create an image of the styles and types in distant galaxies. A remote time and a remote place converge in a shared unreality—an unreality often first conceived by Piranesi. For example, in George Lucas's *Star Wars:*

The city of Coruscant. *Star Wars: Episode II—Attack of the Clones*, directed by George Lucas, 2002.

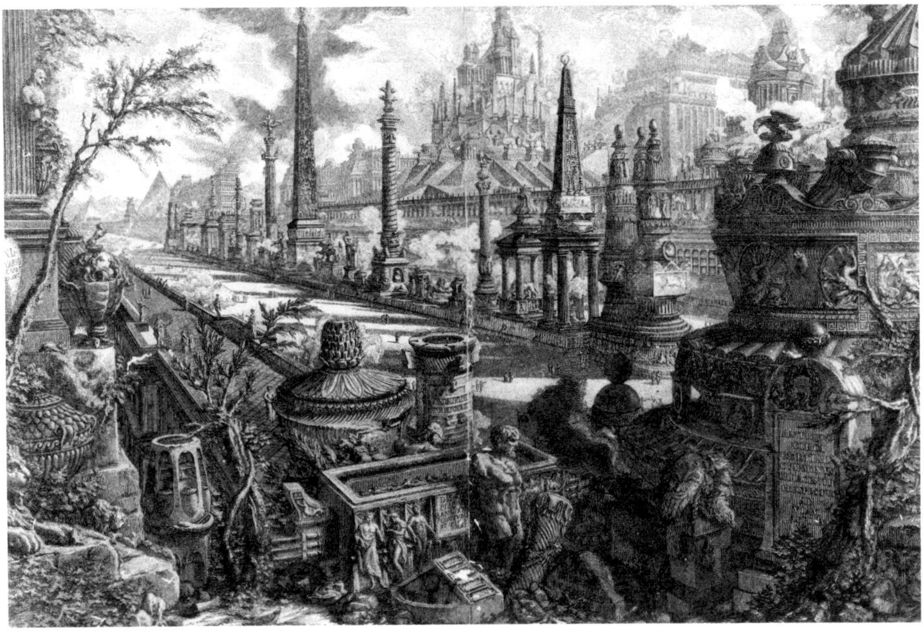

Episode II—Attack of the Clones (2002), the sweeping view of the galactic hub of Coruscant freezes in a frame duplicating Piranesi's mesmerizing panorama of an ancient circus from *Le antichità romane*.

However, it is easy—at times too easy—to link Piranesi's art to film when in reality there are no demonstrable points of connection. One example is the tempting comparison Alexander Kupfer makes between Fritz Lang's *Metropolis* (1927) and Piranesi's *Carceri*: in fact, Lang's images of a strictly class-divided society set to a utopia of skyscrapers rests on no specific Piranesi composition nor on any explicit reliance on Piranesi by the designers or by the director himself. Rather, Lang professed New York as inspiration, a city he visited in 1924.[6] A resemblance is more obvious and also more commensurate between Piranesi's prints and the posters for the film by the Russian designer Boris Bilinsky. The French poster for *Metropolis* can be seen to translate the pile of temples, stelae, and obelisks in Piranesi's Via Appia fantasy from *Le antichità romane* (1756) into starkly modern forms (*see following*): the pyramidal mounds of the buildings correspond even down to the jagged contours of their silhouette, presenting a city long gone and one not yet realized as flipsides to each other.[7]

Neither can an excursion into Piranesian set designs fail to acknowledge how his art helped underpin a plot's psychological level. Stairs are a Piranesian leitmotif in film as well as literature. More precisely, they feature as cinematized manifestations of the Piranesi Pivot, adding to the points I made in chapter one.

Giovanni Battista Piranesi, *Ancient Circus*, second title page to volume III of *Le antichità romane*, ca. 1756.

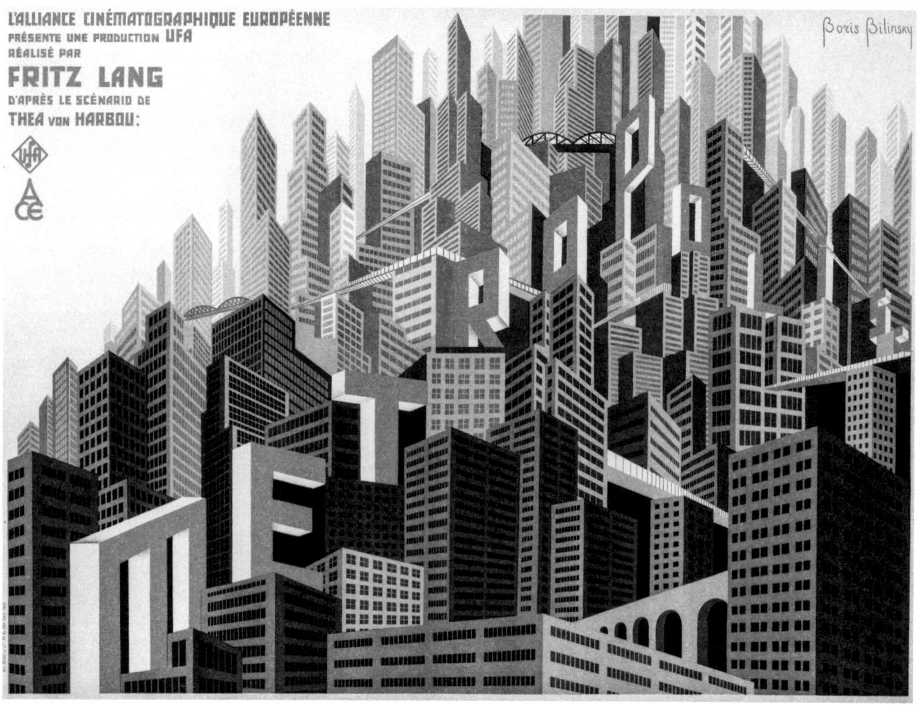

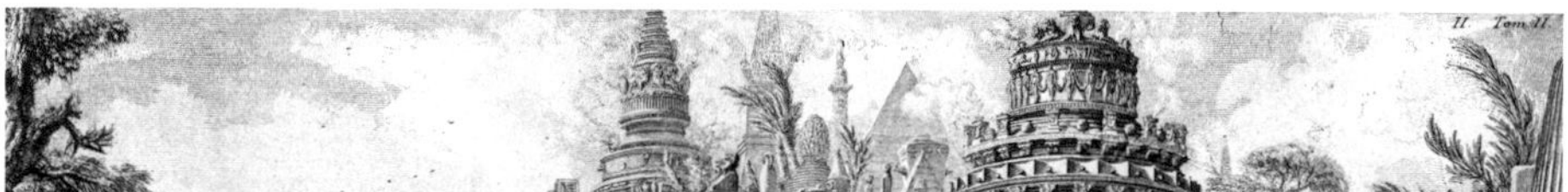

Boris Bilinsky, poster for *Metropolis*, 1927.
Giovanni Battista Piranesi, *Via Appia*, second title page to volume II of *Le antichità romane*, ca. 1756.

The few examples below suggest how stairs make a conspicuous appearance about midway through films; moreover, descending those stairs marks a turning point in the events—a profound shift of some kind.

The Piranesi Pivot is intensely cinematic. The turning point it entails allows the narrative to unfold on multiple levels, as filmmakers realized early on. In *Snow White and the Seven Dwarfs* (1937), produced by Walt Disney, the Queen's castle is furnished with a spiral stair perhaps inspired by the *Carceri*, as has been noted.[8] It has not been noted, however, that the stairs in Disney's classic seem to carry a deeper significance. They make their one and only appearance in a scene where the Queen descends to an underground chamber to mix an extract that will temporarily transform her stately countenance into that of an old woman (*see below*). In an altered guise, she may exit the castle unrecognized and track down her rival beauty, Snow White. For the Queen, as for Disney, the Piranesian stair heralds transfiguration and a sense of mission, no matter how malevolent that mission may be.

What awaits at the bottom of Piranesi's spiral—in film as in literature—is a transformation of the self, like in *Snow White*, and sometimes, too, a self-obliteration. Halfway through the horror-noir *The Spiral Staircase* (1946, dir. Robert Siodmak), the audience gets their first glimpse of the ominous stairs spiraling through the old mansion that is the setting for the action(*see page 143*). A serial

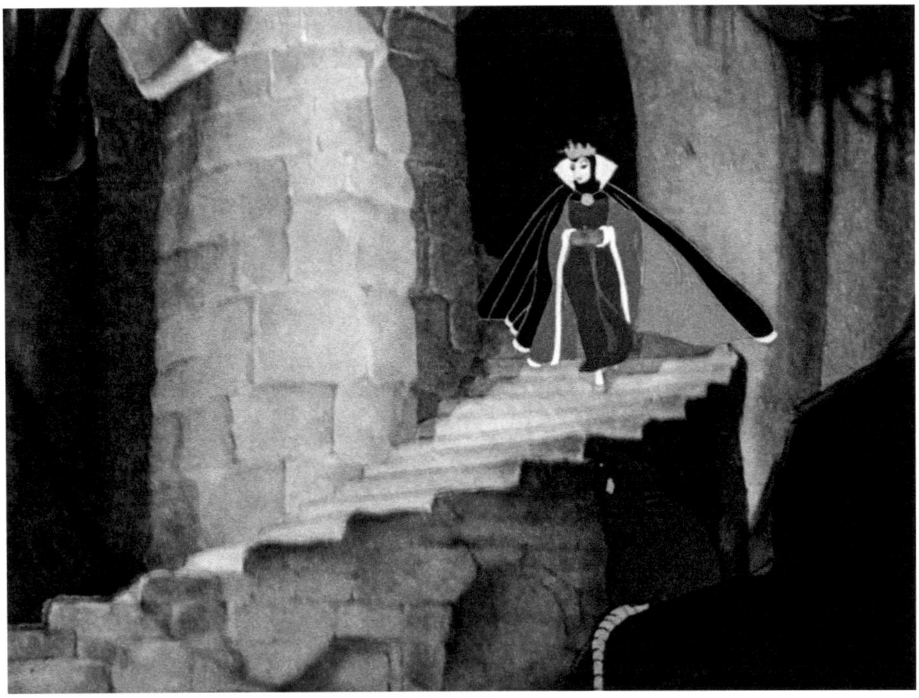

The Queen descending the stairs, *Snow White and the Seven Dwarfs* © 1937 Disney.

killer is on the loose, and it is precisely at the foot of these winding stairs that he kills his first victim. In the end, it is also here that the murderer himself is killed. Both the title of the film and the motif of the spiral stair hark back to an early twentieth-century crime novel—but they also go back further, to a storyboard visually invented in the eighteenth century and psychologically charged in the course of a period that ran from De Quincey's *Confessions* to psychoanalytical literature.

The ploy persists to this day. About halfway into Denis Villeneuve's dystopian *Blade Runner 2049* (2017), the protagonist named "K" (like the protagonist in Kafka's *The Castle*) finds himself atop a narrow stairway. In a majestically conceived future world, he is a police officer on a mission to hunt down an illegal replicant indistinguishable from humans in both form and feelings. He does not know it yet, but after he has descended those stairs, roamed an abandoned furnace, and found in its ashes a toy horse he had hidden there as a boy, he will realize that the replicant is none other than himself. The toy horse triggers "memories" that set K on a quest to find the truth about his own background, about himself. Descending the stairs to a deeper level, architecturally as well as psychologically, is a turning point in Villeneuve's epic, taking the unmistakable form of a Piranesi Pivot.

In film, just as in literature, stairways recur as a symbol of the transition between life and death, as well as between different states of life, profiting from the literary adaptation of Piranesi from De Quincey onwards. As a motif first saturated by Romantic sentiments of awe and horror, then included in the construction of the unconscious, the winding stair never seems to make an appearance in film without an added poignancy. Also in film, "it points to a process of psychic transformation," to borrow the words of Carl Gustav Jung.[9]

ARCHITECTURE IN MOTION

The notion of a "proto-cinematic" Piranesi yields even deeper layers. In the previous chapter we saw that historians and curators promoted modern art not simply as novel, but as supra-historical—as a phenomenon unfolding beyond time. The same rhetoric permeates the discourse on film and cinematography. The idea of film's "timeless aspects," to paraphrase the 1948 MOMA exhibition, exempted cinematic effects from the "stream of time" and enabled writers and filmmakers to see constitutive elements of film, such as moving images or montage, as predating the invention of film proper. In the modern attempts to give such elements a pre-cinematic history, Piranesi proved crucial.

The element that most clearly separates film from other visual arts—namely, the fact that the images are moving—is also the one where Piranesi is cast most interestingly as a forerunner. In the effort to pin down a philosophy of film, Gilles Deleuze states: "When we think of the prehistory of the cinema, we always end up confused, because we do not know where its technological lineage begins, or how to define this lineage."[10] As a point of departure for his two books on cinema, Deleuze refers to the French thinker Henri Bergson and in particular to Bergson's concept of movement. To Bergson, in *Creative Evolution* (1907), movement is more than a transition from one still point to another, no matter how infinitesimal the gaps between them are. True movement cannot be reduced to a string of separate instances on a timeline; rather, it breaks forth in one continuous surge from past to future. However, neither science nor philosophy have been able to grasp this movement in and for itself, according to Bergson. We are placed outside of it, doomed to recompose it artificially. We take snapshots of a passing reality and string it together in imitation of a true flow. This representation of movement he calls "cinematographical." Separated from the true movement by an unsurpassable divide, we "set going a kind of cinematograph inside us."[11] Bergson, therefore, at the turn of the twentieth century, inscribed cinematography in a history of motion that went far back in time, or, seen the other way around, he inscribed early representations of motion in a history of cinematography.

Bergson was by and large negative towards cinema, since it only seemed to trap true flow in crude mechanics. However, the autonomy of the moving picture invited further thinking. Taking a cue from Bergson, Deleuze elaborated on the concept of motion. Contrary to Bergson's conclusion, the surge of true movement is to Deleuze the very essence of film. A shot does not mechanically *represent* movement but extends into the next shot in a fluid reconfiguration of content that itself constitutes movement. Cinema creates a "movement image—that is, pure movement extracted from bodies or moving things."[12] Cinematic movement is thus entirely autonomous, which makes film the last descendant of a lineage that reaches back to the birth of the modern sciences, according to Deleuze, and links to Kepler, Galileo, and Newton, whose accomplishments pointed to the idea of movement as existing in and for itself.[13]

Piranesi, too, although not mentioned by Deleuze, emerges as an early exponent of the idea of autonomous movement, but with a standpoint in architecture. The idea that Piranesi's halls continued indefinitely fostered the corresponding idea that moving through them never ceased, an idea already formulated by De Quincey and Nodier in the eighteenth century, as we saw in chapter one. But Piranesi's complex spatial constructions had a disorientating effect on twentieth-century observers as well, confounding the sense of time and place. "Bridges engender new bridges. Columns new columns. And so on *ad infinitum*. As far as the eye can follow," Sergei Eisenstein noted; Piranesi's perspectives seemed to extend without limit from any imagined standpoint within the compositions.[14] Simply because it appeared to be without a center or an end, the space engendered a sense of motion, a restless wandering of the eye; it unfolded at the very moment of beholding. As Steven Jacobs points out, this multiplicity of standpoints gave his prints a sense of motion—"the essence of the film medium."[15] To recent observers, then, Piranesi heralded a perpetual movement that seemed not only modern but also fundamentally cinematic.

The temptation to "activate" Piranesi's prints—to implant an "I" restlessly on the move through their spaces—responds in particular to what we may define as a French school that builds on Bergson and Deleuze but also on Victor Hugo and other nineteenth-century authors. The *Carceri* series, especially, invites a reading of its individual images as still shots in a cinematic sequence. To realize that sequence as an actual film, however, was left to Grégoire Dupond and Factum Arte in a project made for the 2010 Venice Biennale of Architecture.[16] In what Dupond and Factum Arte called a "virtual animation," they re-envisioned and combined twelve of Piranesi's sixteen *Carceri* prints in a hypnotic itinerary.[17] In a first-person perspective, the spectator of the film floats through a complex composed of interconnected *Carceri* images, all from the second edition. In one continuous take the tour brings us under arches, around pillars and up stairways with "prints" breathtakingly clicking into three dimensions as we enter them. In Dupond's rendering the figure reappearing on successive landings, identified by De Quincey as Piranesi, has become you and me. However, the mesmerizing

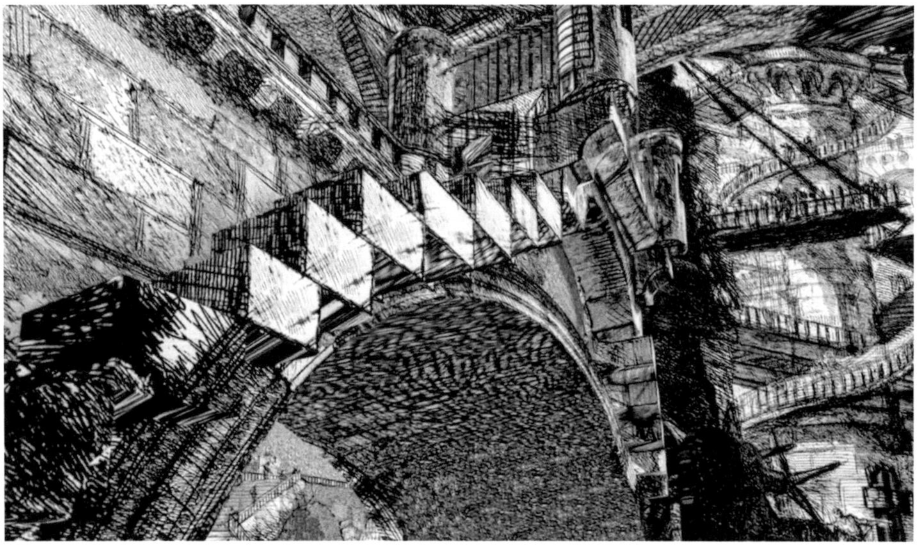

Grégoire Dupond/Factum Arte, still image from *Carceri d'invenzione*, 2010.

movement from one space to the next does not happen without compromises. An ad hoc architecture of stairs and arches, not designed by Piranesi, is invented to enable the transition between the "prints." At other times, details in Piranesi's prints are altered in order to secure a coherent filmic "palace." Overall, Dupond's film creates the illusion that the spaces are intrinsically connected, with the prints representing different parts of a single labyrinthine construction—a megalomaniac fantasy of a kind celebrated by the French since Victor Hugo, who in 1830 referred to the "whirling Babels dreamed of by Piranesi."[18]

In contrast to this literal adaptation of the *Carceri* as a filmic sequence, Sergei Eisenstein presents an alternative model of cinematic movement, no less dependent on Piranesi. According to Eisenstein a succession of still shots creates a sense of narrative not because they form a sequence but because they are superimposed, forming a palimpsest. With every new shot, he argues, the previous one lingers on the retina for the briefest of moments—a time-lag that secures continuity and a sense of motion.

> For, in fact, each sequential element is perceived not *next* to the other, but on *top* of the other. For the idea (or sensation) of movement arises from the process of superimposing on the retained impression of the object's first position, a newly visible further position of the object.[19]

In contrast to Bergson and Deleuze, Eisenstein perceives cinematic movement not as a flow but as a layering of images—a model that approximates printmaking. It comes as no surprise therefore that Piranesi's prints, and more specifically their different editions, appealed to Eisenstein; they conceptualized movement. The film director even resorts to concepts taken from graphic reproduction to explain the rapid stacking of images in the mind: "It is on the [...] ability of retaining imprints of a visual impression that the phenomenon of cinematic movement is built."[20]

The importance of Piranesi was certainly recast in light of film—as was in fact the entire history of art. Cinema is merely the newest form of illustration, according to Anne Hollander: "It encapsulates the whole history of figurative art, helping itself to that history's most effective devices."[21] Conversely, images that date as far back as the Renaissance, she claims, manifest specific cinematic tricks and effects *avant la lettre* in their distinct handling of light, emotional effects, and so on. It is true that Piranesi anticipated many of these solutions.[22] But I would argue that his prints have assumed a special significance as prefigurations of movement not simply because the images themselves appear like flickering camera shots, but because they predict different *forms* of cinematic movement—both the one that structures shots into narratives, as discussed by Deleuze and illustrated by Dupond, as well as the one that stacks them in layers, evolving from Eisenstein's retina–screen relation.[23]

TWO PIONEERS OF MONTAGE

Cinematic Piranesi is to a large extent the invention of film director and theorist Sergei Eisenstein. Eisenstein's bold and perceptive interpretations of the *Carceri* credited Piranesi with a role behind the camera, as one who (pre)formulated the very principles of filmmaking.

Apart from directing classics such as *Battleship Potemkin* (1925), *October: Ten Days that Shook the World* (1928), and *Ivan the Terrible*, part I (1944) and II (1946), Eisenstein wrote extensively on film and film theory. And Piranesi is a frequent reference. In fact, from various accounts of Eisenstein's life, including his own writings, we may piece together a veritable biography of Piranesi appropriations. Eisenstein recalls that his first encounter with Piranesi's art was a reproduction of the *Carcere oscura* (1743) in an Italian book on theater design from 1902.[24] When he first saw an actual print by Piranesi is unclear, but in his memoirs he mentions a dream that had recurred ever since he was a student: he would find himself in a bookshop in Leningrad (St. Petersburg) where cash never was an issue and all the titles he had ever coveted were always available—Rabelais, Ben Jonson, Hegel. "And how often here do I hold in my hands the full set of Piranesi's 'Prisons.'"[25] The trope of Piranesi's "dreams," which we have encountered throughout, comes with a new twist, as the dream in this case refers not to the prison series but to the shop in which they turn up. Fascinated by the *Carceri*, it did not take long for Eisenstein to become aware of the differences between the two editions, and the discovery would profoundly affect his construction of filmic space, as discussed below.[26] However, it was only after World War II that he acquired his own *Carceri* print, namely *The Gothic Arch*, along with an impression of the *Carcere oscura*, after he managed to persuade a provincial museum to part with them in exchange for a small stack of prints—"one Edelinck, one Hogarth, one Nanteuil, and a charming Claude Méllane."[27] By the time of his death, in February 1948, at least four Piranesi prints adorned his Moscow apartment, a small collection he invited his readers to behold in a masterly and very cinematic revival of Piranesi's art in the essay "Piranesi. Or the Fluidity of Form," as we shall see.[28] But for now, and with this biographical prelude in mind, it should come as no surprise that the Russian filmmaker's investigation of Piranesi enabled him to reinvent his art, hinging the results on the concept of montage.

Montage is a play of contrasts. It "is an idea that arises from the collision of independent shots—shots even opposite to one another," Eisenstein wrote in 1929.[29] Unlike the continuous narrative cultivated by Western filmmakers, montage, which was a particularly Russian invention, breaks up such continuity in contrasting images that are intellectually and politically challenging, but genuinely cinematic, and that catapult the spectator out of the comfort of the unfolding of a "good story." While undoubtedly disruptive, the violent cut-and-paste procedure is also able to present a plot on different levels, deepening the meaning of events by setting them against a realm of ideas and symbols. In Eisenstein's work, montage opens film to ideology; the zigzagging between opposing storylines mirrors the dialectic of history at large. With references to Lenin and Engels, dialectic is the very law of the world, indeed of cognition itself, and to the pro-Soviet director, therefore, the legitimate form of film.[30] It is a sweeping perspective, but important, for he also inscribes Piranesi into a dialectic history, as we shall see.[31]

In Eisenstein's oeuvre, Piranesi informs montage on all levels of filmmaking, from the arrangements of contrasting elements within each frame to the structuring of scenes. For example, the director's advice to distribute "[p]ieces of darkness and pieces of lightness" reflects a sensitivity to sharp contrasts typical of the early twentieth-century reaction to Piranesi's prints. Eisenstein also recognizes a montage effect in the diagonals that crisscross Piranesi's compositions and that result from his unique *line*—"a line built from the movements and variations of '*counter-volumes*.'" The arcs and vaults of the *Carceri* collide with their endless stairs, he writes, "breaking the accumulated *spatial fugue* with a *linear fugue*."[32]

According to the Russian filmmaker, Piranesi introduced a form of spatial montage too. Deeply fascinated by the perspective construction in the *Carceri*, Eisenstein observes how Piranesi makes space recede towards the background in what seem like sudden leaps: "Everywhere the initial movement of deepening perspective is interrupted by a bridge, a column, an arch, a passage," he notes.[33] When the perspective picks up again beyond the bridge or the column, the dimensions are reduced; the view keeps receding but in an allover diminished scale of representation. With such perspective jolts, Piranesi manages to create the illusion of extreme remoteness, whereas the montage-like quality lies in the deliberate disruption in perspectival continuity. In Eisenstein's language, one arched construction "explodes" out of its scale to a qualitatively different scale. Piranesi's space thus progresses in "unexpected qualitative leaps" that hurl the viewer from one spatial pocket to the next, towards the depth of the composition.

However, the illusion of depth, according to Eisenstein, derives not only from the manipulation of perspective, but also from the production of prints. The editions of the *Carceri*, or rather the difference between them, made him aware of Piranesi's planar build-up of space. What characterizes Piranesi's reworked second edition, he writes, is the addition of new foregrounds that have the effect of pushing the existing ones further back. In raising the intensity of the etchings from one edition to the next, Piranesi thrusts the entire construction one degree towards the back of the composition: "Plane bursts from plane and by a system of explosions plunges ever deeper into the depths."[34]

It is worth considering this in more detail, since Eisenstein transferred Piranesi's "layering" of space to filmmaking and to *Ivan the Terrible* (1944) in particular. Recounting the life of the medieval tsar, Eisenstein let much of the story about Ivan unfold within vaulted halls and chambers. From a cinematographic perspective, these locations served as a laboratory for the translation of the *Carceri* to cinematic space: in several scenes, he built up expansive foregrounds, layering the space as if the scenes had been etched and then re-etched. The foreground became decorative—a depository of "transferred columns, parts of vaults, stoves, piers, or objects of everyday use," as he wrote on the construction of sets.[35] Although this prop list relates to *Ivan the Terrible*, in a shadow narrative it could also describe the *Carceri* and, more particularly, the features that distinguish the second edition from the first. This fascination with the divergent editions of Piranesi is common to twentieth-century approaches to art at large: to Arthur Hind, as argued in chapter one, the difference between the first and second edition of the *Carceri* represented a modernist–historicist divide; to Alfred H. Barr, it represented a cubist–surrealist one. To Eisenstein, it represented neither, but rather a pronounced discontinuity—one layer on top of another—in a build-up pinpointing the principle of montage.

In a final consideration, the *Carceri* suite demonstrated the principle of montage also as a *series*. I believe any observer of the sixteen fantasies involuntarily tries to combine them as views of the same netherworld. However, one searches in vain for openings or stairs that might lead from one composition to the next. And a connectedness that just about fails is arguably what made the series modern. In other words, Eisenstein's impression of the sequence formed by the *Carceri* prints did not hinge on a continuity of images but on the gaps that just about prevented them from combining. Dupond's animation, as we saw, lures the spectator into believing that the prison interiors form one interlinked space; for Eisenstein, however, they formed a continuously *disrupted* sequence of spaces. That disruption—the essence of filmmaking—was infinitely more cinematic than an unbroken storyline adapted from a novel. In fact, it was the very non-relation between the prints that manifested the concept of montage.[36] In this way the modernity of Piranesi, according to

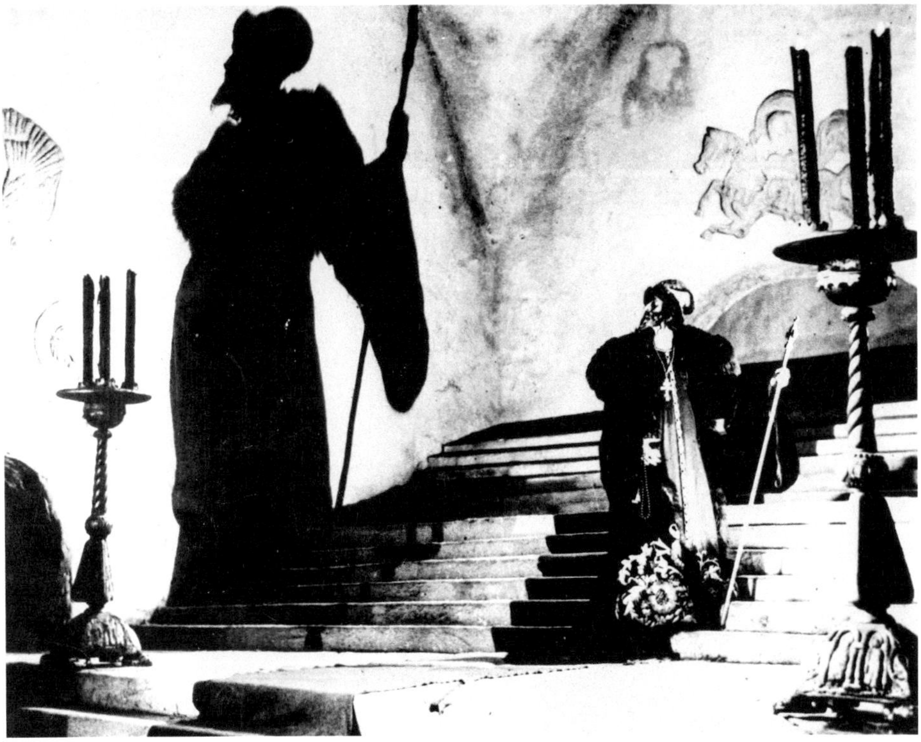

Eisenstein, lay in making unrelated fragments conjoin in a sequence—a fundamentally "deconstructivist" idea with an impact on architects like Bernard Tschumi.[37]

Eisenstein's revival of Piranesi was not confined to writing but also extended to filmmaking, resulting in some of his most memorable imagery. An iconic scene in the director's oeuvre, and a highpoint in twentieth-century Piranesi reception, occurs in *October: Ten Days that Shook the World* from 1928. Here, De Quincey's interpretation of the *Carceri* is combined with Bolshevik propaganda in an arresting montage sequence. De Quincey's description of the climbing figure of Piranesi, mentioned in chapter one, was already uncannily cinematic. The reappearance of Piranesi at different levels within the same image defies temporal and spatial logic, but to Eisenstein it also captured perfectly the cut-and-paste reality of montage. The staircase was as potent a symbol for the Russian film director as it was for other authors and artists figuring in this discussion, but it was a symbol he chose to read politically, and it exemplifies Eisenstein's practical application of Piranesi and/or De Quincey. [38]

Made only ten years after the October revolution, the film recapitulates the dramatic days in 1917. Eisenstein shoots at the actual locations and has extras reenact the parts they played in the real events. He adopts the viewpoint of the Lenin

Ivan the Terrible, part I, directed by Sergei M. Eisenstein, 1944.

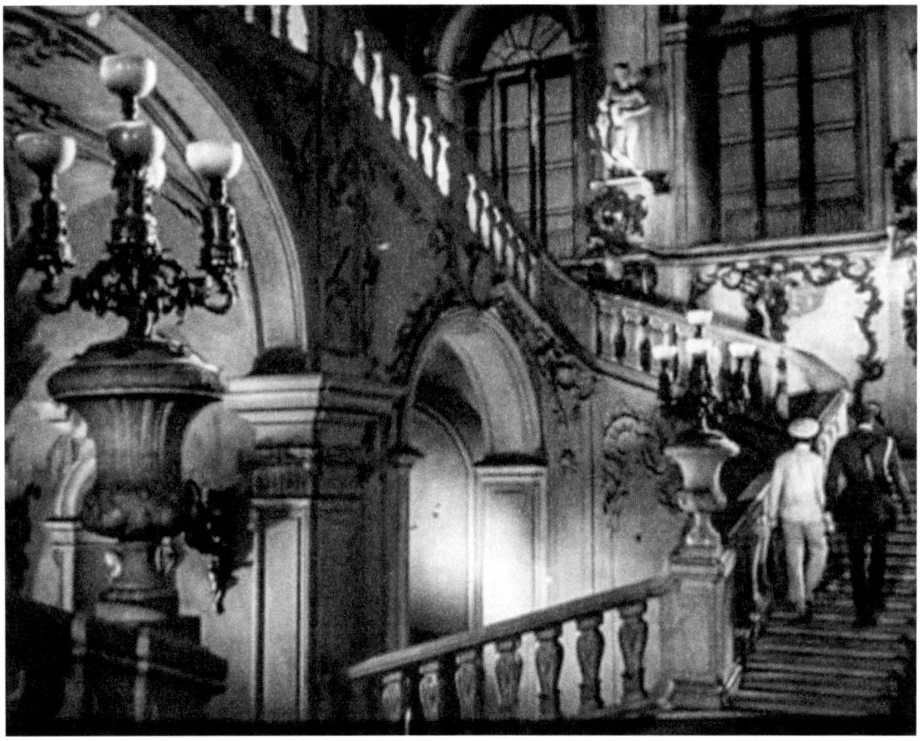

faction, which of course ultimately won the day, displaying an undisguised loathing for the pre-Bolshevik government led by Alexander Kerensky. To Eisenstein, the endlessly climbing figure in De Quincey's description recalls Kerensky's absurd elevation in rank, from one administrative post to the other, until he somehow ended up with the title of prime minister. However, the challenge for the director is how to convert De Quincey's *Carceri* description to film. The solution he arrives at is in fact rather simple; he translates Piranesi's surreal redoubling on the stairway to an equally surreal repetition of the same take. Filming the character of Kerensky ascending the Jordan Staircase in the Winter Palace five times in a row, then gluing the shots together, the endless climb splits into a sequence of takes that could go on endlessly too, according to the director. "As we can see," Eisenstein remarks, "through an essentially simple system of displacement the emotional rise of Piranesi from the visions of De Quincey-Coleridge was transformed into the ironic flight 'in place' of Aleksander Fedorovich Kerensky."[39] If we are to believe Eisenstein's retrospective explanation of the making of *October*, the *Carceri* series presented itself as the solution to his effort to find a suitable cinematic form for a politically charged scene. It instructed him on how to disrupt, or more specifically, break up, the unfolding of events, thus allowing multiple messages to transpire.

Kerensky ascending the Jordan Staircase. Scene from *October: Ten Days that Shook the World*, directed by Sergei M. Eisenstein, 1927.

"I am now looking at this etching on my wall" is the ingenious opening to Eisenstein's essay "Piranesi, Or the Fluidity of Forms." The essay, completed in 1946–47, not long before the director's death, focuses on two etchings in the oeuvre of the Venetian: the *Carcere oscura* (*see following*) and *The Gothic Arch* from the *Carceri*, the same composition d'Harnoncourt selected for his MOMA show (*see following*).[40] Both were prints that Eisenstein owned and had on the wall of his Moscow apartment. In his text, Eisenstein invites the reader—or in fact the spectator—into the apartment, encouraging them to follow his glance in a carefully staged progression from one print to the next. He "looks" at one etching, then lets the eyes "slide along the yellow wall" until "they stop unexpectedly" at the second etching, as if the glance were a movie camera and the two prints were sequential scenes. It is a clever rhetorical device, recreating Eisenstein's argument cinematically: the prints are lifted out of a historical past and recast as timeless in the same way a movie always re-actualizes events in and *as* a present. Like Alfred H. Barr, Eisenstein is using Piranesi as an aid in his championing of modernism.

Six years separate the making of the two prints on the wall and yet, according to the Russian director, they are remarkably connected.[41] In fact, the nature of that connection makes Piranesi a seminal figure in the prehistory of cinema. Eisenstein argues that the *Carcere oscura* develops into *The Gothic Arch* in what is not a development at all, but a jolt—a dimensional leap. The early print "explodes" into the later one, he writes—an observation he sets out to prove by imagining the consequences of that explosion with the precision of an engineer. In texts and diagrams, he documents how the architecture in the *Carcere oscura*, if it had been detonated by an internal blast, would necessarily result in the architecture of *The Gothic Arch* (*see facing*). Finding the arches, columns, and stairs in the early print deepened, expanded, and multiplied in the later one, he concludes: "Piranesi's second etching is actually

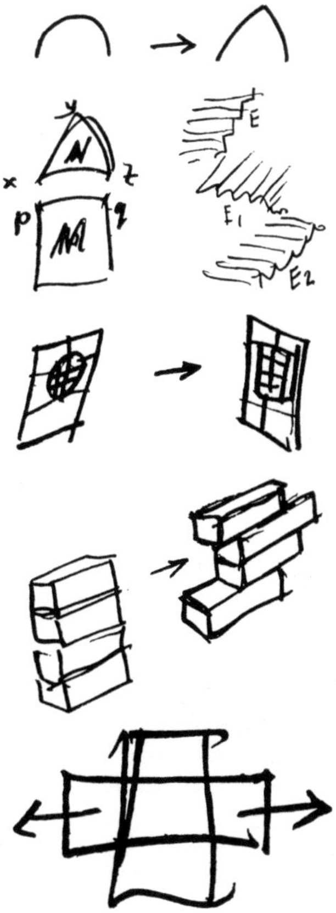

Sergei M. Eisenstein, diagram of the "explosions" in Piranesi's *Carcere oscura* resulting in the architecture of *The Gothic Arch*, ca. 1946–1947.

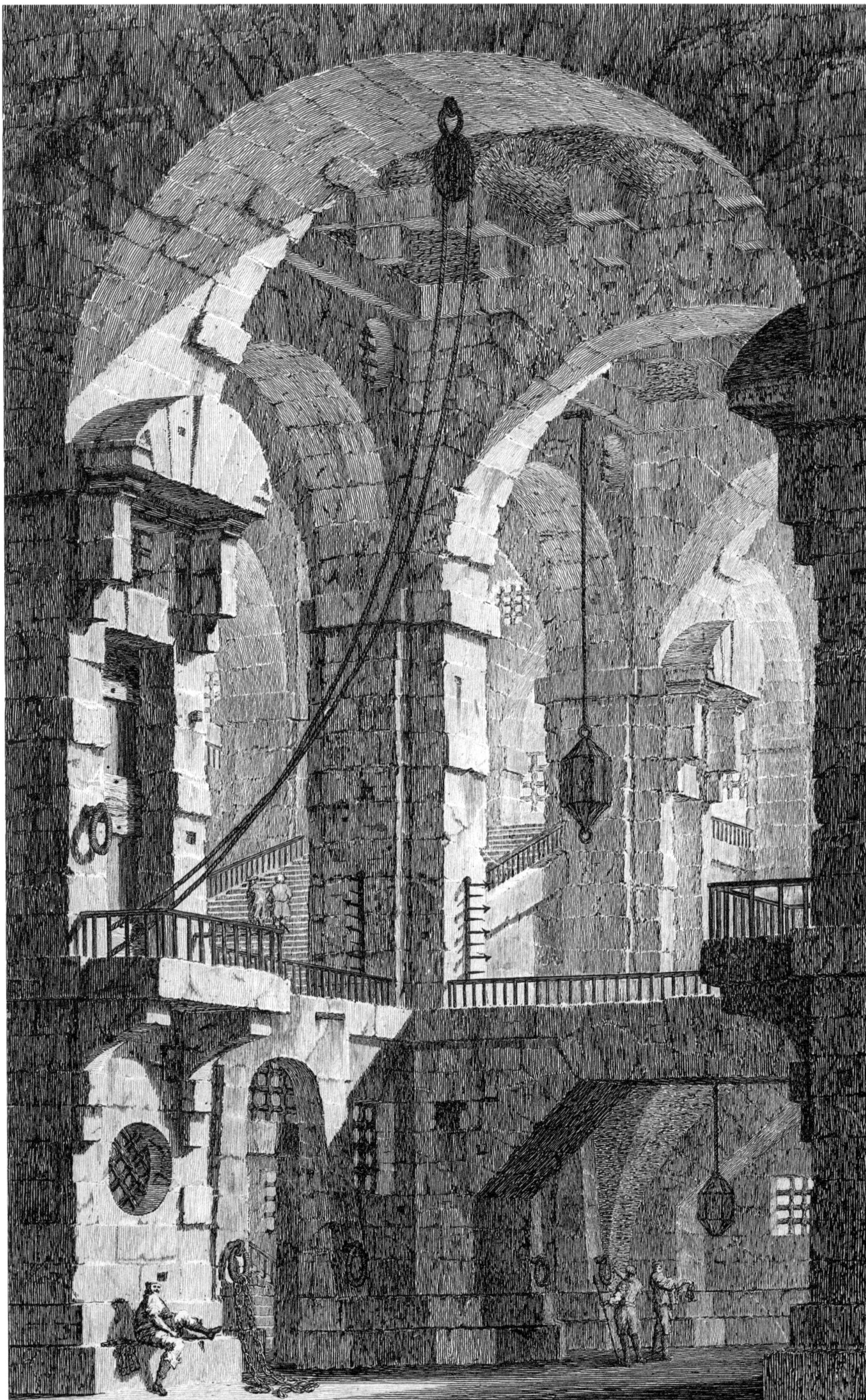

the first one exploding in ecstatic flight."[42] The insight makes him speculate further. It is by leaps, not by gradual transitions, that Piranesi matures as an artist. In other words, for truly great artists, life itself advances according to the principle of montage. A biography founded on "grand leaps and bursts" places Piranesi in fact alongside El Greco, Zola, Whitman, Pushkin, Gogol, Dostoyevsky, and Tolstoy.[43]

However, the blast of force that transformed the *Carcere oscura* is by no means spent. Is it possible to foresee and discover one more "leap," one more "explosion," one more "spurt"? Eisenstein asks rhetorically.[44] Far from petering out with the *Carceri*, the force that propelled the series into existence makes a final surge, pushing beyond Piranesi's oeuvre, even beyond his period, and landing in modern art, and more particularly in cubism.[45] The breathtaking jump across centuries, schools, media brings the creative burst begun by Piranesi to its emotional climax, according to the filmmaker. Although the history that leads from the *Carcere oscura* to cubism via the two editions of the *Carceri* is a history of the dissolution of form, abstraction is not an end in itself for Eisenstein, as it was for Barr. In fact, the endpoint is neither a movement nor a school, but a single work of art, namely Picasso's *Guernica*—the disturbing image painted in 1937 in response to the bombing of the Basque town of that name (*see following*). Looking past *Guernica*'s abstract qualities, Eisenstein directly addresses its emotional content, stating that it would be difficult to find "a more heartrending expression of the inner tragic dynamics of human destruction." The force that began by "exploding" one formal composition to make the next now sees both prints turned "into the emotion of a revolutionary challenge to the Fascism crushing Spain."[46] It is precisely in this capacity that *Guernica*, in Eisenstein's words, represents "the third state" of the *Carceri*. The painting's political and revolutionary significance saturates its eighteenth-century graphic precedents and completes their transformation; one that Piranesi had no chance to foresee, of course.

Manfredo Tafuri questions the validity of this leap in "The Historicity of the Avant-Garde: Piranesi and Eisenstein" (1980). Eisenstein's reference to *Guernica* introduces "a clearly dissonant motif," he writes, because the "ethical-political commitment" of Picasso does not accord with the formal universe of Piranesi.[47] However, I want to argue that Eisenstein envisions this striking leap not in historical terms, but in cinematic ones. As mentioned above, the director's wandering glance along the wall of prints forms a narrative thread in his essay on Piranesi. However, the "looking" serves to punctuate a much broader narrative in which Eisenstein meditates on the history of art and architecture at large. This crosscutting between seeing and reflection, between prints and history, makes the text as such a demonstration of montage. And the montage it manifests, moreover, is of an intellectual kind, reflecting Eisenstein's aim to *create* rather than just represent

facing and foldout Giovanni Battista Piranesi, *Carcere oscura* from *Prima parte di architettura e prospettive*, 1743. Giovanni Battista Piranesi, plate XIV, *The Gothic Arch*, from *Carceri d'invenzione*, second edition, ca. 1761.

reality—"to propose the real as the result of a search and not as a *given*," as Marie-Claire Ropars-Wuilleumier puts it.[48] In summation, the admittedly provocative jump from Piranesi to Picasso, from *Carceri* to *Guernica*, makes sense if seen, or read, as a piece of cinematic montage, structured, that is, not in a sequence of shots but as a sequence of paragraphs.

In the previous chapter, we saw that d'Harnoncourt used Piranesi curatorially to demonstrate the timelessness of abstract art. Arguably, Eisenstein used Piranesi in the same way to demonstrate the timelessness of montage. Remarkably, Piranesi's *The Gothic Arch* served to prove the point simultaneously in the respective fields in Moscow and New York. And the similarity does not stop there.

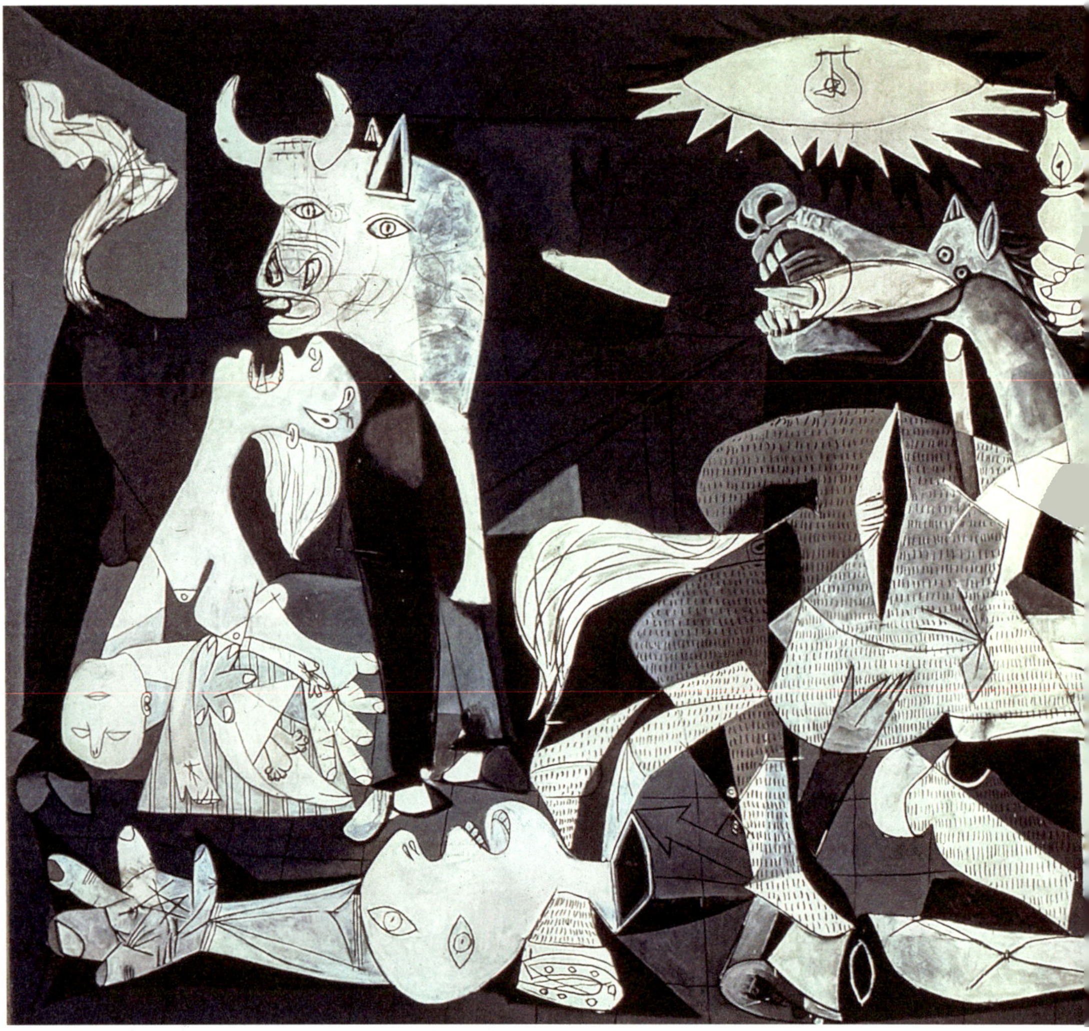

Pablo Picasso, *Guernica*, 1937. Oil on canvas.

The sequence of artworks representing "history" in Eisenstein's essay corresponded to the sequence on display in the first room in d'Harnoncourt's *Timeless Aspects of Modern Art*, which incorporated Piranesi in a history that included early Chinese art, Cézanne, and Picasso.[49] However, the direction history took differed in the two manifestations. At MOMA the counter-chronological loop—Cézanne–Picasso–Piranesi—served to nail abstraction as a universal quality; Eisenstein, more conventionally, stuck to historical chronology, as it was the only way he could pin down a succession leading to the socio-political apotheosis of *Guernica*. Ironically, MOMA flirted more openly with the idea of history as a montage sequence, subjected to crosscutting, than did the moviemaker.

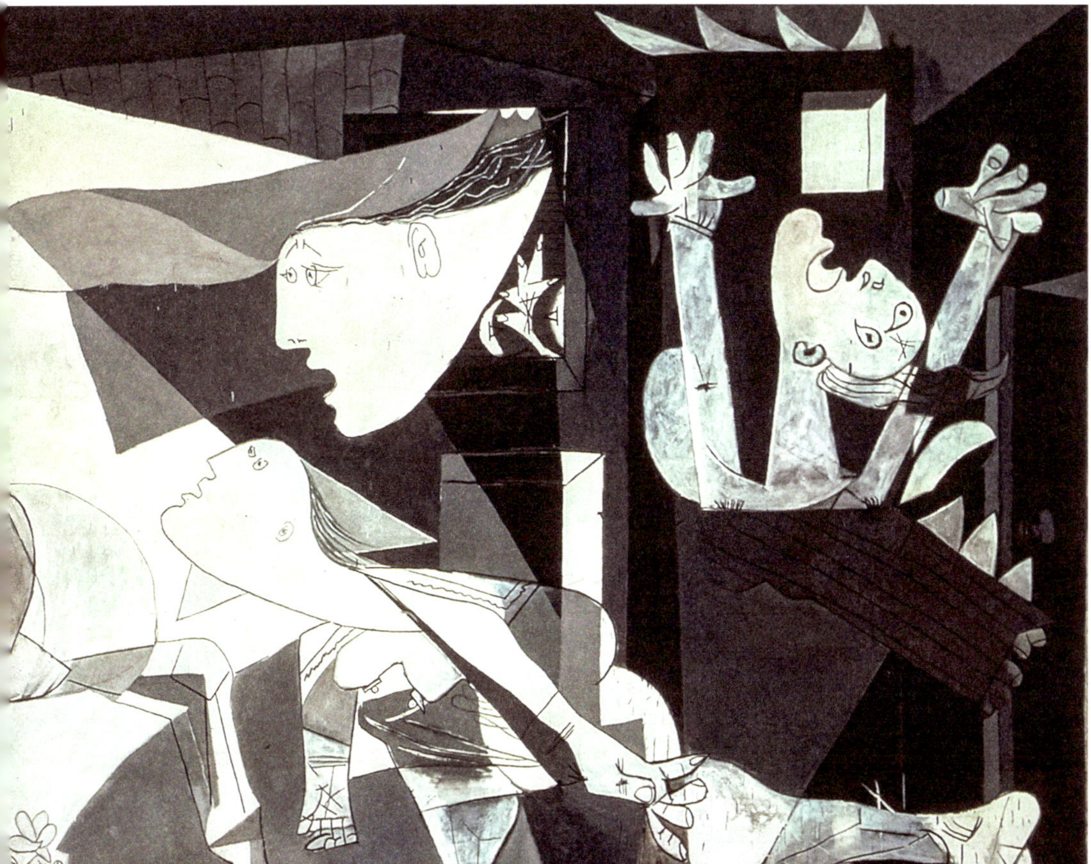

The comparison between MOMA and Eisenstein is far from random and trails back to Barr's two 1936 exhibitions. Barr was a great admirer of Eisenstein and of *October* in particular. He visited the director in his studio twice in early 1928 during his stay in Moscow, and on one of these occasions he was even shown four reels of *October*—"a magnificent accomplishment"—which was then in the process of being edited.[50] Back home, Barr wrote two enthusiastic articles introducing Eisenstein to an American audience and taking care to enlighten his readers on the superior technique of montage: "But to the writer his most interesting technical quality is his masterly kinetic composition achieved through cutting."[51] Because of montage, Barr continued, *October* became "too bold, too abstract, and too subtle" to have any immediate success in Russia and Germany.[52] He could only hope, he added, that Eisenstein would come to America (which he did in 1930). While fearing that the filmmaker would meet with timidity, vulgarity, and prudishness, as well as severe temptations to cheapen his art, he insisted that the encounter would be a significant learning experience for Americans: "The result of such a visit would help us to judge not merely Eisenstein, but America as well."[53]

Barr may well have been one of the Americans who learned from the Russian filmmaker and in due course applied the lesson from *October*—the technique of "cutting"—to the exposition of art. In any event, we may establish a connection between the cinematic form of montage that so impressed the young Barr and the conspicuous dismantling and rearrangement of historical sequences at the exhibitions which he, and later d'Harnoncourt, curated, and which included Piranesi.

To conclude, Eisenstein's primary interest was not to demonstrate that Piranesi was timeless. Rather, Piranesi helped him demonstrate the timelessness of montage. The principle of montage enabled cinema to break free from the diachronic storyline that Western film had uncritically adapted from literature and to reestablish the legitimacy and independence of the medium of film on genuinely cinematic terms. To Eisenstein, therefore, it was of great importance to present the history of art as though it already carried within itself the principle of montage. As Soviet filmmaking marked the fulfillment of history, that fulfillment also altered the stages leading up to it, injecting artworks with an essence that strictly speaking belonged to the future. This is the radical claim in Eisenstein's philosophy of history.[54]

Piranesi's *Carceri* triumph as an example of an art transformed retroactively as *cinematic*. On one level, the eighteenth-century prints inspired countless scenes and settings, but on another, they dictated the very form of film. In this perspective, Piranesi's compositions emerge not simply as proto-cinematic but as a reference by which cinema invented itself historically, conceptually, and technically.

THE SUBVER

SIVE MODERNIST

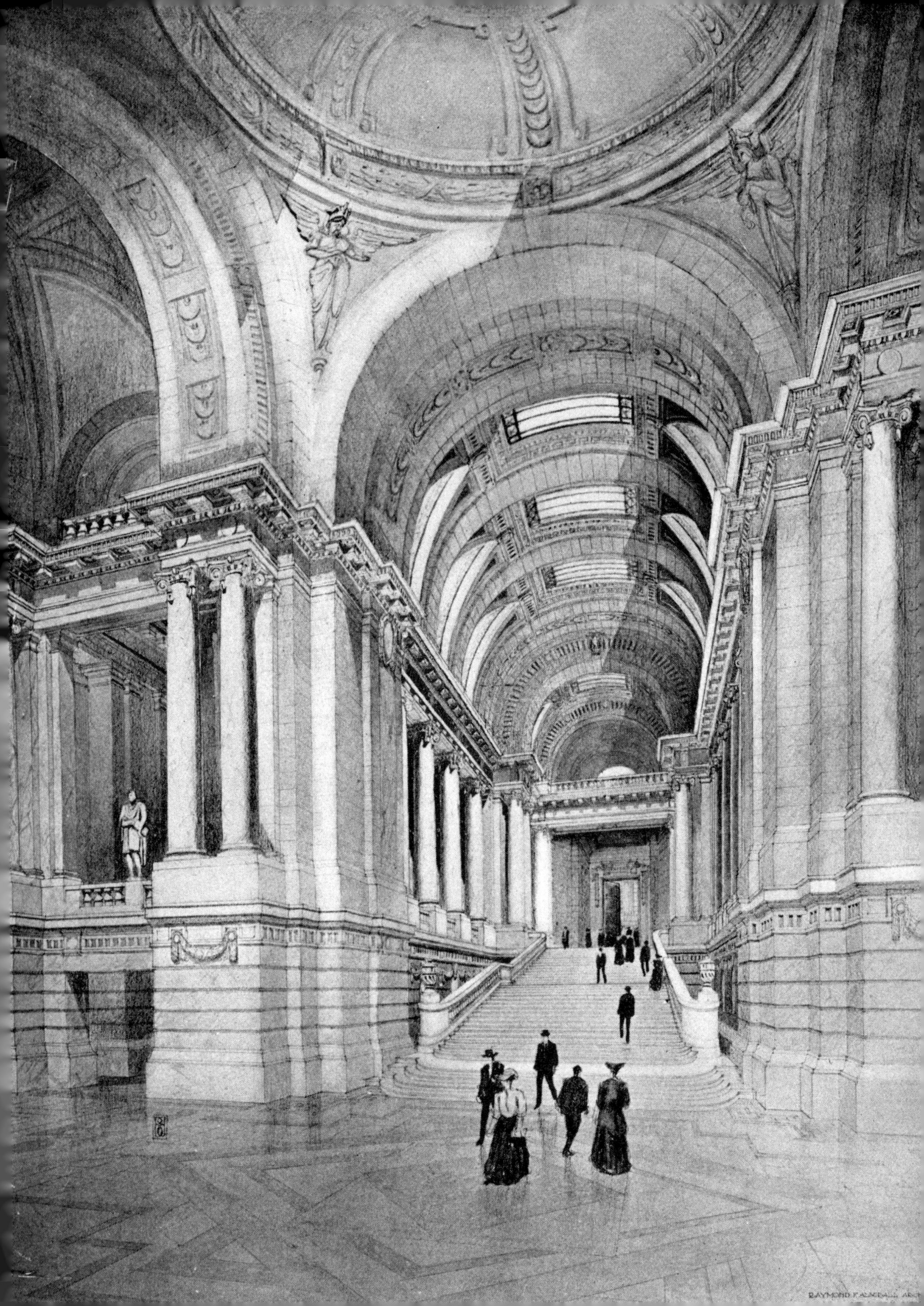
RAYMOND F. ALMIRALL ARC

Although Piranesi considered himself an architect, signing his plates *architetto*, a majority of his prints are archaeological, evoking ancient Rome. From the outset, then, his work seemed to point in two directions. The period after 1900 began to see in the imagined forms not a distorted past but, on the contrary, a possible future—a future that architecturally embraced the modern age itself. The shift of focus from Piranesi the antiquarian to Piranesi the avant-gardist coalesces in several turns in architectural discourse and practice in the twentieth and twenty-first centuries. Rudolf Wittkower, in "Piranesi's 'Parere su l'architettura'" (1938), defined Piranesi's originality in terms of 1930s ideas. Writing at the height of architectural modernism, he describes how Piranesi's *Parere* defends a free and imaginative art: "Archaeological material now becomes a weapon in the hands of a revolutionary modernist."[1] However, Piranesi's architecture held qualities that also challenged mainstream modernism, prompting architects and historians to reconsider the origin and development of the modern movement itself. Piranesi represented a continually disruptive element, at times suppressed, at others exploited. In short, he emerged as a subversive force in the historiography of modern architecture, the full extent of which has not yet been discussed in scholarly literature. As the last two chapters trail through a terrain that may seem familiar, covering a century of modernism and various forms of postmodernism, my hope is that new and surprising paths will open up with Piranesi as guide.

A PIRANESIAN STYLE?

In the years around 1900, monumental buildings erected in Rome and elsewhere often met with the label "Piranesian." But rather than being the kind of architecture that one might call modern, these were buildings that manifested an exaggerated past, with a profusion of motifs that mixed references from different times and places and short-circuited any effort to fit them into a specific "style." Here, the series of neo-Renaissances and neo-baroques that made up nineteenth-century historicism sort of imploded in an architecture that absorbed and transcended them all. After Rome became the capital of a unified Italy in 1871, new ministries and government buildings rose at the rim of the historic center. A city that for centuries had seen its antiquity exported and transformed into classicisms, really defined elsewhere, found its own entangled character expressed in the prints of Piranesi. His "free transformation," to quote Wittkower, reflected an ideal that was decidedly eclectic–archaeological, perhaps the one "style" Rome could claim entirely for itself, emerging from its wealth of ruins and fragments.[2]

Vestibule of the unbuilt version of Brooklyn Central Library, designed by Raymond Almirall, 1908.

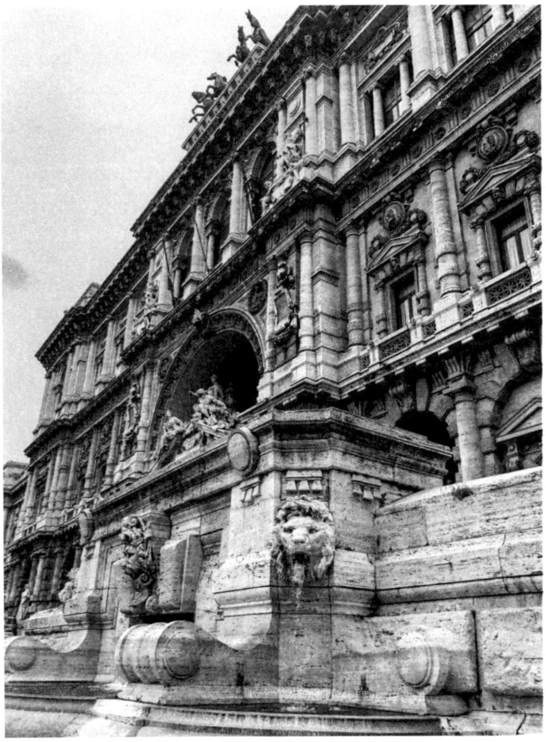

A style that seemingly accumulated *all* styles and elements asserted Rome as a new capital in contrast to the homogeneous neo-antiques cultivated in northern Italy and associated with Renaissance Florence, Palladian Veneto, and, not least, neoclassical Turin.

For example, dominating the embankment of the Tiber, Guglielmo Calderini's immense Palace of Justice (1888–1910) does not evoke a specific Piranesian structure or set of motifs, and somehow it does not need to. The building's overwhelming effect results from its ambition not to be a "building" at all but a world of its own—dense, fragmented, multilayered—conveying the impression of piles upon piles of fragments, manifesting the collapsed and reassembled world of the ancients. Calderini's complex is a Forum Romanum all by itself—albeit as Piranesi might have reconstructed it. More concretely, the superimposition of classical fragments and dramatic chiaroscuro contribute to a structure that seems to recreate Piranesi's Roman fantasies.

Similarly immense, overabundant structures were built in many places around 1900. As Terry Kirk documents, architects themselves occasionally labeled their projects Piranesian, among them Raimondo D'Aronco, who worked in the 1890s and experimented with a bold, dynamic form of classicism.[3] Piranesi's oeuvre also served as a reference for a dumbfounded public trying to process the impression that the vast new monuments made on them. Buildings that shattered the scale and arrangements not only of the historical Renaissance and baroque but also of these periods' neo-evocations seemed a trifle more comprehensible with Piranesi's imaginative prints at hand. Summing up the impression of the Palace of Justice in Brussels, completed by Joseph Poelaert in 1883, the poet Paul Verlaine said, "[t]here is something of the Tower of Babel, plus Michelangelo, with a bit of Piranesi, and a dash—one may say—of madness... Outside, it is a colossus, inside

Palazzo della Giustizia, Rome, designed by Guglielmo Calderini, 1888–1910.

a monster. It wants to be immense, and it is."[4] In Verlaine's description, it is as if the Romantic hallucinations of Victor Hugo had been turned into solids. "Piranesian" represented not so much a style as a category in which to place buildings that transcended styles.

In 1910 Arthur Samuel drew attention to what he perceived as a Piranesi-inspired architecture being erected across the Atlantic. "The American architects have drawn liberally on his entire output, and the result is a delight to the eye," he wrote, and mentions as examples bank buildings and city halls in the United States and Canada as well as public architecture in New York, including the enormous Pennsylvania Station, which opened the year Samuel's book appeared.[5]

The reference to Piranesi in these and other examples is not entirely unfounded. For example, the unbuilt vestibule of Brooklyn Central Library comes close to evoking a specific Piranesi composition, namely *The Vestibule of an Ancient Temple* (1743) (*see following*). A contemporary illustration of the Brooklyn project shows a vaulted gallery receding towards the distance with columns on tall podiums flanking the gallery (*see page 160*). The image of the Brooklyn vestibule also employs the trick of distributing scaled-down human figures across the interior to emphasize its grand dimensions.

However, although monuments from around 1900 invite associations with Piranesi, the exact elements that trigger those associations often elude definition. At what point, or at what level, does a building become "Piranesian"? In the architectural discourse from the early twentieth century to the present the adjective is invoked in countless contexts and denotes a profusion of meanings that range from formal arrangements to emotional responses; Rem Koolhaas even thinks of himself as Piranesian.[6]

More than manifesting a Piranesian style, I would argue that a *fin-de-siècle* architecture from Brussels to Brooklyn highlights the complexity of reproduction—the effect of solutions that are overpoweringly pictorial. A critical mind would ask whether it is truly the architecture that makes interiors Piranesi-like, or simply the vantage point from which a building is seen. Unquestionably, it is from certain positions, and not from others, that stairs and arches align in perspectives comparable to Piranesi's prints. The ambiguity has wider implications. It points to the fact that connections between Piranesi and the architecture of the modern age are locked not to specific materials, volumes, dimensions, but to specific angles. If architects are "building Piranesi" (as Vincent Scully said of Kahn), it is no longer prints that represent architecture but architecture that represents prints.[7] A Piranesian quality is confined to, and realized as, viewpoints popularized in illustrations and then played back into the hands of architects. In other

overleaf Giovanni Battista Piranesi, *Vestibule of an Ancient Temple* from *Prima parte di architettura e prospettive*, 1743.

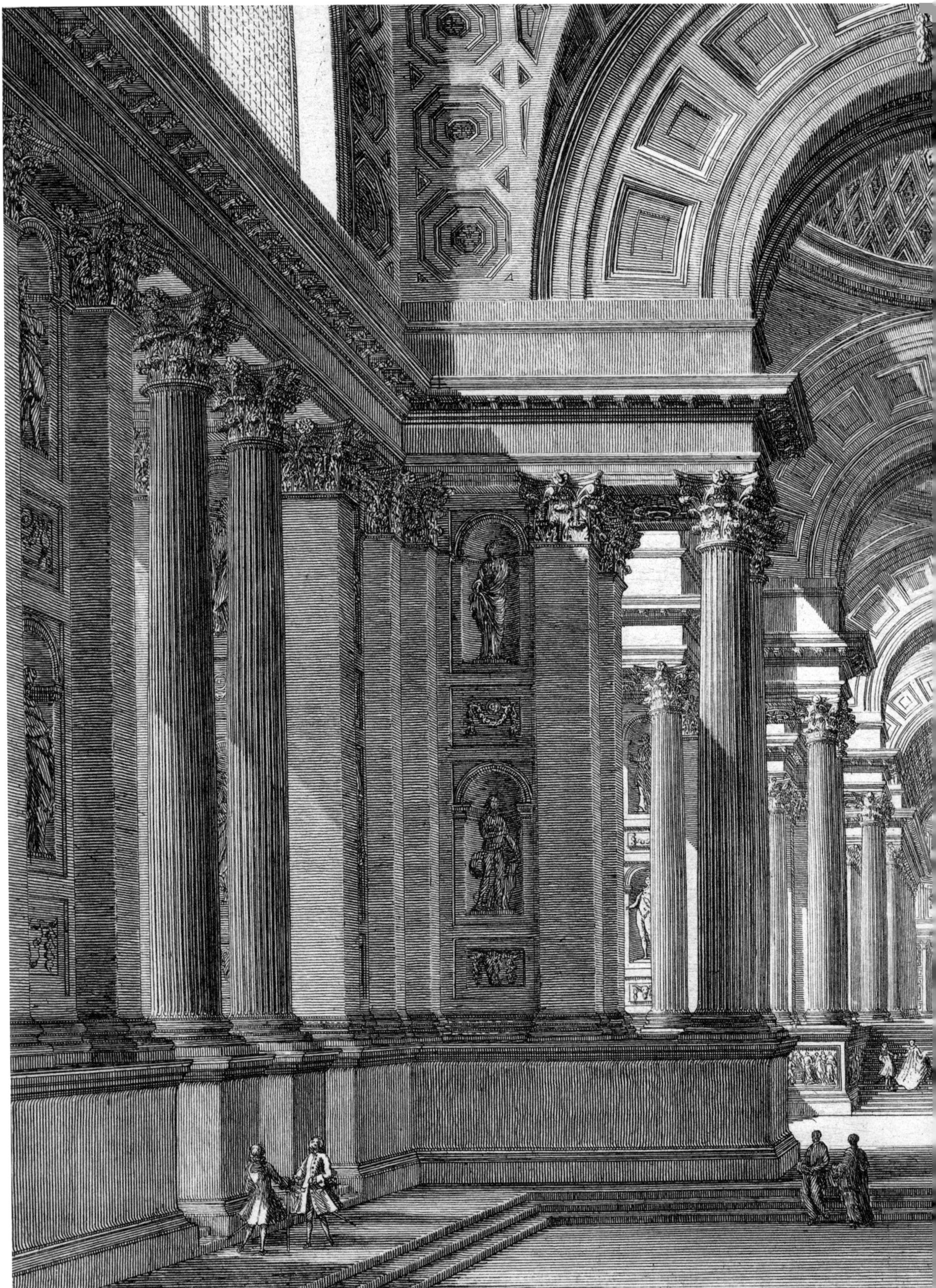

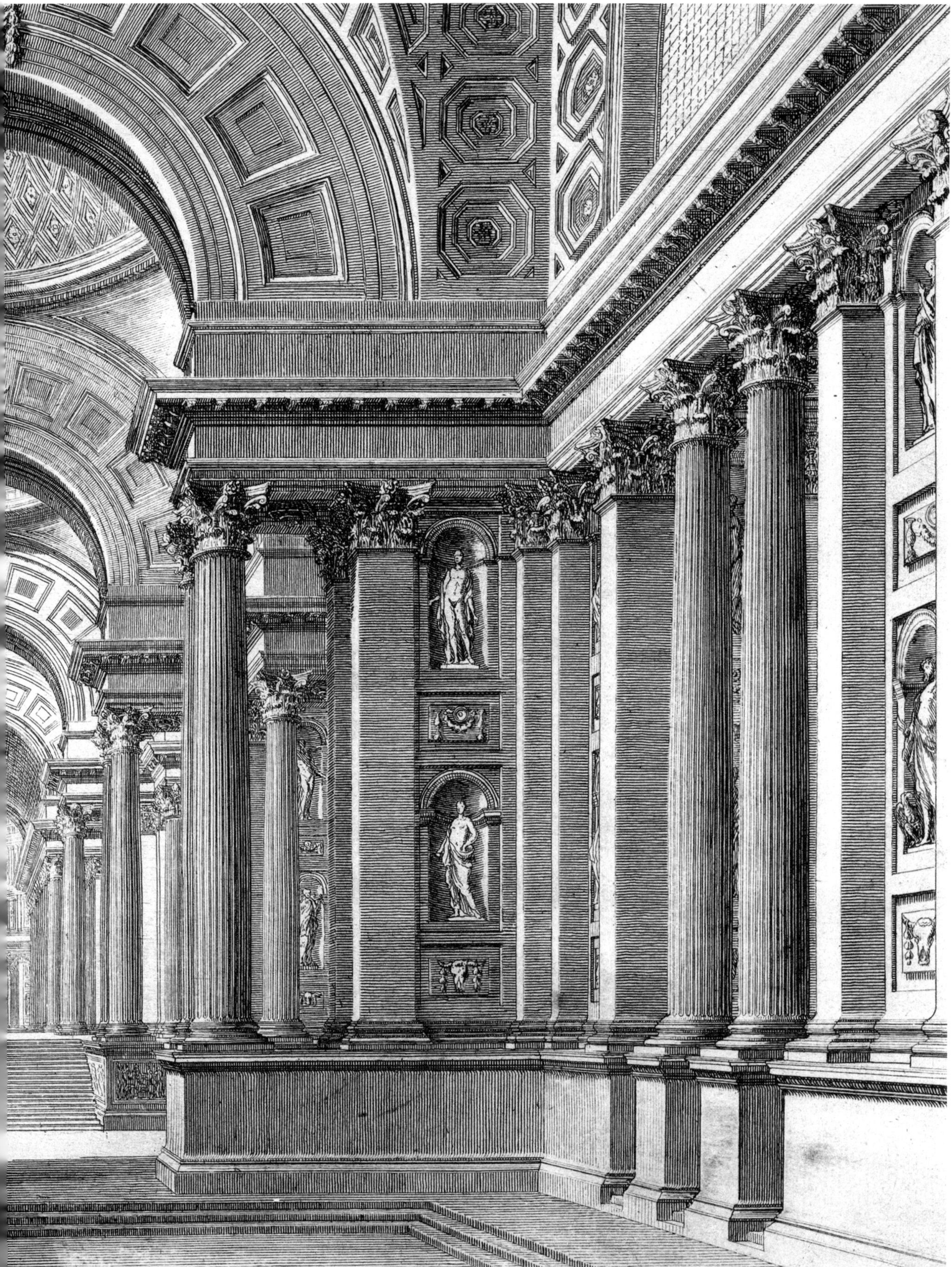

words, we are dealing with the building of prints. Elements are piled on elements, images on images, in what is perhaps less a Roman eclecticism than a print-historicism—a historic style retrieved from prints and recomposed in imitation of such, rather than in depths and volumes. An architecture of grand vistas and infinite perspectives is activated in carefully planned sequences of impressions as the spectator moves through the interiors, akin to how still shots combine in a cinematic movement, an art form excitingly novel at the time.

LE CORBUSIER AND THE AMBIGUITY OF ROME IN PRINT

"To send architectural students to Rome is to cripple them for life," Le Corbusier wrote in *Vers une architecture* in the chapter "The Lesson of Rome" (1923).[8] Rome was "the damnation of the half-educated" because only wise men knew how to resist the kind of monuments that lay in wait in the city. The most abominable examples, grouped under the heading "The Rome of Horrors," included Calderini's Palace of Justice—the Piranesian extravaganza.[9] Though Le Corbusier did not explicitly associate Calderini's building with Piranesi, he expressed a comparable aversion to Piranesi's work. At the same time, however, he carefully studied it. Indeed, Piranesi can be found at the core of the Swiss architect's effort to liberate architectural form from the cladding of historical styles, illustrating the ambiguity governing his approach to the past and, consequently, also his attempt to formulate an architecture of the future.

Arguably, the list of Roman horrors was a didactic necessity. It enabled Le Corbusier to set his vision of a new architecture against a backdrop of overwrought and baroque designs. In order for pure forms and volumes to be revealed, something obscuring those essentials was needed. In *Vers une architecture*, as well as in Le Corbusier's notes and sketches, the dichotomy between surface and mass, between prints and buildings, splits architecture into polar units—but the "lesson of Piranesi," as we might put it, demonstrates that in Le Corbusier's case divisions are never clear cut.

In July 1915—the same year William M. Ivins published his reappraisal of the *Carceri* suite—Le Corbusier, still known by his birth name, Charles-Édouard Jeanneret, installed himself in the print department at the Bibliothèque Nationale in Paris to do what he later would call "a patient and minute research" of their holdings.[10] The idea was to write a book, which in the end came to naught, but the discoveries he made at the library proved nothing less than decisive for his vision of a new architecture and, in a larger perspective, for a nascent modernist outlook. Jeanneret had visited Rome four years earlier and studied, sketched, and photographed the monuments of antiquity and the Renaissance. What interested him now, however, was not the buildings themselves but printed representations of them. He called up one volume after the other—Palladio, Vignola, Scamozzi, Fontana, Fischer von Erlach, Bibiena, Pozzo, re-envisioning Rome based on old prints rather than on his own memories.

He also called up Piranesi. But before we scrutinize his approach to the Venetian, I will make a digression. Jeanneret's staging of himself in the library has striking similarities to Goethe, who a hundred years earlier withdrew to his garden house in Weimar to write an account of his journey to Rome. As an aide-mémoire he took just a few prints, among them Pirro Ligorio's map *Anteiquae urbis imago*, a hallucinatory reconstruction of the ancient city first printed in 1561.[11] Not inconsequentially, this was the same map Jeanneret requested at the Bibliothèque Nationale. Amidst Ligorio's extravagant antiquities, Jeanneret eyed a latent

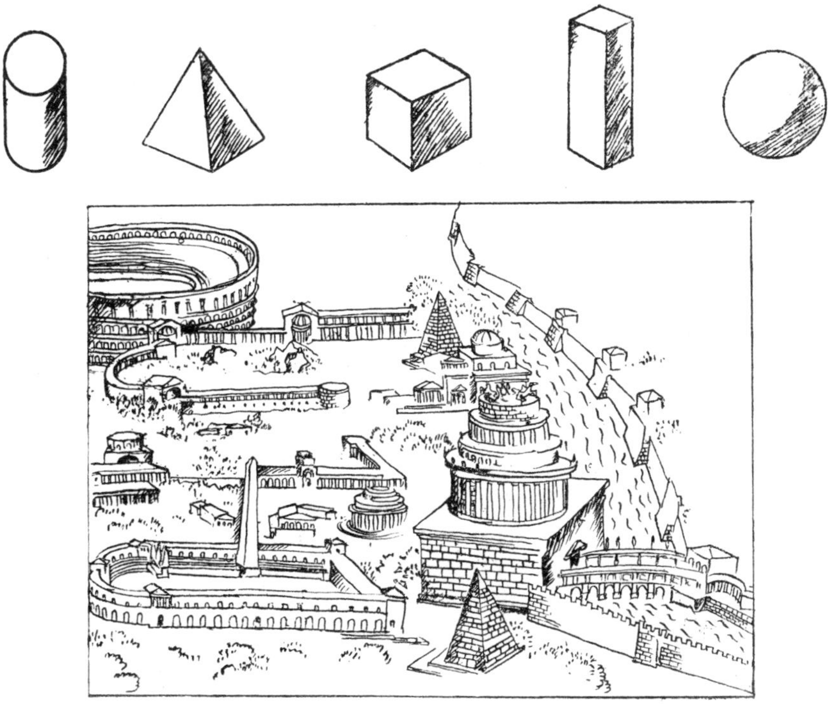

Diagram of the basic forms of architecture extracted from Pirro Ligorio's *Anteiquae urbis imago* (page 128) in Le Corbusier's *Vers une architecture*, 1923.

modernism, as shown by a sketch he made of the area around the ancient Mausoleum of Hadrian. The sketch was first published in 1920, in *L'Esprit Nouveau*, the journal Le Corbusier founded, and then in *Vers une architecture*, and has come to define no less than what the "modern" is in architecture, and, just as significant, how the modern was extricated from prints of Rome (*see preceding*). In the sixteenth-century map, Jeanneret imagined he could discern a set of basic forms nestling within Ligorio's fantastically elaborate edifices. To him, these reconstructions showed in all clarity that, behind the veneer of styles, architecture was reducible to simple geometric shapes: "[C]ubes, cones, spheres, cylinders or pyramids are the great primary forms," was how he explained the didactic importance of the illustration.[12] In this way, Ligorio's printed architecture stood out not as ancient but as essential, and therefore also as *new*. The map's varied and always monumental assembly of buildings, he wrote in the margins of the sketch, made it a "prototype of a modern city."[13] However, the map was obviously not varied *enough*, because before publishing the sketch, Jeanneret (or Le Corbusier at this point) added an amphitheater to the section he copied to exemplify the primary form of a cylinder. In other words, he intervened in the representation of the city and rearranged its buildings in order to present a more complete picture of the essentials of architecture.

At the Bibliothèque Nationale, in the summer of 1915, Jeanneret also studied Piranesi, who triggered not only a mixed response, but also a contrary one, laying bare a discord that was to prevail in his thinking and in the modernist project at large. At first glance, Piranesi did not meet with the architect's approval. In a note included in the study material, he wrote, "All of Piranesi's reconstitutions...map of Rome and acrobatic compositions of which so much has been made at the École des Beaux-Arts: nothing but porticos, colonnades, and obelisks!!! It is crazy. It is horrible, ugly, and idiotic. Make no mistake, it is anything but grandiose."[14] The assessment is damning, of course, but it presents only half the picture. At some level, Piranesi also intrigued the architect and served to strengthen his vision of the "modernism" inherent in past buildings, echoing (or for all we know preceding) the effect Ligorio's map had on him. A drawing from his days at the library contains no less than sixteen prints from Piranesi's *Vedute di Roma*, roughly sketched and pinned to the paper folio as if it were a gallery wall (*see following*).[15] The display includes ancient and modern structures as well as views of gardens and squares. Also from these prints, Jeanneret was able to extract elementary shapes—the structural essence—that defined good architecture, although he never subjected the miniatures to the same kind of didactic reworking as the Ligorio map. Distinct geometries nevertheless characterize the monuments in Jeanneret's Piranesi gallery, monuments such as the Pantheon, the Pyramid of

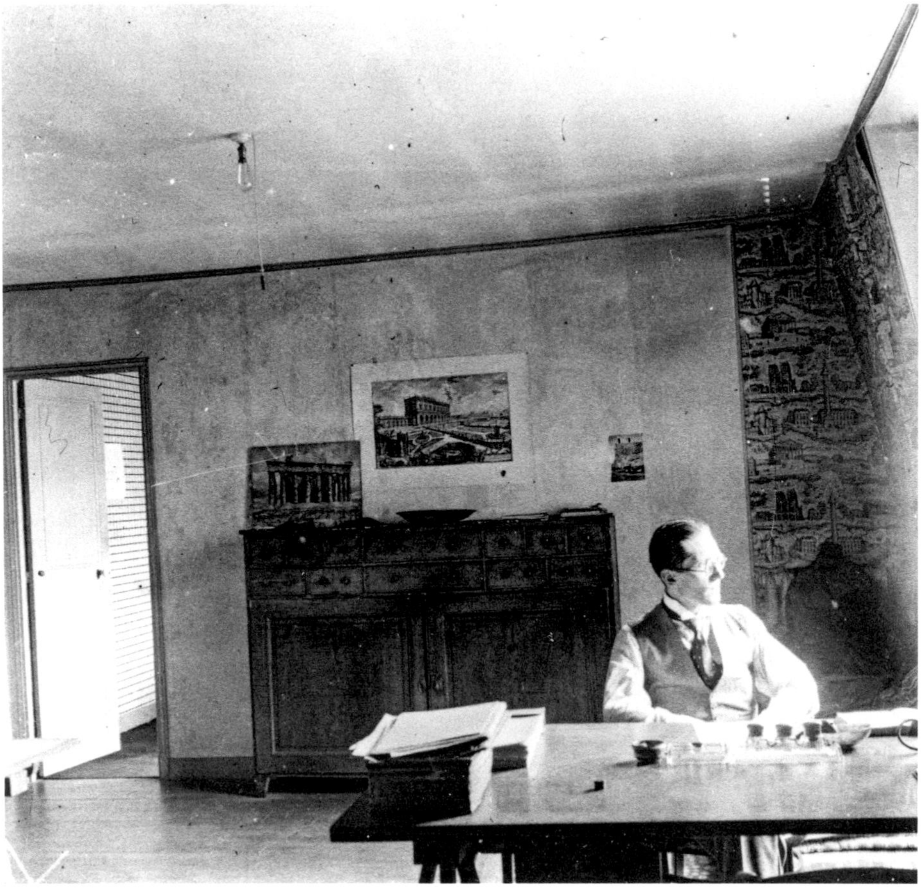

Cestius, and the Villa Albani, which he elsewhere celebrated for their essential forms.[16] Behind the "horrible, ugly, and idiotic," then, were shapes that constituted the vocabulary of an architecture that was modern. Piranesi, more than Ligorio, disclosed the ambiguity that modernism had to gloss over in order to appear sound and wholesome. A further sign of Le Corbusier's fascination with Piranesi is the view he acquired and put up behind his desk in his apartment—a view of the Villa Albani. The print was identical to one that he sketched at the Bibliothèque Nationale—an illustration of the form of the rectangle? Like Eisenstein in Moscow or Borges in Buenos Aires, Le Corbusier also decorated the walls at home with a Piranesi print. Although he may have responded to the decorating advice of Sturgis and Samuel, who wrote books addressed to collectors in these years, it was Le Corbusier the architect who presumably savored the design. More than a mere collectible, the Piranesi print emerged as a key to unlock "the modern."

Le Corbusier in his apartmentwith Piranesi's view of Villa Albani hanging on the wall, 1911.

overleaf Le Corbusier, sketch of sixteen prints by Piranesi from *Vedute di Roma*, 1915. Pencil on paper.

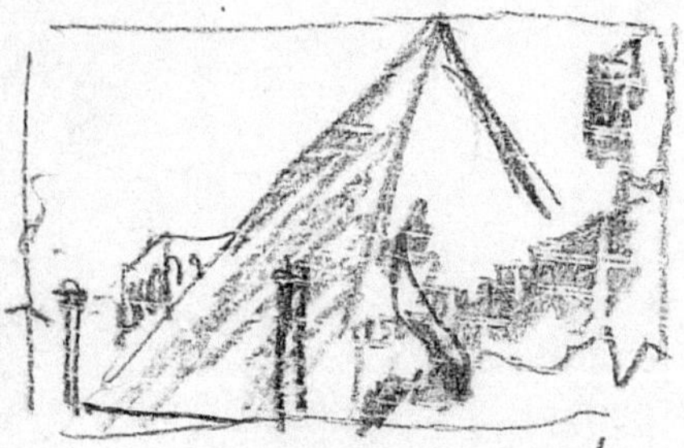

Piramide di Cestio

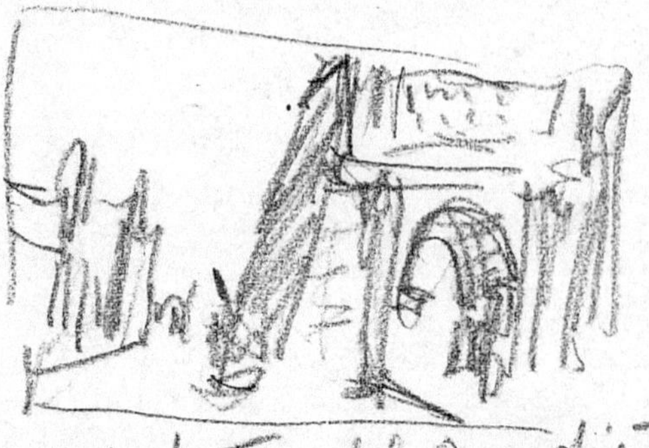

Veduta del Arco di Ti

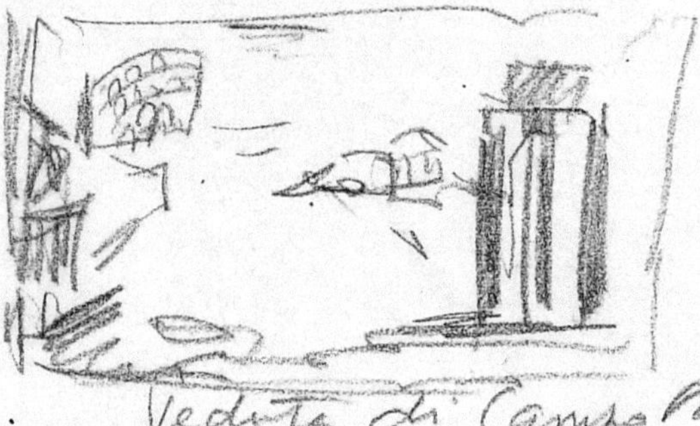

Veduta di Campo Vaccino (Foro)

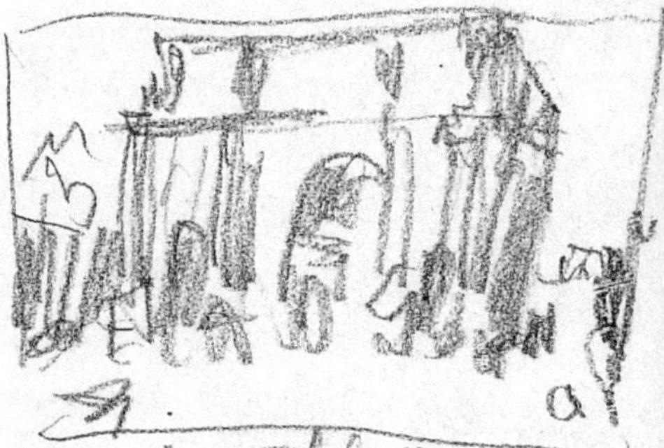

Veduta del Arco di Costantino

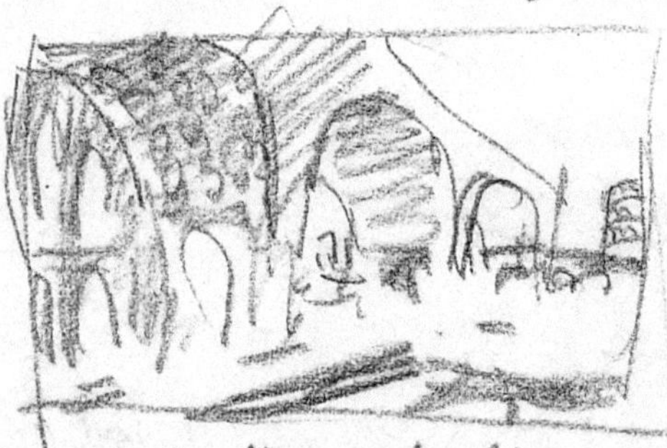

Veduta degli avanzi del Tablino (Basilica di Costantino)

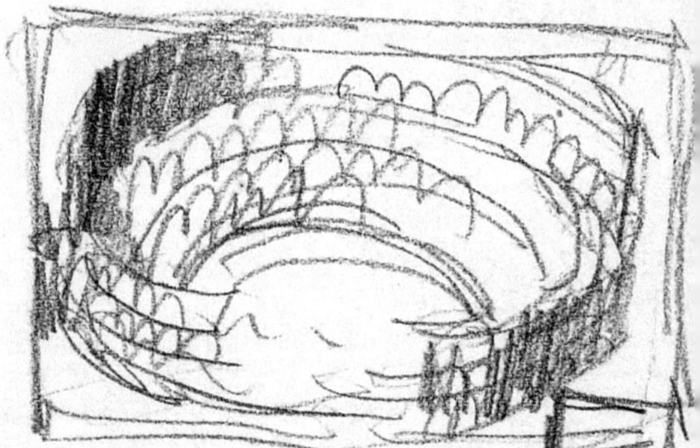

Veduta dell anfiteatro Flavio detto Colosseo (à revoir!)

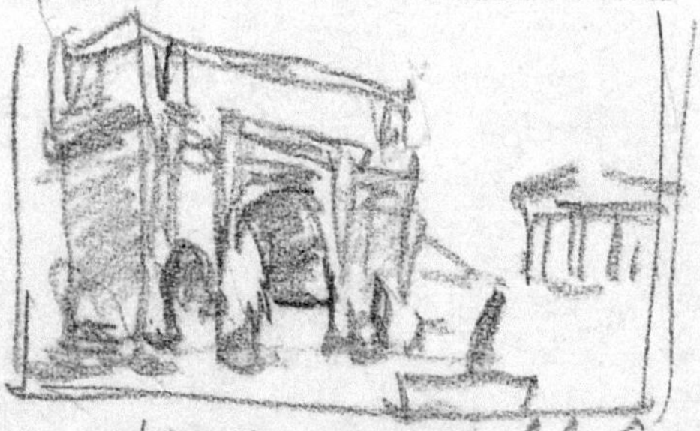

Veduta dell Arco di Settimio Severo

Vil albe

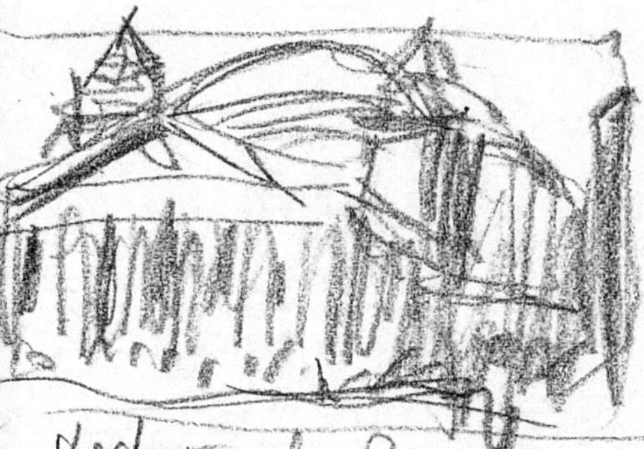

Veduta di Pantheon d'Agrippa

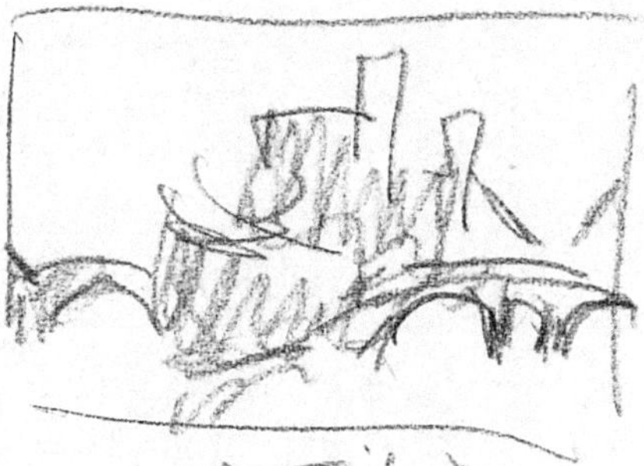

il Tibere

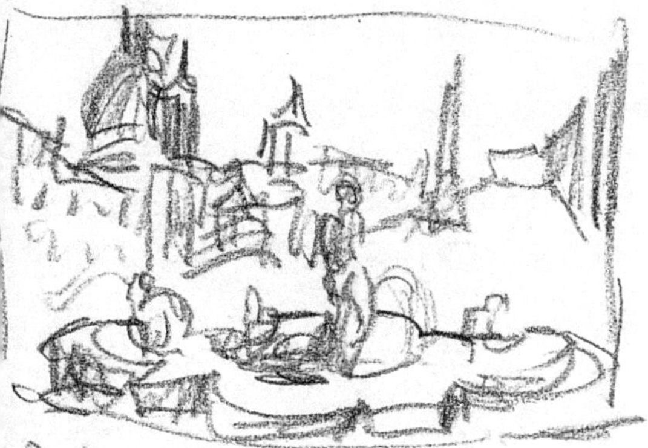

Piazza Navona

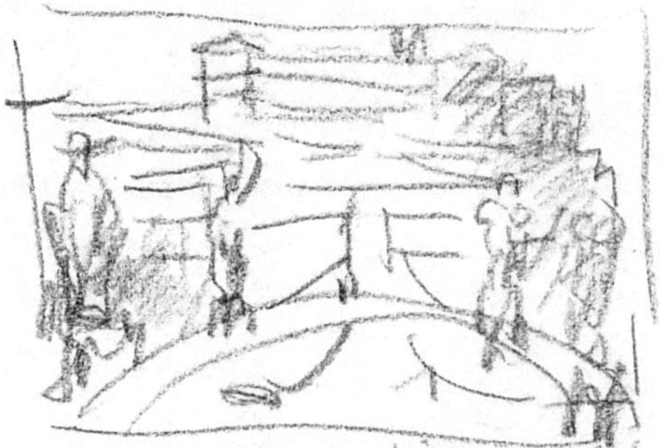

Villa d'este

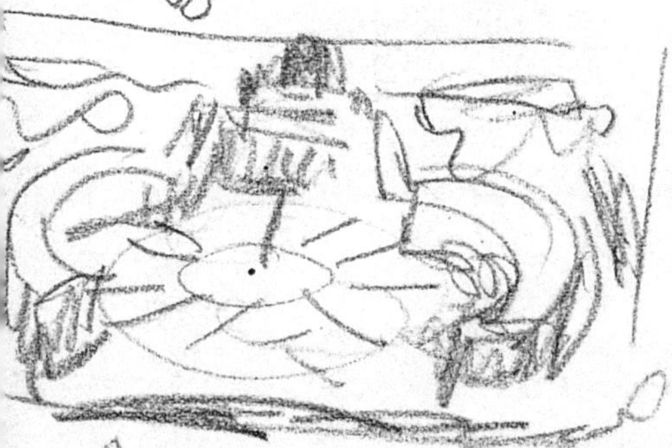

Basilica Vaticana, La vue de dessus.

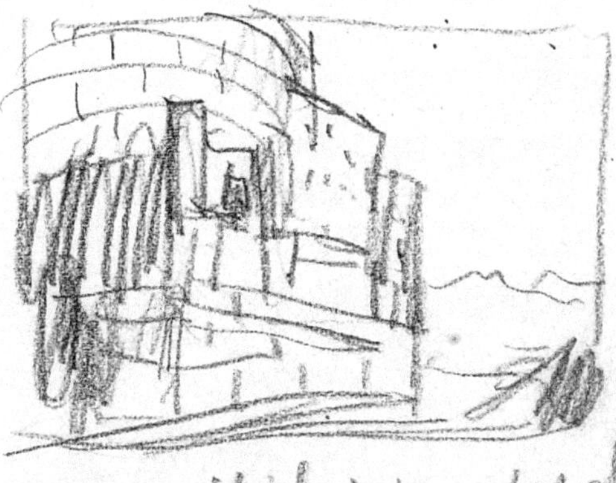

Veduti de sepolcro della famiglia Plauzia

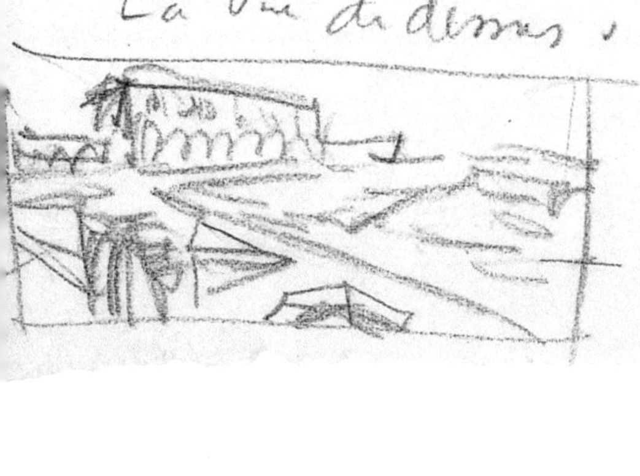

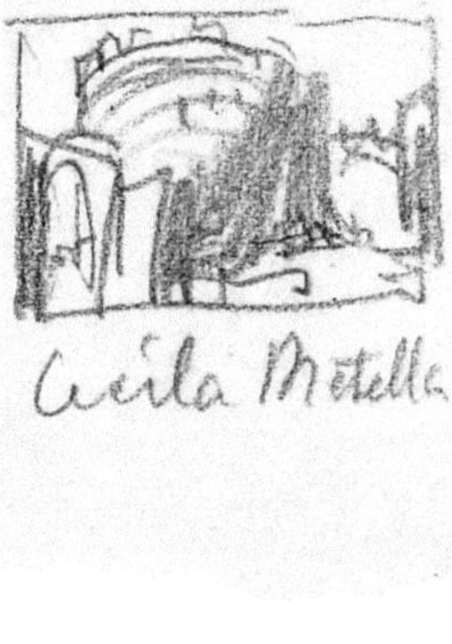

Cecila Metella

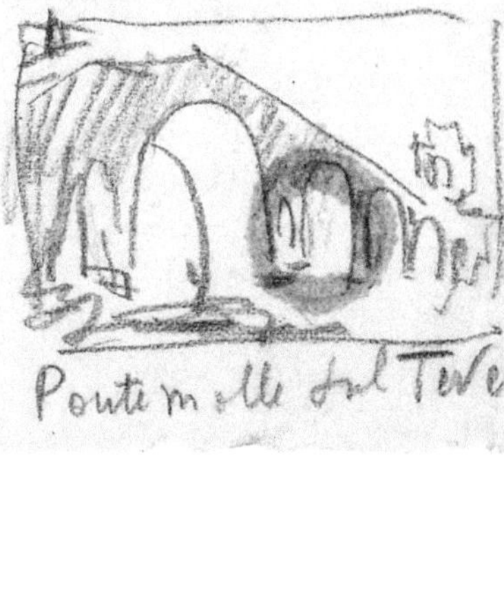

Ponte molle sul Tevere

Le Corbusier's ambivalence towards Piranesi is triggered by an ambivalence inherent in the graphic reproduction itself. Arguably, it was the virtuoso detailing in Piranesi's printed architecture—the "splendid profusion," as Henri Focillon put it—that made Le Corbusier aware of the stark forms "behind" it.[17] As much as he hails "geometric forms," the idea that such forms exist at all depends on the ornately engraved superficies that conveniently "cover" them. In this sense, modern architecture is born from the dichotomy between a veneer of ornament and the purity of forms. Indeed, if we were to pursue the point, prints as such—a veneer by constitution—triggered the idea of the "superficiality" of the historical styles, a view that came to pervade modernist ideas of the past.

Le Corbusier took up a clear position against the print historicism in architecture. But in the next round, as we shall see, the ambivalence Le Corbusier had shown towards Piranesi was exploited by those who were in turn ambivalent towards Le Corbusier. Piranesi's oeuvre—complicated, fantastical, contradictory—was to become a point of reference for architects and historians who sought an escape from a modernism that with time had become abstract and alienating. From the start of the modern movement, then, Piranesi embodied a counterforce which was no less modern, but which represented the unstable and unpredictable dimension of architecture.

BETWEEN THE BAROQUE AND THE INDUSTRIAL

In the historiography of modern architecture, Piranesi represented at first a vaguely discordant element, and one with little potential, it seemed, to explain the origin and development of modernist aesthetics. Nowhere did this become clearer than in the 1932 landmark MOMA exhibition *Modern Architecture* and in the catalogue Henry-Russell Hitchcock wrote together with Philip Johnson and Alfred H. Barr. The event marked a triumphant exposition of architectural modernism. In the catalogue's attempt to pin down principles of modern architecture, history as such turned into a suspect category, reeking of structural dishonesty and aesthetic collapse. The tone was jubilant when Johnson, for example, said that with Frank Lloyd Wright "all ties with the past were finally broken."[18] Yet the history of modern architecture, or more precisely the history of that history, constantly renegotiates questions of origin and developments. Panayotis Tournikiotis reminds us how the modern movement constantly opens up the field for a "number of equally possible discourses about the same actual events"—and indeed about the same houses, one might add.[19] If the historian's task is to look back and identify shifts of meaning, as Tournikiotis suggests, I will argue that Piranesi represents such a shift—or in fact several shifts. This chapter, therefore, asks when and how Piranesi went from being a marginal figure in the history of architectural modernism to become a force that actually structured that history.

It was the American historian Vincent Scully who introduced Piranesi as a catalyst in the development of modern architecture. In the article "Modern Architecture: Toward a Redefinition of Style" (1957) and the subsequent *Modern Architecture: The Architecture of Democracy* (1961) Piranesi offered a corrective to the origin that historians had proposed for modern architecture up to then. Like Yourcenar's "The Dark Brain of Piranesi" or Gombrich's *Art and Illusion*—both published around the same time—Scully's text launched a dynamic, disorderly, ambiguous Piranesi; in his case, the Venetian constituted the origin he needed in order to reread and redirect the path of the modern movement.

To extricate Piranesi from the past and reinvent his art as proto-modern, Scully had to confront the position Piranesi held among his predecessors. In the 1957 article he refers to two founding fathers of the discipline—the American Henry-Russell Hitchcock, Scully's supervisor at Yale, and the Swiss-born Sigfried Giedion, who had arrived in the United States in 1938. What united these two scholars in Scully's mind was their erroneous account of the genesis and development of modernism. Disregarding for a moment everything that actually separates Hitchcock's and Giedion's visions of history, Scully recreated them as a common foe and entered the fray with his own alternative origin story of modern architecture, a beginning for which he recruited Piranesi as guarantor.

Although Hitchcock and Giedion agreed in principle, they presented modernism's *longue durée* in slightly different terms. The Venetian proved a useful figure for both in different ways, although never as a propagator of a countermodernism, which was how Scully revived him. In fact, the Piranesi that makes an appearance in Hitchcock's *Modern Architecture: Romanticism and Reintegration* (1929) is very much the literary recreation of Piranesi cultivated by Romantic authors. To Hitchcock, Piranesi represents a tradition that modern architecture reacts *against,* rather than a force that shapes it. Although Hitchcock placed the origin of modern architecture in the eighteenth and nineteenth centuries, it was not Piranesi's prints that he had in mind, but an architecture of industry and engineering that experimented with materials and construction methods, which he termed "The New Tradition." Piranesi, by contrast, he classed as "baroque"—as an exponent of an anti-classicist impulse that prevailed alongside the growth of industrial architecture, lasting well into the nineteenth century before eventually dying out.[20] Propagating a baroque Piranesi, Hitchcock ultimately revealed himself to be an heir to the Swiss art historian Heinrich Wölfflin and a nineteenth-century Swiss German tradition: in the influential *Renaissance und Barock* (1888), Wölfflin mentions Piranesi once, precisely as an exponent of the baroque.[21]

In *Modern Architecture*, Hitchcock also explicitly recognized as Piranesian the "cult of the 'sublime' expressed through the colossal in architecture."[22] The sublime, as noted in the prelude, is associated with late-eighteenth-century aesthetics and the art of Romantic poets and painters. This questions what architectural value—if any—Hitchcock found in Piranesi's prints. The "sublime" and the "colossal" are terms that lack the architectural precision otherwise permeating Hitchcock's discourse; they depend instead on a tradition reaching back to De Quincey. Hitchcock in fact admitted that the "energies" in the Romantic period were predominantly literary and subjugated even the art of building to their powers. In short, Hitchcock transferred a nineteenth-century poetic vision of Piranesi to the history of modern architecture, the effect being that Piranesi emerged as neither "modern" nor truly "architectural."

Scully also rejected Giedion's account of the genesis of modern forms in *Space, Time and Architecture* (1941), which was based on a 1938–1939 lecture series held at Harvard University.[23] Giedion's error, in his view, was to make a geographically anchored connection between the baroque and modernism; buildings by Francesco Borromini, Guarino Guarini, and Balthasar Neumann manifested "a new power to mold space" that turned the late baroque into a proto-modernism—and Borromini, for example, into a seventeenth-century Le Corbusier.[24] But placing the origins of modern architecture in the European baroque severely limited the transatlantic share in the development of the modern. Always focused on what was happening on American soil, Scully found a more fitting origin for that development in universal and transactional Piranesi prints.

The reader of *Space, Time and Architecture* soon realizes that Giedion sees modern architecture developing along two trajectories, stemming not only from a history of mass and volume emerging from the baroque, but also from a history of engineering constructions originating in the late eighteenth and nineteenth centuries. Among the constructions in the latter category were metal frame buildings such as warehouses, factories, and railroad stations. According to Giedion, these structures had evolved largely hidden from view, curbed by a nineteenth-century eclectic architecture. That is to say, beyond, or beneath, the "masquerade of styles," Giedion recognized a deeper realm in which engineering works pressed forward, playing the part of "architecture's subconsciousness."[25] The metal constructions and their dizzying spaces assumed the quality of a

Galerie des Machines, Paris, designed by Ferdinand Dutert, 1889.

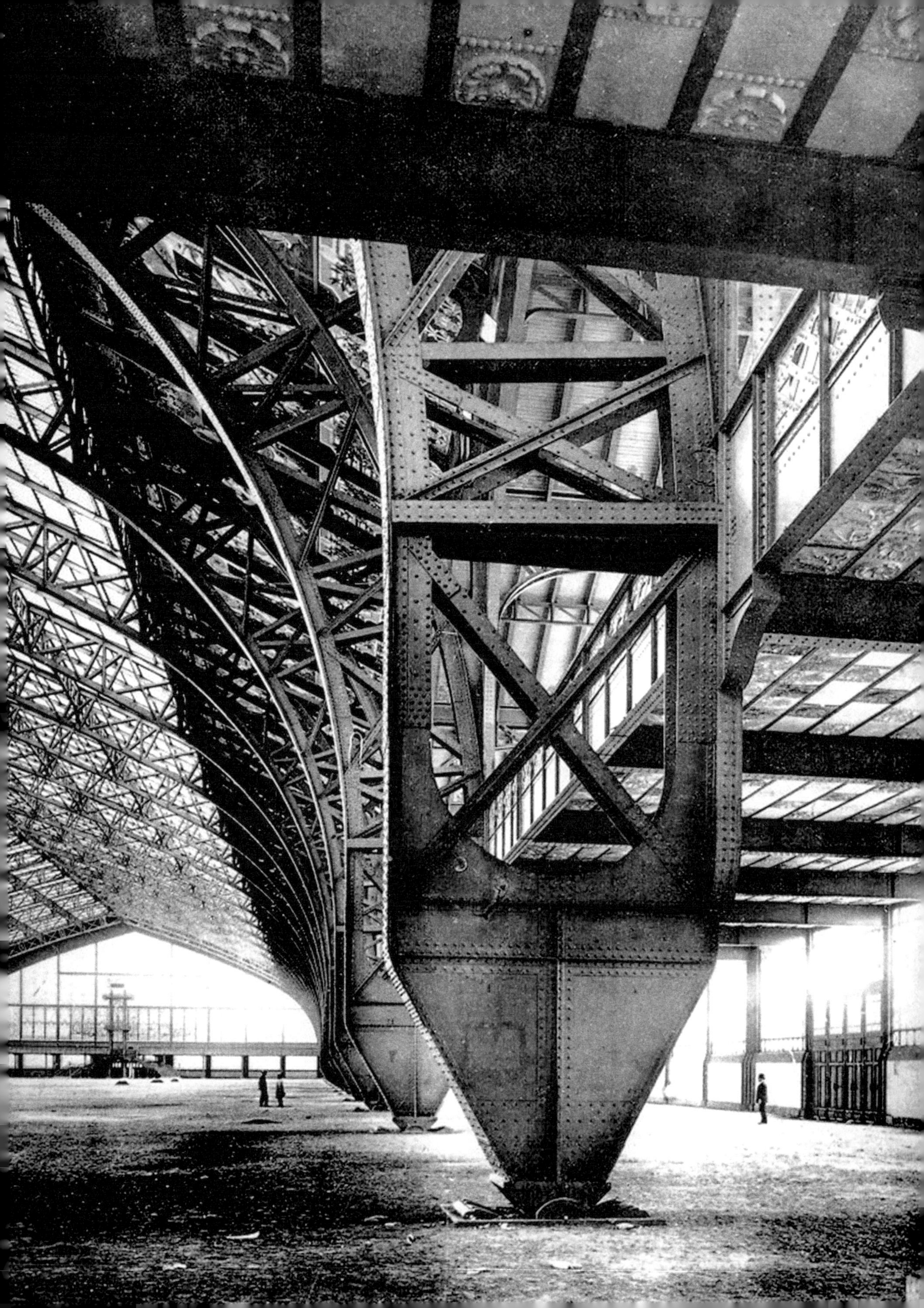

partly suppressed "interiority" developing in the shadows of the historical styles and awaiting integration in everyday building practice and their final, triumphant designation as "modern."[26]

One might think that a common point of origin for Giedion's trajectories towards modern architecture could be found in the dual legacy of the *Carceri* series, as both images of mental depths *and* engineering fantasia. However, Giedion never discussed these prints; the *Carceri*'s twisted notions of space, time, *and* architecture probably signaled nothing more than a false start in the history of modern architecture. In fact, when Giedion looked to Piranesi, it was not for his artistic merits at all, but because the etchings illustrated sites in and around Rome. Only their documentary value mattered, which is why the Piranesi prints illustrating Giedion's books are mostly taken from *Vedute di Roma*. Only Piranesi's view of Piazza del Popolo made it to the pages of *Space, Time and Architecture*, though the Swiss historian failed to name the artist in the caption—an exceptional slip in an otherwise meticulously edited first edition.[27]

To conclude, in the discourse on the origin of modern architecture, the baroque, the modern, and Piranesi were entangled in patterns that overlapped, but in slightly different constellations: Hitchcock connected Piranesi and the baroque but excluded both from the modern project, whereas Giedion connected the baroque and the modern but excluded Piranesi. The solution Scully opted for was the one that remained: he connected the modern and Piranesi but excluded the baroque.

ARCHITECTURE OF MOVEMENT AND EXPANSE

In *The International Style: Architecture Since 1922*, Hitchcock and Johnson claimed that eclecticism in architecture had finally been abolished, replaced by one style, the International Style.[28] The victorious modern movement had prevailed with its supremacy of volume over mass, its regularity, and its abolishing of décor: "This contemporary style, which exists throughout the world, is unified and inclusive, not fragmentary and contradictory," the authors insisted.[29] Hitchcock's student, Vincent Scully, turned that relation upside down. It was precisely in the fragmentary and the contradictory that he saw the tenets of an alternative development towards the modern, and he placed its beginnings with Piranesi.

But Scully was not solely responsible for this reorientation, and again MOMA played a pivotal role in the launching of a modern Piranesi. The reintroduction of the Venetian etcher as bold and forward-looking, not only in painting but also in architecture, was the feat of Arthur Drexler, director of the department of architecture and design. In 1960 Drexler curated the highly influential *Visionary Architecture*, which *The New York Times* hailed as possibly the most important architectural show at the museum since *Modern Architecture* in 1932. In the early 1960s the exhibition toured the world, from Oslo to Tokyo, and left its mark on a global audience of architects and critics. On display were reproductions of three fantastical designs by Piranesi: the ideal harbor, the *Parte di ampio magnifico porto* (1750) (*see following*), a plan of a magnificent college, which I will return to in the next chapter, and one of the *Carceri* prints. Drexler was captivated by Piranesi's "delightful, endless colonnades" and connected these designs to projects by Le Corbusier, Louis Kahn, Frank Lloyd Wright, Frederick Kiesler, Kisho Kurokawa, and many others. The history of unbuilt projects, Drexler claimed, was just as important as the history of built ones: "For the architect, ideal projects afford the sole occasions when he can rebuild the world as he knows it ought to be."[30] The exhibition was a gamechanger, as it turned its back on a strict functionalism in architecture and allowed for the imagined and unattainable. It is important in our context because it demonstrates that when Piranesi entered the history of modern architecture, it was as part of a broader restitution of "fantasy" as a valid category in architectural discourse and practice.

In 1961, the year after the exhibition, Scully (who knew Drexler well) published an extended passage—a meditation almost—on Piranesi. From being a marginal figure in discourses on modern architecture, he now became a reference that restructured the very history of it. In Scully's survey of the recent past, titled *Modern Architecture: The Architecture of Democracy*, Piranesi gave "a new key to comprehension," to quote Jacques Lucan.[31] The Venetian's compositions evinced the idea that modern architecture derived not so much from principles as from a "continuous movement."[32] The *Carceri* in particular caught Scully's imagination—not a specific print, but the associations of movement and expanse collectively evoked by the series. The *Carceri* offered nothing less than a starting point in the revised history of modern architecture.

With this in mind, Scully's first move is to sever the connection between the baroque and the modern that Giedion had insisted on. A comparison between the Spanish Steps in Rome (1721–1725) and Le Corbusier's High Court in Chandigarh, Punjab (1951–1956) serves this purpose. To Scully, the juxtaposition of the two complexes highlights the fundamental difference between the old and the new world, temporally and geographically. The Spanish Steps manifests a playful but ultimately controlled space, which "hardly makes Baroque architecture a kind of prototype of modern work, as some historians have attempted to do," Scully writes (with obvious reference to Giedion).[33] On the contrary, the

overleaf Giovanni Battista Piranesi, *Part of a Magnificent Harbor*, from *Opere varie di architettura, prospettive, grotteschi, antichità*, 1750.

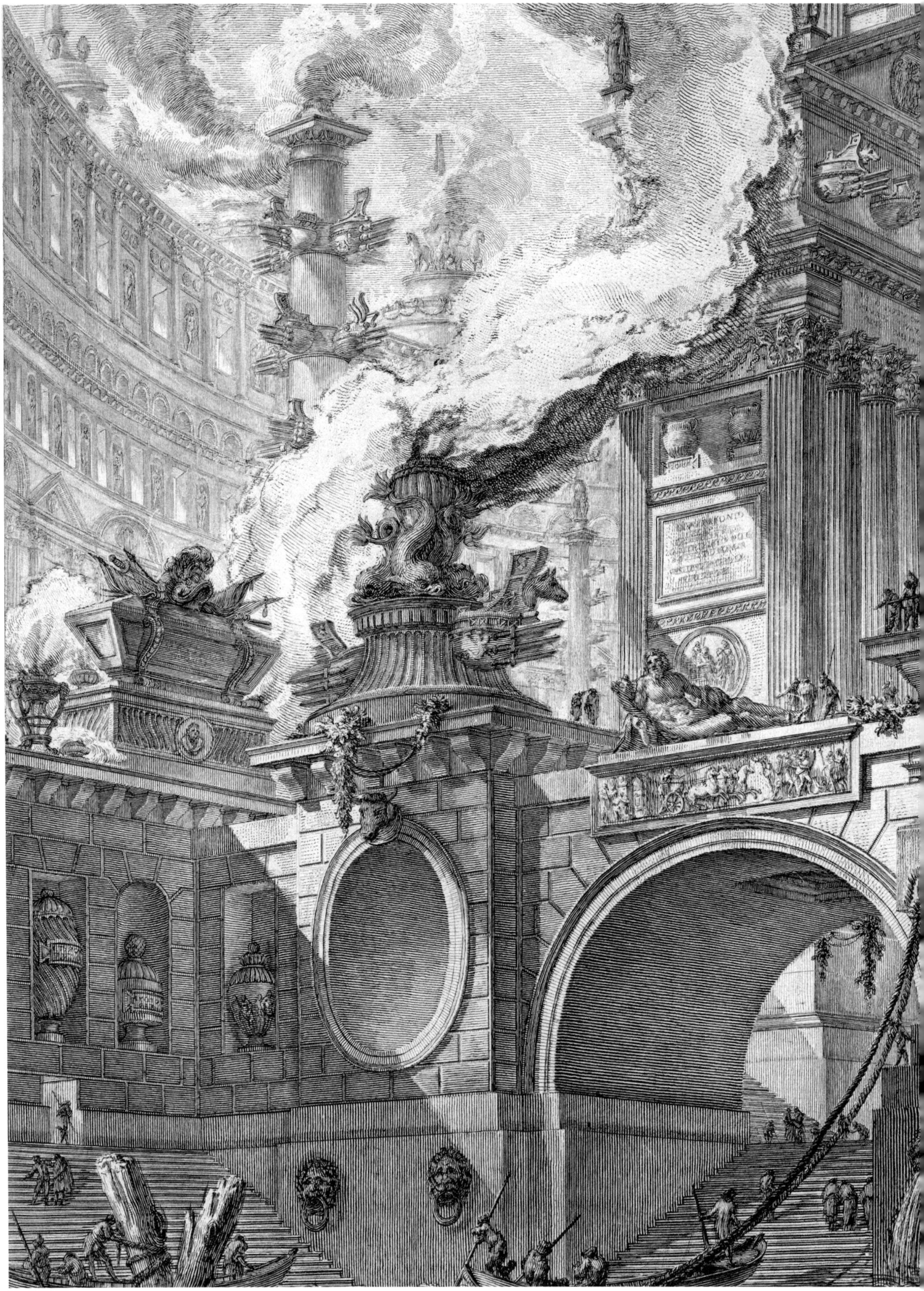

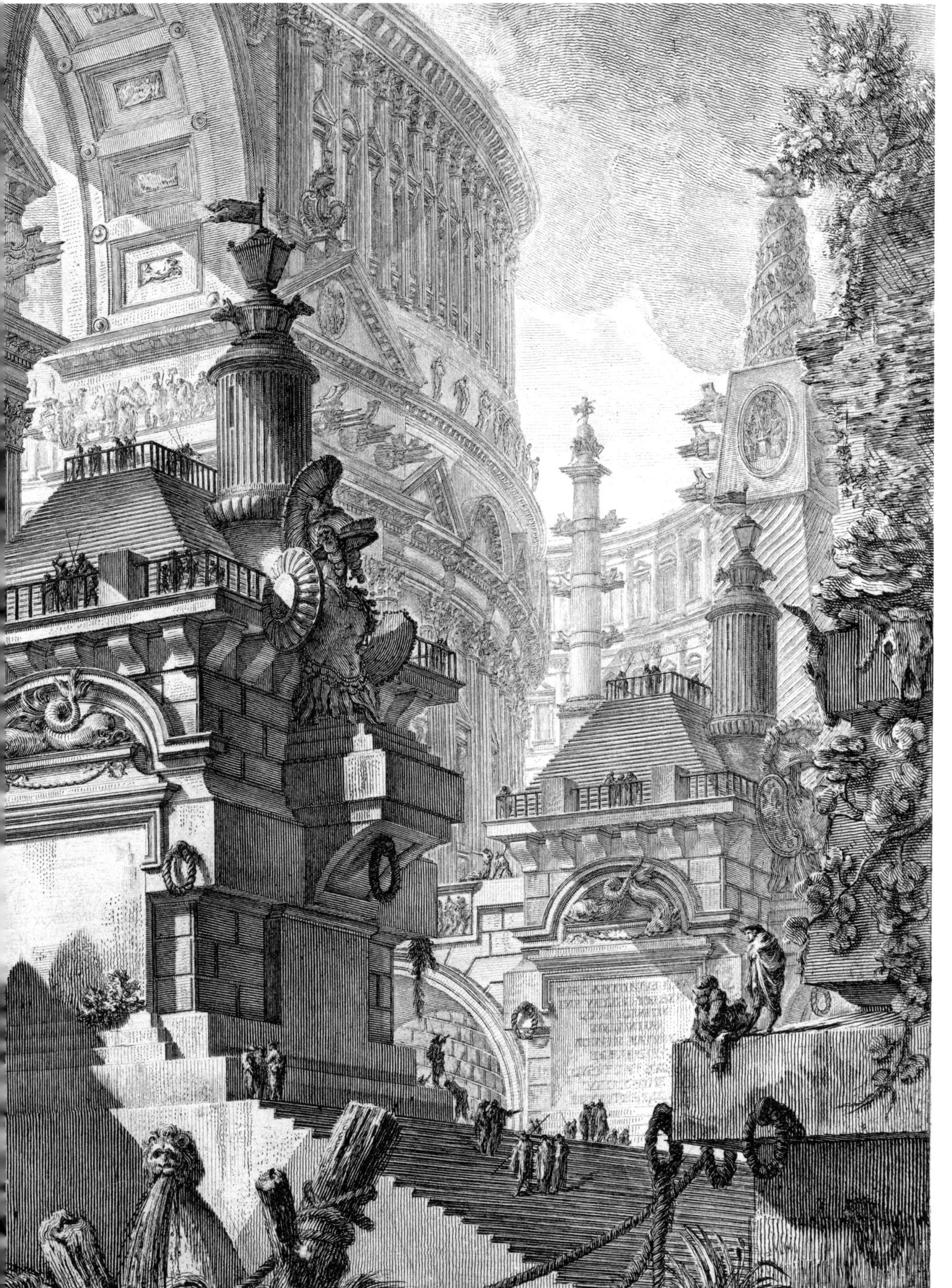

stairs represent a baroque that is essentially unmodern, "an architecture that is intended to enclose and shelter human beings in a psychic sense, to order them absolutely so that they can always find a known conclusion at the end of any journey." By contrast, Le Corbusier's High Court towers as a forbidding mass, "an isolated sculptural image" that provides no shelter but instead stages a confrontation between man and the hostility of his surroundings. Modern architecture, exemplified by Le Corbusier, manifests an almost dystopian quality, exposing humans to a void—a void, however, in which continuities may evolve unrestricted.

In a second move, having broken the bond between the baroque and the modern, Scully breaks the bond between Piranesi and the baroque. That is to say, he relocates the starting point of modern architecture, moving it from Giedion's Spanish Steps to Piranesi and the *Carceri* series. Instead of signaling the end of a bygone era (the baroque), Piranesi is now groomed to represent the beginning of a new one. Thus, Piranesi the Prophet, already a familiar figure in discourses on abstract art and cinema, re-enters the stage. The *Carceri* "prefigure" (Scully's term) the shattering of the baroque world and pave the way for Le Corbusier; they are "prophetic in their forms," Scully writes, using a soothsaying trope employed by modern pioneers from Barr to Eisenstein in an attempt to have Piranesi land on the contemporary side of history.

Cleansed of literary and baroque associations, the *Carceri* project an entirely new imagery in Scully's view:

> In them, the symmetry, hierarchy, climax, and emotional release of Baroque architectural space, like that of the Spanish Stairs, were cast aside in favor of the complicated spatial wandering, in which the objectives of the journey were not revealed and therefore could not be known. Men became small in a threatening environment of terrible masses, and that vertical element, the column, against which they had been accustomed to test their size and uprightness, now disappeared, while the arches swung in colliding orbits continuously from their chain-hung bases on the stairs. It is already the end of the old, humanist, man-centered world with its fixed values—and the beginning of the mass age of modern history, with its huge environments and rushing continuities.[34]

In Scully's narrative, the *Carceri* series returns as a nexus in the historiography of the modern age, on this occasion when its architecture is sorted. More specifically, Piranesi is the pivotal point in a history that shifted from the old ideal of creating spatial enclosures to a new one that pursued continuity and expanse.

Moreover, in Scully's history, and in contrast to Hitchcock's, the designs prevail as *architecture*, no longer hovering as mere poetic translocations but possessing mass and volume. For Scully, looking at the *Carceri*, the angst and disorientation induced by the images do not derive from their bottomless descent but quite concretely from a missing element—the column. The sense of alienation has its source in the architectural space the prints actually represent, not in the psychological space they symbolize. Dispensing with symmetry, hierarchy, and not least the classical column—the very yardstick of man's physiological relation to the world—the *Carceri* in Scully's interpretation usher us into the domain of late modernism.

The magnetic pull of the *Carceri* is an effect Scully cannot resist developing. Drawn into the compositions, wandering within their endless halls, the onlooker is on a journey whose objective "could not be known," in contrast to the "known conclusions" of the Spanish Steps and the baroque. The "unknown" in Piranesi therefore sanctions the element of the unplanned and the open-ended in architecture. The true potential lies beyond the frame of vision. Revolting against the position of Hitchcock and Giedion, a position he in reality forged, Scully shifts the origin of modern building from a baroque unity to a Piranesian complexity

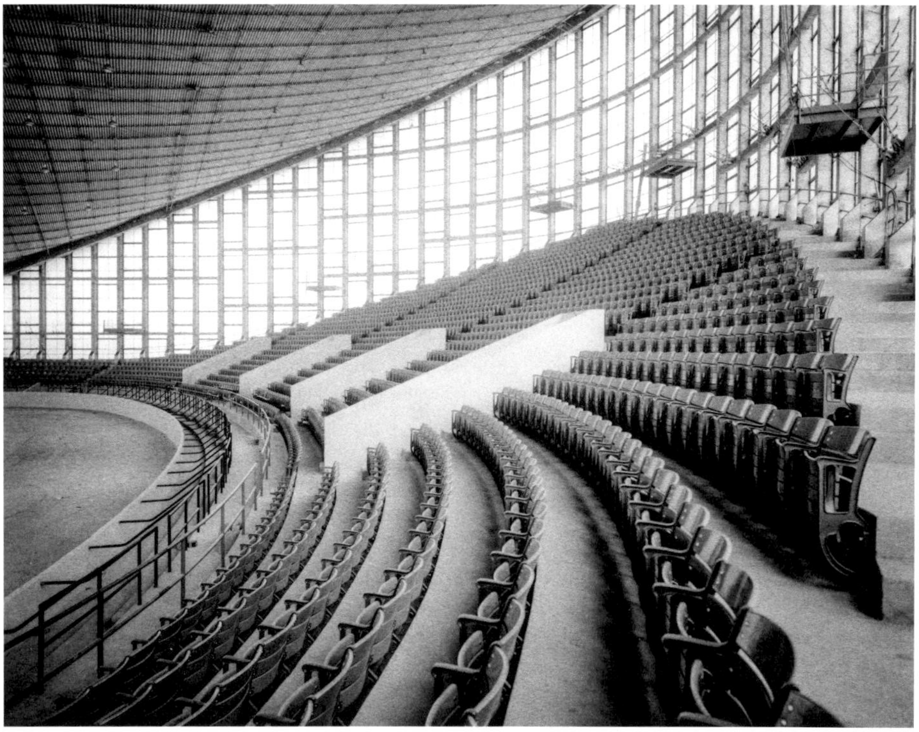

Dorton Arena (The Livestock Pavilion), Raleigh, North Carolina, designed by Matthew Nowicki and William Henley Dietrick, 1952–1953.

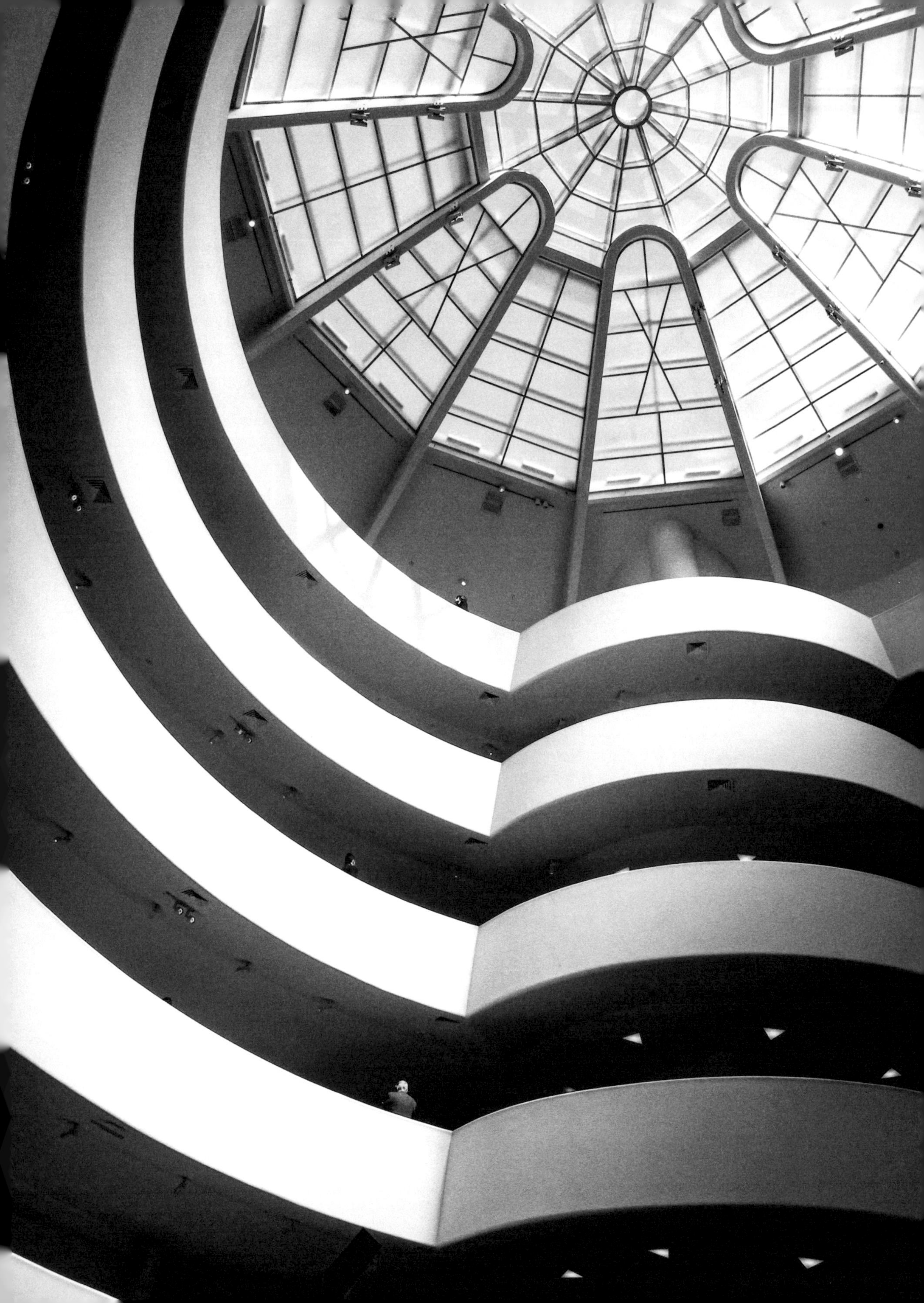

and openness. Resketching history from this beginning—all the time with reference to the *Carceri*—he gives modern, "impossible" constructions in metal and glass a historical and emotional resonance. As Scully writes, "it is the modern engineer—wholly released by his nineteenth-century materialism and positivism from the human tradition—who has, on his own terms, constructed Piranesi's world at its appropriate scale." On new Piranesian foundations, then, Scully presents a genealogy of buildings that literally springs from the arches of the *Carceri*. This history of Piranesi emulations includes Joseph Paxton's "endlessly continuous" Crystal Palace (1851); the Eiffel Tower and Ferdinand Dutert's Galerie des Machines (*see page 175*), both built for the world exhibition in Paris in 1889; as well as Max Berg's Centennial Hall in Breslau (1913). Scully then takes a leap to a recent example, the Livestock Pavilion in North Carolina (1953) with its roof of continuous, intersecting arches leaping out of vision "like Piranesi's arches themselves" (*see preceding*). These were buildings that Giedion too discussed and illustrated, but Scully uproots the whole series and realigns it with a development that starts with Piranesi.

In a bold act of translocation, Piranesi also becomes American, with compositions that in Scully's view manifest the endless expanse of the prairies more than the "controlled environment" of ancient European cities.[35] The continuous movement that the *Carceri* seem to engender corresponds to the American impulse to go west and follow the "Open Road," Scully writes with reference to Walt Whitman—a road "for which there is no goal but forward."[36] Continuous movement also coagulates as a design principle in buildings such as Henry Hobson Richardson's Ames Gate Lodge, with its "great arched swings, like the arches of Piranesi."[37] In this way, the drama of continuity in architecture becomes an American drama enacted through Scully's Piranesian reading of buildings by Louis Sullivan, Mies van der Rohe, and Frank Lloyd Wright. He ends the trajectory with the "time-defeating spiral" of Wright's Guggenheim Museum in New York—the same spiral that the almost blind Borges descended "full of anxiety," fearing it was going to end in empty space.[38] In Scully's tale, everything comes together with this building, which is the final monument, he writes, to the mobility and mass movement enshrined in American democratic mythology.

The Guggenheim Museum rounds off the important first chapter in a revised architectural history that spins out of a deeper story, spiraling from the spaces of the *Carceri*. The Guggenheim "brings the spatially continuous phase of modern architecture, inherent since Piranesi, to its only possible denoument and, probably, its close."[39]

Interior of Guggenheim Museum, New York, designed by Frank Lloyd Wright, 1959.

In the historiography of modern architecture, reformulated in the 1960s, and here exemplified by Drexler and Scully, Piranesi staked out an alternative course that embraced contradictions, impossibilities, yearnings, and fears.

In the same period Robert Venturi and Manfredo Tafuri, although in many respects taking up different positions, expanded on the ambiguity and heterogeneity of Piranesi's structures. Neither was convinced that contemporary architecture, or the history that led to it, accorded with the narratives of modernism cultivated by Hitchcock, Johnson, and Giedion. Venturi's *Complexity and Contradiction in Architecture* (1966), which Drexler published and to which Scully wrote an introduction, hunted for discordances in buildings and challenged the uncompromising, monolithic vision of modernist discourse on architecture. Mixing into the discourse numerous examples from history, the book suggested new, surprising genealogies for recent buildings.

The notion of a Piranesian Le Corbusier—paradoxical as it may seem—must be the surest sign of hardcore modernism in decline. Extraordinarily, Venturi described Le Corbusier's Villa Savoye and Piranesi's *Ancient Baths* (ca. 1750) with the exact same words. These two buildings, so different in time, place, and function, find a point of convergence in Venturi's identically phrased

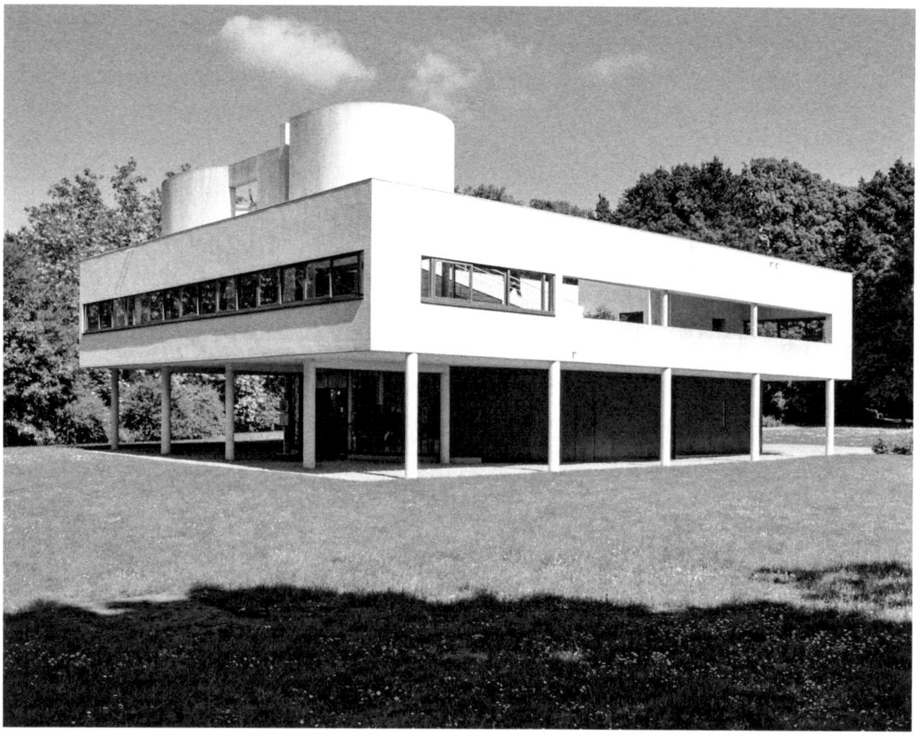

Villa Savoye, Poissy, France, designed by Le Corbusier, 1928.

characterization; both manifest a "crowded intricacy within a rigid frame."[40] How the two structures concretely correspond to this description is something Venturi never gets around to explaining. But if we try to adopt his perspective, we could say they are both obviously top-heavy constructions: Le Corbusier's weighty first floor, impossibly resting on matchstick pilotis, can be seen to correspond to Piranesi's Doric columns, which support a surrealistic load of arches and vaults in willful defiance of classical ideals. The "rigid frame" of architecture contains an "intricacy" that matches Venturi's idea of contradiction. Or at least one could see it that way.

In summation, Venturi's startling comparison reinforced Scully's view of a development in which Piranesi and Le Corbusier combine. Fifty years after the young Le Corbusier studied Piranesi at the Bibliothèque Nationale, the genesis of modern architecture had been redefined. In the revised histories of Scully and Venturi, Le Corbusier's projects ironically found an origin in the prints of Piranesi. The iconic Swiss modernist, if he did not spin in his grave, is bound to have flinched. The "horrible, ugly, and idiotic" in Piranesi's art, which Le Corbusier thought only obscured the essentials of modern architecture, had now become part of the modern itself.

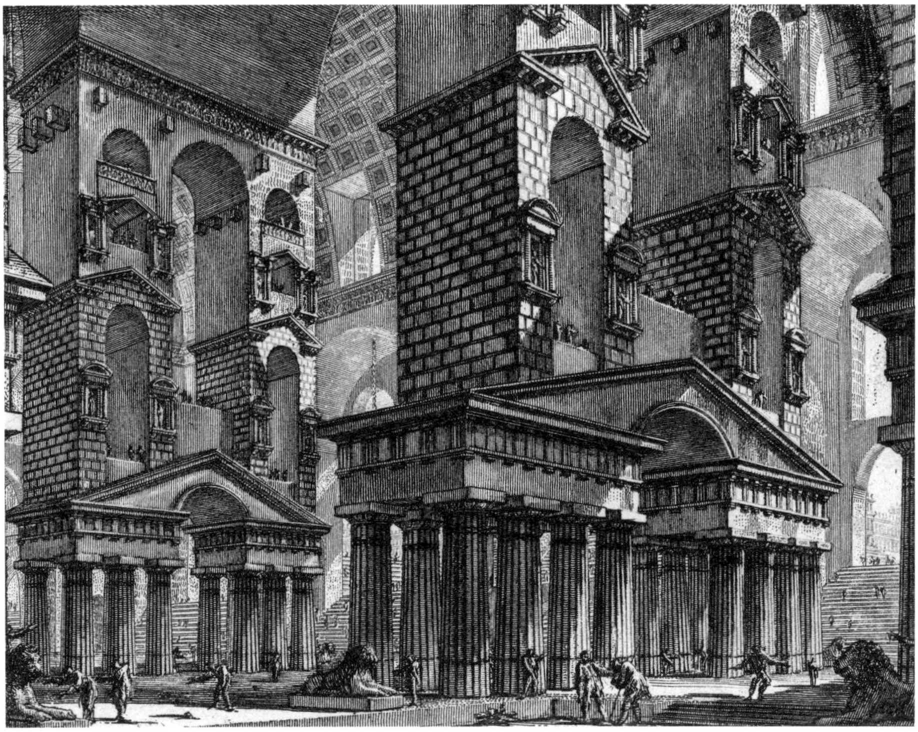

Giovanni Battista Piranesi, *Ancient Baths with Stairs* from *Opere varie di architettura, prospettive, grotteschi, antichità*, 1750.

CAMPO MA

RZIO AS METHOD

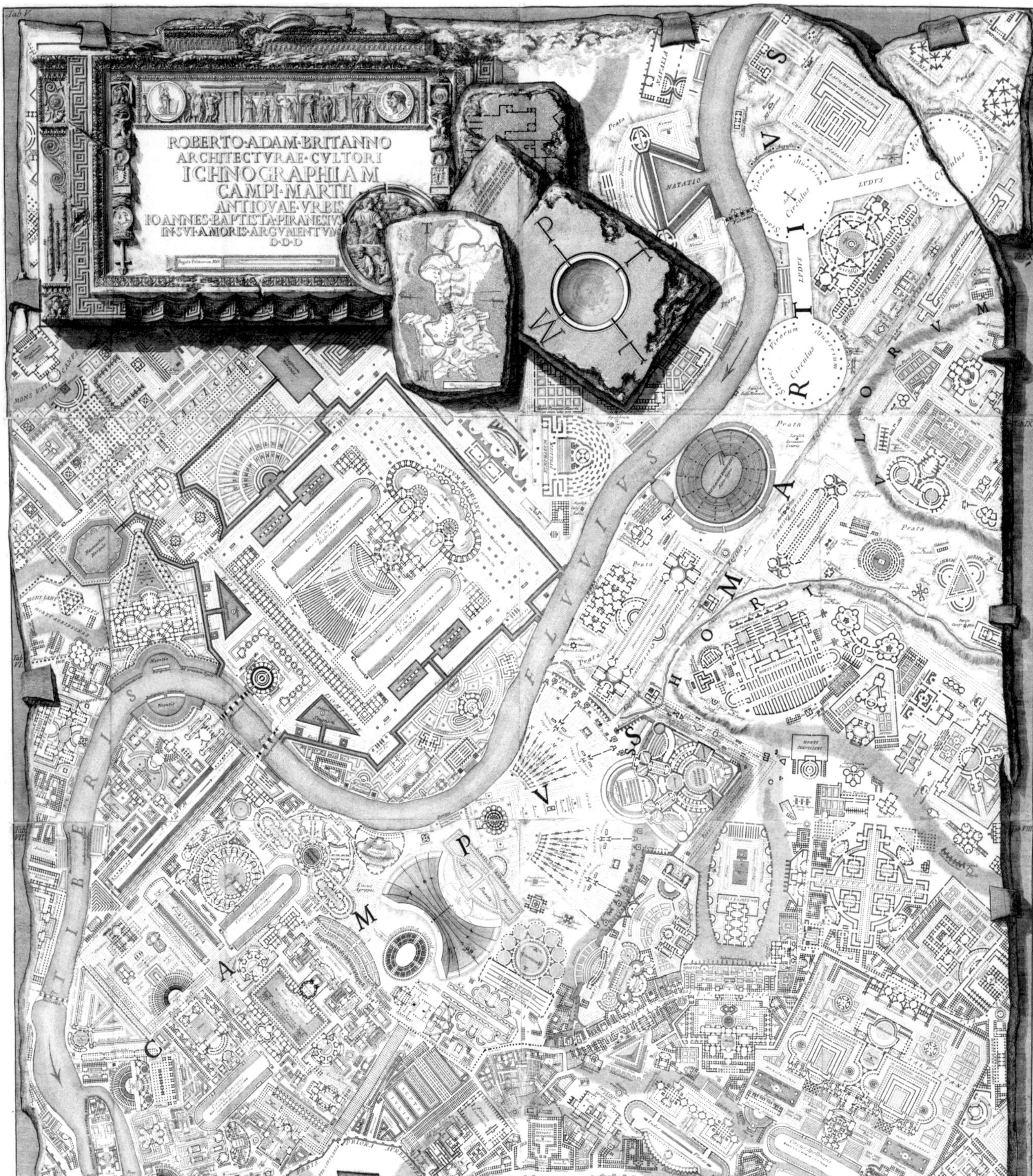

Giovanni Battista Piranesi, plan of the *Campo Marzio* from *Il Campo Marzio dell'antica Roma*, 1762.

The *Ichnographia* from Piranesi's *Il Campo Marzio dell'antica Roma* (1762) is a partly etched and partly engraved map, 1.35m by 1.17m, that shows the area of the Campo Marzio in imperial times.[1] Although incised, the plan is presented not as an engraving but as a stone slab artfully pinned to the wall by iron clamps in emulation of the famous marble plan of Rome, whose remaining fragments were first uncovered in the sixteenth century. Piranesi would have us believe that he is representing an object already incised, and bearing the authority of an antique piece. However, there are few points of connection between the structures shown in the plan and the archaeological record in the corresponding parts of Rome. In Piranesi's take, buildings, complexes, quarters are progressively swept up in a geometric reordering that seems to threaten to overrun the scattered evidence, but in fact only exploits the lacunae in archaeological knowledge and rarely infringes on documented elements. Piranesi understands only too well that appearances as they might have been are more compelling than those that obviously never were.

It is difficult not to view the plan through the eyes of architects and writers who have studied it in the course of the last decades and whose observations are the true subject of this chapter. The question haunting the modern age is not the extent to which Piranesi's hallucinatory reconstruction of the ancient city is accurate, but whether Rome at all was his true subject. The patterns of interlinked geometric modules could equally be an analogy of a city, a claim for the autonomy of architecture. Although the plan contains known landmarks, such as the Pantheon and the Mausoleum of Augustus, other structures exceed the boundaries of time and place; not only did those vast compounds never exist, but they hardly *could* exist, in the way they pushed the reality of architecture to the limits. On the one hand, then, the vision reflects the knowledge Piranesi had of ancient Rome based on an investigation of Roman texts and ruins, as Joseph Connors has discussed.[2] On the other hand, there is reason to take Piranesi at his word when he writes that the plan differs from the rules of the ancients and is "actually closer to the usage of our own times."[3] In this sense, Piranesi used antiquity to convey ideas about his own period in a similar way to those who have used Piranesi to invoke ideas about the modern age.

Existing in an unresolved state between a geometrically generated design and an archaeological reconstruction, the plan has come to question the meaning of the past, the site, and indeed architecture. But the value attributed precisely to this ambiguity is a recent thing. The *Campo Marzio*'s extravagant take on Rome did not appeal to early twentieth-century Piranesi scholars at all. Writers from Sturgis and Samuel to Focillon and Hind failed to take an interest in Piranesi's urban vision, neither reproducing the plan nor mentioning it. It was only from the

1960s onwards that the influence of the *Campo Marzio* on architectural discourse and practices began to grow, coming to rival, and in part supplant, the *Carceri* in fame and significance. A precondition for the plan's change of fortune, I argue, was the idea that an intricate historical design might simply be a veneer covering the essential forms and volumes of architecture, as Le Corbusier had demonstrated in his analysis of Ligorio's *Anteiquae urbis imago* from 1561. Thus, "behind" the map's elaborately contrived past other qualities lay hidden, such as a potential present.

A famous plate in Rudolf Wittkower's *Architectural Principles in the Age of Humanism* (1949) reduced a number of Palladio villas in the Veneto area to simple geometric forms. In "Il Campomarzio di G. B. Piranesi" (1956), Vincenzo Fasolo adopted a similar perspective on the *Campo Marzio* plan, believing he had "uncovered" the skeletal grid on which the ornate designs were based. Mirroring Le Corbusier, Fasolo identified and extracted the simple shapes he thought nestled within Piranesi's reconstructions. The removal of idiosyncratic excesses unveiled a stark contemporaneity that seemed not only to extricate Piranesi the modernist from a historicist guise but to release the *Campo Marzio* design from the domain of (failed) archaeology. "It seems legitimate to consider this *Campo Marzio* as a work of architecture in which the personality of Piranesi the architect configures," Fasolo observed with a simple statement that in fact signaled a complete reorientation.[4] In this new

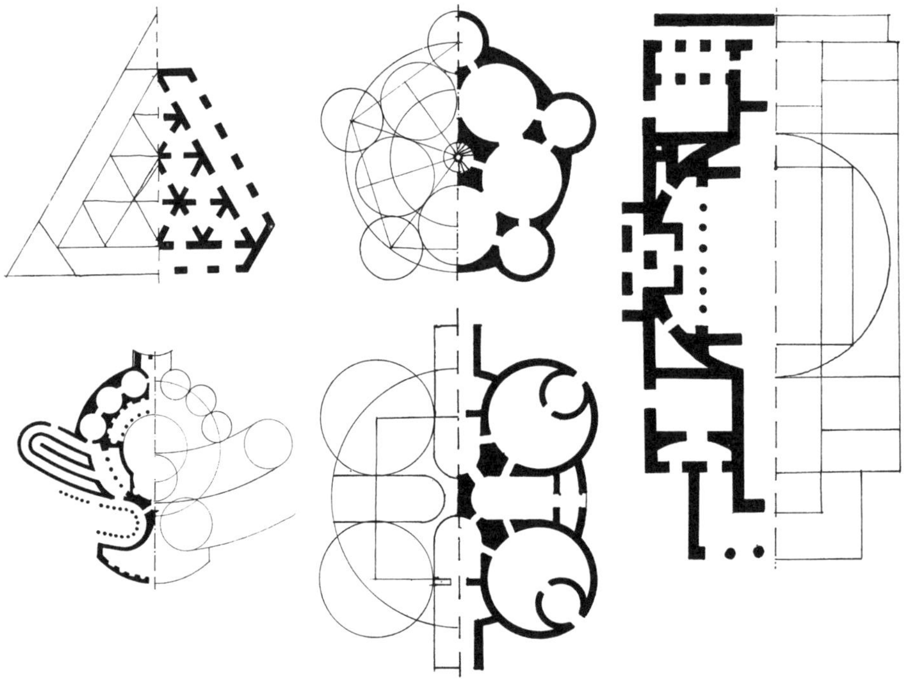

Vincenzo Fasolo, diagram of forms (figure 24) in "Il Campomarzio di G. B. Piranesi," 1956.

and apparently rational light, documented structures such as the Pantheon and the Theater of Marcellus were mere topographical references "in a seemingly limitless web of planning forms," as John Wilton-Ely wrote in recognition of Fasolo's contribution.[5] More than simply a failed reconstruction, the *Campo Marzio* plan became a sign of boundless creativity, rationalizing the world in a geometric order on a par with Enlightenment ideals. Piranesi, a Rembrandt of Architecture to the scholarly community at the beginning of the twentieth century, now emerged at its end as a Newton of Archaeology, re-envisioning Rome itself on mathematical principles.

This chapter investigates the importance of Piranesi's *Campo Marzio* in recent decades, tracing the course architects staked out in a terrain literally mapped by Piranesi. In a history we may think we know well, the focus on the *Campo Marzio* plan will, I hope, bring to light fresh insights and new connections. Based on interviews, catalogue texts, and drawings, among other material, the chapter aims to uncover a transition from copying the design to "excavating" the principles that seemed to underlie it. In the context of 1970s architectural discourse, this shift reflects the widening rift between postmodernism, on the one hand, and a conceptually oriented architecture on the other. The revival of the *Campo Marzio* plan not only illustrates this divide, I argue, but in part also caused it. Whereas postmodernism, in brief terms, signaled a return to history, the conceptual or formalist

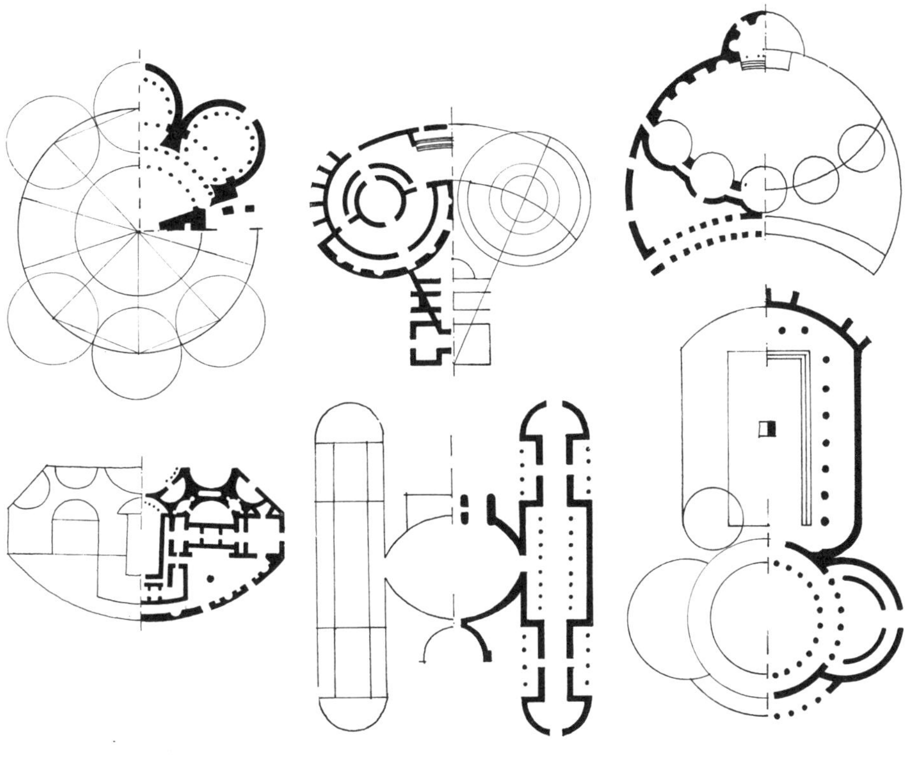

tendency more elusively aspired towards freeing architecture from any context whatsoever. It would be wrong, however, to think that conceptual architects rejected history, for the rejection of history was an idea that also had its past, an idea propagated in particular by Manfredo Tafuri and evinced in Piranesi's *Campo Marzio.* In this perspective, the plan became modern as it changed from being a quarry of historical monuments to become a manual in the very undoing of historicism in building.

POSTMODERN PIRANESI?

In his 1962 monograph on Louis Kahn, Vincent Scully mentions in passing that an impression of Piranesi's *Campo Marzio* plan hung in front of Kahn's desk in his office in Philadelphia.[6] In a photograph of the office taken around the same time, Kahn's 1961 redevelopment scheme for Market Street East in Philadelphia appears to be pinned across that precise impression (*see opposite*).[7] The superimposition is telling. The drawing on top of the print, and a new city on top of an ancient one, summarizes not only Kahn's reliance on the map but also the layers of history that late modern architects had come to acknowledge and to which they themselves self-consciously wished to add.

In 1985, another impression of the Piranesi plan up for sale in a New York shop caught the eye of architect Peter Eisenman. Not being able to afford it at the time, Eisenman made down payments for five years until he was finally able to collect it, but then kept it rolled up under his office desk for another five, embarrassed about how much it had cost. The *Campo Marzio* plan now hangs on the wall of the architect's bedroom: "When I get up in the morning, when I put my clothes on, I look at the Piranesi."[8]

The *Campo Marzio* held both Kahn and Eisenman spellbound, but did so for very different reasons, eliciting different interpretations and, indeed, different solutions in the thinking and practice of architecture. On a deeper level, the battle over the *Campo Marzio* outlined in this chapter reflects a disagreement over the direction architecture should take in the wake of modernism. The diverging opinions on Kahn's practice is a case in point. Kahn himself admitted that Piranesi was an inspiration and Vincent Scully, who knew Kahn well, was able to add that the latter "bought every book by Piranesi that he could find [...] He looked at the pictures, like most architects, and he loved Piranesi, who was really the inventor of what Kahn was doing." Referring to Kahn's National Assembly in Dhaka (1962–1983) Scully revealed that every one of the shapes in the intricate plan derived from the "fantastical reconstruction of the Campus Martius in Rome" (*see following*).[9]

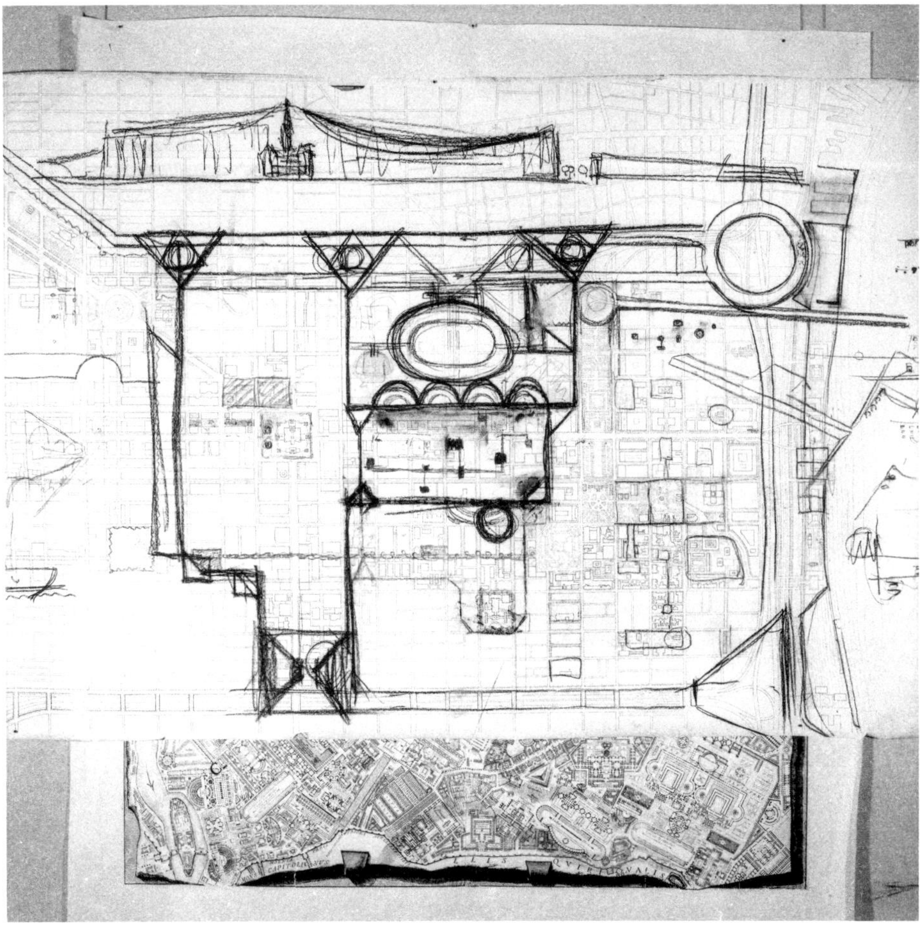

It was precisely this selecting of motifs, as if antiquity were a picture book, that Manfredo Tafuri rejected, accusing Kahn of an approach where "history is only an *ingredient* to be manipulated."[10] To Tafuri, the *Campo Marzio* plan prevailed not as a catalogue of buildings but as a critique of the value of building anything at all. Its radical reinvention of ancient Rome announced a discontinuity with the past, rather than a continuity, according to Tafuri—illustrating that history is above all the historian's own construction. Ultimately, the controversy over what Piranesi "was doing," to say it with Scully, went so deep that it gave rise not only to diverging opinions but to diverging ideologies.

This chapter asks why Piranesi's great plan posed a problem for postmodernists and, conversely, a solution for architects and theorists who looked for a new formal basis in contemporary architecture. The break away from a historical reading of the map to a conceptual one is highlighted by two events that took place in 1978,

Photograph of Louis Kahn's project for Market Street East, Philadelphia, pinned across Piranesi's plan of the *Campo Marzio*, 1961.

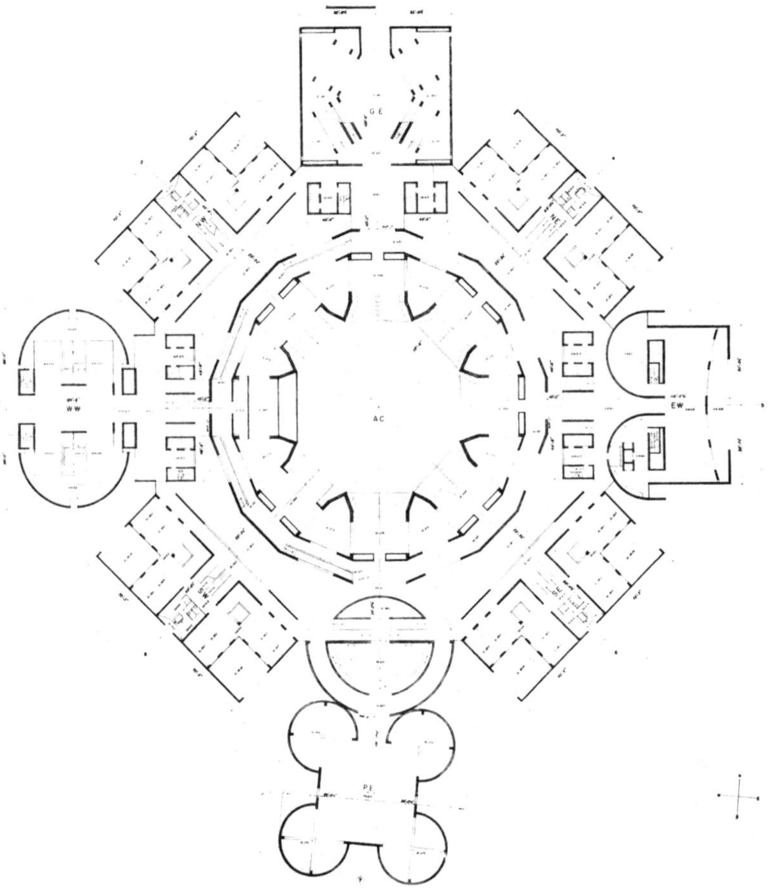

namely the exhibition *Roma interrotta* in Rome and the seminar and exhibition *Progetti per l'area di Cannaregio ovest* (in the following abbreviated to *10 progetti*) in Venice. While these are crucial events, which I will return to, the actual debut of the *Campo Marzio* in the contemporary discourse on architecture took place two years earlier, at the 1976 Venice Biennale. More specifically, fragments of it appeared at a special exhibition where American and European architects presented recent projects.[11] Aldo Rossi was among the European architects participating, and in collaboration with Eraldo Consolascio, Bruno Reichlin, and Fabio Reinhart, he contributed the *Città analoga* (Analogous City), a 2.5m by 2.5m collage composed of printed material that included plans and elevations from old maps and treatise illustrations as well as representations of modern architecture including Rossi's own (*see opposite*).[12] On one level, the *Città analoga* promoted plans and views of actual sites; on another, it displayed prints themselves as

Louis Kahn, drawing for the National Assembly Building of Bangladesh, Dhaka, 1962–1983.

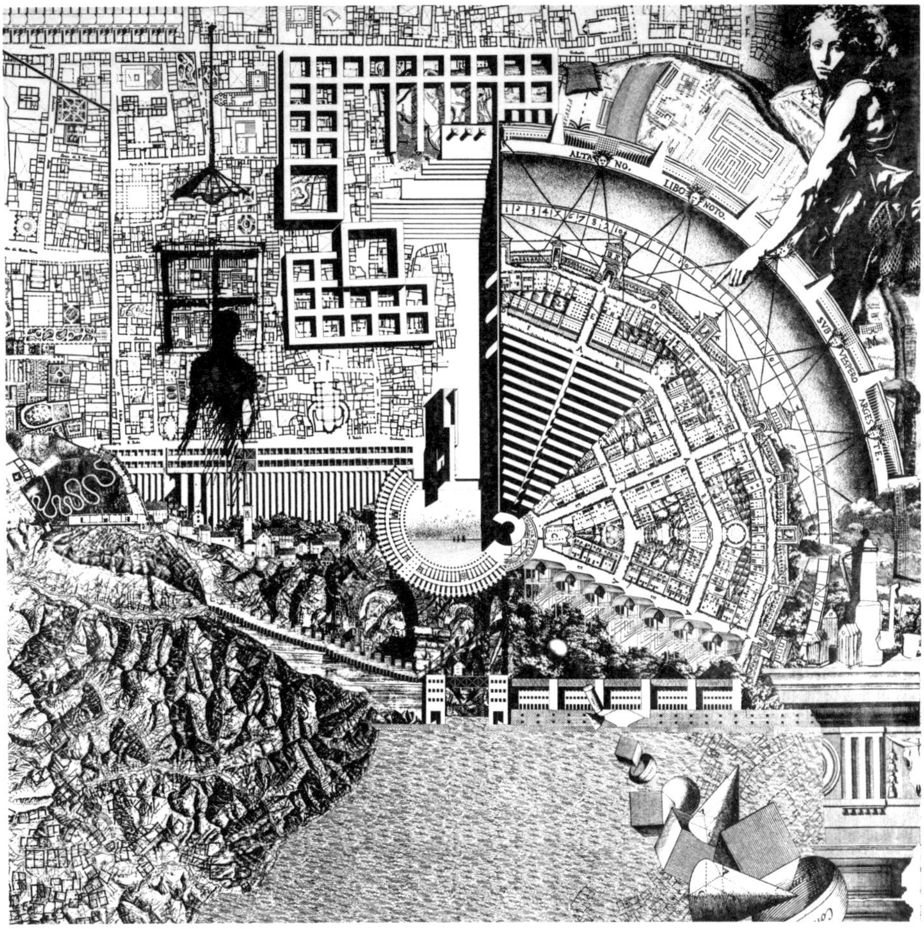

constituents of the ideal metropolis. Prints "become *part* of the city, not just a representation of it," as Peter Eisenman wrote of the work.[13] Incorporated into this collage was a fragment from Piranesi's *Campo Marzio*, along with a fragment combining elements from *Carceri*'s plate III (*The Round Tower*) and plate V (*The Lion Bas-Reliefs*).[14] For the first time Piranesi's plan explicitly figured in and *as* a modern project, rather than as a background reference. Echoing Alfred H. Barr's inclusion of the *Carceri* in his 1936 display of modern art, Rossi—forty years later—integrated the *Campo Marzio* into a display of modern architecture. However, the inclusion of the plan was polemical. The printed fragments formed part of an argument that advanced collage as an urban ideal, and, in a larger context, urged architects to embrace historical types and images.[15] In reintroducing the past into the contemporary discourse, Rossi's *Città analoga* signaled a postmodern turn in architecture, hijacking Piranesi for the cause.

Aldo Rossi, *Città analoga*, 1976.

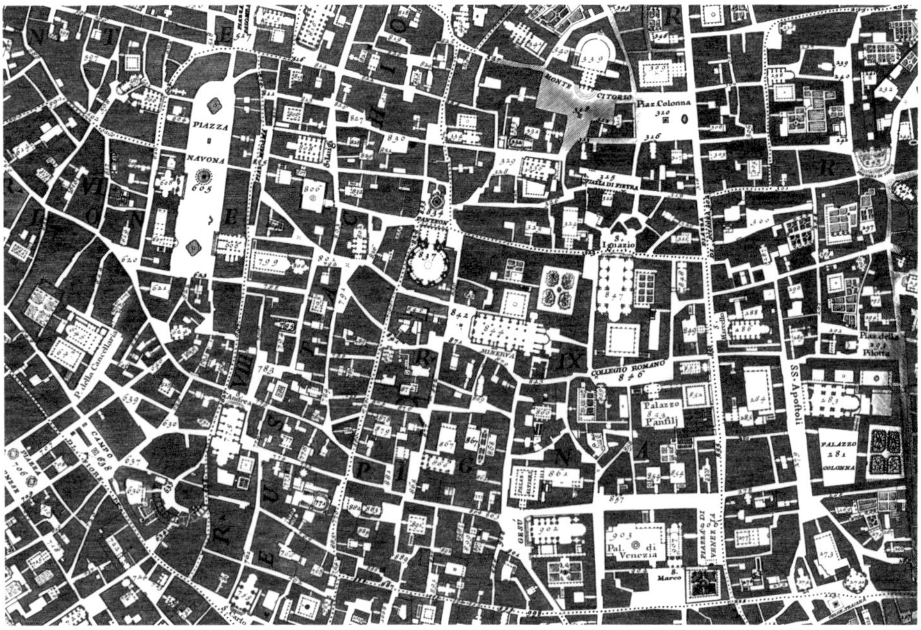

However, Piranesi's prints, and the *Campo Marzio* in particular, proved to be troublesome references. No event illustrates the mixed message of Piranesi's compositions better than the *Roma interrotta* (Rome Interrupted) exhibition organized by Incontri Internazionali d'Arte and the Italian architect Piero Sartogo and staged in the ruins of the Markets of Trajan in the spring and summer of 1978. As it happened, *Roma interrotta* coincided with the bicentenary of Piranesi's death, but the organizers ignored the *Campo Marzio* and focused instead on Giovanni Battista Nolli's *Nuova pianta di Roma* from 1748.[16] A cartographic milestone when it first appeared, Nolli's twelve-folio engraved map represented eighteenth-century Rome—its ruins, churches, palaces, and houses, enclosed by the city walls and surrounded by farmland—with an unprecedented precision. The figure–ground composition allowed the mass of the buildings to stand out darkly against the white background of streets and squares.

Roma interrotta invited twelve European and American architects to elaborate on individual sections of the Nolli map.[17] The result was an idiosyncratic collage of imaginary updates of the eighteenth-century city, "a series of gymnastic exercises for the imagination," as Giulio Carlo Argan wrote in the preface to the catalogue (*see opposite*).[18] Any playfulness apart, the exhibition never hid its objective of discrediting nineteenth- and twentieth-century urban developments—schemes labeled "crude and without substance" by Michael Graves in the special issue of *Architectural Design* devoted to the exhibition.[19] With *Roma interrotta*, the

Giovanni Battista Nolli, *La pianta grande di Roma*, 1748. Detail.

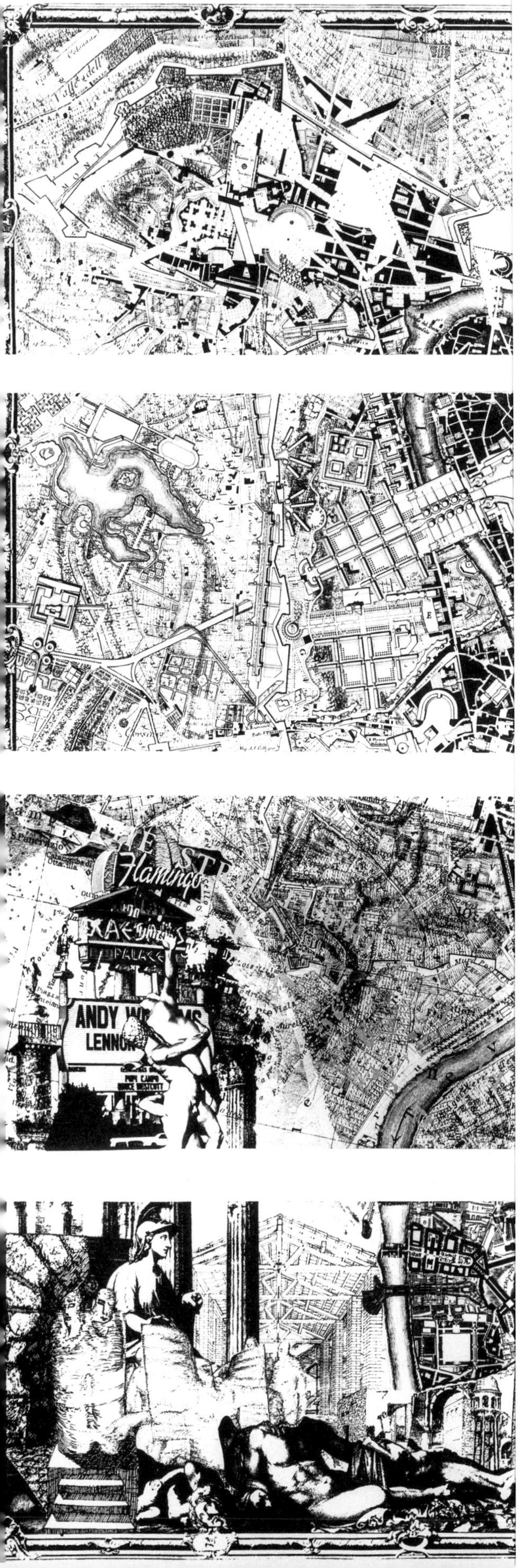

Twelve architects revisiting Nolli's plan of Rome for the exhibition *Roma interrotta*, Rome, 1978.

invited architects accepted the call to pick up where Nolli had left off, as if the intervening centuries never had occurred, presenting twelve variations of a counterfactual history of Rome. However, the exhibition also failed as a critique of the modern city as it became *too* contextual, as Maarten Delbeke points out, with projects that took no account of the reality of Rome as a capital.[20]

Campo Marzio was not on display, but its absence was as telling, and in its own way as influential, as if it had been an exhibit. The contrafactual city conceived by Piranesi was itself a comment on Rome and therefore a solution that in a sense competed with the contributions of the twelve invited architects. The absence of the *Campo Marzio* was necessary in the sense that it allowed the architect-draftsmen participating in the exhibition to act like Piranesi's double. In fact, some of them explicitly adopted Piranesi's role as a radical reinventor. The exactitude of Nolli's *Nuova pianta* prompted both James Stirling and Colin Rowe, for instance, to superimpose onto historical Rome architectures that had never been built, or had been built elsewhere, in a confounding of forms and temporalities reminiscent of the Venetian. The sector given to Stirling, for example, permitted him to arrange his own projects in the unbuilt *vigne* outside the city walls in the same way that the vast northern expanse of Rome had served as a tabula rasa for Piranesi's most extravagant solutions.[21] Distributing thirty buildings of his own design across the realm of a long-gone Rome, it was precisely Piranesi, and not Nolli, that Stirling compared himself to. Both were united by a certain

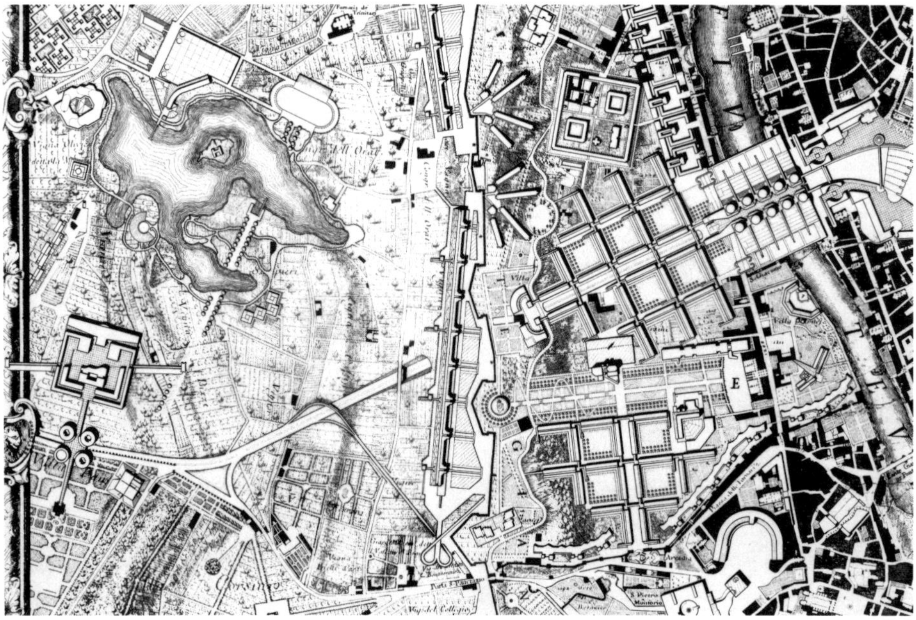

James Stirling, reworked section of Nolli's plan for *Roma interrotta*, 1978.

preposterousness, he wrote, and as his text to *Roma interrotta* declares with no small irony: "Megalomania is the privilege of a chosen few. Piranesi who made his plan in 1762 was surely a Megalomaniac Frustrated Architect (MFA) as also Boullée, Vanbrugh, Soane, Sant'Elia, Le Corbusier etc. and it is in this distinguished company as an MFA architect that we make our proposal."[22]

Special side shows gave the architects space to expand on their projects, which in some instances meant acting like modern-day Piranesis. The assignment for *Roma interrotta* inspired Leon Krier to envision clusters of multi-storied brick towers extending across town, far beyond the confines of his designated Nolli sector. These enormous structures constituted sheltered plazas, which Krier imagined would become "the future centers of urban life."[23] Nolli offered no support for such utopias, but Piranesi did. Leafing through the Venetian's oeuvre, Krier found compositions that he manipulated as foils for his visions. More precisely, at the far end of Piranesi's views of Piazza Navona and Via del Corso, published in *Vedute di Roma*, Krier inserted his own roofed plazas. Thus, Piranesi's *vedute* enabled him to create an impression of how these gigantic structures would look if Nolli's and Piranesi's Rome had been preserved intact up to the modern era.

References to the past as a means to disrupt, if not downright reverse, the progress of modernism is a postmodern strategy that links *Città analoga* and

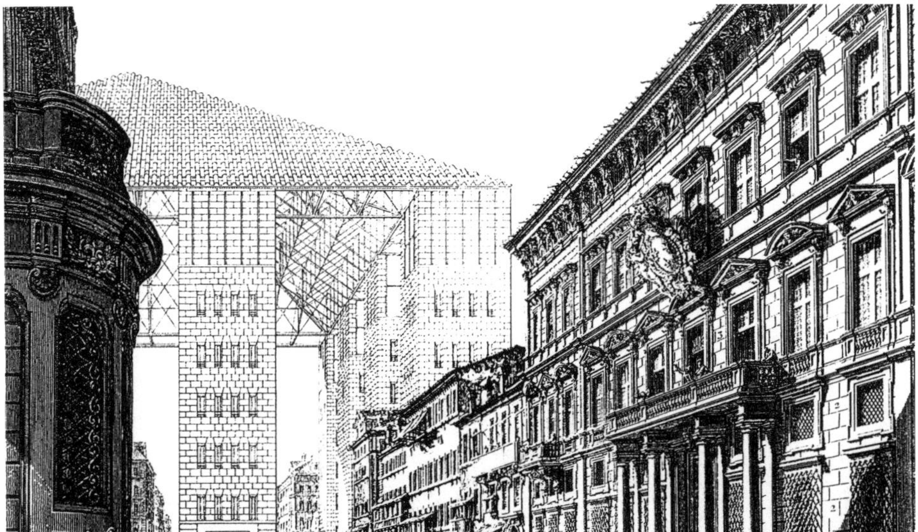

Leon Krier, interpretation of Piranesi's *Via del Corso* for *Roma interrotta*, 1978.

Roma interrotta and their rethinking of cities. The two installations, as Léa-Catherine Szacka points out, were landmark events that not only exhibited the postmodern but also contributed to the construction of postmodernism as such. Thus, the twelve architects' exercises for *Roma interrotta* "correspond to a shift towards a narrative of fragmented and plural subjectivities that is typical of postmodernity."[24] When Charles Jencks in the 1970s introduced "postmodernism" to describe a new turn in architecture, he was using an already established term.[25] With a measure of goodwill, the label "postmodern" could also be applied to a particular appropriation of Piranesi—the kind exemplified by Aldo Rossi, Leon Krier, and others—which involved extracting motifs from his prints and subsequently reinserting them adjacent to, or within, a contemporary setting.[26]

However, in the postmodern revival of historical material, Piranesi's *Campo Marzio* remained at best a substratum. It underscored *Città analoga* and *Roma interrotta* but never surfaced as an explicit point of reference in exhibitions and publications, as the Nolli map did. Neither Aldo Rossi's influential *Architecture of the City* (1966), nor Colin Rowe's and Fred Koetter's *Collage City* (1978), which otherwise promotes the value of the historical layers of cities—exemplified with old prints—so much as mentions the Venetian etcher. Piranesi, who could qualify as "postmodern" himself, given his own insistent recombination of motifs, clearly resisted simple re-use. In fact, and in spite of his rich and varied output, postmodern discourse and aesthetics conspicuously avoided him. The question is why.

Part of the explanation can be found in comments and reviews published in connection with *Roma interrotta*. When Charles Jencks described Leon Krier's manipulated Piranesi compositions for the exhibition, he used a telling choice of words: Krier's towering structures are "collaged into the Roman perspectives of Piranesi."[27] For Krier and for Jencks, the frisson lay in the temporal collision—the time jump—manifested by collages of this kind. But if the juxtaposition of elements from different periods was a point in itself, the suitability of Piranesi for such operations was questionable. Krier wrote that he would have actually preferred to insert his covered plazas into the "bright light" of Percier, Fontaine, and Letarouilly, who all excelled in graphically pure delineations. Piranesi, by contrast, came dangerously close to enmeshing the collage in a psychological and architectural mire. Piranesi would only do justice to the imagined plazas in a distant future, Krier wrote, when these plazas had themselves turned into ruins "linked by a multitude of dark timber bridges" like the ones seen in the *Carceri*.[28]

Obviously, and underlying Krier's ironic distance, Piranesi posed a problem because of the connotations of his images. It is as if Krier regressively shared the opinion of the early twentieth-century print collectors we encountered in chapter two, and perceived a Piranesi contaminated by the *Carceri*'s disquieting content and by the artist's alleged internal anguish. In short, the associations with psychological tension and spatial ambiguity detracted from the decorative function that a postmodern approach assigned to the compositions.

A similar complication arose with regard to the *Campo Marzio* plan. In postmodernism's history parade, the map's value as a record of the past was undermined by the discrepancy between the ancient city and the imaginative form that Piranesi gave to it. A "painful encounter" is how Costantino Dardi characterized the relation between the two in the catalogue to *Roma interrotta*. Michael Graves diagnosed the Piranesi problem more precisely in *Architectural Design*. Comparing Piranesi's *Campo Marzio* with Nolli's plan he concluded that "one is made aware of the extreme differences between these two positions: one is a composition of mutually adjusted set pieces, and the other involves the mutual modification of figure and ground, providing a comprehensible equity between figural object and figural space."[29] The characterization is significant for the 1970s diverging views on the *Campo Marzio* and the conception of it both as a problem and as a solution. Piranesi, in Graves's view, ignored the connection between buildings and geography, creating in effect a parallel Rome that elaborates on rather than represents the past. The plan could never offer a basis for the exhibition in the way Nolli's map could, because it was itself a creative take on Rome—an unnamed "thirteenth" project in the *Roma interrotta* collaboration. When Graves recognized "set pieces" in Piranesi's plans, he identified an architecture unhinged, as it were, from the ground, indeed from any relation to external parameters at all, and accountable only to the enclosed universe formed by the architectural elements themselves. In other words, the *Campo Marzio* offered a faux history that encroached on the postmodern project rather than providing it with the historical raw material it coveted. In contrast to Nolli's figure–ground composition, the *Campo Marzio*'s figure–figure drawing presents a city adrift, detached from topography and to a certain degree from history itself, short-circuiting, and thereby artfully negating, the continuity with the past that the postmodernist project cultivated. A plan in which geometry, not archaeology, generated the design, almost to the point of abstraction, resulted in what Tafuri called a "useless machine" overriding the evidence of topography and archaeology alike.[30] But the same elements that sabotaged the *Campo Marzio*'s validity as a historical document also made it the subject for a faction of architects and historians who by contrast approached the plan as pure form, as we shall see. In short, whereas the postmodernists looked to Piranesi for motifs, mostly in vain, others found certain principles, a method, at work in the *Campo Marzio*'s deeper layer.

TAFURI AND CONCEPTUAL *CAMPO MARZIO*

The transformation of the *Campo Marzio* into a tool to rethink architecture was very much the doing of the Italian architectural historian Manfredo Tafuri. Inspired by his compelling interpretation, architects who defined themselves in opposition to postmodernism looked at the plan with fresh eyes and "activated" it as a method of design. It was Tafuri who fathered the conceptual reading of the plan, with, I argue, lasting consequences for a new formalist turn in architecture.

Tafuri was a disruptive force in the architectural debate of the 1970s, also on the subject of Piranesi. It was in opposition to Tafuri that John Wilton-Ely invoked the rationality of the *Campo Marzio* at the 1978 bicentenary symposium of the Venetian's death. Calling attention to the "challenging interpretations" of the plan, he strongly objected to Tafuri's reading of it as "a veritable Megalopolis—an enormous architectural system turning against itself to produce a state of auto-destruction."[31] The battle over the *Campo Marzio* was in reality a battle over the idea of historical progress. On the one side were those who read into it a confirmation of the paradigm of Enlightenment, on the other, those who read into it the breakdown of that paradigm. To late modernists and postmodernists alike, Tafuri was clearly in the latter faction. "I despise him, and I despise even more what he writes," fumed Aldo van Eyck at the opening debate of the 1976 Venice Biennale, "he has no idea how disgusting is the influence he has."[32] To the postmodernists, Tafuri's interpretation of the *Campo Marzio* in a series of texts to be discussed below corrupted the value of the plan, or at least complicated its use. However, Tafuri's reinvention of Piranesi as an avant-gardist—deconstructive, boundless, political—gave the modern in its post-postmodern guise a recipe to rethink architectural form, urban expansion, and even social and existential freedom within the (megalo)polis.

The reading of the *Campo Marzio* that I call "conceptual" has an origin in two articles by Tafuri originally published in Italian as "Per una critica dell'ideologia architettonica" (1969) and "L'architettura come 'utopia negativa'" (1971). The passages on Piranesi in the first essay were later extended and included in *Progetto e utopia* (1973) (*Architecture and Utopia*), whereas the second essay was reworked to become the chapter, "The Wicked Architect: G. B. Piranesi, Heterotopia, and the Voyage," in *La sfera e il labirinto* (1980) (*The Sphere and the Labyrinth*).[33] Importantly, these texts, and not least Tafuri's revisions of them, testify to a thinking that itself matures or deepens over the course of a few years as Tafuri's attention shifts from the formal qualities of Piranesi's designs to their existential and political dimensions—a progression this discussion will attempt to retrace.

In an overall perspective, Piranesi became an ally in the critique Tafuri directed at his own discipline and its grand sweeping narratives, which did little more than create their own "architectures." With the notion of operative criticism, Tafuri aimed to purge the retelling of architectural history of its abstractness—of its framework precisely as *history*—and to restore to the historian's and architect's awareness the raw, indecipherable components that actually constitute the past.[34] If Vincent Scully recreated Piranesi as a point of origin in an alternative history of modern architecture, Tafuri, by contrast, placed Piranesi not *in* history but somewhat outside it, enlisting him as a witness to history's inadequacy to guarantee continuity at all. In *Teorie e storia dell'architettura* (1968) (*Theories and History of Architecture*) he states his case: the continuity that history represents is just that—a "representation." The reality of the past, by contrast, remains forever enigmatic, leaving posterity with fragments that are mute. As the architect is condemned to use these fragments, but unable to comprehend or reconstitute the order to which they once belonged, architecture remains gridlocked between a past that is beyond recovery and a future that cannot free itself from the past. Piranesi's honest response to that gridlock was to give it an expression, rather than trying to escape it or cover it up, and in this sense he also heralded a 1970s conceptual architecture. "He opens the doors to modern architecture and, at the same time, becomes its most merciless critic," Tafuri declared.[35] Piranesi would

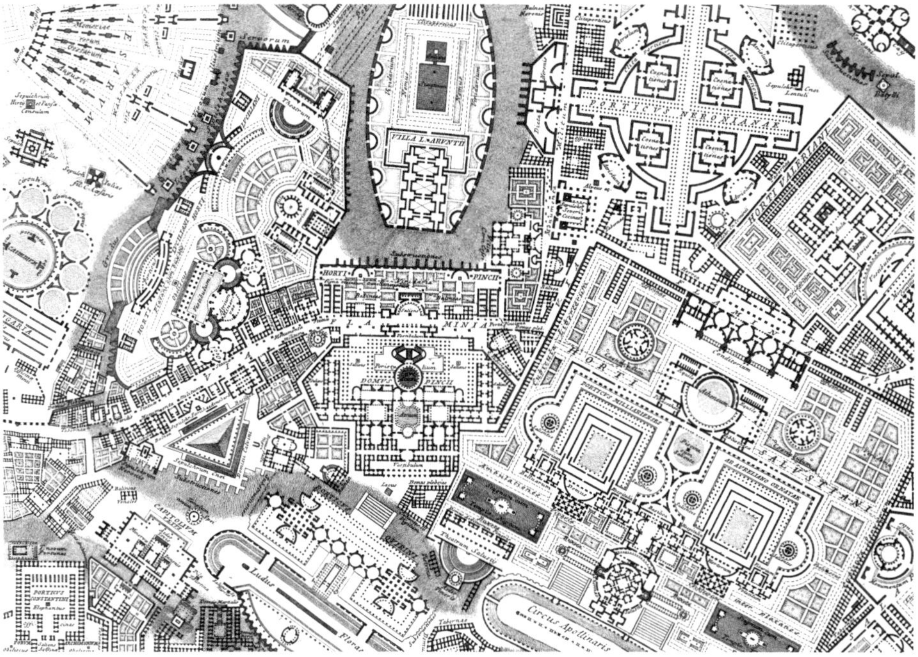

Giovanni Battista Piranesi, detail of the *Campo Marzio* plan, 1762.

become the "wicked architect," in the title Tafuri gave his 1971 essay when he reworked it as a chapter in *The Sphere and the Labyrinth*.

To Tafuri, antiquity was hardly a concern for Piranesi: "The archaeological mask of *Campo Marzio* fools no one. It is an experimental design and the city, therefore, remains an unknown," he wrote in *Architecture and Utopia*.[36] Tafuri was not the first to recognize the architectural value of the *Campo Marzio*. Vincenzo Fasolo, as we recall, considered the plan "a work of architecture" rather than an archaeological reconstruction.[37] Tafuri, however, went further and found in it a manual, a methodology, for an approach to architecture that could confront history without resorting to historicism. In the plan, "we witness an epic representation of the battle waged by architecture against itself," Tafuri claimed.[38] The self-generating pattern produced by the expanding geometric modules in Piranesi's plan departs from, but also transcends, the fragmented documentary evidence; it displays the wish for unity through the very elements that prevent it from achieving this (*see preceding*). The result is the city as a gigantic "useless machine."[39] In other words, the fragment and the whole, the past and the present, are never reconciled but are frozen at the very moment of their non-reconciliation. On this basis, Tafuri connected Piranesi to modern architectural practices, securing the plan's significance in a post-1968 discourse. Learning from Piranesi, the architect as critic needed to turn that unbearable tension into a principle of design. As Tafuri would claim in his essay on the group of architects known as the New York Five:

> Today, he who wishes to make architecture speak is thus forced to resort to materials devoid of all meaning; he is forced to reduce to degree zero every ideology, every dream of social function, every utopian residue. In his hands, the elements of the modern architectural tradition are all at once reduced to enigmatic fragments—to mute signals of a language whose code has been lost—shoved away haphazardly in the desert of history.[40]

To Tafuri, Piranesi demonstrated the effort required to create an autonomous architecture, to emancipate the *built* from the many narratives that encroach on it, and to display it in its raw form. "Piranesi's intent in *Campo Marzio* is to draw attention to the birth—necessary and terrifying—of an architecture bereft of the signified, split off from any symbolic system, from any 'value' other than architecture itself."[41]

The precision of Tafuri's critique increased when he set out to analyze the generic principle at work in the *Campo Marzio* plan. The "monstrous pullulation of form" that seemed to override the archaeological evidence also transcended the limits of architecture *per se*. Piranesi launched transgression as an aim in itself, an

Giovanni Battista Piranesi, *Plan of Magnificent College*,
from *Opere varie di architettura, prospettive, grotteschi, antichità*, 1750.

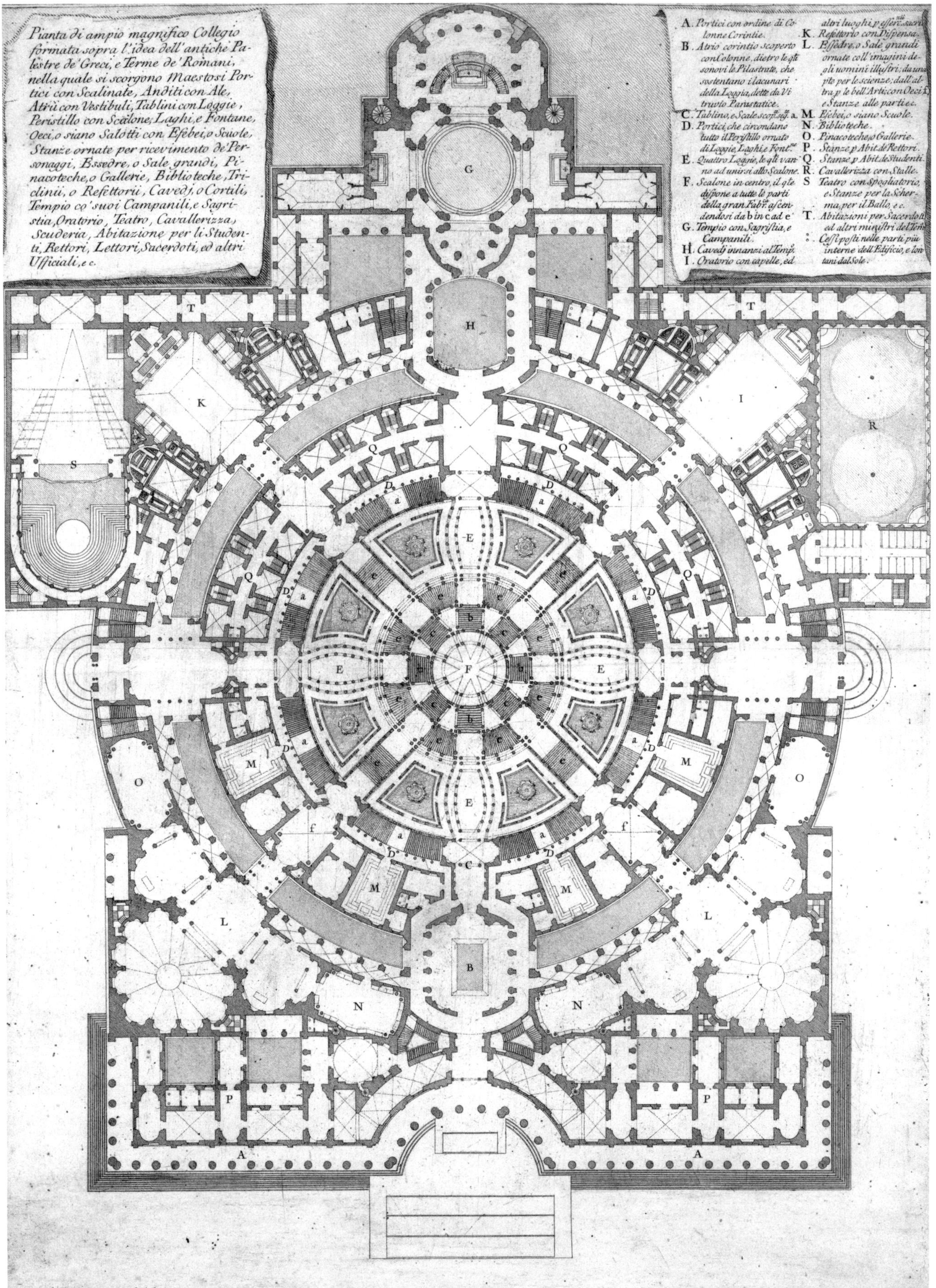
Pianta di ampio magnifico Collegio formata sopra l'idea dell'antiche Palestre de' Greci, e Terme de' Romani, nella quale si scorgono Maestosi Portici con Scalinate, Anditi con Ale, Atrii con Vestibuli, Tablini con Loggie, Peristillo con Scalone, Laghi, e Fontane, Oeci, o siano Salotti con Efebei, o Scuole, Stanze ornate per ricevimento de' Personaggi, Essedre, o Sale grandi, Pinacoteche, o Gallerie, Biblioteche, Triclinii, o Refettorii, Cavedj, o Cortili, Tempio co' suoi Campanili, e Sagristia, Oratorio, Teatro, Cavallerizza, Scuderia, Abitazione per li Studenti, Rettori, Lettori, Sacerdoti, ed altri Ufficiali, e c.
A. Portici con ordine di Colonne Corintie.
B. Atrio corintio scoperto con Colonne, dietro le qli sonovi le Pilastrate, che sostentano i lacunari della Loggia, dette da Vitruvio Parastatice.
C. Tablino, e Scale scop.te seg.te a.
D. Portici, che circondano tutto il Peristillo ornato di Loggie, Laghi, e Font.ne
E. Quattro Loggie, le qli vanno ad unirsi allo Scalone.
F. Scalone in centro, il qle dispone a tutte le parti della gran Fabr.ca ascendendosi da b in c ad e
G. Tempio con Sagristia, e Campanili.
H. Cavedj innanzi al Temp.o
I. Oratorio con capelle, ed altri luoghi p esserc.zii sacri
K. Refettorio con Dispensa.
L. Essedre, o Sale grandi ornate coll'imagini degli uomini illustri; da una pte per le scienze; dall'altra p le bell'Arti; con Oeci f, e Stanze alle parti e c.
M. Efebei, o siano Scuole.
N. Biblioteche.
O. Pinacoteche, o Gallerie.
P. Stanze p Abit. de Rettori.
Q. Stanze p Abit. de Studenti.
R. Cavallerizza con Stalle.
S Teatro con Spogliatorio, e Stanze per la Scherma, per il Ballo, e c.
T. Abitazioni per Sacerdoti, ed altri ministri del Tem.
⁘. Cessi posti nelle parti più interne dell'Edificio, e lontani dal Sole.
Giambattista Piranesi inventore Scolpì.

endless architectural mutation that in many ways responded to 1960s and 1970s radical thinking about urbanism. However, Tafuri's understanding of the plan gradually deepened, revealing an increasingly empathic reading that also drew on other parts of Piranesi's work—a deepening we can retrace by considering his passages on the *Campo Marzio* in the chronological order they appeared. At first, in the 1971 "L'architettura come 'utopia negativa,'" and with a focus purely on the formal aspects, it was Piranesi's dismantling of a *center* that caught his attention. The radiating plan in the *Pianta di ampio magnifico collegio* (1750) is "endlessly expandable" (*see preceding*). Likewise, "The independence of the parts and their montage obey no other law than that of pure *contiguity*."[42] Neither can the *Campo Marzio* have a true center, according to Tafuri. It is a "colossal piece of *bricolage*" that evolves with no real end in sight. The privileged point of view (or of governance, if we were to read it politically) evaporates alongside the institutions constructed around such points. "Piranesi's engravings [...] present to us not merely a set designer's whim, but rather a *systematic criticism of the concept of 'center*.'"[43]

The boundlessness Tafuri saw potentially unfold in the plan recalls the connection Scully made between Piranesi and the endless plains of America, but to Tafuri this endlessness did not imply freedom but ultimately the opposite—incarceration. The sense of confinement that only the boundless can induce is a subjective experience associated with Piranesi through a tradition going back to De Quincey. Turning his attention to the *Carceri*, Tafuri observed the same absence of center that characterized the *Campo Marzio* but coupled it specifically with the confinement indicated by their prison label. He noted that "In the *Carceri*, the constriction comes not from the absence of space, but from an opening toward the infinite," which led him to conclude that Piranesi's prison extended across space and time, constituting "a whole *universe*—which includes [...] the spectator himself."[44]

With no center and no boundaries, temporal or spatial, it seems that architecture for Tafuri is on the point of renouncing its corporeality and becoming a psychological unit—a metaphor, one could argue. In *Architecture and Utopia* from 1973, Tafuri made what I consider a significant addition to what otherwise is an adaptation of his 1969 essay, building on ideas he had developed in the text from 1971. In the added passage he looks inward, reflecting on the psychological impact of Piranesian infinity, writing that what we see in the *Carceri* is "the existential condition of human collectivity, liberated and condemned at the same time."[45] In other words, the infinite—the expression of ultimate freedom—closes in on modern man and becomes a source of oppression. Two years after Tafuri's observations, Michel Foucault published *Surveiller et punir: naissance de la prison* (1975) (*Discipline and Punish: The Birth of the Prison*) in the same 1970s spirit of institutional critique. In his history of the prison, Foucault compared Piranesi's *Carceri* to the eighteenth-century panopticon devised by Jeremy Bentham. The panopticon is built around a central surveillance platform from which isolated cells spread out radially, making the inmates "perfectly individualized and constantly visible."[46] In contrast to the "cruel, ingenious cage" of the panopticon, Piranesi's "ruined prisons, littered with mechanisms of torture" represent an *expanse*.[47] Although he did not stretch that expanse *ad infinitum* as Tafuri did, Foucault went on to draw the ultimate conclusion of the incarcerated "human existence." In modern history, he wrote, regimes of power have grown so extensive that society not only controls human beings, but produces them. The modern soul is born out of methods of punishment and constraint, and on that new reality our subjectivity—our inner self—is constructed; "the soul is the prison of the body."[48]

To put it differently, our own psyche is the contraption that keeps us chained, in Foucault's view. To speculate further, if the soul imprisons the body, that leaves our bodies somewhat innocent, as involuntary victims. One could argue, then, that the "soul" for Foucault and "history" for Tafuri are both ideological constructions contaminated by mechanisms of power, and, consequently, the body (Foucault) and the building (Tafuri) are corporealities that elude the grip of semiotics and exist outside the world of meaning. In any case, the comparison between the two suggests that the historiography of architecture entwined with institutional critique in a way that gave Piranesi a renewed relevance.

However, the "confinement" Tafuri pointed to in his reading of Piranesi was more explicitly political than Foucault's. In the 1960s and 1970s Tafuri was committed to the neo-Marxist movement in Italy. In his texts, the "liberation" of architecture always means the liberation of its forms from ideologies and thus from the typologies that serve these ideologies—church, palace, court, college. Buildings become protagonists in a universal class struggle. When Tafuri places Piranesi in the "pre-capitalist bourgeoisie" of the eighteenth century, it is very much as his own alter ego. Therefore, besides the proto-cubist and the proto-filmmaker, Tafuri's reinvention of the Venetian etcher

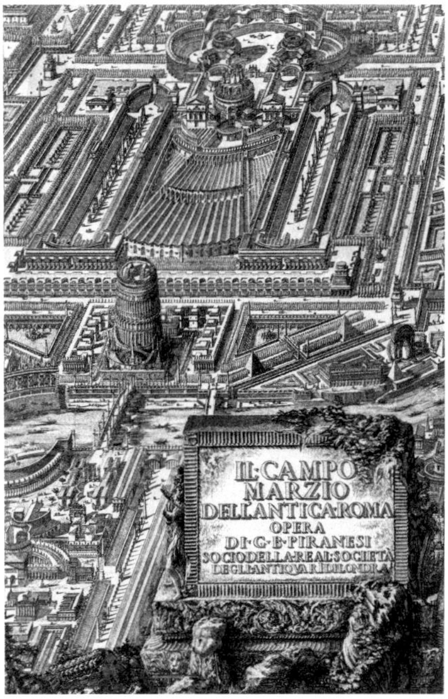

Giovanni Battista Piranesi, frontispiece, *Il Campo Marzio dell'antica Roma*, 1762.

as a proto-Marxist adheres to the temporal loops typical of the modern age. To Tafuri, the *Campo Marzio* signals precisely Piranesi's revolt against the absolutism of his day—its boundless geometry an expression of the struggle for social and political freedom. The "monstrous pullulation" of form in the *Campo Marzio* is "a merciless satire of late-baroque typology to reproduce itself metamorphically."[49] At the same time, the plan's seemingly relentless unfolding of geometries, reaching towards infinity, holds a promise, a prophecy even, of a new political and social order, however ideal. The "ambiguous evocation" of the plan, Tafuri writes in *Architecture and Utopia*, "is the graphic monument of that tentative opening of late-baroque culture to revolutionary ideologies."[50] By casting a future city in the same mold in which he reconstructs the old, Piranesi creates a tension that architectural history cannot gloss over. In fact, the tension is what structures that history.

To conclude, Tafuri paved the way for Piranesi in an architectural discourse that broke not only with modernism, but also with postmodernism—formally, existentially, politically. Piranesi seemed to sanction a purely conceptual architecture, dissolving the very parameters that conventionally condition the art of building, leaving posterity with designs that were centerless and boundless, that had no future or past. In the final count, the *Campo Marzio* plan, as reinvented by Tafuri, seemed to codify the predicaments and challenges, fears and possibilities, of a new architectural and urban reality.

A PAST THAT LIES AHEAD

In 1978, while audiences flocked to *Roma interrotta*, the city of Venice, together with the Istituto Universitario di Architettura (Faculty of Architecture), organized a seminar on the redevelopment of the district of Cannaregio at the city's north end. Under the influence of Manfredo Tafuri, the organizers invited proposals from ten architects, among them Peter Eisenman, John Hejduk, and Carlo Aymonino, resulting in an exhibition and a catalogue.[51] *10 progetti* was not only the antithesis of *Roma interrotta*, but was also partly conceived in reaction to it, with the express aim of rescuing architecture from the lure of postmodernism and its "nostalgia for the past."[52] Like their Roman counterparts, the proposals were hypothetical, but unlike *Roma interrotta* their attitude towards history was defiant, consciously severing ties to past practices and motifs. The attempt to cleanse the projects of all ideological content—of any references outside architecture itself—represented a new "conceptual" architecture, as Eisenman would call it, or an "architecture as such," in Tafuri's words.[53] In these experiments "each stage of the project becomes potentially an end and each moment of the creative process tends towards being a completed 'part,'" Francesco Dal Co wrote in the introduction to the catalogue, issued in 1980.[54] Simply put, in contrast to *Roma interrotta*'s mooring of architecture in history, *10 progetti* promoted an architecture moored in nothing but itself.

These two ideologically opposed events represented a sharp divide in the architectural scene at the time.[55] And the *Campo Marzio* plan, I argue, came to the rescue for architects who sought an alternative to postmodernism. "I became an enemy [. . .] of *Roma interrotta* and of contextualism and figure–ground urbanism. And to combat that, the only name that I could have was Piranesi," Peter Eisenman said.[56] At the heart of Eisenman's fascination with Piranesi's *Campo Marzio*, repeatedly voiced in publications, is the quality of the buildings as pure forms, as signs with no signifier: "In this sense, Piranesi presented a virtual Rome outside of real time and real space."[57] The plan and its simulacra of buildings served as explicit references in the project he submitted in 1978 for the renovated city square of Cannaregio.[58] And as I see it, its use was contrapuntal. Whereas Piranesi had projected an artificial city on the real grounds of Rome, Eisenman created an artificial ground for the real city of Venice. More precisely, Eisenman invented a richly articulated underground, in a city famously devoid of it, by digging fake holes and slicing vertical diagonals across the designated spot. At intervals, he also distributed references to an unbuilt hospital planned for an adjacent site (by Le Corbusier) as well as to his own *House XI* (*see following*).[59] A compound of structures that never had been built was thus "unearthed" in imitation of an archaeological site. Eisenman, then, fabricated not the buildings of the past but the future traces of them—the substratum on which the architecture stood, or would have been standing on if it had existed. He excavated buildings that were yet to be realized, and that in fact would always remain unbuilt. This supremely formalist message trapped the course of time in a gridlock: by uncovering a past that lay ahead, the Cannaregio project also held the future captive. When what is yet to come already lies behind us, history itself collapses.

Not only does Eisenman consider Cannaregio his most significant project, he also describes it as the first time he did "a Tafuri-Piranesian project."[60] It was Tafuri's reading, rather than Piranesi's work itself, that led Eisenman to the *Campo Marzio* and to its potential as a tool in the design process.[61] The intervention of Tafuri shows that Piranesi's ambiguous representations had again acquired an eloquent interpreter who translated his compositions into words and pointed out what to look for, a role De Quincey had once taken in the mediation of the *Carceri*.

In fact, strong bonds were forged between Tafuri and the so-called New York Five, comprising Eisenman, John Hejduk, Michael Graves, Charles

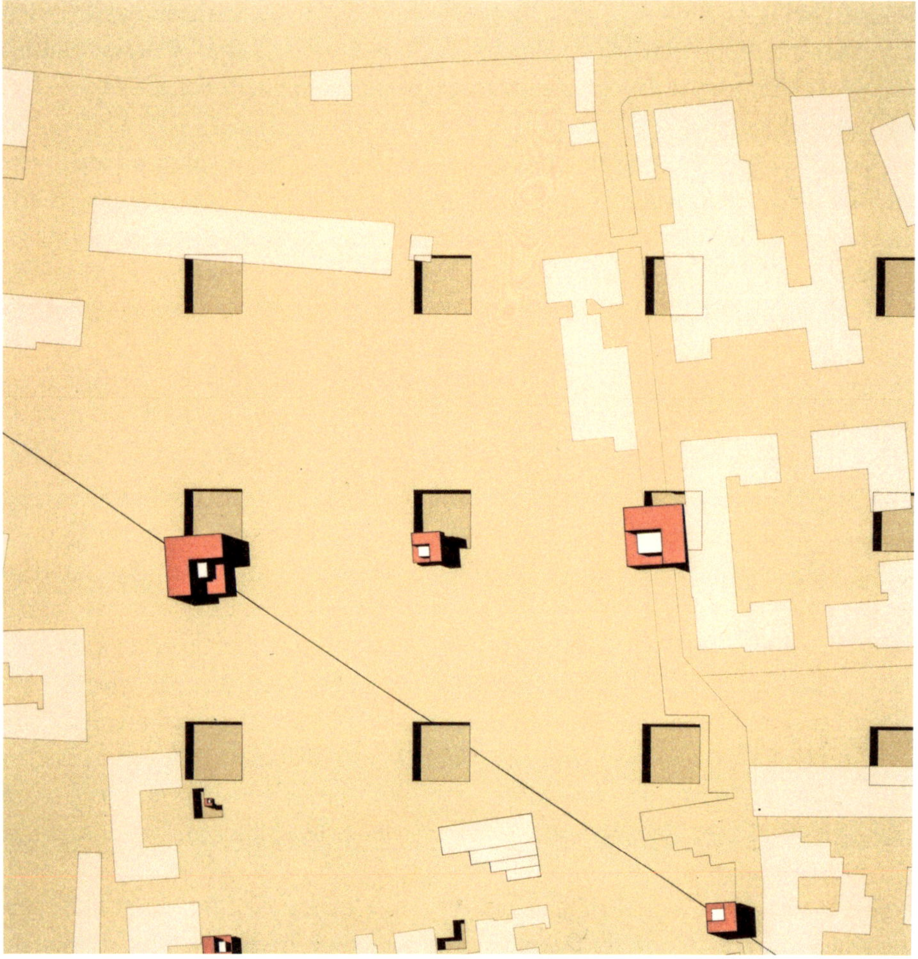

Gwathmey, and Richard Meier.[62] In the 1970s Tafuri also became associated with the Institute for Architecture and Urban Studies in New York (IAUS), which Eisenman had directed since 1967, and published essays, among them "The Dialectics of the Avant-Garde: Piranesi and Eisenstein," in *Oppositions*, the journal co-edited by Eisenman. Moreover, *Progetto e utopia* was published with the MIT Press in 1976 as *Architecture and Utopia* and sold no less than 21,000 copies over the following two decades.[63] So, even though the name of Tafuri at times remained unacknowledged, the idea of the Piranesi plan as an "experimental design" reached a wide group of theoretically inclined architects in the 1970s and 1980s, who besides Eisenman included Stanley Allen, Steven Holl, Bernard Tschumi, and Rem Koolhaas.[64] While they did not necessarily adopt Tafuri's interpretation, they embraced the idea of the plan as methodology—as an

Peter Eisenman, project for Cannaregio town square, plan, 1978.

instrument to help emancipate architecture from the "false" tradition propagated by postmodernism. How that instrument was wielded, however, differed from one architectural practice to the next, as the following will show.

Architect and author Stanley Allen proclaimed the *Campo Marzio* a "plane" where modernism played out its aspirations and fantasies, and "the horizons of classicism and the most radical project of modernity coincide."[65] Allen structured his 1989 essay "Piranesi's *Campo Marzio*: An Experimental Design" in explicit imitation of an architectural project, dividing the text into three sections, "site," "context," and "program," and illustrating it with images of his own model of the Piranesi plan. Although Allen filtered his interpretation of the *Campo Marzio* through a sieve of modern and postmodern references—Le Corbusier, Man Ray, Freud, Eisenstein, Shklovsky, Foucault, Derrida—he nevertheless emerged as a follower of Tafuri. First, he referred to the idea that classical architecture was already from the beginning an amalgam, forged from all kinds of influences. "The original is thus already contaminated," he wrote, recuperating an assessment Tafuri had applied not only to Piranesi's *Campo Marzio* in *The Sphere and the Labyrinth* but also to his own (and Allen's) discipline, characterizing the historiography of architecture as "rotten to the core," a reference Allen failed to mention.[66] Allen's second Tafurian point concerns the recognition of the "overriding principle" at work in the *Campo Marzio*. In the plan, he observed, the whole and the parts submit to the same geometric rules, but these rules refer to nothing but themselves. Although geometry is understood in this plan for the first time as instrumental, "this instrumentality undercuts the rational principle that underlies it." What is left is an endless chain of combinations unable to constrain the mechanisms that produce them. Thus, the "useless machines" of the *Campo Marzio*, Allen concluded—with a direct quote from Tafuri's *Architecture and Utopia*—are self-perpetuating.[67]

Tafuri had obviously turned the *Campo Marzio* into a fashionable reference for writers and architects who defined themselves in opposition to a historically oriented postmodernism and who were in need of principles—a conceptual basis—for alternative visions. The attempts to assimilate Piranesi into the design process were always ambitious, but not always successful. American architect Steven Holl recalls that he read *Architecture and Utopia*, as well as Tafuri's *Oppositions* essay on Piranesi and Eisenstein, soon after joining the IAUS in New York in 1977.[68] It was a belated introduction: in 1970, as a student on the University of Washington Rome program, Holl had lived only a block away from Tafuri, but they never met. In fact, Holl claims that he remained unmoved by Tafuri's ideas, though he did not remain indifferent to the possibility of extracting from the *Campo Marzio* a method to use as a design principle.

Porta Vittoria was a project to redevelop a disused railyard on the old railroad belt outside the historic center of Milan.[69] Commissioned by the XVII Triennale of Milan for the 1987 exhibition *The Imagined Cities: An Italian Journey*, Holl's design counts among his most significant, contributing to the search for new methodologies in architecture at the time. Like many architects of his generation, Holl wanted to invent not just buildings but the entire system from which they were derived. In the case of Porta Vittoria, he began by ditching traditional urban planning schemes based on city blocks and building types. At some point in the process of dispensing with these conventions, the *Campo Marzio* plan emerged as a solution. Holl's early watercolors show extravagant and arbitrary geometric modules from Piranesi's plan entwined with the more functional architecture required for Milan (*see following*). However, by clinging to the *Campo Marzio*, Holl found that he reinforced the very approach he renounced—the "postmodern attempts to reintroduce history" represented by Krier, Venturi, and Jencks. By following Piranesi, he risked turning his own project into a historical pastiche. He abandoned the attempt, deeming the mere "mimicking" or "aping of the *Campo Marzio* a failure."[70]

The method he finally arrived at in the project for Porta Vittoria was to reverse the design process itself. Instead of starting with the ground plans, as architects normally do, he started by drawing perspectives, as if the buildings were already standing; only afterwards were they worked out in plan and section. These perspectives, while they show fully developed forms and volumes, record an architecture that does not yet exist. For Holl, as for Eisenman, a standpoint in the future marks the greatest possible distance from a postmodern yearning for the past. In both cases, too, the attempt not to predict but to *reconstruct* a future already spent prompts new design methods. Interestingly, Piranesi's plan, with its fanciful look at ancient Rome, can equally be seen to present a city of the future, a Rome that never came to pass. As such, the plan defies linear temporality, or rather compresses it into a single vision. Holl's perspectives also presented the Milan complex as a collection of poetically glimpsed fragments. And as Holl sees it in retrospect, piecing together an urban space from fragments brought the whole project back into the orbit of Piranesi. Porta Vittoria became "another version of the *Campo Marzio*," in the sense that both display a "fragmentary process" that generates a new and loosely connected wholeness.[71]

Other architectural practices, too, exploited the *Campo Marzio* plan but took its implementation to a new level, as the remainder of this chapter will show. No longer was its impact confined to single buildings, as was the case with Kahn, or even pockets of urban planning, as exemplified by Eisenman or Holl; now it became an instrument for rethinking the city itself, for outlining alternative ways of urban living. From the ideological skirmish of the 1970s, it emerged as an emblem of a new urbanism that addressed the challenges of the unchecked expansion of megacities around the world. It codified the generic city, as Rem Koolhaas was to demonstrate. In short, and somewhat paradoxically, the apparent unhinging of Piranesi's plan from the historic city it represented gave cities without pasts a historical alibi.

KOOLHAAS AND BUILDING THE BOUNDLESS

The term "deconstructivism" was coined by Mark Wigley when he and Philip Johnson mounted the *Deconstructivist Architecture* exhibition at MOMA in 1988. Evoking both philosophical deconstruction and early twentieth-century Russian constructivism, it summed up a tendency in architecture that Wigley had observed for some time, represented in the show by seven architects: Frank Gehry, Daniel Libeskind, Rem Koolhaas, Peter Eisenman, Zaha Hadid, Coop Himmelblau, and Bernard Tschumi. "This is an architecture of disruption, dislocation, deflection, deviation, and distortion," Wigley wrote in the catalogue, pointing out that deconstructivist architecture "inhabits the center of the tradition in order to demonstrate that architecture is always infected, that pure form has always been contaminated."[72] The words and ideas that Wigley conveyed are interchangeable with those that had characterized Piranesi's *Carceri* for almost two centuries. Wigley never mentioned Piranesi, however—neither in his PhD dissertation, later turned into a book, nor in the exhibition catalogue. But the architects he exhibited did. "Piranesi speaks to the present in a profound and mysterious way," Daniel Libeskind wrote in 1982 in connection with the Hannover exhibition *Inventionen: Piranesi und Architekturphantasien in der Gegenwart*, to which Rem Koolhaas among others also contributed.[73] Bernard Tschumi drew a parallel between the *Campo Marzio* plan, which he calls "not compositional," and his own *Parc de la Villette* (1982), pointing out how they both strike a precarious balance between the arbitrary and the systematic.[74] Eisenman too, as we have seen, consulted the Venetian's oeuvre. But it was on Koolhaas that Piranesi would have the greatest impact.[75] The Dutch architect strongly objected to being classified as a "deconstructivist," stating it was more rewarding to construct things than to break them apart.[76] In his attempt to stake out an alternative course, Piranesi's *Campo Marzio* would become operative in a way that I argue contrasted with earlier "static" applications of the plan.

Koolhaas called Tafuri an "anti-force."[77] If Eisenman had approached Piranesi through Tafuri, Koolhaas found little that resonated in the theories of the Italian and preferred instead to examine the historical and archaeological reality

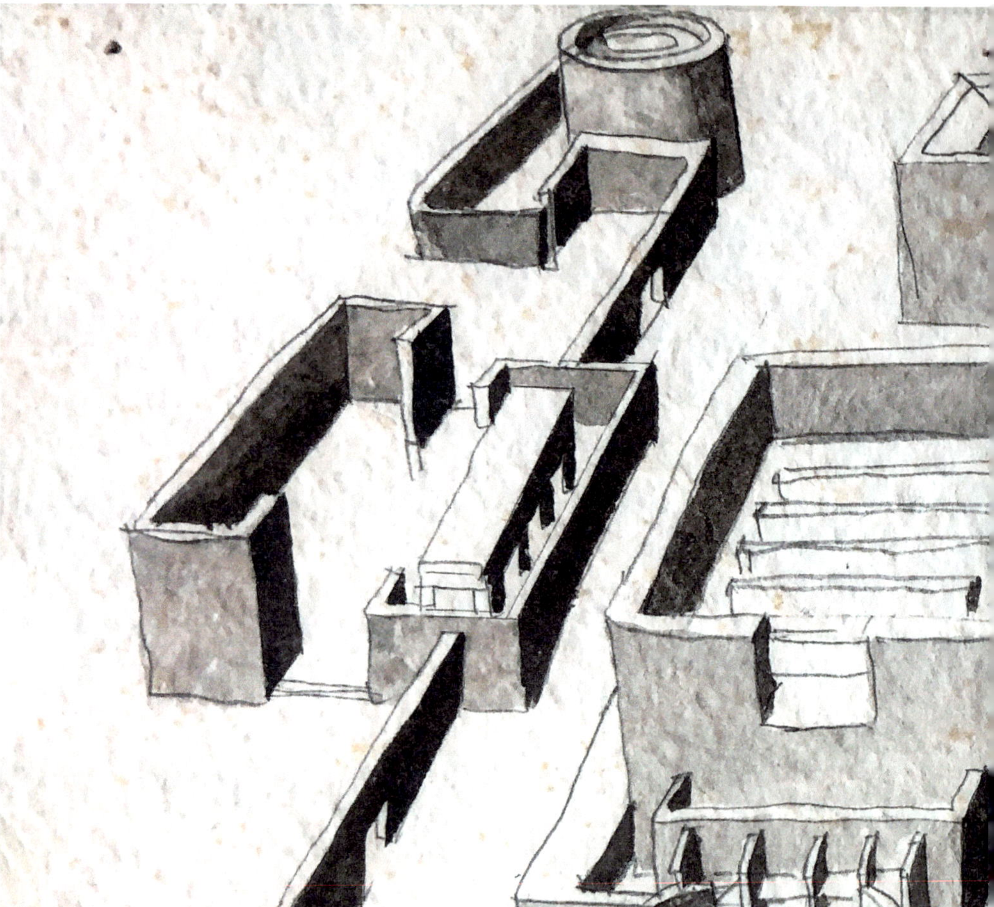

Steven Holl, design for Porta Vittoria, Milan, correlated with Piranesi's *Campo Marzio*, 1986. Watercolor.

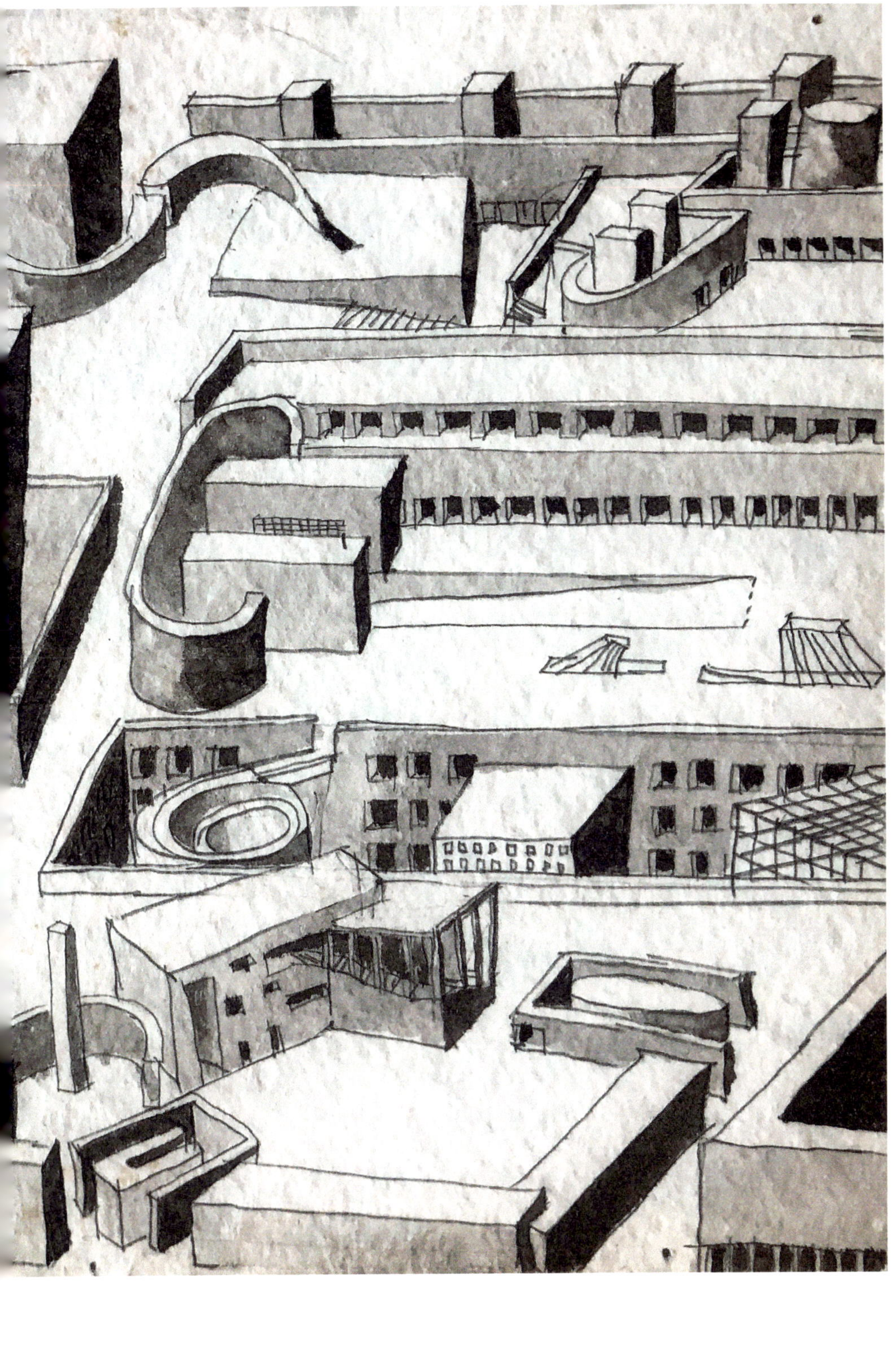

in Piranesi's compositions. According to Koolhaas himself, the Piranesi he was initially attracted to, and, indeed, felt an affinity with, was Piranesi as an artist *and* researcher.[78] Koolhaas graduated from the Architectural Association (AA) in London in 1972, and his particular vision of Piranesi was inspired both by the AA lectures of the erudite Thomas Stevens and by the German architect Oswald Mathias Ungers, who he met in late 1972 at Cornell University. It was together with Ungers, Koolhaas recalls, that he first leafed through Piranesi's volumes and "unfolded those amazing images."[79]

Nonetheless, the very idea of interpreting the *Campo Marzio* conceptually was indebted to Tafuri. And Koolhaas's projects offer a veritable microhistory of reappearances of the plan. Traces of the plan's significance are already apparent in Koolhaas's AA diploma project, *Exodus, or the Voluntary Prisoners of Architecture* (1972), developed in collaboration with Elia Zenghelis, Zoe Zenghelis, and Madelon Vriesendorp. *Exodus* envisions London as an ancient, derelict metropolis skewered by a chillingly ideal and yet inherently diversified "strip" that partly replaces, partly incorporates the English capital (*see following*). Two walls enclose identically partitioned squares that reconstitute the city allegorically, pocketing urban life into sections of recreation and entertainment. As a modern-day Ark, *Exodus* invites the citizens to enjoy the pleasures of the "strip" at the cost of leaving their former lives behind and willingly embracing their confinement within its walls. So, if *Exodus* formally evokes the *Campo Marzio*, psychologically it relates to the *Carceri*'s infinitely extending prisons. But whereas earlier writers and artists represented those Piranesian confines as a dystopia, Koolhaas turns them into a self-imposed exile, a life-long resort: "The inhabitants of this architecture, those strong enough to love it, would become its Voluntary Prisoners, ecstatic in the freedom of their architectural confines."[80] The disconcertingly unresolved state between freedom and confinement, also addressed by Borges, Sebald, and Tafuri, is implemented here as an urban vision.

Obvious architectural sources for *Exodus* are Superstudio's *Continuous Monument* (1969) and Archizoom's *No-Stop City* (1968–1972).[81] Both projects formulate the idea of the infinite as a dimension growing uncontrollably from within the modern city itself, so to speak, in a critique of modern urban expansion. However, the endlessly repeatable modules proposed by Archizoom, for example, produced a "bad infinity"—"a continuous city with no attribute other than its infinite quantity," to quote Pier Vittorio Aureli.[82] If we consider the *Campo Marzio* plan as an alternative source for *Exodus*, it suggests a solution that by contrast preserves the particulars of the historical city—be it ancient Rome or London: "London is a mess and it is a mess that like the *Campo Marzio* also contains perfect sections," Koolhaas himself observed. The importance of the plan, in other words, is that Piranesi articulated the urban by means of an endless variety of forms—"an unbelievable proliferation of potential incidents and conditions," according to the Dutch architect.[83] The *Campo Marzio* manifests infinity as a multiplicity rather than an abstraction. In other words, it was not simply the utopia of the plan that appealed to Koolhaas, but the relation of the utopian whole to the precisely shaped and archaeologically founded compounds within it. The tension between defined units and an expanding whole, between the built and the boundless, activated the plan somehow.

It is this perception of colliding dimensions that explains, I believe, Koolhaas's enduring interest in Piranesi's plan, which is evident in his present-day assessment of its importance:

> At one point I took the *Campo Marzio* as the symbol of the urban. It is also a kind of cliché or an emblem—an emblem of the urban condition in its duality of being both planned and unplanned. That is what is so appealing about this particular plan, that it is chaotic and organized at the same time, or, rather, that it is an assembly of organized pieces in a chaotic whole.[84]

In projects executed by Koolhaas and his office OMA from the 1990s to 2020, Piranesi's plan reappears in various guises, though it is always approached as if it were a code—a formula—that allows buildings bound by their physical limits to exist also in a limitless dimension—as a city within the city. The references to the *Campo Marzio* over those three decades amount to a history in itself—a history, however, in which the application of the plan develops from being a decorative element dabbed onto the building plans to become a principle generating their design. True enough, Koolhaas never actually attempted to build Piranesi's structures; in that sense, the plan always remained an emblem, even as its power to activate forms and layouts increased. In projects ranging from libraries to airports, from Paris to Doha, the *Campo Marzio* plan progressively "sank" into the architecture, implanting at its very core the idea of an infinite multiplicity. The plan emerged as a cartographic quotation understood by everyone; "a code that I have experienced is very efficient in almost any culture—Thai, Chinese, the Italians, the Americans, the French; everyone understands it, even if they don't know what it is."[85]

The following brief survey of Koolhaas's *Campo Marzio* architecture starts with the project for "Two Libraries for Jussieu" in Paris (1992). Here, the reference to *Campo Marzio* is merely cosmetic. Fragments from the printed plan are used to decorate parts of the drawings that represent service functions and

overleaf Rem Koolhaas, *Exodus, or the Voluntary Prisoners of Architecture*, 1972. (Aerial view of London.)

following spread Rem Koolhaas/OMA, section and plan of the Hyperbuilding, Bangkok, 1996.

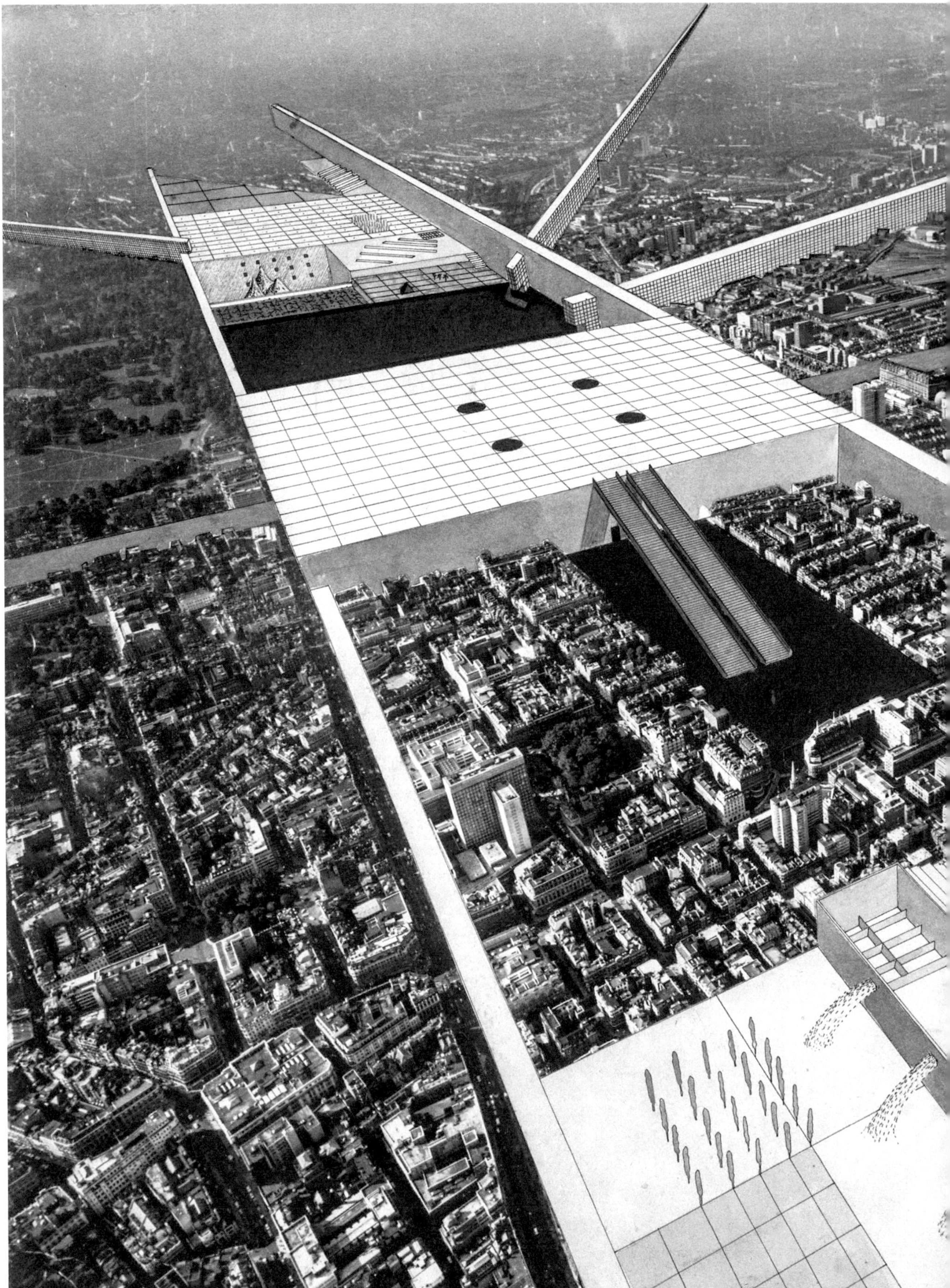

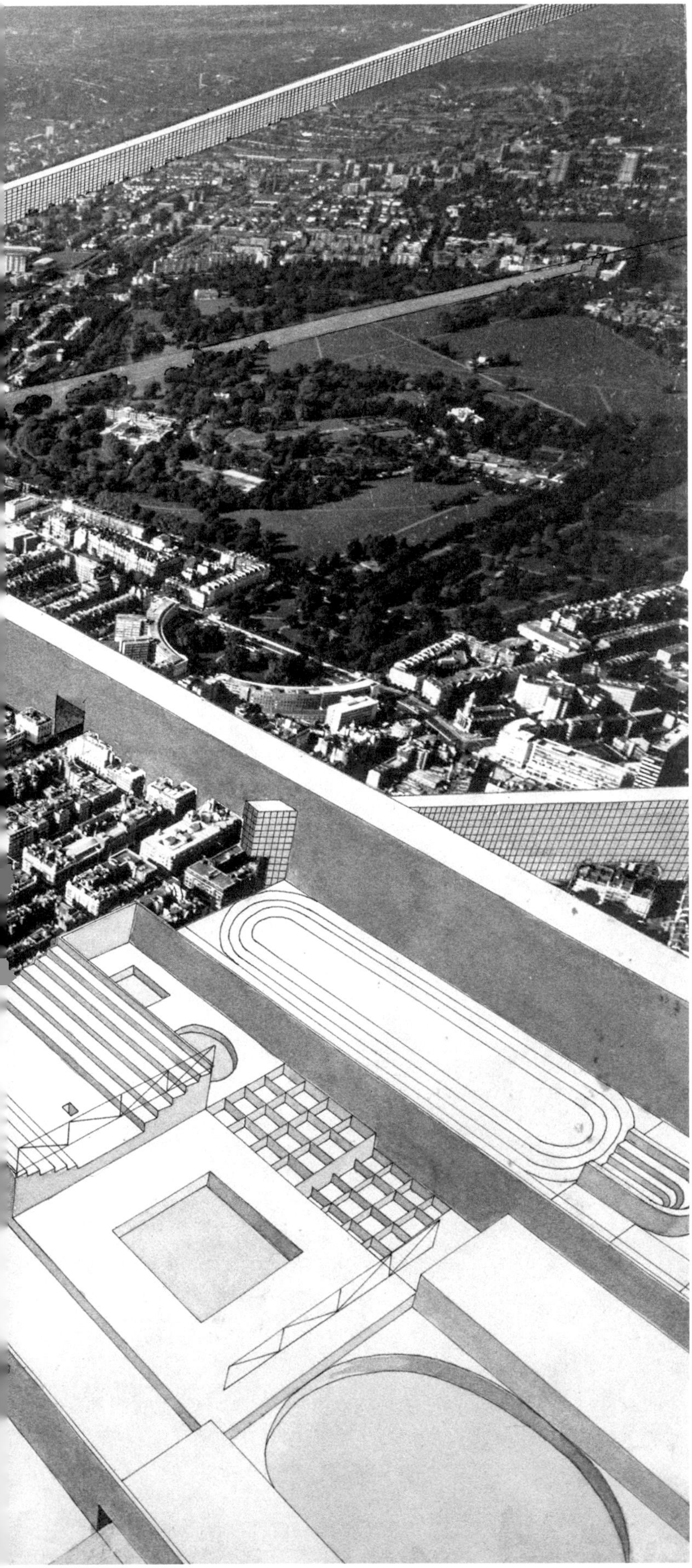

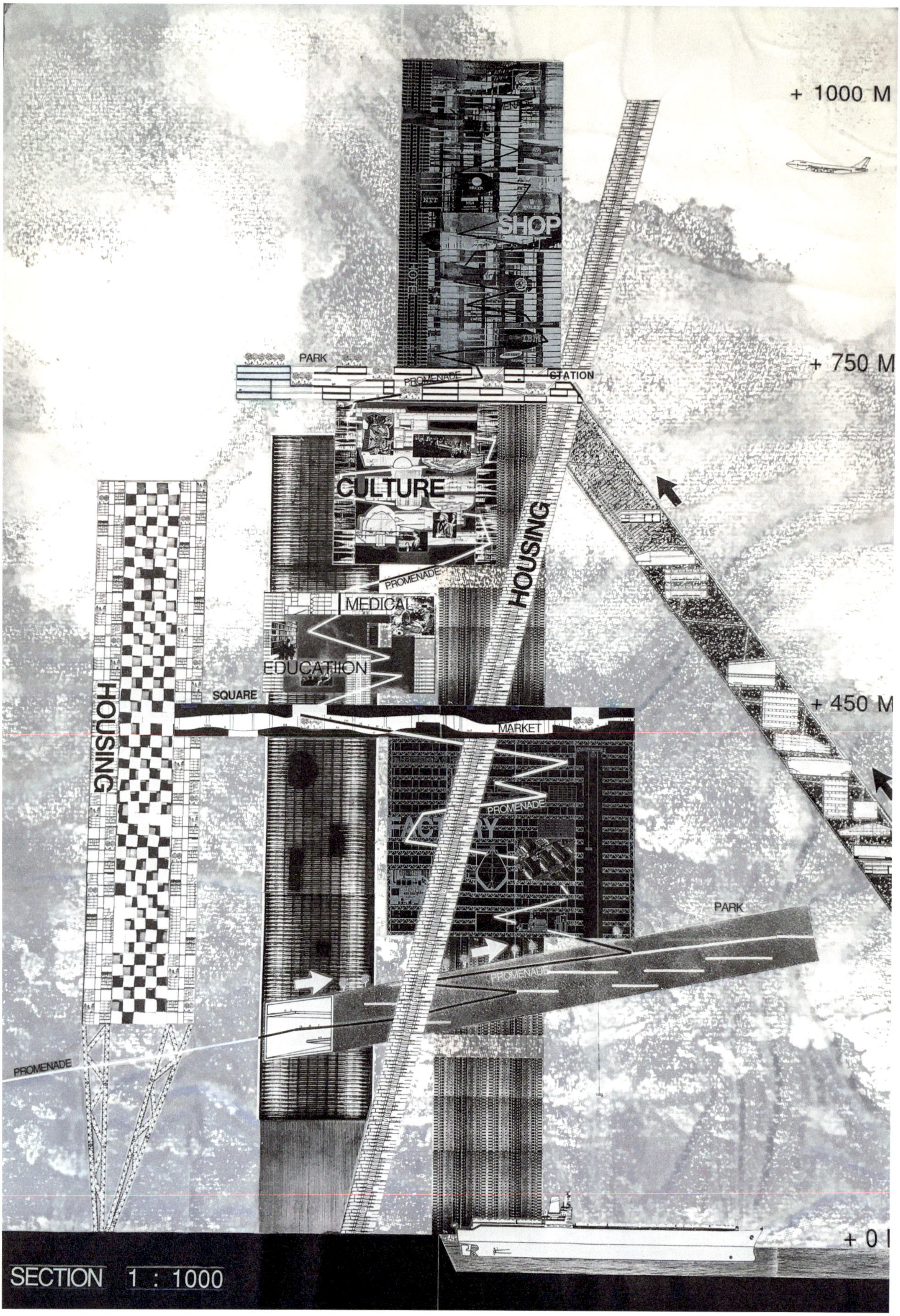
+ 1000 M
SHOP
PARK
PROMENADE
STATION
+ 750 M
CULTURE
HOUSING
PROMENADE
MEDICAL
EDUCATIION
SQUARE
HOUSING
+ 450 M
MARKET
PROMENADE
FACTORY
PARK
PROMENADE
PROMENADE
+ 0
SECTION 1 : 1000

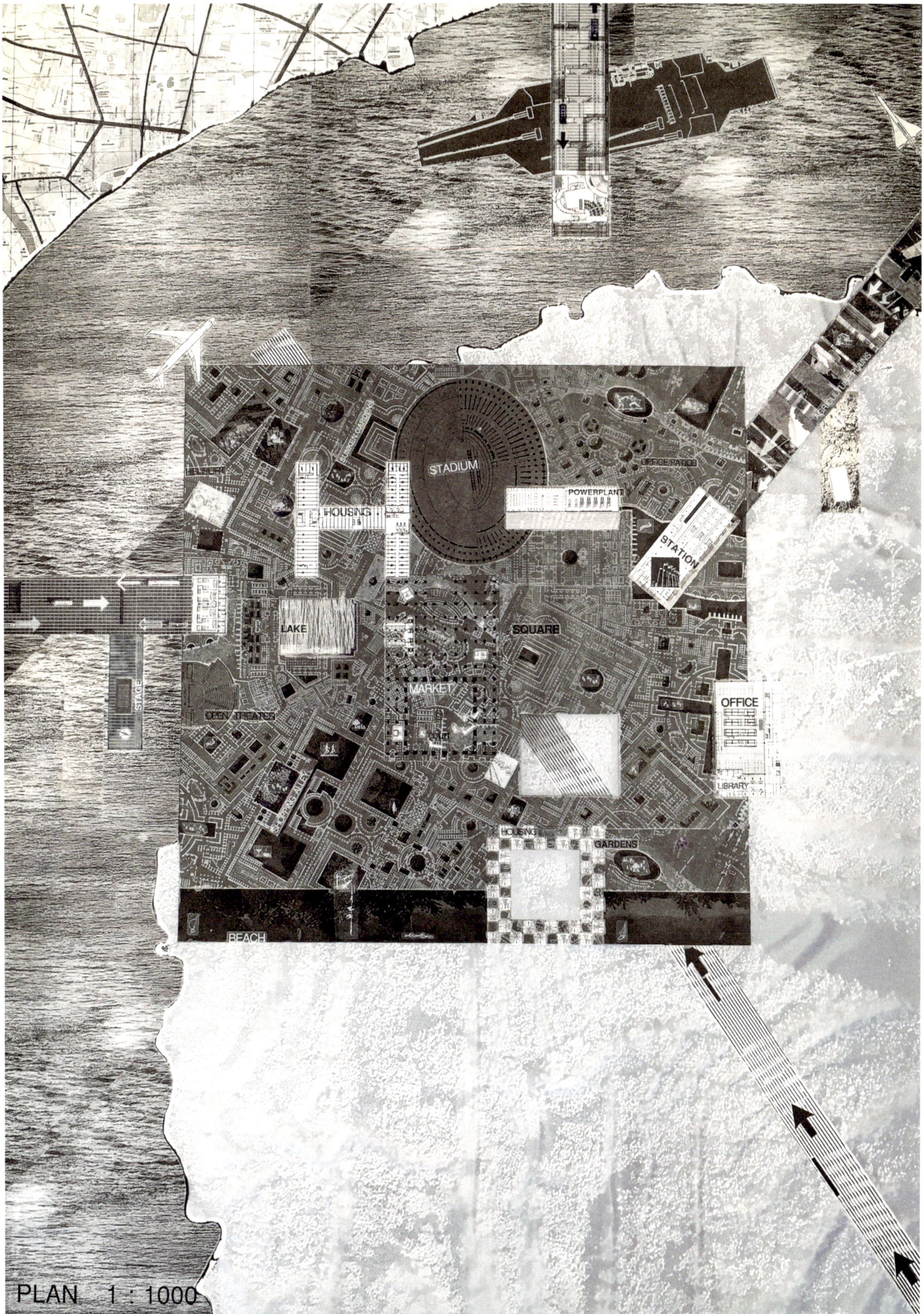
STADIUM
HOUSING
POWERPLANT
OFFICE PATIOS
STATION
LAKE
SQUARE
STAGE
MARKET
OPEN THEATRES
OFFICE
LIBRARY
HOUSING
GARDENS
BEACH
PLAN 1 : 1000

storage facilities, and for no other reason than to create variety. The plan is an efficient way to introduce contrast without losing interest, the architect admits.[86] Nevertheless, cultivating the building's "urban condition" is an expressed aim. The succession of floors alludes to a city, vertically stacked, and "urbanized" by means of bookshelves, desks, tables, and so on—as if the entire interior were a toy town. According to Koolhaas, the elements of the library were distributed "like buildings in a city."[87]

Although the plan remained decorative in the case of the Paris library, the idea of the building as a container of cities would bring the *Campo Marzio* into play in future projects by Koolhaas and OMA. The more Koolhaas incorporated the plan, the more it appeared to him "the most intellectually profound representation of the whole idea of the city."[88] A case in point is the immense Hyperbuilding in Bangkok (1996), envisioned as a bundle of towers, up to a thousand meters tall, accommodating 120,000 inhabitants across five million square meters. It is "structured as a metaphor of the city: towers constitute streets, horizontal elements are parks, volumes are districts, and diagonals are boulevards."[89] No longer located *within* the ground plan, the Hyperbuilding projects the *Campo Marzio* onto its surroundings: an early collage produced by OMA shows Piranesi's printed city superimposed on Bangkok itself. In this sense the plan replaces the real hub with an antique megalopolis, counterbalancing the Hyperbuilding with a corresponding hypercity, as it were (*see preceding*). A vision emerges of the Piranesian *urbs* as the only realm suited to supporting Koolhaas's megastructure—the only one in which its footprint does not appear absurdly oversized. In contrast to the Jussieu libraries, the *Campo Marzio* plan asserts itself as a mediator between the monument and the metropolis, but also as an expression of the boundlessness the Hyperbuilding attempts to capture. In this sense Koolhaas's interpretation of the *Campo Marzio* plan is tied to his idea of "bigness" as the shattering of scale and proportion in modern corporate architecture(*see overleaf*).[90]

In 1996 Koolhaas and his team planned a super high-rise in Seoul, named the Togok Towers. It was never built, but exists in a series of collages. Reminiscent of Rossi's *Città analoga*, the footprint of the building is glued onto segments cut from *Campo Marzio*. The stark beauty of these designs almost reconsecrates them as formalist art (*see pages 232–233*).

Six years later, Koolhaas and OMA exported Piranesi's great plan to Beijing. The CCTV and TVCC television center and headquarters, along with the service building and the so-called media park, were begun in 2002, designed by Koolhaas in collaboration with David Gianotten and Ole Scheeren (*see opposite*).[91] The complex of buildings, roads, paths, and gardens forms a city within the city and is laid

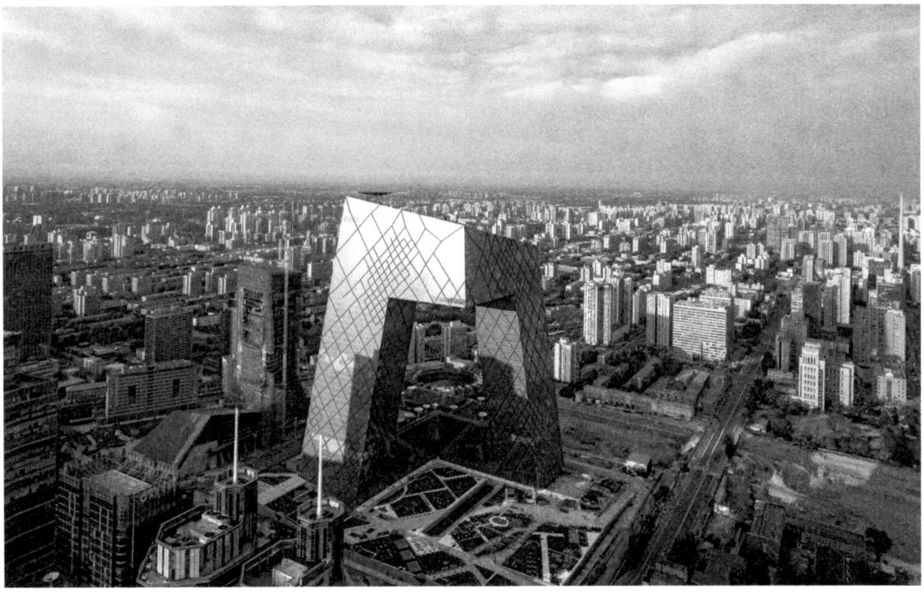

out explicitly on the grid of Piranesi's *Campo Marzio*. A ceaselessly expanding Beijing finds a "historic" model for that expansion in a representation of an equally transgressive ancient Rome.

Early plans and models show how Koolhaas and OMA positioned the television and media compound right across the part of Piranesi's reconstructed Rome that represents the Via Flaminia, one of ancient Rome's main thoroughfares, legitimizing the roads that dissect the building plot in Beijing. The *Campo Marzio* also sanctions the project when seen, somewhat grandiosely, from the perspective of the Chinese capital itself: if in Bangkok the Piranesi city offered an ideal ground on which the Koolhaas buildings might exist, that "ideal" ground would now be built in a very real Beijing. Beijing, as a modern *Campo Marzio*, can therefore list the Koolhaas compound as its first "correct" construction.

Whether there was any intention to erect Piranesi's structures three-dimensionally remains mere speculation. The circular service building in the media center certainly recalls Roman amphitheaters and arenas for water games, so-called *naumachia*, linking structures across millennia in a typology of public entertainment.[92] Although no pendant to this circular building is found in the corresponding spot in *Campo Marzio*, an extraordinarily direct adaptation of Piranesi's print determined the distribution of other elements in Koolhaas's compound. That said, the translation from an eighteenth-century engraving to a functional city complex required adjustments. In a first stage, the architect and his team translated Piranesi's incised architecture into simplified pixels. These were in turn individualized and

Rem Koolhaas/OMA, CCTV and TVCC headquarters and television center, Beijing, 2002–2012.

foldouts Rem Koolhaas/OMA, two collages showing imagined views from within the Hyperbuilding, Bangkok, 1996.

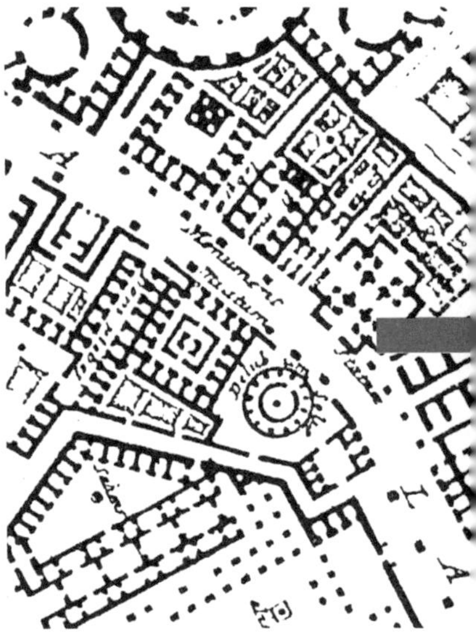

articulated as trees, greenery, benches, as well as pavement patterns (*see facing*). The pixelated *Campo Marzio* surprisingly continues inside the CCTV tower, leaving visible imprints of Piranesi's Rome on the floor and walls of the lobby area.[93] So, the plan of *Campo Marzio* does not simply illustrate the compound's "urban condition," but comes close to informing the shape and interrelation of its concrete parts. Grafted onto the architecture—indeed onto an entire city quarter—it seems on the verge of subjugating Beijing itself to an eighteenth-century printmaker's fantasy of Rome.

"It is constantly there. It is difficult to erase," Koolhaas has said of the *Campo Marzio* plan.[94] And the Qatar National Library in Doha, completed in 2017, can be seen as a final stage, to date, in the implementation of Piranesi's plan in built form. Koolhaas has admitted that he had the *Campo Marzio* in mind when designing the library, but in contrast to the mere decorative function it had at Jussieu, I would argue that in this instance it determined the very concept and structure of the building. In a strikingly concrete interpretation of the plan's archaeology, part of the library's ground floor is carved out, masquerading as an excavation site dramatically sunk six meters below the lobby area. Complete with subterranean walls partitioning the site, the fake archaeological dig pretends to uncover the antique evidence for the building rising in tiers above it. In contrast to Eisenman, who used Piranesi's plan as a launch pad to advance the complete autonomy of form, Koolhaas, as a second Piranesi, first "exposes" the ancient world and then reimagines it in geometrically patterned strata of ramps and bookshelves dabbed into the air and zigzagging across space as if he were etching them (*see following*). Rather than a specific site in Piranesi's *Campo Marzio*, then, the library evokes its very build-up. It is the stratigraphy of the plan that is the true "subject" of the Doha library.

The *Campo Marzio* plan also connects to the library conceptually. The excavated part of the ground floor contains the "heritage library," which holds the most precious books and manuscripts in the Doha collection. Knowledge, then, is given the concrete expression of an "unearthed" stratum of the past. For all its fantastic elements, the *Campo Marzio* plan is also based on knowledge of what lies beneath. The scattered remnants of the submerged ancient city enabled Piranesi to reconstruct its aspect, but also, and equally importantly, to divert from it in a spectacular way. The lacunae of evidence gave him space to maneuver, casting him as "an intermediary between knowledge and the representation of knowledge," in

Conversion from etching to pixels. Illustration from OMA, *CCTV New Site Construction & Development Program. Extended Preliminary Design. EPD Landscape Report*, 4.1, 2004.

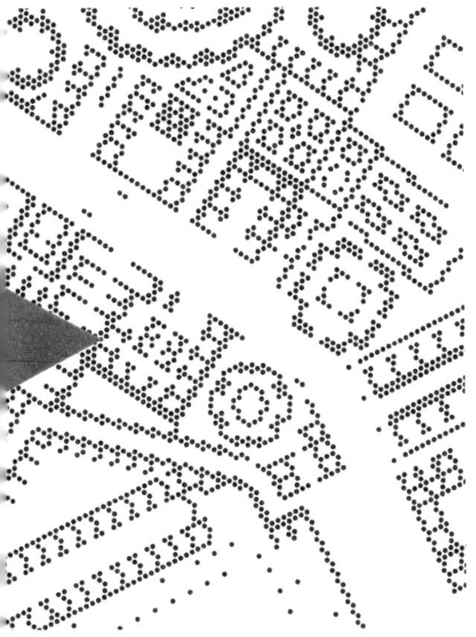

Koolhaas's words.[95] It is a relation that plays out in the interior of the Doha library, I believe, with knowledge manifested in the form of a dig and the interpretation of that knowledge materialized as the very library soaring Piranesi-like on top, urging the ideal library user, in its implicit symbolism, never to lose their foothold in a common past as they embark on indvidual flights of fancy. In this way, the *Campo Marzio* plan illustrates learning itself.

To Koolhaas, the *Campo Marzio* captures the modern urban condition in a concise emblem. When applied to Bangkok, Seoul, Beijing, Doha, and other cities, this emblem makes them in turn Piranesian; it gives expanding cities a historical reference for precisely that expansion.[96] In the essays "Whatever Happened to Urbanism?" (1994) and "The Generic City" (1994), the *Campo Marzio* forms a backdrop to Koolhaas's diagnosis of contemporary urban planning, in which he laments an urbanity that has surrendered to chaos, and "chaos is what happens when nothing happens, not something that can be engineered or embraced."[97] The Generic City, in Koolhaas's definition, is uncontrollable and monotonous, "an endless repetition of the same simple structural module"[98]—a description that evokes the kind of unstoppable cellular division of spaces that made authors from De Quincey to Borges sense architecture as an existential entrapment. Like Italo Calvino's Leonia, mentioned in chapter one, Koolhaas's Generic City expands, renews, and replaces itself; it has no center and no past, or rather it is all center and constantly self-reproducing. What is therefore required, Koolhaas writes, is a new urbanism, one with "enabling fields" that allow processes to take place but "that refuse to be crystallized into definitive form." In other words, Koolhaas searches for a principle that can structure and diversify urban growth, in the same way that Piranesi used geometric patterns to hold expanding Rome in check. Urbanism will have to imagine a "new newness," Koolhaas claims—a newness which is at the same time old, one could add, and embodied in Piranesi's *Campo Marzio*. It is not accidental, then, that a section of Piranesi's plan illustrates the title page of Koolhaas's essay "Whatever Happened to Urbanism?"[99]

Compared to Eisenman or Holl, the *Campo Marzio* plan figures in a wider perspective in Koolhaas's projects, or, more precisely, it figures as a negotiator *between* perspectives. It allows buildings to contain within their very limited enclosures the idea of an infinitely extending city, exemplified by the library in Paris and the CCTV center in Beijing. In other instances, the plan points

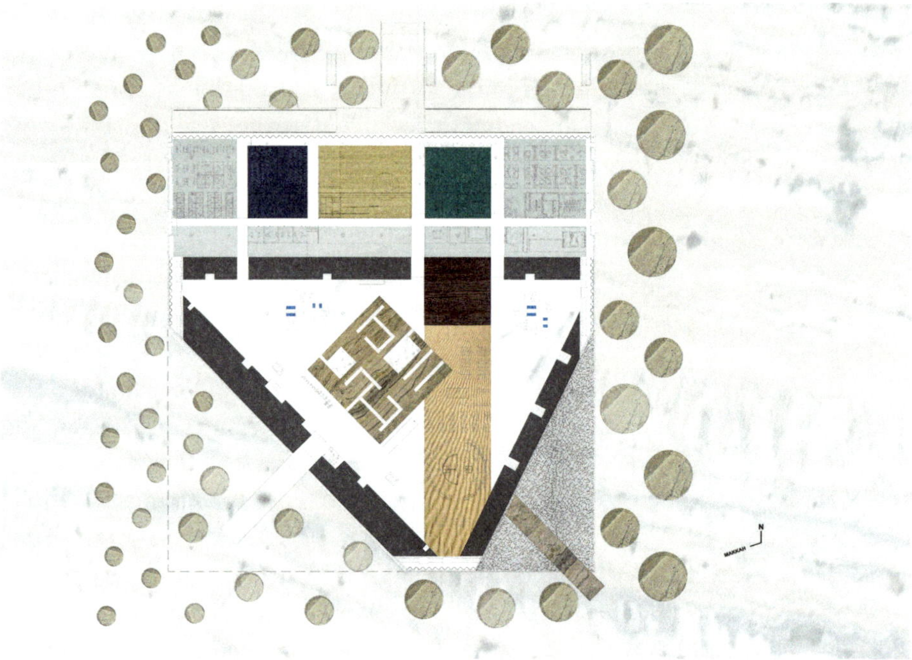

further—to intangible spheres: the library in Doha, for instance, harbors concepts that are themselves unbuildable but that nonetheless condition the building. And to the extent that these concepts can be tentatively named, as "knowledge" and "learning," Koolhaas finds them codified in the *Campo Marzio* plan.

INHABITING *CAMPO MARZIO*

Continuing from Koolhaas, the idea that we actually already inhabit the *Campo Marzio* plan, for better or for worse, marks the endpoint in this chapter's trajectory. So far, I have traced successive stages in the exploration of the plan's conceptual layers and identified Manfredo Tafuri and Rem Koolhaas as instrumental players. In a final stage of this development, the *Campo Marzio* plan again became "habitable," so to speak, in projects that did not, however, return to the idea of the historic city but, almost on the contrary, departed from the abstract city that lingered within Piranesi's exaggerated geometric rendering.

Across disciplines, manifestations of "built infinities" are often Piranesian in origin. For example, in "The Immortal," discussed in chapter one, Borges envisioned an infinite structure that embraces human life itself. Tafuri, twenty years later, explicitly ascribed endlessness in built form to Piranesi: "In these etchings the space of the building [...] is an infinite space."[100] Architecturally, resonances

Rem Koolhaas/OMA, Qatar National Library, plan, 2017.

of the Piranesian infinity structure can also be seen in Koolhaas's *Exodus,* with its voluntary prisoners, as well as in Dutch architect Constant Nieuwenhuys's imagined *New Babylon*—a vast labyrinthine metropolis on pillars that girds the entire Earth.[101] While bringing out the latent utopianism of *Campo Marzio*, such projects also underscore its frenzied permutation of forms, its "perpetuum mobile," in Koolhaas's words, or "endless chain of combinations," as Stanley Allen saw it.[102] In a mutation of elements that potentially has no end, infinity itself is caught within the plan's geometries, conveying a vague sense of thralldom.

Others have challenged this disquieting view of the plan and read into it possibilities that potentially improve the quality of urban living. In contrast to a history of appropriation, in which the plan has served as backdrop for the development of the architect's own design, a new generation of architects and theorists have reversed the focus and imagined how the plan—as an image of an actual city—would accommodate potential inhabitants. For the 2012 Venice Biennale of Architecture, three teams developed separate interpretations of the *Campo Marzio* in the exhibition *The Piranesi Variations.* Apart from Peter Eisenman, who had taken the initiative, and headed a team of students from Yale University, the triad included Jeffrey Kipnis with students from Ohio State University, and Pier Vittorio Aureli and Martino Tattara with a team from their firm Dogma.

It was the younger pair of Aureli and Tattara who addressed real urban conditions most explicitly in their project, *A Field of Walls*, which targets the "predefined trajectories"—the "compulsion to flow within given channels"—that cities force upon their populations, resulting in apathy.[103] In response, the project's authors sought to obstruct this involuntary circulation, as a means to free the bodies from urban sleepwalking and recast the social and political space of cities. Instead of enhancing circulation, *A Field of Walls* speculates on its limits. The project identifies the *wall* as the primary constituent in Piranesi's *Campo Marzio.* Multiplying that constituent, Aureli and Tattara superimposed onto the plan fifteen habitable walls running in parallel across Piranesi's Rome, adjusted to the "existing" structures (*see following*). Drawing in part on Roman aqueducts and in part on Koolhaas's *Exodus*, the wall that "contains, defines, channels, constrains, limits, stops, articulates and divides" is meant as a wake-up call: "This city made of walls reintroduces a spatiality in which movement is liberated from the predetermined trajectories of streets."[104] Unlike Tafuri's interpretation, liberation for the Dogma architects lies not in freedom from types but in the tactile sensation of interruption experienced by the inhabitants. There is nonetheless an obvious political dimension to the project: the walls serve to sharpen senses dulled by bourgeois urbanity and rouse the population from a cultural and political slumber.

In *Archescape: On the Tracks of Piranesi* (2014), Gijs Wallis de Vries borrowed Gilles Deleuze's concept of "flight line" to reintegrate the *Campo Marzio* plan into an urban vision that is almost the inverse of the one proposed by Aureli and Tattara. Flight lines are those continuities that link reality and art, city and landscape, according to de Vries. He writes that "rather than a line between two points, with a beginning and an end, a flight line explores the space between."[105] Flight lines shoot outward but also inward, to a city's staged escapes of gardens, arcades, academies, museums, theaters, unraveling niches of recreation—landscapes—within Piranesi's dense geometries. "A vision of a city as a landscape," *Campo Marzio* becomes paradigmatic of a new urbanism not because of its forms, but because of the open spaces that separate them.[106] With de Vries's poetic recreation of a city right inside the plan, the boundlessness of the *Campo Marzio* turns introspective, so to speak, and extends along lines to a point where psychology and architecture converge. In contrast to Aureli and Tattara, but publishing around the same time, de Vries proposed the *Campo Marzio* as a city of voids, rather than walls, demonstrating the versatility of the plan as a reference in contemporary thinking about urbanity.

To conclude, the *Campo Marzio* plan has functioned as a table on which architects have drafted and redrafted solutions to increasingly complex urban situations at the cost of disregarding the antique monuments Piranesi's designs profess to reconstruct. Just as Nolli's map served the postmodernists at the *Roma interrotta* exhibition in 1978, so Piranesi's map served a succession of architects who extracted, added, or rearranged elements of the design, advancing it as a perpetually updated corrective to modern city planning. "In a single map, Piranesi suggested that there was no one scale, no one time, no one location, and no one reality," Peter Eisenman wrote in 2007, highlighting the plan's potential for endless reuse.[107] However, the formalist annexation of the plan also made the reading of it more abstract. Its archaeology faded from view, along with other elements, like columns, statues, and ornaments, that Piranesi had taken care to articulate. Therefore, as a reference in a conceptual architecture from the 1970s on, the *Campo Marzio* helped establish a new formal basis at the cost of relinquishing the plan's own basis on Roman soil.

In this chapter, I have argued that the *Campo Marzio* plan resisted a simple revival in postmodern pastiches and collages, instead yielding principles that were evoked expressly to counter postmodernism and to help formulate new formal syntaxes in architecture. While the nature of those principles differs from one project to the next, there is no doubt that their interpretation has contributed in various ways to the redefinition of contemporary architecture. Paradoxically, the

DOGMA, *A Field of Walls*, 2012.

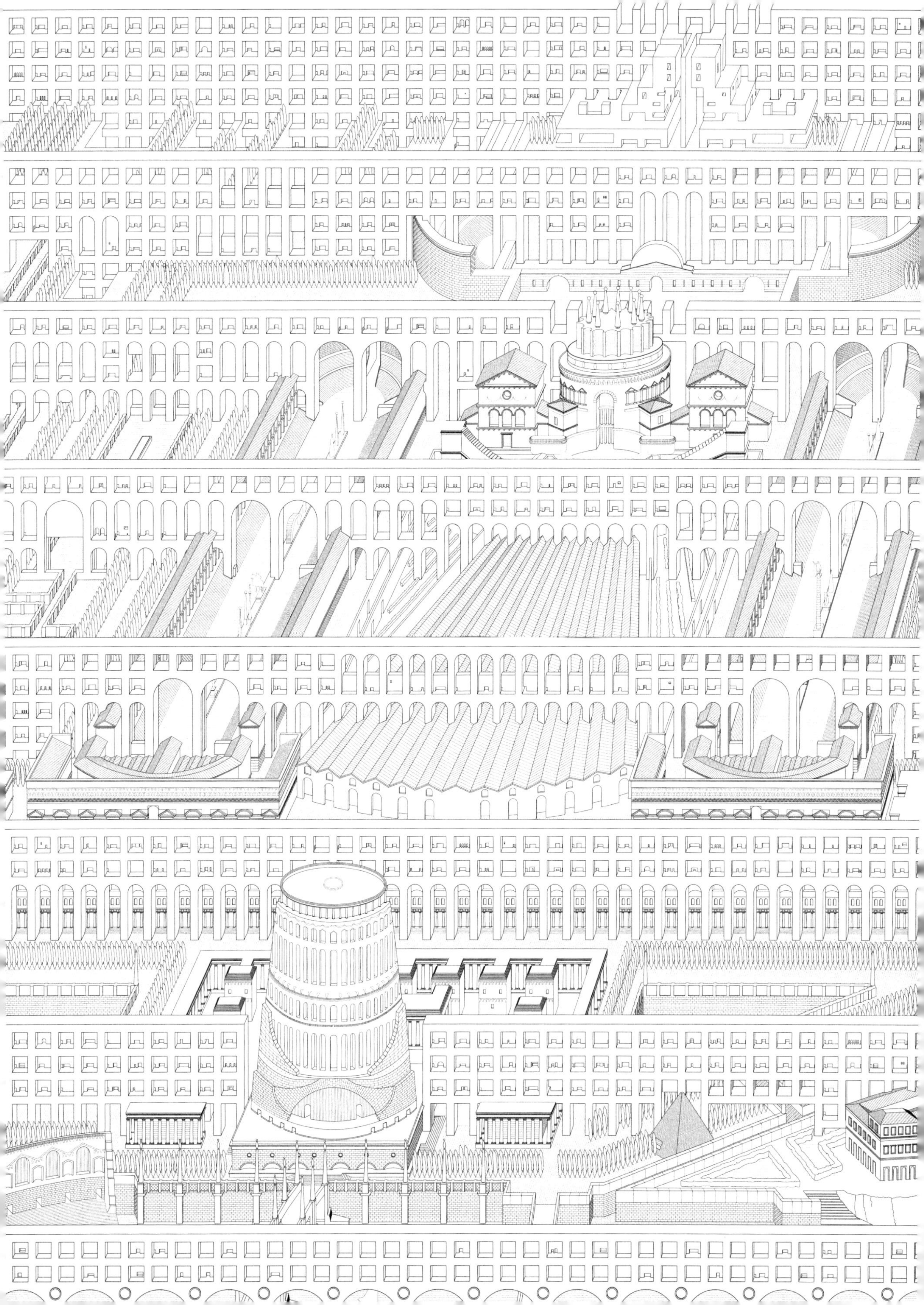

recourse to such principles almost brought the contemporary discourse from Eisenman to Koolhaas back to a modernist stance, represented in this discussion by Le Corbusier, and to the conviction that certain formal systems lay dormant beneath historical or historicist arrangements. However, the similarity is only superficial. What distinguishes references to Piranesi's plan in recent decades is the dynamic relation to history and temporality that they are meant to signal. Looking at the built and unbuilt projects discussed in this chapter, the reader discovers soon enough that the implementations of the *Campo Marzio* engage them precisely in contemplations about history.

Through a historiographic approach, at times laden with a plethora of references, from Proust to Sebald, from De Quincey to Walt Disney, this study has aimed to show how literature, art, film, and architecture have appropriated Piranesi, not so much to make projects appear novel, as to recreate their novelty as timeless—to lift the quality of "modern" above and beyond the confines of a mere "age." Such aspirations reduced Piranesi's compositions to stepping-stones for modernists like Barr and Eisenstein in their efforts to secure the status of painterly cubism and cinematic montage as atemporal phenomena. And where art historians and filmmakers discerned "timeless" qualities in Piranesi's compositions, architects and city planners were prepared to see a "boundless" architecture of infinity. The sense of being lost in the midst of perpetually expanding perspectives is shared by a number of Piranesi observers; center and periphery, entrances and exits, all evaporate at the moment of beholding.

So, if limitlessness can have a form, Piranesi can be said to have created it.

But to many that limitlessness soon turned vicious, and, far from signaling freedom, engendered a sense of entrapment, diagnosed in psychoanalytical and existential literature. In Piranesi's art, modern culture saw reflected an inner world partitioned into labyrinths, stairs, narrow landings, and bottomless pits extending *ad infinitum*. The artist seemed to say that the reality we perceive, whether conceived in texts, pictures, film, or architecture, carries with it a shadowy counterpart, or, in fact, that it is itself a mere projection. An inner and an outer realm, entwined to the point where the reality of both becomes uncertain, characterizes a fundamental Piranesian experience.

In modern interpretations, Piranesi's prints have rarely existed in and for themselves—as prints. Various mediums have appropriated the compositions as if they were, and always had been, cornerstones of their own coming-into-being. The prints' transformation into psychological literature, abstract art, cinematic sequences, and postmodern architecture reinvented the conditions by which they became meaningful. But the succession of mediums in itself forms a telling itinerary. Recapturing this route through the decades, this study has shown how Piranesi moved from constituting an emotional stratum in fiction, to becoming an abstract configuration in art and cinema, and ending as a tangible grid in architecture. It is a sequence by which Piranesi seems to shape the modern age into a distinct narrative. It could be the story of how the application of Piranesi in the course of a century or so gradually became more manifest, more *material*, from delineating the chambers of the soul to providing the schema for new cities. Alternatively, the narrative might be read as one that goes from the individual to the collective—from framing the idea of the self, as in Victor Hugo, to fashioning societies, as Manfredo Tafuri saw it. Reviewing the last century in one sweeping glance, we might even glimpse, through the lens of Piranesi, an interior world of instability and discontinuity turning inside out to become our exterior one.

But then again, the succession of topics in this book may not give cause to picture a development at all. A development easily ties history to a teleology where the point is to predict where we head next. Can Piranesi tell us where we are heading? History forms a wholeness only in the mind of the historian, not in the multifarious, heterogeneous reality of its actual unfolding. But Piranesi is a reference precisely as that—as multifarious and heterogeneous; it is in the attempts to break up, move on, refract, and undo existing conditions that his influence is most strongly felt. Piranesi is a patron of pasts that never were and futures that never will be.

I end this trajectory of Piranesi in our age at a time when the outlook is truly global and his *Campo Marzio* grid underpins projects of urbanization around the world. Looking ahead, we may imagine the endless modulation of the plan generating worlds that are no longer real, but virtual. In the *New Campo Marzio* (2020), developed by Damjan Jovanovic and others, Piranesi's Rome is the model for an "open-ended" simulation game. As experimental software, the plan has transferred to a realm where its potential and its limits are once again redefined.[108]

This book admittedly offers an ambiguous conclusion to the story it tells. By imposing a thematic order on the material, it contradicts the discontinuity and disruption it has defined as distinctive of Piranesi's influence. It short-circuits the very history which it has unraveled, and of which it undeniably forms part. The organization of this text, then, somehow betrays the content; other, more radical forms of presentations would surely reflect the material more imaginatively. Still, in its ambiguity, I hope this monograph may be inscribed into an esteemed genealogy of Piranesi emulations, for nothing can be more noble in this tradition than the ambition to rein in the endless and contain the infinite, only to be deceived by the format.

overleaf Rem Koolhaas/OMA, footprint of building projected onto Piranesi's *Campo Marzio*. Togok Towers, Seoul, 1996

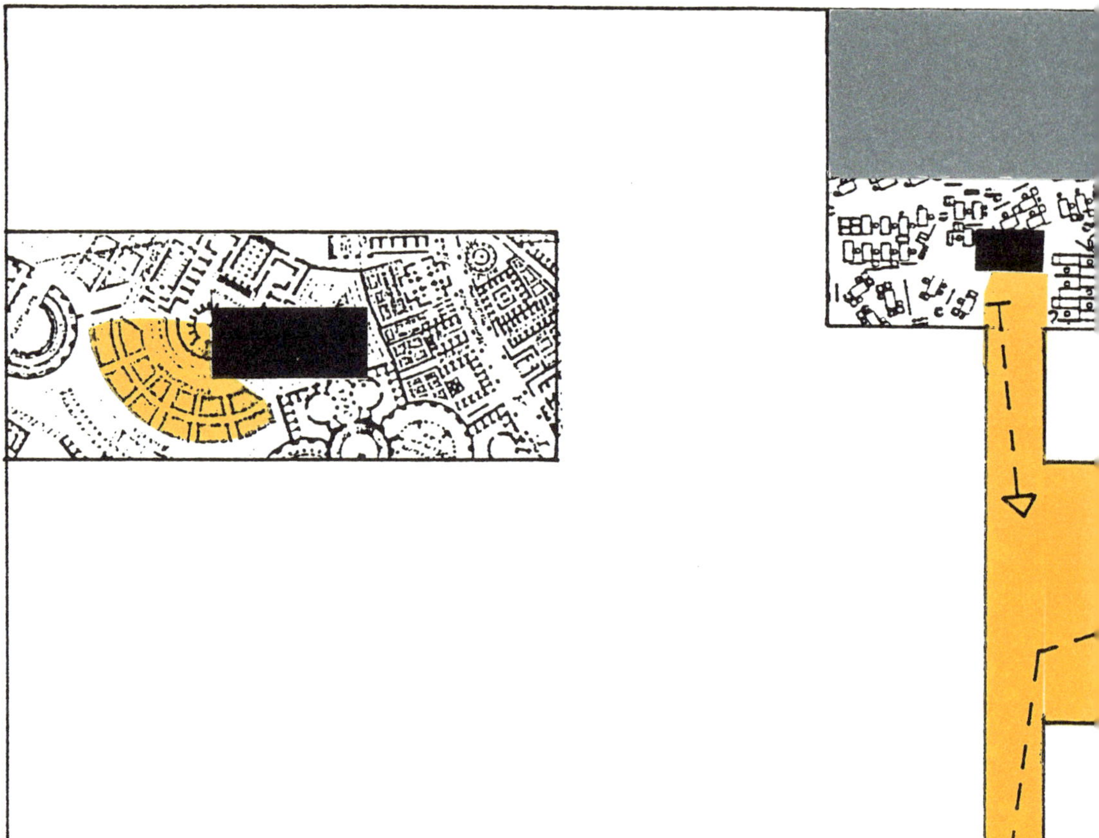

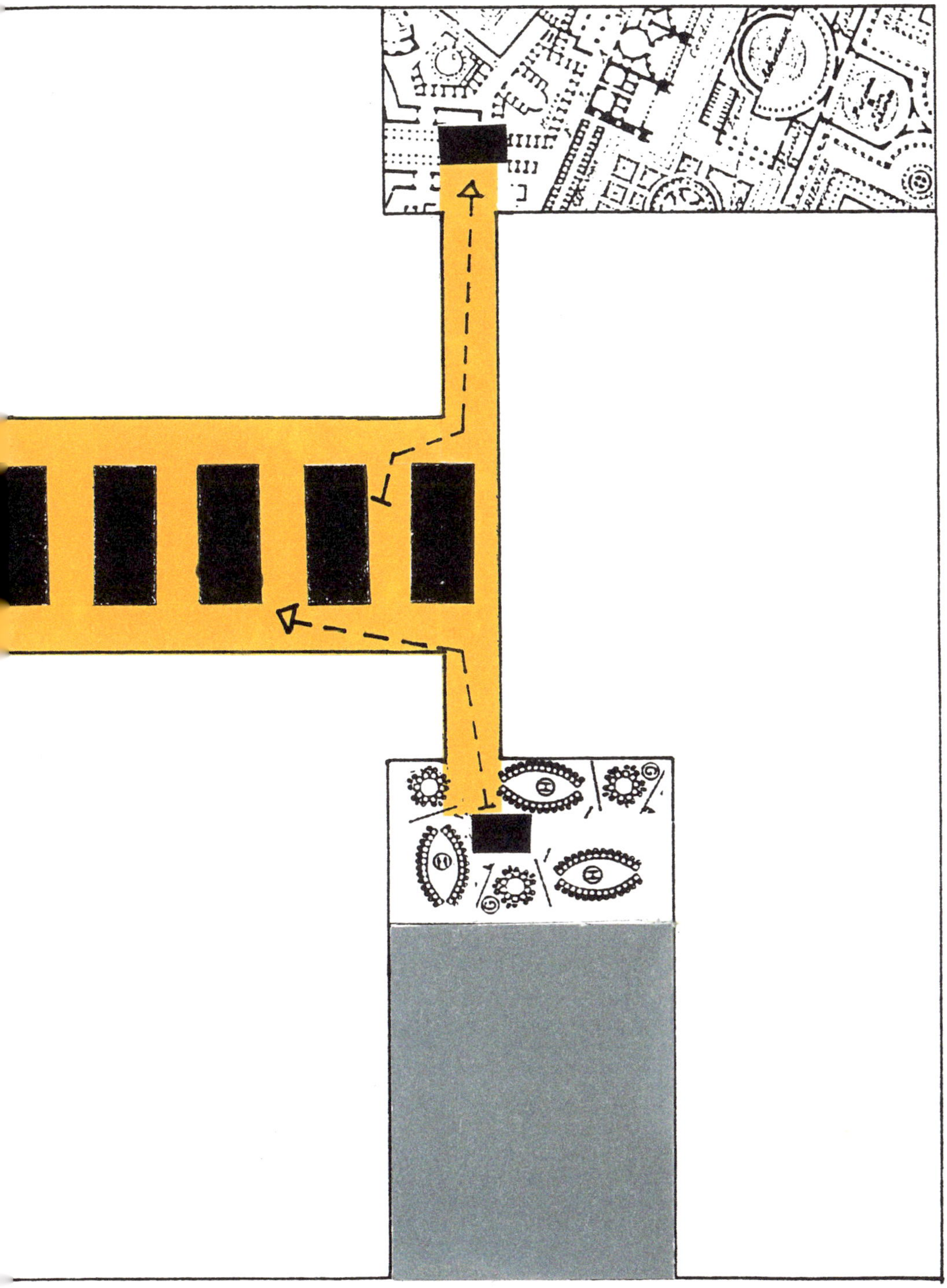

CODA—P

OPLE'S PIRANESI

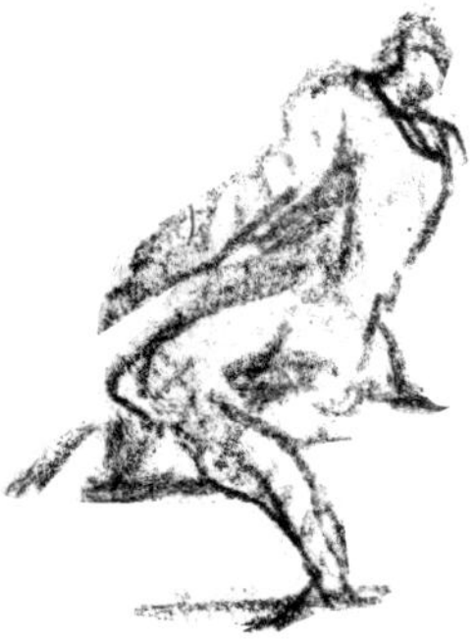

An important undertaking in a new urbanism, according to the *Mémoires* of Asger Jorn and Guy Debord (1959), is to replace the stairs of Piranesi with lifts.[1] Jorn and Debord obviously had in mind the *Carceri* and the prints' association with fateful descents that lead to nothing but angst and confusion in the tradition of Hugo and Baudelaire. The lift would do away with any tortuous climbing, and consequently with any sense of disquiet, in the emotionally based restructuring of cities that Debord and his fellow Situationists dubbed "psychogeography."

In the transit hall of the Euralille train station (completed 1994), Rem Koolhaas replaced the stairs of Piranesi not only with lifts but also with escalators, easing access from the street level to the metro system below. The crisscrossing escalators of OMA's "Espace Piranesien" take commuters past a large mural by Jean Pattou that depicts arches and piers entwined by spiral stairs and ramps, ramming home the evocation of the *Carceri*.

As these two examples suggest, Piranesi still casts a spell over the downward journey, even in its technologically updated forms. Not even lifts and escalators manage to quite dispel two centuries of associating the idea of going underground with the dystopian Venetian. And just as the underground descent is conceptually monopolized by Piranesi, so too is the subway's labyrinth of tunnels. Despite its conspicuous modernity, the typology of the subway has elicited parallels to the *Carceri* and the *Campo Marzio* as well as to Piranesi's renderings of vaults and reservoirs from Roman times. The inner earth, according to Lars Lerup, escapes the typologies of architectural history; it represents an "otherness" that brings out affinities between the deep interiorities conceived by Piranesi and the underground tunnel makers: "As normally experienced, deliberate space is constructed—it is materialized labor. In the Piranesi print, however, space is carved out of the metal etching plate, much as a station in Stockholm's metro is blasted out of the *urberg* (using Alfred Nobel's dynamite)."[2] The materiality of stone and copper yields a different space to the one that architects construct.

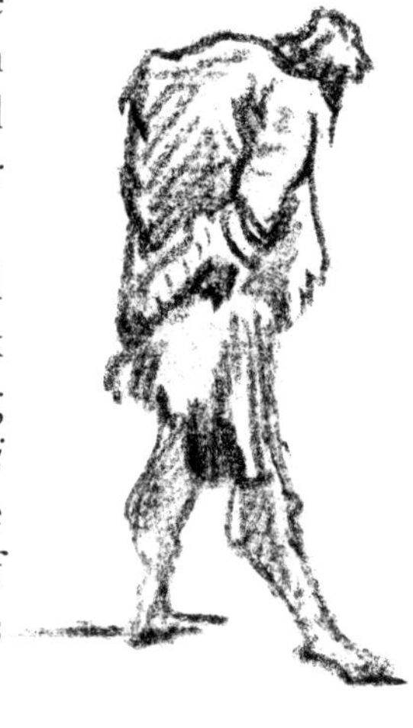

The lifts and escalators lead to an underground ruled by Piranesi. As soon as one enters the subway system, Mark Pimlott observes, the entire architecture of interlocking spaces traversed by bridges confines the traveler to a *Carceri* paradigm.[3] Similarly, in Marshall Berman's opinion, the *Carceri* etchings prefigure the oppressive environment of the Washington DC Metro in particular, where platforms

Giovanni Battista Piranesi, "Five Male Figures." Red chalk on paper.

seem to stretch into infinity and passengers are "encased in enormous voids shaped by barrel-vaulted ceilings, and by vast blots of blackness at the platform's ends."[4] Lifts, escalators, subways—tokens of modernity—move through spaces carved out on copper by the eighteenth-century etcher. The modern engineered world is but a veneer, for the experience of it already seems to reside deep in the underground of our own psyche, prefigured in the "impossible" architecture of Piranesi's prints.

However, the sublime, disturbing effect of the Piranesian underground also wears off. "Mass Communication on the People Freeway: Or Piranesi Is Too Easy" is the title of the studio course Robert Venturi and Denise Scott Brown gave at Yale University in 1967, later published in *Perspecta* (1969).[5] The course addressed the 1960s' redesign of subways, with a focus on Herald Square in New York. Venturi denounced attempts to include "Piranesian bridges" in subway stations, criticizing architects who tried too hard to "make" neat architecture out of these spaces. Venturi's point was that the whole Piranesian vocabulary—bridges, vaults, gangways—offers picturesque motifs that are too easily evoked to dramatize, or, in fact, contextualize, subterranean spaces that are unencumbered by an architectural history.

To Venturi and his students, Piranesi was no longer dangerous. His compositions conveyed a stylized space, a domesticized cavity. To them, rawer and more primal forebears of subways could be found in the prehistoric caves of Lascaux and Altamira and in the early Christian catacombs. Whereas those underground spaces connected at a deeper human level, they wrote, the world of Piranesi was neither primordial nor cavernous but remained what it had always been, of course, namely prints on paper.

According to Borges, as we saw in chapter one, the *Carceri* were the inspiration for the endless subterranean halls in William Beckford's story *Vathek* (1787), in his view, the first representation in literature of a truly unbearable hell. It was not the solitude that made these halls so frightening. On the contrary, there were people everywhere, but no one communicated: "They all avoided each other; and, though surrounded by a multitude that no one could number, each wandered at random unheedful of the rest," Beckford wrote.[6] Two hundred years later, Yourcenar made a similar observation, saying that the true horror of the *Carceri* is the indifference expressed by people "roaming through enormous spaces, whose various groups seem almost never to communicate among themselves or even to take note of their respective presences."[7] Returning to the subway, the scenario that Beckford and Yourcenar evoke is hardly shocking to the millions of commuters who each day descend into subway

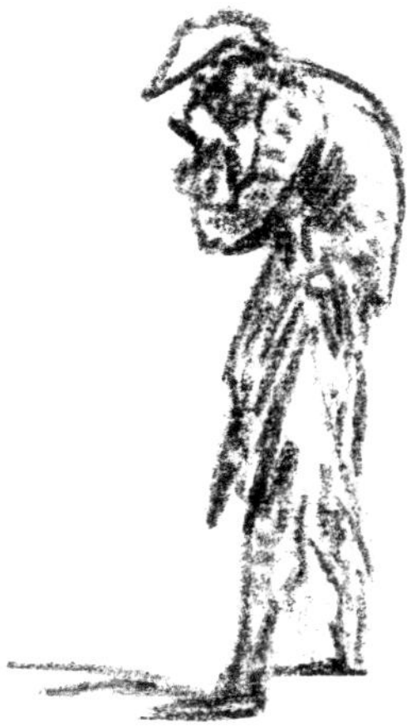

systems around the world. In fact, both descriptions capture quite accurately the apathy of the early morning rush hour on platforms worldwide. Whether the world is therefore tragically fulfilling the dystopia prophesied in Piranesi's etchings, or whether the nightmare can be dispelled by an unexpected free seat on the train and the first, blissful sip from a takeaway coffee, is an open question.

All the same, Piranesi's architecture induces a particular sense of oppression that signals not merely confinement but also the seemingly infinite extent of that confinement—a devious superstructure equaling society itself. Piranesi's spacious interiors convey a freedom that is useless, or, more correctly, they convey the *imitation* of freedom, and as such they illustrate the existential condition of modern men and women who find themselves "liberated and condemned at the same time," to quote Tafuri.[8] This reading of Piranesi's work was pivotal in bringing the artist to prominence in the twentieth century. The confinement–liberation theme appealed to the Marxist convictions shared by a surprisingly large number of his admirers: already in the 1930s, German philosopher Ernst Bloch identified in Piranesi's oeuvre not an ancient world but the plans for a future one and connected Piranesi's symmetries with Soviet architecture.[9] Indeed, Marxist thought permeates the Piranesi interpretations of Eisenstein, Tafuri, Berman, Aureli, and Tattara. His art could serve as either a promise or a warning, but always as an incentive to emancipate crowds from oppression—architectural, political, and existential.

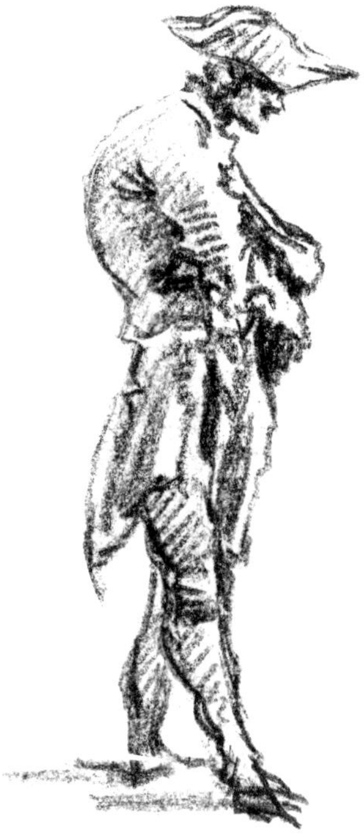

People, in Piranesi's prints, amount to a disquieting entity, hovering over bottomless depths, crouching in the shadow of gigantic ruins—alone, brooding, and seldom communicating. Their moods and gestures seem to express the disruption, discontinuity, and conflict of the architecture itself. They are intermediaries who dictate our reaction to Piranesi's world, without our being aware of it at first. In the end, who are the people Piranesi frames in his art? Modern interpreters from Eisenstein to Gombrich have pointed out that his objective was not to portray people, but to include the beholder—to make *us* the subject of his compositions. His many tricks to dissolve time and space reduce architecture to a mere instrument. Contradictions and ambiguities, disguised as architecture, were for Piranesi means to ensnare spectators in the compositions. In this, he succeeded; for centuries later we have still not found our way out.

Prelude

1 Rem Koolhaas, interview with the author, Apr. 9, 2019, Amsterdam. According to Koolhaas, this must have been in the late 1940s.

2 Johann Wolfgang von Goethe, *Goethe's Boyhood*, trans. Wilhelm Wagner (Cambridge: The University Press, 1894).

3 On Goethe's collection of prints, see Johannes Grave, *Der "Ideale Kunstkörper": Johann Wolfgang Goethe als Sammler von Druckgraphiken und Zeichnungen* (Göttingen: Vandenhoeck & Ruprecht, 2006). On Goethe's collection of Piranesi in particular, see Victor Plahte Tschudi, "Goethe in the Hall and His Journeys in Printed Rome," *Architectural Histories* 3, no. 1 (2015): 11–15, www.doi.org/10.5334/ah.cx.

4 On the history of the church and Piranesi's intervention, the most comprehensive study remains John Wilton-Ely, *Piranesi as Architect and Designer* (New Haven, CT: Yale University Press, 1993).

5 Marcia Reed, "Reading Piranesi: The Architecture of the Book," in *The Art of Exaggeration: Piranesi's Perspectives on Rome*, ed. Eunice D. Howe (Los Angeles: Fisher Gallery, University of Southern California, 1995), 24.

6 See for example Heather Hyde Minor and Carolyn Yerkes, *Piranesi Unbound* (Princeton: Princeton University Press, 2020).

7 The essence of modernity, Georg Simmel wrote in 1911, is "the experience and interpretation of the world in terms of the reactions of our inner life and indeed as an inner world." Quoted from K. Michael Hays, "Introduction to Manfredo Tafuri 'Toward a Critique of Architectural Ideology,'" in *Architecture Theory since 1968* (Cambridge, MA: MIT Press, 1998), 4–5, note 2.

8 Rudolf Wittkower, "Piranesi's 'Parere su l'architettura,'" *Journal of the Warburg Institute* 2, no. 2 (October 1938): 155.

9 Sergei Eisenstein, "Piranesi, Or the Fluidity of Forms," trans. Roberta Reeder, *Oppositions* 11 (1977): 83–110. Aldous Huxley, *Prisons* (London: Trianon Press, 1949).

10 Ulya Vogt-Göknil, *Giovanni Battista Piranesi: Carceri* (Zürich: Origo Verlag, 1958). Patricia May Sekler, "Notes on Old and Modern Drawings: Giovanni Battista Piranesi's Carceri Etchings and Related Drawings," *Art Quarterly* 25 (1962): 331–363.

11 Vincent Scully, "Modern Architecture: Towards a Redefinition of Style," *Perspecta* 4 (1957): 4–11. On Debord, see Simon Sadler, *The Situationist City* (Cambridge, MA: MIT Press, 1998), 75. See also Günther Feuerstein, "Function, Provocation," in *The Situationists and the City*, ed. Tom McDonough (London: Verso, 2009), 134. "Piranesi titled a few projects *Carceri* (prisons). These are grandiose rooms, without utilization in the end." Feuerstein's essay was originally published in *Aujourd'hui* 53 (May–June 1966): 26–27.

12 Major publications on Piranesi from this period include Lola Kantor-Kazovsky, *Piranesi as Interpreter of Roman Architecture and the Origins of His Intellectual World* (Florence: Leo S. Olschki, 2006). Joseph Connors, *Piranesi and the Campus Martius: The Missing Corso: Topography and Archaeology in Eighteenth-Century Rome* (Milan: Jaca Book, 2011). Mario Bevilacqua, Heather Hyde Minor, and Fabio Barry, *The Serpent and The Stylus: Essays on G. B. Piranesi* (Ann Arbor: University of Michigan Press, 2006). John A. Pinto, *Speaking Ruins: Piranesi, Architects, and Antiquity in Eighteenth-Century Rome* (Ann Arbor: University of Michigan Press, 2012). Heather Hyde Minor, *Piranesi's Lost Words* (University Park: Pennsylvania State University Press, 2015). See also Giuseppe Pavanello, Michele De Lucchi, and Adam Lowe, *Le arti di Piranesi: architetto, incisore, antiquario, vedutista, designer* (Venice: Marsilio, 2010). Dirk De Meyer, Bart Verschaffel, and Pieter-Jan Cierkens, eds., *Aspects of Piranesi: Essays on History, Criticism and Invention* (Ghent: A&S/books, 2015).

13 The Piranesi-related projects of Rem Koolhaas are discussed in chapter six. See Pier Vittorio Aureli and Martino Tattara, "A Field of Walls (2012)," in *Dogma: 11 Projects* (London: AA Publications, 2015), 32–41. The project is based on Aureli's and Tattara's contribution to the exhibition *The Piranesi Variations*, organized by Peter Eisenman, at the 2010 architectural biennale in Venice. See also Pier Vittorio Aureli, *The Possibility of an Absolute Architecture* (Cambridge, MA: MIT Press, 2011). Gijs Wallis de Vries, *Archescape:*

On the Tracks of Piranesi (Amsterdam: Thousand & One Publishers, 2014).

14 The catalogues include Henri Focillon, *Giovanni Battista Piranesi. Essai de catalogue raisonné de son oeuvre* (Paris, 1918) and Arthur M. Hind, *Giovanni Battista Piranesi: A Critical Study with a List of His Published Works and Detailed Catalogues of the Prisons and the Views of Rome* (London, 1922), and lastly John Wilton-Ely, *Giovanni Battista Piranesi: The Complete Etchings*, vol. 1 and 2 (San Francisco: Wofsy, 1994).

15 The work was published in Latin with the title *Campus Martius antiquae urbis.*

16 Prints come in different editions but also in different states, which may be confusing. In the literature on Piranesi, "editions" and "states" are used interchangeably. However, an "edition" refers to the reissue of a print, or a series of prints, whereas a "state" refers to eventual alterations done to the copper plate before new prints are being pulled. With these definitions in mind, the *Carceri* exist in multiple states but only in two editions, the first published in 1749–1750, and the second in 1761. On the editions and states of the *Carceri*, see in particular Andrew Robison, *Piranesi: Early Architectural Fantasies: A Catalogue Raisonné of the Etchings* (Chicago: University of Chicago Press, 1986), 139–210.

17 The prison etchings, or *Carceri d'invenzione*, are discussed in detail in the first chapter. On Herbert Batsford's discovery and his friendship with Arthur Samuel, see Harry Batsford, *A Batsford Century: The Record of a Hundred Years of Publishing and Bookselling 1843–1943*, ed. Hector Bolitho (London: B. T. Batsford, 1944), 46. Batsford's discovery happened just in time for Samuel to include examples of both editions in his book: see Arthur Samuel, *Piranesi* (London: B. T. Batsford, 1910). See also Hind who attributes the "discovery" of the *Carceri*'s first edition to Batsford in Arthur M. Hind, "Giovanni Battista Piranesi and His 'Carceri,'" *Burlington Magazine* 19, no. 98 (May 1911): 81. The British Library acquired the Batsford set in 1911.

18 *The Drawbridge* occurs for example in Focillon's *The Life of Forms in Art* (1934) and in Alfred H. Barr's exhibition *Cubism and Abstract Art* (1936), whereas *The Gothic Arch* was subjected to analysis in Sergei Eisenstein's "Piranesi, Or the Fluidity of Form" (1946–1947) and exhibited at MOMA's *Timeless Aspects of Modern Art* (1948). In the following, I will use titles to refer to the individual prints in the *Carceri d'invenzione* in accordance with established practice. See for instance Robison, *Piranesi: Early Architectural Fantasies*, 1986. And Wilton-Ely, *Giovanni Battista Piranesi: The Complete Etchings.* These titles, however, do not originate with Piranesi.

19 Huxley, *Prisons*, 1949, 22.

20 Manfredo Tafuri, "'The Wicked Architect': G. B. Piranesi, Heterotopia, and the Voyage," in *The Sphere and the Labyrinth: Avant-Gardes and Architecture from Piranesi to the 1970s* (Cambridge, MA: MIT Press, 1987), 27. The text is a translation of Tafuri's *La sfera e il labirinto: Avanguardie e architettura da Piranesi agli anni '70* (1980). An original version of this last text appeared in Manfredo Tafuri, "Per una critica dell'ideologia architettonica," *Contropiano* 1 (1969): 31–79.

21 See Brian Ferneyhough, "Carceri d'Invenzione (1986)" in *Collected Writings*, ed. James Boros and Richard Toop (Amsterdam: Harwood Academic Publishers, 1995), 131–138.

22 See for instance Richard Anderson, *Russia: Modern Architectures in History* (London: Reaktion Books, 2015), 62, 83–85, 288–290. Also see Semën Michajlovskij and Nikolaj Molok, "Piranesi in URSS," in *Piranesi prima e dopo: Italia-Russia XVIII-XXI secolo*, ed. Federica Rossi (Moscow: Antiga Edizioni, 2016), 127–38.

23 Roland Barthes, "The Death of the Author," in *Image, Music, Text*, trans. Stephen Heath (New York: Hill and Wang, 1977), 146.

24 Harold Bloom, *The Anxiety of Influence: A Theory of Poetry*, second edition (Oxford: Oxford University Press, 1997), 5. The first edition of this classic text of criticism was published in 1973.

The De Quincey Effect

1 The literature on these prints is extensive. Giovanna Scaloni gives an analysis of the copper plates in the holdings of the Istituto Nazionale per la Grafica in Rome in "Carceri,"

in *Giambattista Piranesi: matrici incise 1743–1753*, ed. Ginevra Mariani (Rome: Mazzotta/Istituto Nazionale per la Grafica, 2010), 52–69. On the execution of the drawings, see in particular Sekler, "Notes on Old and Modern Drawings." On the *Carceri*'s various editions and states, see Robison, *Piranesi: Early Architectural Fantasies*, 1986, 139–210. Memorable interpretations of the series are offered by Aldous Huxley, *Prisons* (London: Trianon Press, 1949). Marguerite Yourcenar, "The Dark Brain of Piranesi," in *The Dark Brain of Piranesi and Other Essays*, trans. Richard Howard (in collaboration with the author) (Henley-on-Thames: Aidan Ellis, 1985), 88–128. See also Ola Granli, *Omöjliga Rum* (Oslo: OCCAS/Oslo School of Architecture and Design, 2017). A history of the influence of the *Carceri* is found in Alexander Kupfer, *Piranesis "Carceri": Enge und Unendlichkeit in den Gefängnissen der Phantasie* (Stuttgart: Belser Verlag, 1992).

2 Jacques Guillaume Legrand, "Notice historique sur la vie et les ouvrages de J. B. Piranesi architecte, peintre et graveur. Manuscript (Paris, Bibliothèque Nationale Ms. Nouv. Acq. Fr. 5968) Transcribed and published in Erouart, Gilbert, and Monique Mosser, 'À propos de la "Notice historique sur la vie et les ouvrages de J.-B. Piranesi": origine et fortune d'une biographie,'" in *Piranèse et les Français*, ed. Georges Brunel (Rome: Edizioni dell'Elefante, 1978), 235.

3 William M. Ivins, "Piranesi and Le Carceri d'Invenzione," *Print Collector's Quarterly* 5, no. 2 (April 1915): 213–214.

4 Erika Naginski, "Romanticism's Piranesi," in *The Built Surface: Architecture and the Pictorial Arts from Antiquity to the Enlightenment*, ed. Christy Anderson and Karen Koehler, vol. 1 (Aldershot: Ashgate, 2002), 237–259.

5 Oscar Wilde, *Intentions* (London: Methuen, 1908), 245–246.

6 This is not the place to elaborate on the eighteenth-century idea of the sublime and the emotional effect of phenomena in art and nature; I refer to Edmund Burke's *A Philosophical Enquiry into the Origin of Our Idea of the Sublime and Beautiful* (1757) and Archibald Alison's *Essays on the Nature of the Principle of Taste* (1790).

7 Horace Walpole in *Anecdotes of Painting in England* (1771) quoted from John Wilton-Ely, *The Mind and Art of Giovanni Battista Piranesi* (London: Thames and Hudson, 1978), 109. The relation of British Romantic poets to Piranesi is the subject in Martin Christadler, "Giovanni Battista Piranesi und die Architekturmetapher der Romantik," in *Miscellanea Anglo-Americana: Festschrift für Helmut Vierbock*, ed. Kuno Schumann, Wilhelm Hortmann, and Armin Paul Frank (Munich: Karl Pressler, 1974), 78–108. See also Jørgen Andersen, "Giant Dreams: Piranesi's Influence in England," *English Miscellany* 3 (1952): 49–59.

8 The passage is from Beckford's *Dreams, Walking Thoughts and Incidents* (1783) quoted from Anderson, "Giant Dreams," 55.

9 Elizabeth Fay, "Hallucinogesis: Thomas De Quincey's Mind Trips," *Studies in Romanticism* 49, no. 2 (2010): 296. For a brief survey on recent interpretations of the *Confessions*, see pp. 296–297. Curtis Perry argues that the dreams and hallucinations in the book are not so much due to intoxication and oblivion as elaborate forms of self-staging within the narrative. See Curtis Perry, "Piranesi's Prison: Thomas De Quincey and the Failure of Autobiography," *Studies in English Literature, 1500–1900* 33, no. 4 (1993): 809–824.

10 Thomas De Quincey, *The Confessions of an English Opium Eater*, ed. David Masson, vol. 3, *The Collected Writings of Thomas De Quincey* (Edinburgh: Adam and Charles Black, 1890), 438–439.

11 See Michael Bryan, *Bryan's Dictionary of Painters and Engravers*, vol. 4 (London: George Bell and Sons, 1904), 125. This is an enlarged edition of Michael Bryan, *A Biographical and Critical Dictionary of Painters and Engravers* (London: Carpenter and Son, 1816). The latter edition does not include the fever anecdote.

12 See for example Edgar Allan Poe's short story "The Pit and the Pendulum" (1842). The impact of the *Carceri* on American literature is discussed in Kupfer, *Piranesis "Carceri,"* 123–134.

13 De Quincey, *The Confessions of an English Opium Eater*, 3:439.

14 V. A. De Luca does not draw exactly this parallel but discusses similar biblical analogies in De Quincey's writings. See V. A. De Luca, "De Quincey's Icons of Apocalypse: Some Romantic Analogues," in *Thomas De Quincey: Bicentenary Studies*, ed. Robert Lance Snyder (Norman: University of Oklahoma Press, 1985), 20–34.

15 There is consensus among historians that De Quincey based his description on the *Carceri*. See for example J. Hillis Miller, *The Disappearance of God: Five Nineteenth-Century Writers* (Urbana and Chicago: University of Illinois Press, 2000), 68. And also Laurence Stapleton, *The Elected Circle: Studies in the Art of Prose* (Princeton: Princeton University Press, 1973), 139.

16 The point is made by Christopher Warwick Thompson, *Victor Hugo and the Graphic Arts (1820–1833)* (Geneva: Librairie Droz, 1970), 98, 100–102, 109. Thompson refers in particular to Hugo's poem "Légende de la nonne" (1828).

17 For a lively account of the transportation of the plates to Paris, see Arthur Samuel, *Piranesi* (London: B. T. Batsford, 1910), 164–168. On the Piranesi sons' efforts to repossess the plates, see Heather Hyde Minor, *Piranesi's Lost Words* (University Park: Pennsylvania State University Press, 2015), 193–194. On the Paris editions in general, see Andrew Robison, *Piranesi: Early Architectural Fantasies: A Catalogue Raisonné of the Etchings* (Chicago: University of Chicago Press, 1986), 214.

18 On Musset's 1853 translation, published in the short story "La mouche,"see Paul F. Jamieson, "Musset, de Quincey, and Piranesi," *Modern Language Notes* 72, no. 2 (1956): 105–108.

19 On Baudelaire's translation of De Quincey, see Luzius Keller, *Piranèse et les romantiques français: le mythe des escaliers en spirale* (Paris: Librairie José Corti, 1966), 198–199.

20 Keller, *Piranèse et les romantiques français*, 1966. Georges Poulet, *Trois essais de mythologie romantiques* (Paris: Librairie José Corti, 1966). A general survey of the French nineteenth-century "Piranesi cult" is offered by Kupfer, *Piranesis "Carceri,"* 85–122. For a discussion on the preconditions for a predominantly French interest in Piranesi during the Romantic period, see Naginski, "Romanticism's Piranesi."

21 Keller, *Piranèse et les romantiques français*, 1966, 197. Poulet, *Trois essais de mythologie romantiques*, 175.

22 To judge from Nodier's choice of words, he based his reading of De Quincey on Musset's 1828 translation. The point is made by Keller, *Piranèse et les romantiques français*, 1966, 65.

23 Charles Nodier, "Piranèse: contes psychologiques: à propos de la monomanie réflective," in *Oeuvres complètes*, vol. XI (Geneva: Slatkine Reprints, 1998), 167–204. See in particular pp. 189–193. The translation is mine.

24 See Théophile Gautier, "The Club of Assassins," in *Hashish, Wine, Opium: Charles Baudelaire, Théophile Gautier*, trans. Maurice Stang (Richmond: Alma Classics, 2009), 48. The connection between this passage and De Quincey's Piranesi reference was noted by Randolph Hughes, "Vers la contrée du rêve: Balzac, Gautier et Baudelaire, disciples de De Quincey," *Mercure de France* 8 (1939): 569. It was also pointed out by Keller, *Piranèse et les romantiques français*, 1966, 94–96. On Gautier and Piranesi, see also Poulet, *Trois essais de mythologie romantiques*, 166–174.

25 On this point, see Victor Brombert, "Victor Hugo, la prison et l'espace," *Revue des sciences humaines* (January–March 1965): 69.

26 "Devant vos profendeurs j'ai pâli bien souvent/Comme sur une abîme ou sur une fournaise,/Effrayantes Babels que rêvait Piranèse."

27 Poulet, *Trois essais de mythologie romantiques*, 179.

28 On this point, see Keller, *Piranèse et les romantiques français*, 1966, 180.

29 "Le noir cerveau de Piranèse/Est une béante fournaise/Où se mêlent l'arche et le ciel,/L'escalier, la tour, la colonne;/Où croît, monte, s'enfle et bouillonne/L'incommensurable Babel!" The poem *Les mages* appears in Victor Hugo, *Les contemplations*, 1856, VI, 23. The suggestion that Hugo must have seen actual prints by Piranesi by the time he wrote it is made by Keller, *Piranèse et les romantiques français*, 1966, 183.

30 "Je sens s'élargir dans mon être/un abîme béant; cet abîme est mon coeur." See Charles Baudelaire, *The Flowers of Evil*, trans. James McGowan (Oxford: Oxford University Press,

2008), 244. The translation is mine. The quote is from the poem "Femmes damnées: Delphine et Hippolyte." A court ruling banned this and five other poems on grounds of indecency, a ban that was not lifted until 1949.

31 Rafael Argullol writes about Piranesi and Baudelaire but offers less a comparison and more a juxtaposition of their oeuvres. See Rafael Argullol, "La pérdida del centro: Piranesi y Baudelaire," *Revista de Occidente*, no. 115 (December 1990): 27–40. On Baudelaire and his adaptation of De Quincey's passage on Piranesi, see also Keller, *Piranèse et les romantiques français*, 1966, 200–203.

32 "Je vous écris d'une prison où sont les fosses si profondes/qu'on y devine entre les murs des escaliers sans fin, tournant/jusqu'au plus noir du noir comme au coeur du silence." Pierre Seghers, *Piranesi*, trans. Ian Higgins (London: Forest Books, 1993), 2–3.

33 Huxley, *Prisons*, 1949, 18.

34 Samuel, *Piranesi*, 1910, 107. Hind calls them "dreams of prisons" in Arthur M. Hind, *Giovanni Battista Piranesi: A Critical Study with a List of His Published Works and Detailed Catalogues of the Prisons and the Views of Rome* (London: Holland Press, 1968), 11. They are "the dreams of Piranesi" in Andersen, "Giant Dreams," 1952, 54. Yourcenar names them dreams too in "The Dark Brain of Piranesi," 1985, 110. See also Huxley, *Prisons*, 1949, 16. Ernst H. Gombrich, *Art and Illusion: A Study in the Psychology of Pictorial Illusion* (London: Phaidon Press, 1960), 207.

35 John Wilton-Ely, *The Mind and Art of Giovanni Battista Piranesi* (London: Thames and Hudson, 1978), 81. See also Myra Nan Rosenfeld, "Picturesque to Sublime: Piranesi's Stylistic and Technical Development from 1740 to 1761," in *The Serpent and the Stylus: Essays on G. B. Piranesi*, ed. Mario Bevilacqua, Heather Hyde Minor, and Fabio Barry (Ann Arbor: University of Michigan Press, 2006), 83. John A. Pinto, *City of the Soul: Rome and the Romantics* (Hanover: University Press of New England, 2016), 16.

36 Yourcenar, "The Dark Brain of Piranesi," 1985, 110.

37 Huxley, *Prisons*, 1949, 20.

38 Andersen, "Giant Dreams," 1952, 49.

39 Introductory text in booklet accompanying Grégoire Dupond and Factum Arte, *Carceri d'invenzione di G. Battista Piranesi*, Booklet and DVD (Madrid: Julio Soto impresores/ Factum Arte, 2010).

40 On De Quincey's coinage, use, and meaning of the term "subconscious," see Markus Iseli, *Thomas De Quincey and the Cognitive Unconscious* (Basingstoke: Palgrave Macmillan, 2015), 30–42.

41 Charles L. Proudfit, "Thomas De Quincey and Sigmund Freud: Sons, Fathers, Dreamers—Precursors of Psychoanalytical Developmental Psychology," in *Thomas De Quincey: Bicentenary Studies*, ed. Robert Lance Snyder (Norman: University of Oklahoma Press, 1985), 98. See also Iseli, *Thomas De Quincey and the Cognitive Unconscious*, 5–6. The connection between De Quincey and Freud is also pointed out by Perry, "Piranesi's Prison," 812.

42 Sigmund Freud, *Civilization and Its Discontents*, trans. James Strachey (New York: W. W. Norton, 1961), 16–18. The book was originally published in 1930.

43 Sigmund Freud, *Dream Psychology: Psychoanalysis for Beginners* (New York: James A. McCann, 1921), 114.

44 Kasimir's print is a drypoint and etching, executed between 1890 and 1910. Freud probably acquired the print in Vienna and brought it with him to London. It is now in Freud Museum London, cat. no. 3981.

45 Sigmund Freud, *The Interpretation of Dreams (1900)*, trans. James Strachey, vol. 4, *The Standard Edition of the Complete Psychological Works of Sigmund Freud* (London: Vintage Books, 2001), 194.

46 Tarnya Cooper, "Forgetting Rome and the Voice of Piranesi's 'Speaking Ruins,'" in *The Art of Forgetting*, ed. Adrian Forty and Susanne Küchler (Oxford: Berg, 2001), 107.

47 See Pinto, *Speaking Ruins: Piranesi, Architects, and Antiquity in Eighteenth-Century Rome*, 116.

48 Ulrike Brunotte, "The Construction of the Underworld: On the Architecture of Memory in Cults and Psychology," *Daidalos* 48 (1993): 81.

49 Susan Stewart, *Crimes of Writing: Problems in the Containment of Representation* (Durham: Duke University Press 1994), 164.

50 Sigmund Freud, "The 'Uncanny,'" in *Art and Literature*, trans. James Strachey, vol. 14, The Pelican Freud Library (London: Penguin Books, 1985), 356.

51 De Quincey, Piranesi, and the uncanny are discussed in Anthony Vidler, *The Architectural Uncanny: Essays in the Modern Unhomely* (Cambridge, MA: MIT Press, 1992), 37–40.

52 See for instance definition in Carl Gustav Jung, *The Archetypes and the Collective Unconscious*, trans. R. F. C. Hull, Bollingen Series (Princeton: Princeton University Press, 1990), 4. This collection of essays was first published in English with this title in 1959.

53 Jung, 43.

54 Jung, 7.

55 For example, when stairs and ladders occur in dreams, Jung claims, they usually connect to subjects related to our childhood although they may also point "to the process of psychic transformation, with all its ups and downs." See Carl Gustav Jung, *Indvidual Dream Symbolism in Relation to Alchemy*, trans. R. F. C. Hull (Princeton: Princeton University Press, 2010), 136. (The book was originally published as *Psychologie und Alchemie* in 1944). Jung considers the spiral as a form of "inner development" in Jung, 251. In other instances he connects the spiral specifically to stairs, such as in Jung, 128–129.

56 Carl Gustav Jung, "Picasso," in *The Spirit in Man, Art, and Literature*, trans. R. F. C. Hull (Princeton: Princeton University Press, 1971), 135–141. The essay was first published in *Neue Zürcher Zeitung*, CLIII, 2 (Nov. 1932), then republished in 1934, and translated into English in 1940.

57 Letter to Walter Mertens, Nov. 24, 1932. Carl Gustav Jung, *Letters*, ed. Gerhard Adler and Aniela Jaffé, trans. R. F. C. Hull, vol. 1: 1906–1950, Bollingen Series (Princeton: Princeton University Press, 2014), 108.

58 Letter to Hans Welti, Dec. 23, 1932 in Jung, 1: 1906–1950:114–115.

59 Jamieson, "Musset, de Quincey, and Piranesi," 108. Jamieson offers the precision with reference to Alpheus Hyatt Mayor, who in his book on Piranesi a few years earlier had called the prisons Piranesi's only landscapes of the mind. See A. Hyatt Mayor, *Giovanni Battista Piranesi* (New York: H. Bittner and Company, 1952), 30.

60 Keller mentions Jung as a source in an appendix tellingly titled "Les points de vue de la psychologie" (The points of view of psychology) in Keller, *Piranèse et les romantiques français*, 1966, 243–247.

61 With Baudelaire and Mallarmé "the spiral loses all its value as an ornament and becomes the naked expression of ontological anguish." Keller, 198.

62 J. Hillis Miller, *The Disappearance of God: Five Nineteenth-Century Writers* (Urbana and Chicago: University of Illinois Press, 2000), XVI.

63 Henri Focillon, *The Life of Forms in Art*, trans. Charles Beecher Hogan and George Kubler (New York: Zone Books, 1992), 127–130. The book was originally published in French as *Vie des formes* in 1934 and first published in English in 1948.

64 Gombrich, *Art and Illusion*, 244.

65 From the fourth edition (1972) onward, the layout of *Art and Illusion* changed from representing Escher in a small format and Piranesi on an entire page to showing them equally sized across a double spread, as illustrated.

66 Miller, *The Disappearance of God*, 2000, 67.

67 Patrick Bridgwater, *De Quincey's Gothic Masquerade* (Amsterdam: Rodopi, 2004), 157. Bridgwater makes the connection between Kafka's *The Castle* and De Quincey's *Confessions* also in Patrick Bridgwater, *Kafka, Gothic and Fairytale* (Amsterdam: Rodopi, 2003), 64. The latter book even flaunts one of Piranesi's prison drawings on its cover.

68 Bloomer also invokes the great plan of Rome from *Campo Marzio* (1762) and the print *Pianta di ampio magnifico collegio* (1750) as references in her discussion of *Finnegans Wake*. For the quote, see Jennifer Bloomer, *Architecture and the Text: The (S)Crypts of Joyce and Piranesi* (New Haven, CT: Yale University Press, 1993), 15.

69 Jennifer Bloomer, 17.

70 Bloomer, 122–123. She also sees a deeper structural parallel between De Quincey and Joyce's works (p. 122): "The *abîme* of de Quincey's recollection of the *Prisons* is, in manifold multiplication, a major structuring element in *Finnegans Wake*."

71 Italo Calvino, *Invisible Cities* (London: Vintage Books, 1997), 117.
72 Calvino, 102–103.
73 Sam J. Lundwall, *Fängelsestaden: en roman* (Stockholm: Norstedt, 1978), 8. The translation is mine. On the many levels of interaction between Lundwall's novel and the *Carceri*, see Svante Landgraf, "Drömmar av sten: Mot en posthumanistisk estetik i Sam J. Lundwalls Fängelsestaden," *Tidskrift för litteraturvetenskap* 49, no. 1 (2019): 41–50.
74 William Beckford, *Vathek* (1787) in *Three Gothic Novels* (London: Penguin Books, 1968), 245–246.
75 Jorge Luis Borges, "About William Beckford's Vathek," in *Other Inquisitions 1937–1952*, trans. Ruth L. C. Simms (Austin: University of Texas, 1995), 137–140.
76 "Yo conocí a Piranesi a través de Thomas de Quincey." See Cristina Grau, *Borges y la arquitectura* (Madrid: Ediciones Cátedra, 1989), 150.
77 Jorge Luis Borges, "The Immortal," in *The Aleph and Other Stories*, trans. Andrew Hurley (London: Penguin Books, 2000), 8. The story was first printed in 1947 and included in the collection *El aleph* published in 1949.
78 Cristina Grau, *Borges y la arquitectura* (Madrid: Ediciones Cátedra, 1989), 141–142.
79 See point made by Ricardo Romera Rozas, *L'univers humoristique de Jorge Luis Borges et Adolfo Bioy Casares* (Paris: L'Harmattan, 1995), 110.
80 See Grau, *Borges y la arquitectura*, 1989, 82.
81 Jorge Luis Borges and Adolfo Bioy-Casares, *Chronicles of Bustos Domecq*, trans. Thomas di Giovanni Norman (New York: E. P. Dutton, 1976), 78.
82 Romera Rozas, *L'univers humoristique de Jorge Luis Borges et Adolfo Bioy Casares*, 110.
83 Borges and Bioy-Casares, *Chronicles of Bustos Domecq*, 78–79.
84 Jorge Luis Borges, "The Circular Ruins," in *Labyrinths: Selected Stories and Other Writings*, ed. Donald A. Yates and James East Irby, trans. James East Irby (London: Penguin, 2000), 77. The short story originally appeared in the 1941 collection *The Garden of Forking Paths*, which was republished in the augmented *Ficciones* (*Fictions*) (1944).
85 Borges, 72.
86 The identification of the print in Borges's apartment was made by Grau, *Borges y la arquitectura*, 1989, 144–145. In an interview with Borges for *The Paris Review* in 1966, the journalist Ronald Christ noted several (unidentified) etchings by Piranesi on the wall in Borges's office in the Biblioteca Nacional in Buenos Aires. See Ronald Christ, "Jorge Luis Borges, the Art of Fiction No. 39," *Paris Review*, no. 40 (Winter–Spring 1967).
87 Borges, "The Circular Ruins," 77.
88 Goethe speaks of images being imprinted—*gedrückt*—on his mind in his autobiography, mentioned in chapter one. Johann Joachim Winckelmann also envisioned art in this way, noting that concepts of beauty are "imprinted" in the artist's mind from early youth. Johann Joachim Winckelmann, *History of the Art of Antiquity*, trans. Harry Francis Mallgrave (Los Angeles: Getty Research Institite, 2006), 192–193.
89 Marcel Proust, *Remembrance of Things Past*, trans. C. K. Scott Moncrieff, vol. 1 (New York: Henry Holt, 1922), 65.
90 When referring to Piranesi, Proust writes "ces petites gravures"—a term which denotes prints in general, including etching. Interestingly C. K. Scott Moncrieff's English translation from 1922 (known to Proust) substitutes the original "gravure" with the more specialized "etching," responding to the period's heightened sensitivity to Piranesi's technique championed by Arthur Hind and others. Thus, the translator overrides Proust's original but in graphic terms imprecise distinction with a definition that corresponds to Piranesi's actual method.
91 Théophile Gautier, *Travels in Spain*, trans. Frederick C. de Sumichrast (Boston: Little, Brown and Co, 1912), 106.
92 "...où chaque phrase, sans qu'il s'en doute, accentue et poursuit le trait plein de grâce et de gaieté de sa personnalité..." Marcel Proust, *Sur la lecture*, vol. 401 (Québec: La Bibliothèque électronique du Québec, n.d.). Proust's comment on Gautier's *Voyage en Espagne* appears on pp. 62–65. *Sur la lecture* (*On Reading*) was printed as introduction to Proust's translation of John Ruskin's *Sesame and the Lilies*, published in Paris 1906. I am grateful to Prof.

Karin Gundersen for this information. The translation into English is mine.

93 W. G. Sebald, *Austerlitz*, trans. Anthea Bell, 2002, 190–191.

94 The connection between Austerlitz' epiphany and Piranesi's *Carceri* (but not De Quincey's *Confessions*) has been made by Mari Lending, "Historisk Røntgen: Arkitekturfremstillinger i W. G. Sebalds 'Austerlitz,'" *Vinduet*, no. 1 (2010): 98–101.

95 Sebald, *Austerlitz*, 193.

The Etcher Exposed

1 Eighteenth- and nineteenth-century travelers who blamed Piranesi for their disappointment with Rome include the sculptor John Flaxman and the writers William Beckford and William Hazlitt. See Cooper, "Forgetting Rome," 113–114.

2 Joseph Pennell, *Etchers and Etching* (New York: Macmillan, 1919), 176.

3 See Bryan, *Bryan's Dictionary of Painters and Engravers*, 4:125. This is an enlarged edition of Bryan, *A Biographical and Critical Dictionary of Painters and Engravers*. The latter edition does not include the fever anecdote.

4 On printed copies after Leonardo's *Last Supper*, see for instance Leo Steinberg, *Leonardo's Incessant Last Supper* (New York: Zone Books, 2001), appendix E. On Morghen's reproduction in particular, see Victor Plahte Tschudi, "Recollecting Prints: Remembrance and Reproduction in Goethe's Italian Journey," in *From Site to Sight: The Transformation of Place in Art and Literature*, ed. Victor Plahte Tschudi and Turid Karlsen Seim (Rome: Scienze e Lettere, 2013), 139–163.

5 Russell Sturgis, *The Etchings of Piranesi* (New York: Frederick Keppel & Co, 1900), 3–4.

6 W. J. Woodworth, "Piranesi, the Rembrandt of Architecture," *Brush and Pencil* 10, no. 5 (1902): 277, 284.

7 Samuel, *Piranesi*, 1910, 101–102.

8 Quoted from A. Hyatt Mayor, *Giovanni Battista Piranesi* (New York: H. Bittner and Company, 1952), 28.

9 Hind, "Giovanni Battista Piranesi and His 'Carceri,'" 81.

10 Sturgis, *The Etchings of Piranesi*, 5.

11 Samuel, *Piranesi*, 1910, 118–119.

12 Hind, "Giovanni Battista Piranesi and His 'Carceri,'" 82.

13 Woodworth, "Piranesi, the Rembrandt of Architecture," 281.

14 Woodworth, 278.

15 Sturgis, *The Etchings of Piranesi*, 6.

16 Sturgis, 7–8.

17 Albert Giesecke, *Giovanni Battista Piranesi* (Leipzig: Verlag von Klinkhardt und Biermann, 1911), 89.

18 Yourcenar, "The Dark Brain of Piranesi," 1985, 105–106.

19 Henri Focillon, *Giovanni-Battista Piranesi 1720–1778* (Paris: Librairie Renouard—Henri Laurens, 1918), 255. The translation is mine.

20 On photographic emulations of Piranesi, see for instance Pinto, *City of the Soul*, 160–163. See also Luigi Ficacci, "Gabriele Basilico traduce Piranesi vedutista," in *Le arti di Piranesi: architetto, incisore, antiquario, vedutista, designer* (Venice: Marsilio Editore, 2010), 205–281.

21 László Moholy-Nagy, *Painting, Photography, Film* (London: Lund Humphries, 1969), 33.

22 A useful reference book is Beaumont Newhall, *The History of Photography from 1839 to the Present* (New York: Museum of Modern Art, 1982).

23 Robert Demachy, "The Straight and the Modern Print," *Camera Work*, no. 18 (1907): 358–359. *Camera Work* was the influential magazine founded and edited by Alfred Stieglitz. In this book I refer to issues of the magazine collected in Alfred Stieglitz, *Camera Work: The Complete Illustrations 1903–1917* (Cologne: Taschen, 1997).

24 See Alvin Langdon Coburn, *Alvin Langdon Coburn: Photographer*, ed. Helmut Gernsheim and Alison Gernsheim (New York: Dover Publications, 1978), 18.

25 George Bernard Shaw, "Bernard Shaw's Appreciation of Coburn," *Camera Work*, no. 15 (1906): 314.

26 Charles H. Caffin, "Some Prints by Alvin Langdon Coburn," *Camera Work*, no. 6 (1904): 170.

27 See Marius de Zayas, "Photography and Artistic-Photography," *Camera Work*, no. 42/43 (1913): 709.

28 Apparently, Demachy coined the term "pure photography." See Alfred Stieglitz, Sarah Greenough, and Juan Hamilton, *Alfred*

Stieglitz: Photographs and Writings (Washington, DC: National Gallery of Art, 1983), 20.

29 Stieglitz in a letter to R. Child Bayley, Nov. 1, 1916, cited in Stieglitz, Greenough, and Hamilton, 201.

30 László Moholy-Nagy, *The New Vision: From Material to Architecture*, trans. Hoffmann (New York: Brewer, Warren & Putnam, 1930), 193.

31 "Se dovessimo compararlo a qualche altro artefice non sapremmo dire se non che egli è il Rembrand delle antiche rovine." Giovanni Ludovico Bianconi, "Elogio storico del cavaliere Giambattista Piranesi celebre antiquario ed incisore di Roma. Published in *Antologia*, nos. 34, 35, and 36 (1779)," *Grafica* II, no. 2 (1976): 129.

32 See Sturgis, *The Etchings of Piranesi*, postscript.

33 Samuel, *Piranesi*, 1910, 104.

34 Hind, "Giovanni Battista Piranesi and His 'Carceri,'" 91.

35 For the ensuing discussion, see Focillon, *Giovanni-Battista Piranesi 1720–1778*, 241–260.

36 "Ni le dessin ni la peinture n'étaient capables d'atteindre à cette puissance d'expression, supérieure aux impressions ordinaires de la vue. Rome, cent fois l'objet de l'étude des peintres et des graveurs, apparaît ici pour la première fois majestueuse et vraie. Sur les murailles grises et délabrées, le coup de soleil de l'eau-forte fait briller un rayon plus beau que celui du soleil de chaque jour, il les éclaire avec tant de force qu'il leur restitue leur relief et leur prestige." Focillon, 267. The translation is mine.

37 Hind, *Giovanni Battista Piranesi: A Critical Study*, 10. Although Hind in the 1911 article recognized a "wonderful simplicity" in the *Carceri's* first edition, he seems to prefer the second edition, which, he writes, "has gained enormously in variety and in effect" (Hind, "Giovanni Battista Piranesi and His 'Carceri,'" 82). This means that Hind changed his opinion in the course of the decade.

38 Hind, *Giovanni Battista Piranesi: A Critical Study*, 23.

39 David Rosand, *Drawing Acts: Studies in Graphic Expression and Representation* (New York: Cambridge University Press, 2002), 282.

40 Rosand, 285.

41 Robison, *Piranesi: Early Architectural Fantasies*, 1986, 42.

42 Robison, 44.

43 Rosenfeld, "Picturesque to Sublime," 85–86.

44 "Les ruines de Piranèse vont crouler. Elles gémissent, elles crient." Nodier, "Piranèse: contes psychologiques: à propos de la monomanie réflective," 188. The translation is mine.

45 Wallis de Vries, *Archescape*, 178. Huxley, *Prisons*, 1949, 25.

46 Focillon, *The Life of Forms in Art*, 123.

47 Focillon, 126–127.

48 Caroline van Eck, "Architectural History without Words: Piranesi's Representation of Rome, Anachronism and Historical Experience," in *Aspects of Piranesi: Essays on History, Criticism and Invention*, ed. Dirk De Meyer, Bart Verschaffel, and Pieter-Jan Cierkens (Ghent: A&S/books, 2015), 115.

49 "We are confronted with inner and outer historical surfaces. Of these only the outer surfaces of the completed past are accessible to historical knowledge." George Kubler, *The Shape of Time: Remarks on the History of Things* (New Haven, CT: Yale University Press, 1962), 30. Reinterpreting Piranesi's church, Santa Maria in Priorato, explicitly in terms of Kubler, Irene Small observes a construction that is nothing but surface. See Irene Small, "Piranesi's Shape of Time," *Image [&] Narrative*, no. 18 (2007), www.imageandnarrative.be/inarchive/thinking_pictures/small.htm.

50 Yourcenar, "The Dark Brain of Piranesi," 1985, 100–101.

51 Mayor, *Giovanni Battista Piranesi*, 1952, 29.

52 Richard Wendort, "Piranesi's Double Ruin," *Eighteenth-Cantury Studies* 34, no. 2 (2001): 176.

53 Andreas Huyssen, "Authentic Ruins: Products of Modernity," in *Ruins of Modernity*, ed. Julia Hell and Andreas Schönle (Durham, NC: Duke University Press, 2010), 23.

54 See Wittkower, "Piranesi's 'Parere su l'architettura.'" On Piranesi and the Greek-Roman controversy, see also Kantor-Kazovsky, *Piranesi*. Maarten Delbeke, "Piranesi's Parere and the Beauty of Architecture," in *Aspects of Piranesi: Essays on History, Criticism and Invention*, ed. Dirk

De Meyer, Bart Verschaffel, and Pieter-Jan Cierkens (Ghent: A&S/books, 2015), 55–70.

55 Texts forming part of Piranesi's controversy with the French are *Della magnificenza ed architettura de' romani* (1761) and *Osservazioni di Gio. Battista Piranesi sopra la Lettre de M. Mariette* (1765), which included the polemic dialogue *Parere su l'architettura*. Piranesi's texts are translated in Giovanni Battista Piranesi, "Opinions on Architecture: A Dialogue," in *Observations on the Letter of Monsieur Mariette*, trans. Caroline Beamish and David Britt (Los Angeles: Getty Research Institite, 2002), 102–114.

56 Kantor-Kazovsky, *Piranesi*, 220.

57 Manfredo Tafuri, *Architecture and Utopia: Design and Capitalist Development* (Cambridge, MA: MIT Press, 1976), 16.

58 On this point, see Sigrid de Jong, "Piranesi and Primitivism: Origin as Invention," in *Aspects of Piranesi: Essays on History, Criticism and Invention*, ed. Dirk De Meyer, Bart Verschaffel, and Pieter-Jan Cierkens (Ghent: A&S/books, 2015), 89.

59 In his analysis of Piranesi in *La sfera e il labirinto* (1980) Tafuri adapted the term "heterotopia" from Foucault's essay "Des espaces autres: utopies et hétérotopies" (1968), p. 56. On this point, see for instance Jacques Lucan, *Composition, Non-Composition: Architecture and Theory in the Nineteenth and Twentieth Centuries* (Lausanne: EPFL Press, 2012), 527, note 22.

60 Walter Benjamin, "Theses on the Philosophy of History," in *Illuminations*, ed. Hannah Arendt, trans. Harry Zohn (London: Pimlico, 1999), 249.

Piranesi at MOMA

1 Norman Rosenthal, "Giovanni Battista Piranesi and the Recurring Prisons of Art," in *Carceri d'invenzione di G. Battista Piranesi* (Madrid: Julio Soto impresores/Factum Arte, 2010), 18.

2 William M. Ivins, "Piranesi and Le Carceri d'Invenzione," *Print Collector's Quarterly* 5, no. 2 (April 1915): 218.

3 Eisenstein, "Piranesi, Or the Fluidity of Forms," 1977, 94–96.

4 Huxley, *Prisons*, 1949, 24.

5 Tafuri, "Per una critica dell'ideologia architettonica," 53. The quote is from the translation of the text in Manfredo Tafuri, "Toward a Critique of Architectural Ideology," trans. Stephen Sartarelli, in *Architecture Theory since 1968*, ed. K. Michael Hays (Cambridge, MA: MIT Press, 1998), 18.

6 André Salmon, "La jeune peinture française (1912)," in *André Salmon on French Modern Art*, trans. Beth S. Gersh-Nešić (New York: Cambridge University Press, 2005), 27–91. Albert Gleizes and Jean Metzinger, *Du "Cubisme"* (Paris: Eugène Figuière, 1912). The book was published in English in the following year as Gleizes and Metzinger, *Cubism* (London: T. Fisher Unwin, 1913). For Apollinaire's text, I refer to the English translation: Guillaume Apollinaire, *The Cubist Painters: Aesthetic Meditations*, trans. Lionel Abel (New York: Wittenborn and Company, 1944).

7 See for instance Gleizes and Metzinger, *Cubism*, 16. "To understand Cézanne is to foresee cubism," the authors claimed.

8 Ardengo Soffici, *Cubismo e oltre* (Florence: Libreria della Voce, 1913), 23–24.

9 Willard Huntington Wright, *Modern Painting: Its Tendency and Meaning* (New York: John Lane Company, 1915). See chapter "Precursors of the New Era."

10 Alfred H. Barr, *Cubism and Abstract Art* (New York: Museum of Modern Art, 1936), 19.

11 Barr, 46, 221.

12 Installation list, *Cubism and Abstract Art*, undated. MOMA Exhs., 46.2. MOMA Archives, NY.

13 Barr, *Cubism and Abstract Art*, 29.

14 Barr, 78.

15 Sybil Gordon Kantor points to Barr's borrowing from Kahnweiler's *Der Weg zum Kubismus* (1920): Sybil Gordon Kantor, *Alfred H. Barr Jr. and the Intellectual Origins of the Museum of Modern Art* (Cambridge, MA: MIT Press, 2002), 321–323.

16 On the visual paradoxes in this composition, see Vogt-Göknil, *Giovanni Battista Piranesi*, 32–33.

17 For both the 1936 exhibitions, Barr relied on Carl Zigrosser, a longtime curator at the print department of the Philadelphia Museum of Art. In 1919, Zigrosser founded the Weyhe Gallery, and in the name of the gallery lent

several items to *Cubism and Abstract Art*, including works by Paul Klee and Picasso. The catalogue also credits each loan to the Weyhe Gallery, including the Piranesi print. *Fantastic Art, Dada, Surrealism* included twenty-two loans from Zigrosser compiled in a list that counted drawings, etchings, woodcuts, and engravings, mostly by modern artists. See list, *Fantastic Art, Dada, Surrealism*, dated Oct. 31, 1936. MOMA Exhs., 55.3. MOMA Archives, NY.

18 Insurance list, *Cubism and Abstract Art*, dated July 11, 1936. MOMA Exhs., 46.2. MOMA Archives, NY.

19 For example, James Johnson Sweeney and his *Plastic Redirections in 20th Century Painting* (1934) was an important inspiration for Barr and for *Cubism and Abstract Art*. See chapter 2 in Marcia Brennan, *Curating Consciousness: Mysticism and the Modern Museum* (Cambridge, MA: MIT Press, 2010). However, Sweeney took no particular interest in Piranesi.

20 The preserved correspondence between Barr and Moholy-Nagy is dated between Dec. 14, 1936 and Nov. 9, 1937. MOMA Exhs., 55.3. MOMA Archives, NY.

21 Moholy-Nagy, *The New Vision*, 60–61.

22 Barr, *Cubism and Abstract Art*, 19. In modern culture, the reference for the Apollonian and Dionysian opposites ultimately derives from Nietzsche's *The Birth of Tragedy* (1872).

23 Letter from Duane Livingston Knickerbocker Pell to Joseph Madden, Dec. 15, 1936. MOMA Exhs., 55.10. MOMA Archives, NY.

24 Alfred H. Barr, "Introduction," in *Fantastic Art, Dada, Surrealism*, ed. Alfred H. Barr, 2nd ed. (New York: Museum of Modern Art, 1936), 9.

25 Georges Hugnet, "In the Light of Surrealism," in *Fantastic Art, Dada, Surrealism*, 2nd ed., 52.

26 Alfred H. Barr, "Preface," in *Fantastic Art, Dada, Surrealism*, ed. Alfred H. Barr, 1st ed. (New York: Museum of Modern Art, 1936), 7.

27 Barr, "Introduction," 9.

28 Barr, 11.

29 Anne Umland et al., *Dada in the Collection of the Museum of Modern Art* (New York: Museum of Modern Art, 2008), 15.

30 André Breton, "Manifesto of Surrealism (1924)," in *Manifestoes of Surrealism*, trans. Helen R. Lane and Richard Seaver (Ann Arbor: University of Michigan Press, 1969), 10, 14.

31 Letter from Barr to Allen, Aug. 7, 1936. MOMA Exhs., 55.2. MOMA Archives, NY.

32 Letter from Barr to Allen, Oct. 1, 1936. MOMA Exhs., 55.2. MOMA Archives, NY.

33 In a letter that includes a list of Allen's loans, Dorothy H. Dudley, registrar at MOMA, writes, "As far as I know Mr. Barr has selected the first ten items for the exhibition." Letter from Dudley to Allen, Nov. 19, 1936. MOMA Exhs., 55.2. MOMA Archives, NY. We do not know which prints from the *Carceri* Barr excluded.

34 Alberto Giacometti, "I Can Only Speak Indirectly of My Sculptures," in *Alberto Giacometti: Works, Writings, Interviews*, ed. Ángel González (Barcelona: Ediciones Polígrafa, 2006), 131. The text was first published in *Minotaure* 3–4 (Dec. 1933): 46.

35 Museum of Modern Art, gallery label from 2006 www.moma.org/collection/works/80928

36 Glenn D. Lowry, "Giacometti," in MOMA *Highlights* (New York: Museum of Modern Art, 2004), 153.

37 Tafuri's observation was published in *La sfera e il labirinto* (1980), which was translated into English in 1987, and included in the book's chapter on Piranesi. See Tafuri, "The Wicked Architect," 25. Optics and the nature of seeing have always been themes associated with Piranesi and his experimentation with multiple viewpoints. On this subject, see Alberto Pérez-Gómez and Louise Pelletier, *Architectural Representation and the Perspective Hinge* (Cambridge, MA: MIT Press, 1997), 216–217.

38 See www.moma.org/collection/works/78938?classifications=any&date_begin=Pre-1850&date_end=2019&locale=en&page=1&q=Magritte%2C+the+-false+mirror&with_images=1

39 There were only two other works figuring in both shows: Paul Klee's *Sacred Island* (1926) and Pablo Picasso's *Green Still Life* (1914).

40 *Timeless Aspects* was on d'Harnoncourt's mind at least from 1947, as shown by a series of early drafts of his proposal for the exhibition. MOMA Exhs., 393.2. MOMA Archives, NY.

41 René d'Harnoncourt, ed., *Timeless Aspects of Modern Art* (New York: Museum of Modern Art, 1949), unpaginated. By all accounts, d'Harnoncourt wrote the text.

42 Cf. second draft of the proposal for the exhibition titled "Proposed Twentieth Anniversary Exhibitions," p. 3. MOMA Exhs., 393.2. MOMA Archives, NY.
43 Later draft of the proposal for the exhibition titled "Proposed Twentieth Anniversary Exhibitions," p. 4. MOMA Exhs. 393.2. MOMA Archives, NY.
44 D'Harnoncourt, *Timeless Aspects of Modern Art*, unpaginated.
45 Draft of letter from d'Harnoncourt to Taylor, Oct. 27, 1948. MOMA Exhs., 393.3. MOMA Archives, NY.
46 Letter from the registrar to Fred Hahn, Nov. 5, 1948. MOMA Exhs. 393.3. MOMA Archives, NY.
47 See receipt of insurance drafted by The Metropolitan Museum of Modern Art. MOMA Exhs., 393.2. MOMA Archives, NY.
48 MOMA Exhs., 393.2. MOMA Archives, NY.
49 Mayor, *Giovanni Battista Piranesi*, 1952, 29.
50 Letter from the registrar to Fred Hahn, Jan. 27, 1949. MOMA Exhs., 393.3. MOMA Archives, NY.

Moving Prints

1 These terms are employed to connect Piranesi and film by Manfredo Tafuri, "The Historicity of the Avant-Garde: Piranesi and Eisenstein," in *The Sphere and the Labyrinth: Avant-Gardes and Architecture from Piranesi to the 1970s* (Cambridge, MA: MIT Press, 1987), 55. Anne Hollander, *Moving Pictures* (Alfred A. Knopf: New York, 1989), 4. See also Steven Jacobs, "Eisenstein's Piranesi and Cinematic Space," in *Aspects of Piranesi: Essays on History, Criticism and Invention*, ed. Dirk De Meyer, Bart Verschaffel, and Pieter-Jan Cierkens (Ghent: A&S/books, 2015), 143, 154. Alberto Pérez-Gómez and Louise Pelletier, *Architectural Representation and the Perspective Hinge* (Cambridge, MA: MIT Press, 1997), 223.
2 André Bazin, "The Myth of Total Cinema," in *What Is Cinema?*, by André Bazin, trans. Hugh Gray, vol. 1 (Berkeley: University of California Press, 2005), 17.
3 Sergei Eisenstein, "On the Close-Up (in Place of a Foreword)," in *Metod*, vol. 1, *Grundproblem*, ed. Naum Kleiman (Moscow: Muzei kino and Eizenshtein tsentr, 2002), 38, quoted in Luka Arsenjuk, *Movement, Action, Image, Montage: Sergei Eisenstein and the Cinema in Crisis* (Minneapolis: University of Minnesota Press, 2018), 12.
4 Arsenjuk, 12.
5 Wilton-Ely, *The Mind and Art of Giovanni Battista Piranesi*, 1978, 10.
6 Lang's thoughts on New York and *Metropolis* are quoted in Fred Gehler and Ulrich Kasten, *Fritz Lang: Die Stimme von Metropolis* (Berlin: Henschel Verlag, 1990), 9. Visual sources mediating relevant "Piranesi"-like impressions of New York include Hugh Ferriss's imaginary visions of Manhattan and other such images produced at the time. However, the sets for *Metropolis* were not worked out by Lang alone but resulted from a collaboration between Lang, the designers Erich Kettelhut, Otto Hunte, and Karl Vollbrecht, and Thea von Harbou, who wrote the book/screenplay on which the film was based.
7 On the set designs for *Metropolis* and their visual sources, see Dietrich Neumann, *Film Architecture: Set Designs from Metropolis to Blade Runner* (Munich: Prestel, 1999), 33–38, 94–103. On Boris Bilinsky and the posters to *Metropolis*, see also https://documents.uow.edu.au/~morgan/metrojc.htm
8 The observation was made by Bruno Girveau, "La Nostalgie bâtisseuse: Architecture et décor chez Disney," in *Il était une fois Walt Disney: Aux sources de l'art des studios Disney* (Paris: Galeries nationales du Grand Palais, 2006), 208–236 and here quoted from Steven Jacobs, "Eisenstein's Piranesi and Cinematic Space," in *Aspects of Piranesi*, 152.
9 Jung, *Individual Dream Symbolism in Relation to Alchemy*, 136.
10 Gilles Deleuze, *Cinema I: The Movement-Image*, trans. Hugh Tomlinson and Robert Galeta (London: Bloomsbury, 2018), 5.
11 Henri Bergson, *Creative Evolution* (Mineola, NY: Dover Publications, 1998), 306.
12 Deleuze, *Cinema I: The Movement-Image*, 27.
13 Deleuze, 5. See also Bergson, *Creative Evolution*, 329–336.
14 Eisenstein, "Piranesi, Or the Fluidity of Forms," 1977, 104.
15 Jacobs, "Eisenstein's Piranesi and Cinematic Space," 2015, 143.

16 The film was produced for the special exhibition *Le arti di Piranesi: architetto, incisore, antiquario, vedutista, designer*. A DVD with the film and an accompanying booklet were issued in connection with the exhibition. See also the online version www.factum-arte.com/pag/154/-i-The-Arts-of-Piranesi-architect-engraver-antiquarian-vedutista-designer-i-The-exhibition. Already Eisenstein liked to think of the sixteen images in the *Carceri* as still shots in a film, observing how the architectural visions of Piranesi "float into each other." See Sergei Eisenstein, "Piranesi, Or the Fluidity of Forms," trans. Roberta Reeder, *Oppositions* 11 (1977): 100.

17 The order in which the prints appear does not correspond to the numbered plates. In Dupond/Factum Arte's film the order is reorganized as follows: I, II, XII, XVI, XIII, IX, XIV, XV, V, IV, IX, VII, X. Plates lacking from the animation are III, VI, and VIII. On the sequence of the execution of Piranesi's *Carceri* prints, see Sekler, "Notes on Old and Modern Drawings," 345–357.

18 "...tournoyantes babels que rêvait Piranèse/ vous n'êtes rien près des dédales du sort." Victor Hugo, *Feuilles Paginées*, quoted from C. W. Thompson, *Victor Hugo and the Graphic Arts (1820–1833)* (Geneva-Paris: Librairie Droz, 1970), 108–109.

19 Sergei Eisenstein, "A Dialectic Approach to Film Form," in *Film Form: Essays in Film Theory*, trans. Jay Leyda (San Diego: Harcourt, 1977), 49.

20 Eisenstein, "Piranesi, Or the Fluidity of Forms," 1977, 105–106.

21 Hollander, *Moving Pictures*, 1989, 9.

22 On the parallel between the effects of light in Piranesi's prints and the film screen, see Hollander, *Moving Pictures*, 1989, 232. See also Steven Jacobs, "Eisenstein's Piranesi and Cinematic Space," in *Aspects of Piranesi*, 143.

23 See Hollander, *Moving Pictures*, 1989, 231–234.

24 Eisenstein identifies the book as *La scenografia* by Giulio Ferrari. Eisenstein, "Piranesi, Or the Fluidity of Forms," 1977, 85.

25 Sergei Eisenstein, *Beyond the Stars: The Memoirs of Sergei Eisenstein*, ed. Richard Taylor, trans. William Powell (Calcutta: Seagull Books, 1995), 362–364. The memoir's mixture of reflection and actual recollection, of dream and reality, resists any attempt to date events precisely.

26 Eisenstein refers to prints from both editions reproduced in Giesecke's monograph (1911), which might well be where he first detected the difference. Eisenstein, "Piranesi, Or the Fluidity of Forms," 1977, 103–104.

27 Eisenstein, 85. The acquisition took place "only just now," Eisenstein notes in the Piranesi essay written in 1946–1947, which suggests a postwar date.

28 Gathering from his memoirs, Eisenstein owned three *Carceri* etchings by June 1946, in addition to the *Carcere oscure*. Sergei Eisenstein, *Beyond the Stars: The Memoirs of Sergei Eisenstein*, ed. Richard Taylor, trans. William Powell (Calcutta: Seagull Books, 1995), 364. A sketch of Eisenstein's study from 1948 shows a print from the *Carceri* on the wall. See Eisenstein, "Piranesi, Or the Fluidity of Forms," 1977, 103–104.

29 Eisenstein, "A Dialectic Approach to Film Form," 54.

30 On this argument, see David Bordwell, *The Cinema of Eisenstein* (London and New York: Routledge, 2005), 127–128.

31 The key point in Eisenstein's revolution, in Deleuze's words, is that "he gives the dialectic a proper cinematographic meaning." Deleuze, *Cinema I: The Movement-Image*, 45.

32 Sergei Eisenstein, "Form and Content: Practice," in *Film Sense* (San Diego: Harcourt Brace & Company, 1947), 171.

33 Eisenstein, "Piranesi, Or the Fluidity of Forms," 1977, 105.

34 Eisenstein, 104.

35 Eisenstein, 108.

36 Tafuri formulates this point when he writes that "Eisenstein sees in the entire series of the *Carceri* a totality composed of disconnected fragments belonging to a single sequence," in Tafuri, "The Historicity of the Avant-Garde: Piranesi and Eisenstein," 56. A similar point is made by Jacobs, "Eisenstein's Piranesi and Cinematic Space," 2015, 154.

37 Tschumi admits that he got to know and became fascinated with Piranesi through Eisenstein's essay "Piranesi, Or the Fluidity of Form" and the director's drawings based

on *Carceri*. The notion of montage has been important to Tschumi. *The Manhattan Transcripts* (1976–1981), for instance, is "influenced by Eisenstein but it also has to do with the depths and the repetition of the *Prisons*." Bernard Tschumi, interview with the author, Nov. 26, 2018, New York.

38 Eisenstein, "Piranesi, Or the Fluidity of Forms," 1977, 100–103.

39 Eisenstein, 103.

40 On the date of the manuscript see Eisenstein, n. 1. The manuscript "Piranesi, ili tekuchest' form" was printed in Eisenstein, *Izbrannye proizvedeniia* 3 (Moscow: Iskusstvo, 1964), 154–187. The text was translated by Roberta Reeder with the title "Piranesi, Or the Fluidity of Forms" and published in *Oppositions* 11 (1977). It appeared as an appendix to Manfredo Tafuri's chapter on Eisenstein in *La sfera e il labirinto* (1980), 89–11 (translated by Maria Fabris) and reappeared in Reeder's translation in the English edition of Tafuri's book (*The Sphere and the Labyrinth* (1987), 65–90.

41 It remains unclear which edition of *The Gothic Arch* Eisenstein owned. Presuming he owned an impression from the first edition, six or seven years separate the making of it from the publication of the *Carcere oscure* (1743).

42 Eisenstein, 91.

43 Eisenstein, 96.

44 Eisenstein, 94.

45 Eisenstein, 95.

46 Eisenstein, 95–96.

47 Tafuri, "The Historicity of the Avant-Garde: Piranesi and Eisenstein," 62–63. "Storicità dell'avanguardia: Piranesi e Ejzenštejn" originally appeared in *Oppositions* and then as chapter 2 in Tafuri's *La sfera e il labirinto* (1980), 77–88.

48 Marie-Claire Ropars-Wuilleumier, "The Function of Metaphor in Eisenstein's 'October,'" trans. Mary Christopher Baseheart, *Film Criticism* 2, no. 2/3 (1978): 29.

49 The MOMA exhibition displayed a grisaille which at the time was attributed to Ch'ên Jung and executed in 1235–1255 but later identified as a work by an anonymous artist from the Chinese Yuan (1271–1368) or early Ming (1368–1644) dynasty. In his essay on Piranesi, Eisenstein mentions a painting by Chu Chi-Kuei as an example of a particular Eastern montage, a sort of "ecstatic quietism." However, the exact landscape he has in mind remains unknown. In *Nondifferent Nature* (pp. 229–243), Eisenstein displays a considerable knowledge on the literature on Chinese art, including art from the period from which the MOMA exhibit dates. Eisenstein argues that Chinese and Japanese art, too, demonstrate "ecstatic flight," but whereas *Carceri* exploded the elements, the Eastern counterparts rather dissolve them.

50 In his Russian diary, Barr records visits to Eisenstein on January 14 and February 2. See Alfred H. Barr, "Russian Diary 1927–28," *October* 7 (Winter 1978): 10–51. On Barr and Eisenstein, see also Kantor, *Alfred H. Barr*, 169–172.

51 Alfred H. Barr, "The Researches of Eisenstein," *Drawing & Design* 4 (1928): 155.

52 Barr, 156.

53 Alfred H. Barr, "Sergei Michailovitch Eisenstein," *Arts*, no. 14 (1928): 321.

54 A similar point is made by Arsenjuk, *Movement, Action, Image, Montage*, 13. See also Martino Stierli: "Eisenstein used Piranesi to historicize and legitimize the avant-garde principle of cinematic montage," in Martino Stierli, *Montage and the Metropolis: Architecture, Modernity, and the Representation of Space* (New Haven, CT: Yale University Press, 2018), 23.

The Subversive Modernist

1 Wittkower, "Piranesi's 'Parere su l'architettura,'" 155. Alina Payne views Wittkower's *Architectural Principles in the Age of Humanism* (1949) in a similar perspective. See Alina A. Payne, "Rudolf Wittkower and Architectural Principles in the Age of Modernism," *Journal of the Society of Architectural Historians* 53 (1994): 322–342.

2 Wittkower, "Piranesi's 'Parere su l'architettura,'" 155.

3 D'Aronco applied the term Piranesian to a project for a new bridge in Turin (1893) and a house in Istanbul (1896). See Terry Kirk, "Piranesi's Poetic Licence: His Influence on

Modern Italian Architecture," in *The Serpent and the Stylus: Essays on G. B. Piranesi*, ed. Mario Bevilacqua, Heather Hyde Minor, and Fabio Barry (Ann Arbor, MI: University of Michigan Press, 2006), 258–262.

4 Quoted from Nikolaus Pevsner, *A History of Building Types* (Princeton: Princeton University Press, 1976), 60.

5 Samuel, *Piranesi*, 1910, 132–134.

6 Referring to his education in London, Koolhaas states, "I think I would not have been Piranesian without England." Koolhaas, interview with the author, Apr. 9, 2019.

7 Vincent Scully, "Louis I. Kahn and the Ruins of Rome," in *Modern Architecture and Other Essays* (Princeton: Princeton University Press, 2003), 313. The essay was originally published in *MOMA: The Members Quarterly of the Museum of Modern Art*, 12 (1992): 1–13.

8 Le Corbusier, *Towards a New Architecture*, trans. Frederick Etchells (Mansfield Centre, CT: Martino Publishing, 2014), 173. This is a reprint of the first American-English edition from 1927.

9 The other examples are the baroque painted interiors in Castel Sant'Angelo, Palazzo Colonna, and Palazzo Barberini.

10 On his studies at Bibliothèque Nationale, see H. Allen Brooks, *Le Corbusier's Formative Years: Charles-Edouard Jeanneret at La Chaux-de-Fonds* (Chicago: Chicago University Press, 1997), 403–405.

11 Tschudi, "Goethe in the Hall and His Journeys in Printed Rome."

12 Le Corbusier, *Towards a New Architecture*, 29.

13 The translation is mine. The drawing is kept at the Fondation Le Corbusier, Paris.

14 "Toutes les reconstitutions de Piranèse… plan de Rome et compositions funambules qui ont terriblement servi à l'école des Beaux-Arts: vue de portiques, de colonnades, d'obélisques!!! C'est fou. C'est atroce, laid, imbécile. Ce n'est pas grandiose, il ne faut pas s'y tromper." The text is transcribed in Philippe Duboy, "Ch. E. Jeanneret à La Bibliothèque Nationale Paris 1915," *Architecture-mouvement-continuité*, no. 49 (Numéro spécial Le Corbusier) (September 1979): 12.

15 On Jeanneret/Le Corbusier's sketch of Piranesi prints, see Stanislaus von Moos and Arthur Rüegg, *Le Corbusier Before Le Corbusier: Applied Arts, Architecture, Interiors, Painting, and Photography, 1907–1922* (New Haven, CT: Yale University Press, 2002), 188. See also Joost van Gorkom, "The Dialectic of the City," in *Thing Theory and Urban Objects in Rome*, ed. J. G. Wallis De Vries and K. Wuytack, vol. 5 (Eindhoven: Technische Universiteit Eindhoven, 2013), 198–200.

16 Le Corbusier returns to many of these monuments in the chapter titled "The Lesson of Rome," praising "Absence of verbosity, good arrangement, a single idea, daring and unity in construction, the use of elementary shapes. A sane morality." Le Corbusier, *Towards a New Architecture*, 158–159.

17 Henri Focillon, *Giovanni-Battista Piranesi: Essai de catalogue raisonné de son oeuvre* (Paris: Librairie Renouard-Henri Laurens, 1918), 286.

18 Johnson in "Historical Note" in Alfred H. Barr, Philip Johnson, and Henry-Russell Hitchcock, *Modern Architecture: International Exhibition* (New York: Museum of Modern Art, 1932), 18.

19 Panayotis Tournikiotis, *The Historiography of Modern Architecture* (Cambridge, MA: MIT Press, 1999), 3.

20 Henry-Russell Hitchcock, *Modern Architecture: Romanticism and Reintegration* (New York: Da Capo Press, 1993), 7.

21 Heinrich Wölfflin, *Renaissance and Baroque* (London: Collins, 1984), 87. On the subject of baroque Piranesi Wölfflin in turn quoted Carl Justi's *Winckelmann und seine Zeitgenossen*, 2nd ed. (1898), vol. 1, p. 254.

22 Hitchcock, *Modern Architecture*, 7.

23 A detailed account of Giedion's years in the United States is found in Reto Geiser, *Giedion and America: Repositioning the History of Modern Architecture* (Zurich: gta Verlag, 2018), 74.

24 Sigfried Giedion, *Space, Time and Architecture: The Growth of a New Tradition* (Cambridge, MA: Harvard University Press, 1941), 43.

25 Giedion, 24. Obviously inspired by the approach of Freud and Jung, Giedion lands architecture in the territory of psychoanalysis. On p. 117 he writes: "It was out of those technical innovations which appear only behind the scenes in nineteenth-century architecture that the architecture of the future had to grow.

Construction was, as it were, the subconsciousness of architecture; there lay dormant in it impulses that only much later found explicit theoretical statement."

26 Giedion, 101.

27 Piranesi's view of Piazza del Popolo, from *Vedute di Roma*, appears in Giedion, 85. Prints by Piranesi occur purely as documentation of sites also in Sigfried Giedion, *Architecture and the Phenomena of Transition: The Three Space Conceptions in Architecture* (Cambridge, MA: Harvard University Press, 1971). In this publication, Piranesi is correctly identified in the captions.

28 Henry-Russell Hitchcock and Philip Johnson, *The International Style: Architecture Since 1922* (New York: W. W. Norton, 1995), 35. The edition referred to here is a reprint of the original 1932 edition.

29 Hitchcock and Johnson, 35.

30 *Visionary Architecture* at the MOMA ran from Sept. 29 to Dec. 4, 1960. Drexler is most likely the author of the introductory statement accompanying the press release. See www.moma.org/calendar/exhibitions/2554.

31 Lucan, *Composition, Non-Composition*, 52.

32 Vincent Scully, *Modern Architecture: The Architecture of Democracy* (New York: George Braziller, 1961), 16.

33 Scully, 11. Subsequent quotes are taken from Scully's *Modern Architecture*, 11–13

34 Scully, 12.

35 Scully, 27.

36 Scully, "Modern Architecture: Towards a Redefinition of Style," 6–7.

37 Scully, *Modern Architecture*, 18.

38 The translation is mine. Grau, *Borges y la arquitectura*, 1989, 82.

39 Scully, *Modern Architecture*, 32.

40 Robert Venturi, *Complexity and Contradiction in Architecture* (New York: Museum of Modern Art, 1966), 72–73.

Campo Marzio as Method

1 The literature on Piranesi's *Campo Marzio* is extensive. On the dates and execution of the copper plates, see Ginevra Mariani and Giovanna Scaloni, "Il Campo Marzio dell'antica Roma," in *Giambattista Piranesi: matrici incise 1761–1765*, ed. Ginevra Mariani (Rome: Editalia/Istituto Centrale per la Grafica, 2017), 302–304. Important interpretations include Vincenzo Fasolo, "Il Campomarzio di G. B. Piranesi," *Quaderni dell'Istituto di Storia dell'Architettura* 15 (1956): 1–14. A basic reference in this discussion is Tafuri, *Architecture and Utopia*. Other approaches to the map, for example the ones advanced by Joseph Connors and Stanley Allen, are mentioned below. For a reception study of Piranesi's *Ichnographia*, see Angelo Marletta, *Il Campo Marzio dell'antica Roma: Giovanni Battista Piranesi e l'arte del contemperare* (Rome: Ermes, 2016). The idea that Piranesi as an architect is an invention of the modern period is the subject of a forthcoming PhD thesis by Giacomo Pala, University of Innsbruck.

2 Joseph Connors, *Piranesi and the Campus Martius: The Missing Corso: Topography and Archaeology in Eighteenth-Century Rome* (Milan: Jaca Book, 2011), 81–104.

3 Piranesi in the preface to *Campo Marzio dell'antica Roma*, quoted from Jonathan Scott, *Piranesi* (London: Academy Editions, 1975), 166–167.

4 Vincenzo Fasolo, "Il Campomarzio di G. B. Piranesi," *Quaderni dell'Istituto di Storia dell'Architettura* 15 (1956): 12.

5 John Wilton-Ely, "Utopia or Megalopolis? The 'Ichnographia' of Piranesi's 'Campus Martius' Reconsidered," in *Piranesi tra Venezia e l'Europa*, ed. Alessandro Bettagno (Florence: Leo S. Olschki, 1983), 302.

6 Vincent J. Scully, *Louis I. Kahn* (New York: George Braziller, 1962), 37.

7 Scully includes the photograph in his book but fails to mention the *Campo Marzio* plan underneath the drawing.

8 Peter Eisenman, interview with the author, Nov. 27, 2018, New York.

9 Vincent Scully, "Louis I. Kahn and the Ruins of Rome," in *Modern Architecture and Other Essays* (Princeton: Princeton University Press, 2003), 313, 315. In connection with the Fine Arts Center, Fort Wayne (1961–1973), Kahn wrote: "Piranesi made beautiful drawings of Rome as it never could have been. He made drawings of visionary prisms and great spaces where art can be displayed. He envisioned things like Jules Verne. He envisioned things that later turned out to be not at all

fantastic. His visions of entering great spaces were always an inspiration to architects. And I envision them." See Richard Saul Wurman, ed., *What Will Be Has Always Been: The Words of Louis I. Kahn* (New York: AccessPress and Rizzoli, 1986), 9. Also see Christian Devillers, "L'Indian Institute of Management ad Ahmedabad 1962–1974 di Louis I. Kahn," *Casabella*, no. 571 (1990): 61. On Kahn in Rome and his fascination with Piranesi, see Maria Bonaiti, "La lezione della storia," in *Roma e l'eredità di Louis I. Kahn*, ed. Elisabetta Barizza and Marco Falsetti (Milan: Francoangeli, 2014), 95–96. Kahn's precise adaptations from the *Campo Marzio* plan were the subject of Angelo Marletta's paper "Forma urbis forma architecturae. Piranesi, Kahn e i frammenti di Roma" at the international conference *Piranesi@300* (Rome, May 21, 2021).

10 Manfredo Tafuri, *Theories and History of Architecture* (London: Granada, 1980), 56. Tafuri's critique of Kahn became gradually more pronounced in the course of the 1960s and 1970s. On this point, see Marco Biraghi, *Project of Crisis: Manfredo Tafuri and Contemporary Architecture*, trans. Alta Price (Cambridge, MA: MIT Press, 2013), 51–67.

11 On the exhibition *Europa–America: Centro storico–suburbio*, see Léa-Catherine Szacka, "Debates on Display at the 1976 Venice Biennale," in *Place and Displacement: Exhibiting Architecture*, ed. Thordis Arrhenius et al. (Zurich: Lars Müller Publishers, 2014), 99.

12 *Città analoga* had also been the title of an exhibition curated by Rossi and collaborators for the 1973 Milan Triennale, but for the biennale he produced an entirely new piece. On Rossi's *Città analoga* of 1973 and 1976, see Léa-Catherine Szacka, "Città Analoga: Aldo Rossi's Visual Theory on Display," in *Terms of Appropriation: Modern Architecture and Global Exchange*, ed. Amanda Reeser Lawrence and Ana Miljački (London: Routledge, 2017), 263–277. See also Léa-Catherine Szacka, *Exhibiting the Postmodern* (Venice: Marsilio, 2016), 59–74. M. Christine Boyer adopts a Jungian perspective and sees Rossi's analogous city as a recuperation of deep-lying units from memory and culture. See M. Christine Boyer, *The City of Collective Memory: Its Historical Imagery and Architectural Entertainments* (Cambridge, MA: MIT Press, 1994), 178–201. However, I disagree with the reasons Boyer gives for the claim that Piranesi's prints of Rome (she does not specify which ones) prefigured the "analogous city." She claims Piranesi did not search for the origin of architecture in "stones and ornaments" but "moved instead into an arbitrary, utopian, and entirely subjective sphere of subjective experience" (pp. 177–178). This point I would contest and say that even the most fantastical designs evolve around Piranesi's ideas on the origin of architecture, as evidenced for example by the *Campo Marzio* and *Parere su l'architettura* volumes.

13 Peter Eisenman in the introduction to the first American edition of Rossi's *L'architettura della città* (1966) in Aldo Rossi, *The Architecture of the City* (Cambridge, MA: MIT Press, 1982), 10.

14 The section copied from the *Campo Marzio* plan includes two structures at the north end of Piranesi's city, the "Lavacrum publicum" (public bath) and the "Vivarium fulvii" (water reservoir).

15 On the *Campo Marzio* as an inspiration for Aldo Rossi, see Marletta, *Il Campo Marzio dell'antica Roma*, 177–180. Marletta mentions in particular Rossi's project for the San Cataldo cemetery in Modena (1971).

16 On the importance of Nolli's plan in postwar architectural discourse, see Thomas Weaver, "Civitas Interruptus," in *Postmodernism: Style and Subversion, 1970–1990* (London: Victoria and Albert Museum, 2011), 126–131.

17 The invited architects included Piero Sartogo, Costantino Dardi, Antoine Grumbach, James Stirling, Paolo Portoghesi, Romaldo Giurgola, and Robert Venturi with John Rauch, Colin Rowe, Michael Graves, Leon Krier, Aldo Rossi, and Robert Krier. After Rome, *Roma interrotta* traveled in spring 1979 to the AA in London and in the summer to the Cooper-Hewitt Museum in New York. A catalogue was published in Italian and English, republished and commented as Piero Sartogo et al., *Roma Interrotta: Twelve Interventions on the Nolli's Plan of Rome* (Johan & Levi Editore, 2014). The exhibition was also the theme of a special issue of *Architectural Design* 49, no. 3–4 (1979).

18 Argan in foreword to Sartogo et al., 23.

19 Michael Graves, "Roman Interventions," *Architectural Design* 49, no. 3–4 (1979): 4.

20 Maarten Delbeke, "Roma Interrotta: The Urbs That Is Not a Capital," *Incontri. Rivista Europea di Studi Italiani* 26, no. 2 (2011): 47–48.
21 On Stirling's contribution to *Roma interrotta*, see Amanda Reeser Lawrence, *James Stirling: Revisionary Modernist* (New Haven, CT: Yale University Press, 2012), 186–202.
22 James Stirling in Sartogo et al., *Roma Interrotta*, 87.
23 Leon Krier in Sartogo et al., 195.
24 Szacka, *Exhibiting the Postmodern*, 59, 81.
25 Charles Jencks first explained postmodernism in architecture in "The Rise of Post-Modern Architecture" published in *Architectural Association Quarterly* in 1975. An extended discussion appeared in *The Language of Post-Modern Architecture* in 1977. For Jencks's own account of his use of the term, see Charles Jencks, *The Language of Post-Modern Architecture*, fourth revised enlarged edition (London: Academy Editions, 1984), 8.
26 German architect Gerd Neumann also "intervened" in Piranesi's views, adding, extracting, and rearranging their contents in cross-temporal collages. On Neumann's Piranesi pastiches from the late 1970s, see Günter Krawinkel, Wolfgang-M. Pax, and Katrin Sello, *Inventionen: Piranesi und Architekturphantasien in der Gegenwart* (Hannover: Kunstverein Hannover and Deutscher Werkbund Niedersachsen und Bremen, 1982), 119–131.
27 The quote reads "The drawings, when seen collaged into the Roman perspectives of Piranesi, actually stand up to these grand and disturbing images." See Jencks, *The Language of Post-Modern Architecture*, 135–136. The observation is repeated in Charles Jencks, "Towards Radical Eclecticism," in *The Presence of the Past: First International Exhibition of Architecture. La Biennale di Venezia 1980*, ed. Gabriella Borsano (Edizioni La Biennale di Venezia, 1980), 35.
28 Leon Krier in Sartogo et al., *Roma Interrotta*, 205.
29 Graves, "Roman Interventions," 4.
30 Tafuri, *Architecture and Utopia*, 15.
31 Wilton-Ely, "Utopia or Megalopolis? The 'Ichnographia' of Piranesi's 'Campus Martius' Reconsidered," 303.
32 The quote is taken from Szacka, "Debates on Display," 108. The transcript is kept in the IAUS archive, CCA, Montreal.
33 "Per una critica dell'ideologia architettonica" was published in *Contropiano*, no. 1 (1969) whereas "L'architettura come 'utopia negativa' first appeared in *Angelus Novus* (1971). The latter was partially republished in French as "Giovan Battisa Piranesi: L'utopie négative dans l'architecture," *L'Architecture d'aujourd'hui*, no. 184 (March–April, 1976) before it was reworked into the chapter "'L'architetto scellerato': G. B. Piranesi, l'eterotopia e il viaggio" in *La sfera e il labirinto: Avanguardie e architettura da Piranesi agli anni '70* (1980), 33–75, translated as "The Wicked Architect: G. B. Piranesi, Heterotopia, and the Voyage" in *The Sphere and the Labyrinth: Avant-Gardes and Architecture from Piranesi to the 1970s* (1987).
34 An analysis of Tafuri's most important book on history, *Teorie e storia dell'architettura* (1968) and the central concepts it advances is offered by Panayotis Tournikiotis, *The Historiography of Modern Architecture* (Cambridge, MA: MIT Press, 1999), 193–219. For an extended discussion on Tafuri's theory of history, see Andrew Leach, *Manfredo Tafuri: Choosing History* (Ghent: A&S Books, 2007). On the role of Piranesi in relation to the notion of critical operativity, see in particular pp. 232–248. Tafuri and contemporary architecture is discussed by Marco Biraghi, *Project of Crisis: Manfredo Tafuri and Contemporary Architecture*, trans. Alta Price (Cambridge, MA: MIT Press, 2013).
35 Tafuri, *Theories and History of Architecture*, 26.
36 Tafuri, *Architecture and Utopia*, 15.
37 Fasolo, "Il Campomarzio di G. B. Piranesi," 12. On Tafuri's relation to Fasolo, see Andrew Leach, *Manfredo Tafuri: Choosing History* (Ghent: A & S Books, 2007), 16.
38 Tafuri, "Toward a Critique of Architectural Ideology," 10. The essay is a translation of "Per una critica dell'ideologia architettonica" (1969).
39 Tafuri, *Architecture and Utopia*, 14, 15.
40 Tafuri, *The Sphere and the Labyrinth*, 267. The essay "L'architecture dans le boudoir" was first published in *Oppositions* 3 (1974). On the publication history of the essay, see Biraghi, *Project of Crisis*, 2013, 87–101.
41 Manfredo Tafuri, "L'architettura come 'utopia negativa,'" *Angelus Novus*, no. 20 (January 1971): 111. The quote is taken from the translation of the text in Tafuri, "The Wicked Architect," 40.

42 Tafuri, "L'architettura come 'utopia negativa,'" 97. For the translations see Tafuri, "The Wicked Architect," 27–31.

43 Tafuri, "L'architettura come 'utopia negativa,'" 93.

44 Tafuri, 97. An obvious contradiction in Tafuri's critique is that although he claims that the *Carceri* are shown "without any didactic or narrative intent" (p. 90), he allows the label of "prison" to guide his reading of them.

45 Tafuri, *Architecture and Utopia*, 18.

46 Michel Foucault, *Discipline and Punish: The Birth of the Prison*, trans. Alan Sheridan (London: Penguin Books, 1991), 200.

47 For a comparison between Bentham and Piranesi in Foucault, see Paul Hirst, "Foucault and Architecture," *AA Files* 26 (1993): 59.

48 Foucault, *Discipline and Punish*, 29–30.

49 Tafuri, "L'architettura come 'utopia negativa,'" 108.

50 Tafuri, *Architecture and Utopia*, 13.

51 The seminar, titled *Progetti per l'area di Cannaregio ovest* (Projects for the area of west Cannaregio), was organized by Carlo Aymonino and Francesco Dal Co. Besides Eisenman, Hejduk, and Hoesli, the participants included Raimund Abraham, Carlo Aymonino, Rafael Moneo, Aldo Rossi, Valeriano Pastor, Gianugo Polesello, and Luciano Semerani. In addition, Oswald Mathias Ungers was invited to the seminar. See Francesco Dal Co, ed., *10 immagini per Venezia: Raimund Abraham, Carlo Aymonino, Peter Eisenmann, John Hejduk, Bernhard Hoesli, Rafael Moneo, Valeriano Pastor, Gianugo Polesello, Aldo Rossi, Luciano Semerani. Mostra dei progetti per Cannaregio ovest; Venezia, 1 aprile–30 aprile 1980* (Venice: Officina Edizioni, 1980). See also Jean-François Bédard, "Cannaregio (Project History)," in *Cities of Artificial Excavation: The Work of Peter Eisenman, 1978–1988* (New York: Rizzoli International, 1994), 54. Szacka, *Exhibiting the Postmodern*, 2016, 81–83.

52 Peter Eisenman, "Cannaregio (Three Texts for Venice)," in *Cities of Artificial Excavation*, 47. The antithetical nature of the *10 progetti* seminar and exhibition was stressed by Eisenman, interview with the author, Nov. 27, 2018.

53 Tafuri, *The Sphere and the Labyrinth*, 281. The quote does not refer to the architects in *10 progetti* exclusively but to the New York Five, a group that included Peter Eisenman and John Hejduk, and that Tafuri at the time saw as heading a new movement. Tafuri's chapter on the New York Five titled "L'architecture dans le boudoir" is a modification of an essay originally published in *Oppositions* 5 (1976).

54 "Ogni passaggio del progetto diviene potenzialmente un fine; ogni momento del processo creativo tende a essere un 'parte' conchiusa [...]" Dal Co, *10 immagini*, 22. The translation is mine.

55 Szacka, *Exhibiting the Postmodern*, 2016, 82.

56 Eisenman, interview with the author, Nov. 27, 2018.

57 Peter Eisenman, "The Wicked Critic," in *Written into the Void: Selected Writings 1990–2004* (New Haven, CT: Yale University Press, 2007), 154. Originally published in 2000.

58 The simulacrum-definition of the plan's architecture is found in Peter Eisenman, "Written into the Void," in *Written into the Void: Selected Writings 1990–2000* (New Haven, CT: Yale University Press, 2007), 81. The manuscript was composed in 1997.

59 For Eisenman's description of the project, see Eisenman, "Three Texts for Venice."

60 Eisenman, interview with the author, Nov. 27, 2018.

61 Eisenman, "The Wicked Critic," 158. Tafuri's interpretation of Piranesi is a recurrent theme in Eisenman's writings from 1978 onwards. More specifically, he addresses the interpretation of the *Campo Marzio* plan in Tafuri's *Progetto e utopia* (1973), published in the United States in 1976. See Peter Eisenman, "The Graves of Modernism," in *Eisenman Inside Out: Selected Writings, 1963–1988* (New Haven, CT: Yale University Press, 2004), 110. The article was first published in *Oppositions* 12 (Spring 1978): 36–41; Peter Eisenman, "The House of the Dead as the City of Survival," in *Aldo Rossi in America: 1976 to 1979* (New York: Institute for Architecture and Urban Studies, 1979), 4. Eisenman, "Written into the Void," 81, 84. The most substantial discussion of Tafuri and Piranesi is in Eisenman, "The Wicked Critic."

62 Tafuri had seen the works of these architects at the 1973 Milan Triennale and invited them to exhibit in Naples in 1975.

63 On Tafuri's impact in America, see Joan Ockman, "Venice and New York," *Casabella: International Architectural Review*, no. 619–620 (1995): 57–71. On Tafuri and the New York Five, see chapter 4 in Biraghi, *Project of Crisis*, 2013. On Tafuri's five essays in *Oppositions*, written between 1974 and 1979, see Biraghi, 214–15, note 32.

64 Koolhaas and Tschumi were at the IAUS in the 1970s. See Ockman, "Venice and New York," 9, note 9. Ockman also points to Tafuri's influence on architectural historians like Kenneth Frampton and Anthony Vidler, two of the editors of *Oppositions* (p. 59).

65 Stanley Allen, "Piranesi's 'Campo Marzio': An Experimental Design," *Assemblage*, no. 10 (1989): 71.

66 In a 1976 interview, Tafuri looked back on his own research as an architectural historian and to the discovery of the discipline's theoretical foundations: "We found—and personally speaking, I was appalled—that even these foundations were rotten to the core, as Piranesi said." See Françoise Very and Manfredo Tafuri, "The Culture Markets," *Casabella: International Architectural Review*, no. 619–620 (1995): 37. The interview was originally published as "Entretien avec Manfredo Tafuri," *Architecture-Mouvement-Continuité* 39 (June 1976): 64–68. Tafuri here refers to a passage in Piranesi's *Parere* in which Piranesi's mouthpiece, Didascolo, claims that the Romans never corrupted Greek architecture; on the contrary. On finding they had adopted an architecture that already was "infected to the core," and unable to cure its ills, they attempted to mitigate them (Piranesi, "Opinions on Architecture: A Dialogue," 106.)

67 Allen, "Piranesi's 'Campo Marzio,'" 97.

68 The quotes and references are largely based on my interview with Steven Holl, August 4, 2019, Hamarøy, Norway.

69 On Holl's project for Porta Vittoria, see Steven Holl, *Steven Holl* (Basel: Birkhäuser, 1993), 100–103. See also Robert McCarter, *Steven Holl* (London: Phaidon Press, 2015), 30–33.

70 Holl, interview with the author, Aug. 4, 2019.

71 Holl, interview with the author, Aug. 4, 2019.

72 Philip Johnson and Mark Wigley, *Deconstructivist Architecture* (New York: Museum of Modern Art, 1988), 17–18. On the making of the term and concept of "deconstructivism," see Tina Di Carlo, "The Construction of an Exhibition within Architecture Culture: Deconstructivist Architecture, The Museum of Modern Art, 1988" (PhD, Oslo, Oslo School of Architecture and Design, 2016), 29–47.

73 Krawinkel, Pax, and Sello, *Inventionen: Piranesi und Architekturphantasien in der Gegenwart*, 109. The translation is mine. The other participants in the exhibition included Raimund Abraham, Peter Cook, Günther Günschel, Adolfo Natalini, Gerd Neuman, Gaetano Pesce, and Hans Dieter Schaal. On this exhibition, see also José Juan Barba, *Invenciones: Nueva York vs Rem Koolhaas, Bernard Tschumi, Piranesi* (Alcalá: Universidad de Alcalá, 2014), 65–97. On Libeskind and Himmelblau and their connection to Piranesi, see Max Stemshorn, "Zur Piranesi-Rezeption in der Architekturavantgarde," in *Vision Piranesi*, ed. Max Stemshorn and Susanne Grötz (Stadthaus Ulm/Hemsbach: Druckhaus Beltz, 2002), 85–104.

74 Tschumi, interview with the author, Nov. 26, 2018.

75 The participants at *Deconstructivist Architecture* were not comfortable with being called "deconstructivist," neither did they think that they belonged to a school. Bernard Tschumi recalls the situation as absurd: "Immediately all seven said we are not a movement, we are not a school. That's very important." Tschumi, interview with the author, Nov. 26, 2018. Eisenman, too, objected to the term "deconstructivist" and never used it in interview with the author, Nov. 27, 2018.

76 Koolhaas rejected deconstructivist aesthetics, declaring it was "ten times more interesting to *make* things than to *explode* things," seeing no future for the movement within architecture. See Alejandro Zaera Polo and Rem Koolhaas, "Finding Freedom: Conversations with Rem Koolhaas," *El Croquis*, no. 53 (1992): 29.

77 Koolhaas, interview with the author, Apr. 9, 2019.

78 Koolhaas, interview with the author, Apr. 9, 2019.

79 Koolhaas remembers Stevens as "the dominant intellectual idiot savant type in the school, who could hold forth on almost

anything in the most unbelievably brilliant way." See Rem Koolhaas and Robert Somol, "Being O.M.U.'s Ghostwriter: Rem Koolhaas in Conversation with Robert Somol," in *Reckoning with Colin Rowe: Ten Architects Take Position*, ed. Emmanuel Petit (New York: Routledge, Taylor & Francis Group, 2015), 87. I also refer to Koolhaas's interview with author, Apr. 9, 2019.

80 Rem Koolhaas, "Exodus," in *S, M, L, XL* (Rotterdam, 1995), 7.

81 Koolhaas's encounter with the Berlin Wall in 1971 was also important for the project. See Rem Koolhaas, "Fieldtrip, (A)A Memoir," in *S, M, L, XL* (New York: Monacelli Press, 1995), 570–578.

82 Aureli, *The Possibility of an Absolute Architecture*, 19.

83 Koolhaas, interview with the author, Apr. 9, 2019.

84 Koolhaas, interview with the author, Apr. 9, 2019.

85 Koolhaas, interview with the author, Apr. 9, 2019.

86 Koolhaas, interview with the author, Apr. 9, 2019. See also the presentation of the project in Rem Koolhaas and OMA, "Two Libraries for Jussieu," *El Croquis*, no. 79 (1996): 124.

87 Koolhaas and OMA, 124.

88 Koolhaas, interview with the author, Apr. 9, 2019.

89 Rem Koolhaas and OMA, "Hyperbuilding," *El Croquis*, no. 131–132 (2006): 66. See also Rem Koolhaas, Simon Brown, and John Link, "The Hyperbuilding," in *Content* (Cologne: Taschen, 2004), 420–421.

90 Rem Koolhaas, "Bigness, or the Problem of Large," in *S, M, L, XL* (Rotterdam: 010 Publishers, 1995), 494–517.

91 See Rem Koolhaas and OMA, "CCTV & TVCC," *El Croquis*, no. 131–132 (2006): 270–311. For this discussion see in particular OMA, CCTV *New Site Construction & Development Program. Extended Preliminary Design.* EPD *Landscape Report* (OMA, 2004), section 4.

92 Referring to the *Campo Marzio* plan in relation to the CCTV and TVCC center and headquarters, Koolhaas remarks: "I particularly like this version [of *Campo Marzio* implementations], because in certain cases it is simply decorative, but in this version it really had a role beyond that. I was looking at it in terms of which elements could be three-dimensional and which elements we would be happy to keep as two-dimensional." Koolhaas, interview with the author, Apr. 9, 2019.

93 Koolhaas, interview with the author, Apr. 9, 2019.

94 Koolhaas, interview with the author, Apr. 9, 2019.

95 Koolhaas, interview with the author, Apr. 9, 2019.

96 In several other projects, not discussed here, Koolhaas and his team "anchored" their building designs in the *Campo Marzio* plan. One of the program presentations, circulated in a small number and kept in the OMA archives, shows Piranesi's plan juxtaposed with a photo of Los Angeles and thus underpinning OMA's proposal for an extended LACMA (2001). The Axel Springer Campus in Berlin (2020) is Koolhaas's latest "*Campo Marzio* project." One telling image shows how Piranesi's plan constitutes the lowest stratum of the building, a situation that resembles the build-up of the Qatar National Library. I am grateful to Talitha van Dijk for granting access to this material.

97 Rem Koolhaas, "What Ever Happened to Urbanism," in *S, M, L, XL* (Rotterdam: 010 Publishers, 1995), 969.

98 Rem Koolhaas, "The Generic City," in *S, M, L, XL* (Rotterdam: 010 Publishers, 1995), 1251.

99 Koolhaas, "What Ever Happened to Urbanism," 971.

100 Tafuri, *Architecture and Utopia*, 18.

101 Simon Sadler writes "The fantastic spaces and vistas of New Babylon would be truly reminiscent of the sublime visions of Piranesi and John Martin." In Sadler, *The Situationist City*, 141.

102 Koolhaas, interview with the author, Apr. 9, 2019. Allen, "Piranesi's 'Campo Marzio,'" 1989, 97.

103 Aureli and Tattara, "A Field of Walls (2012)," 32.

104 Aureli and Tattara, 36.

105 Wallis de Vries, *Archescape*, 30.

106 Wallis de Vries, 178.
107 Peter Eisenman, "Piranesi and the City," in *Piranesi as Designer*, ed. Sarah E. Lawrence (New York: Cooper-Hewitt, National Design Museum, Smithsonian Institution, 2007), 303.
108 See https://lifeforms.io/New-Campo-Marzio-1

Coda — People's Piranesi

1 Guy Debord and Asger Jorn, *Mémoires: structures portantes d'Asger Jorn* (New York: Wittenborn and Company, 1959). The book is unpaginated. For the quote, see Sadler, *The Situationist City*, 108.
2 Lars Lerup, *The Continuous City: Fourteen Essays on Architecture and Urbanization* (Zurich: Park Books, 2017), 125.
3 Pimlott takes as an example the Bonaventure metro in Montréal. See Mark Pimlott, *Without and Within: Essays on the Territory and the Interior* (Rotterdam: Episode Publishers, 2007), 252.
4 Marshall Berman, "Notes from Underground: Plato's Caves, Piranesi Prisons and Subways," *Harvard Design Magazine*, 2001: 70.
5 Robert Venturi, Bruce Adams, and Denise Scott Brown, "Mass Communication on the People Freeway: Or Piranesi Is Too Easy," *Perspecta* 12 (1969): 49–56. An abbreviated description of the project was printed in Venturi and Scott Brown's *Learning from Las Vegas* (1972).
6 William Beckford, "Vathek," in *Three Gothic Novels* (London: Penguin Books, 1968), 246.
7 Yourcenar, "The Dark Brain of Piranesi," 1985, 117–118.
8 Tafuri, *Architecture and Utopia*, 18.
9 Ernst Bloch, *The Principle of Hope*, trans. Neville Plaice, Stephen Plaice, and Paul Knight, vol. 2 (Cambridge, MA: MIT Press, 1995), 741. *The Principle of Hope* in three volumes was written in 1938–1947.

overleaf Rem Koolhaas/OMA, collage showing the imagined view from within the Hyperbuilding, Bangkok, 1996.

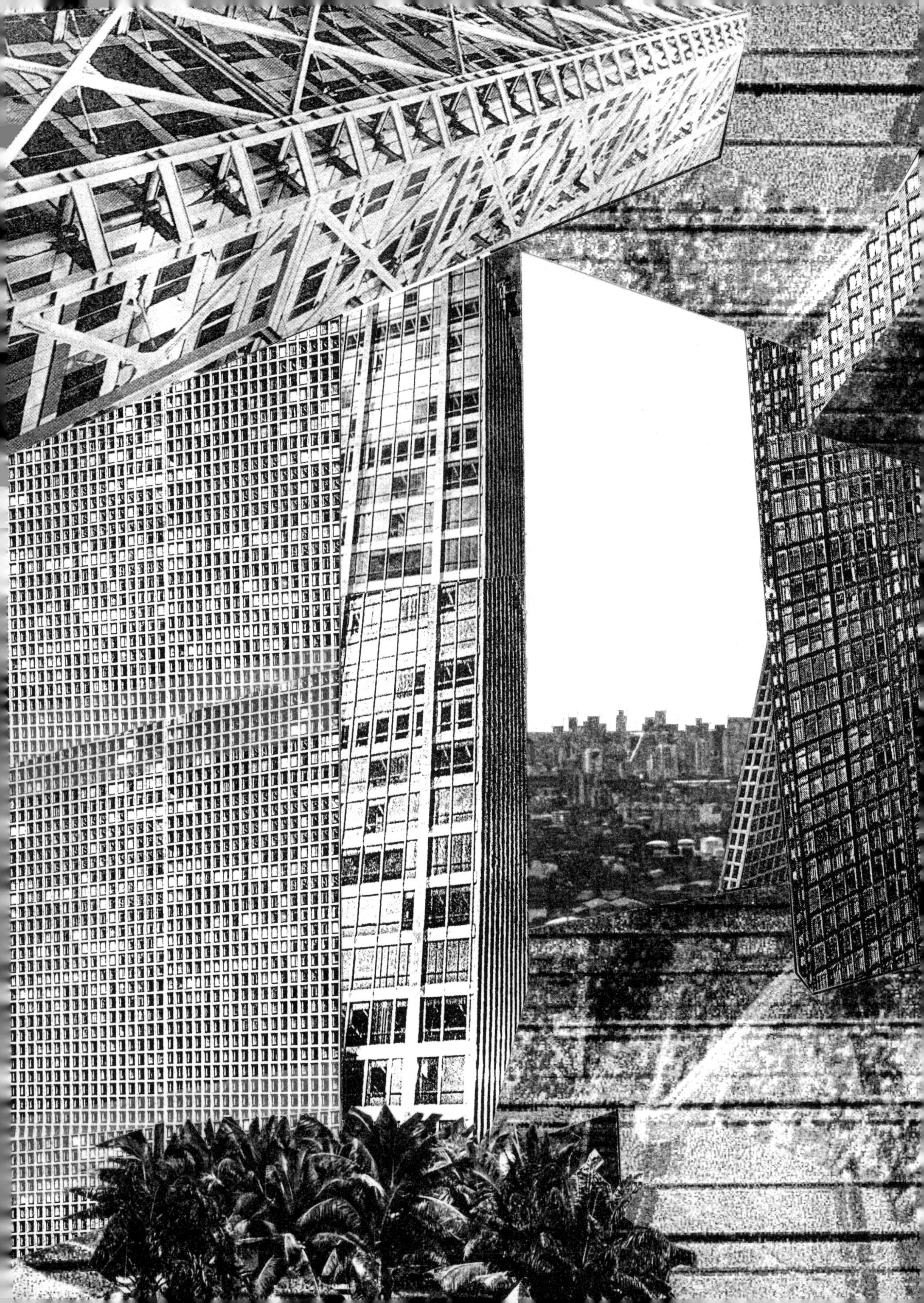

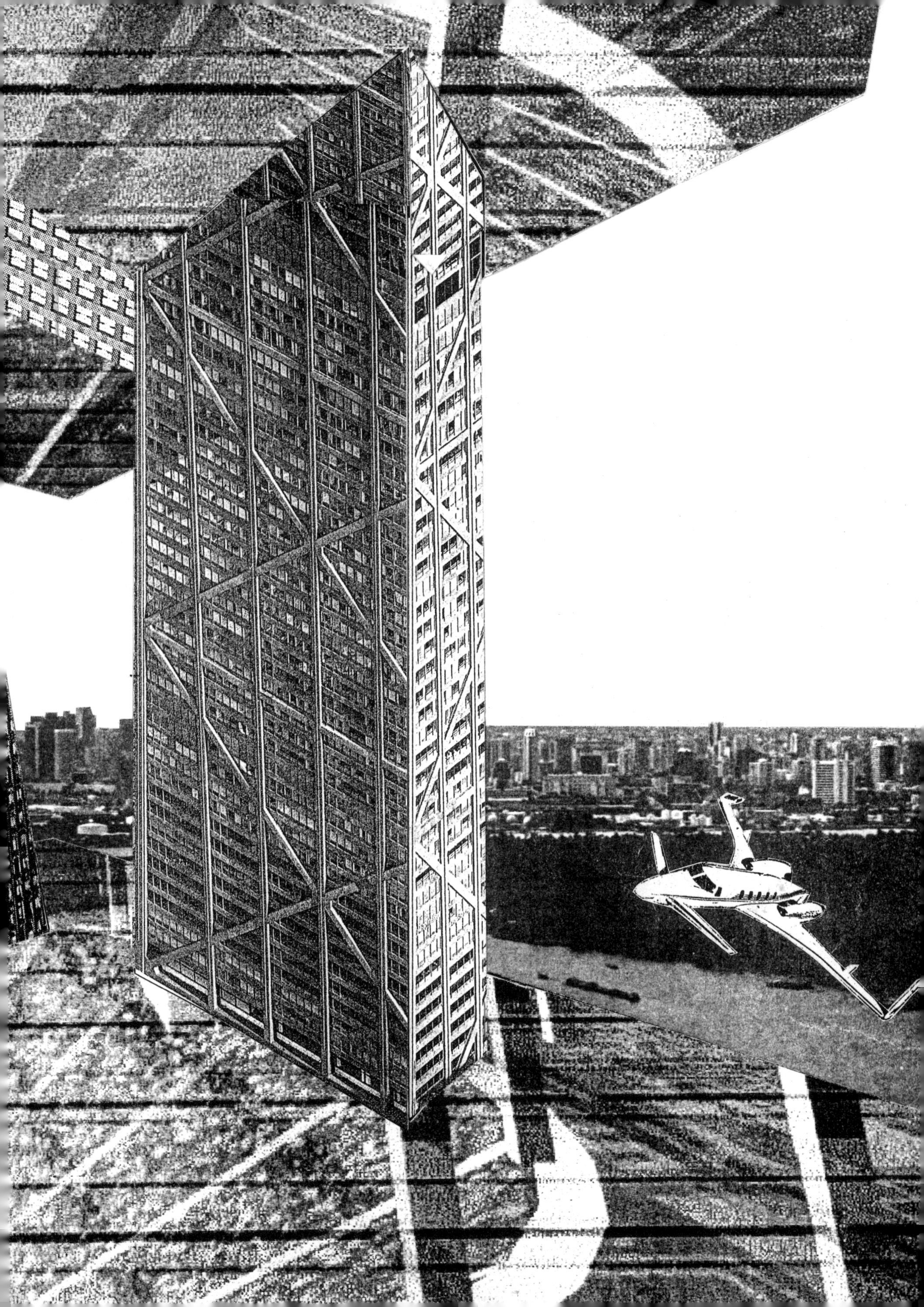

Archival sources

MOMA Exhs. 46.1-3. Museum of Modern Art Archives, New York.
MOMA Exhs. 55.1-12. Museum of Modern Art Archives, New York.
MOMA Exhs. 393.1-3. Museum of Modern Art Archives, New York.

Bibliography

Allen, Stanley. "Piranesi's 'Campo Marzio': An Experimental Design." *Assemblage*, no. 10 (1989): 70–109.

Andersen, Jørgen. "Giant Dreams: Piranesi's Influence in England." *English Miscellany* 3 (1952): 49–59.

Anderson, Richard. *Russia: Modern Architectures in History*. London: Reaktion Books, 2015.

Apollinaire, Guillaume. *The Cubist Painters: Aesthetic Meditations*. Translated by Lionel Abel. New York: Wittenborn and Company, 1944.

Argullol, Rafael. "La pérdida del centro: Piranesi y Baudelaire." *Revista de Occidente*, no. 115 (December 1990): 27–40.

Arsenjuk, Luka. *Movement, Action, Image, Montage: Sergei Eisenstein and the Cinema in Crisis*. Minneapolis: University of Minnesota Press, 2018.

Aureli, Pier Vittorio. *The Possibility of an Absolute Architecture*. Cambridge, MA: MIT Press, 2011.

Aureli, Pier Vittorio, and Martino Tattara. "A Field of Walls (2012)." In *Dogma: 11 Projects*, 32–41. London: AA Publications, 2015.

Barba, José Juan. *Invenciones: Nueva York vs Rem Koolhaas, Bernard Tschumi, Piranesi*. Alcalá: Universidad de Alcalá, 2014.

Barr, Alfred H. "Introduction." In *Fantastic Art, Dada, Surrealism*, edited by Alfred H. Barr, 2nd ed., 9–13. New York: Museum of Modern Art, 1936.

Barr, Alfred H. "Sergei Michailovitch Eisenstein." *Arts*, no. 14 (1928): 316–321.

Barr, Alfred H. *Cubism and Abstract Art*. New York: Museum of Modern Art, 1936.

Barr, Alfred H. "Preface." In *Fantastic Art, Dada, Surrealism*, edited by Alfred H. Barr, 1st ed., 7–8. New York: Museum of Modern Art, 1936.

Barr, Alfred H. "Russian Diary 1927–28." *October* 7 (Winter 1978): 10–51.

Barr, Alfred H. "The Researches of Eisenstein." *Drawing & Design* 4 (1928): 155–156.

Barr, Alfred H., Philip Johnson, and Henry-Russell Hitchcock. *Modern Architecture: International Exhibition*. New York: Museum of Modern Art, 1932.

Barthes, Roland. "The Death of the Author." In *Image, Music, Text*, translated by Stephen Heath, 142–148. New York: Hill and Wang, 1977.

Batsford, Harry. *A Batsford Century: The Record of a Hundred Years of Publishing and Bookselling 1843–1943*. Edited by Hector Bolitho. London: B. T. Batsford, 1944.

Baudelaire, Charles. *The Flowers of Evil*. Translated by James McGowan. Oxford: Oxford University Press, 2008.

Bazin, André. "The Myth of Total Cinema." In *What Is Cinema?*, by André Bazin, 17–22. Translated by Hugh Gray. Berkeley: University of California Press, 2005.

Beckford, William. "Vathek." In *Three Gothic Novels*, 149–255. London: Penguin Books, 1968.

Bédard, Jean-François. "Cannaregio (Project History)." In *Cities of Artificial Excavation: The Work of Peter Eisenman, 1978–1988*, 54–60. New York: Rizzoli International, 1994.

Benjamin, Walter. "Theses on the Philosophy of History." In *Illuminations*, edited by Hannah Arendt, translated by Harry Zohn, 245–255. London: Pimlico, 1999.

Bergson, Henri. *Creative Evolution*. Mineola, NY: Dover Publications, 1998.

Berman, Marshall. "Notes from Underground: Plato's Caves, Piranesi Prisons and Subways." *Harvard Design Magazine*, no. 15 (2001).

Bevilacqua, Mario, Heather Hyde Minor, and Fabio Barry. *The Serpent and the Stylus: Essays on G. B. Piranesi*. Ann Arbor: University of Michigan Press, 2006.

Bianconi, Giovanni Ludovico. "Elogio storico del cavaliere Giambattista Piranesi celebre antiquario ed incisore di Roma. Published in *Antologia*, Nos. 34, 35, and 36 (1779)." *Grafica* II, no. 2 (1976): 127–135.

Biraghi, Marco. *Project of Crisis: Manfredo Tafuri and Contemporary Architecture*. Translated by Alta Price. Cambridge, MA: MIT Press, 2013.

Bloch, Ernst. *The Principle of Hope*. Translated by Neville Plaice, Stephen Plaice, and Paul

Knight. Vol. 2. Cambridge, MA: MIT Press, 1995.
Bloom, Harold. *The Anxiety of Influence: A Theory of Poetry*, 2nd ed. Oxford: Oxford University Press, 1997.
Bloomer, Jennifer. *Architecture and the Text: The (S)Crypts of Joyce and Piranesi*. New Haven, CT: Yale University Press, 1993.
Bonaiti, Maria. "La lezione della storia." In *Roma e l'eredità di Louis I. Kahn*, edited by Elisabetta Barizza and Marco Falsetti, 89–98. Milan: Francoangeli, 2014.
Bordwell, David. *The Cinema of Eisenstein*. London and New York: Routledge, 2005.
Borges, Jorge Luis. "About William Beckford's Vathek." In *Other Inquisitions 1937–1952*, translated by Ruth L. C. Simms, 137–140. Austin: University of Texas, 1995.
Borges, Jorge Luis. "The Circular Ruins." In *Labyrinths: Selected Stories and Other Writings*, edited by Donald A. Yates and James East Irby, translated by James East Irby, 72–77. London: Penguin, 2000.
Borges, Jorge Luis. "The Immortal." In *The Aleph and Other Stories*, translated by Andrew Hurley, 3–19. London: Penguin Books, 2000.
Borges, Jorge Luis, and Adolfo Bioy-Casares. *Chronicles of Bustos Domecq*. Translated by Thomas di Giovanni Norman. New York: E. P. Dutton, 1976.
Boyer, M. Christine. *The City of Collective Memory: Its Historical Imagery and Architectural Entertainments*. Cambridge, MA: MIT Press, 1994.
Breton, André. "Manifesto of Surrealism (1924)." In *Manifestoes of Surrealism*, translated by Helen R. Lane and Richard Seaver. Ann Arbor: University of Michigan Press, 1969.
Bridgwater, Patrick. *De Quincey's Gothic Masquerade*. Amsterdam: Rodopi, 2004.
Bridgwater, Patrick. *Kafka, Gothic and Fairytale*. Amsterdam: Rodopi, 2003.
Brombert, Victor. "Victor Hugo, la prison et l'espace." *Revue des sciences humaines*, January–March 1965: 59–79.
Brooks, H. Allen. *Le Corbusier's Formative Years: Charles-Edouard Jeanneret at La Chaux-de-Fonds*. Chicago: Chicago University Press, 1997.
Brunotte, Ulrike. "The Construction of the Underworld: On the Architecture of Memory in Cults and Psychology." *Daidalos* 48 (1993): 78–86.
Bryan, Michael. *A Biographical and Critical Dictionary of Painters and Engravers*. London: Carpenter and Son, 1816.
Bryan, Michael. *Bryan's Dictionary of Painters and Engravers*. Vol. 4. London: George Bell and Sons, 1904.
Caffin, Charles H. "Some Prints by Alvin Langdon Coburn." *Camera Work*, no. 6 (1904): 169–171.
Calvino, Italo. *Invisible Cities*. London: Vintage Books, 1997.
Christ, Ronald. "Jorge Luis Borges, the Art of Fiction No. 39." *Paris Review*, no. 40 (Winter–Spring 1967).
Christadler, Martin. "Giovanni Battista Piranesi und die Architekturmetapher der Romantik." In *Miscellanea Anglo-Americana: Festschrift für Helmut Vierbock*, edited by Kuno Schumann, Wilhelm Hortmann, and Armin Paul Frank, 78–108. Munich: Karl Pressler, 1974.
Coburn, Alvin Langdon. *Alvin Langdon Coburn: Photographer*. Edited by Helmut Gernsheim and Alison Gernsheim. New York: Dover Publications, 1978.
Connors, Joseph. *Piranesi and the Campus Martius: The Missing Corso: Topography and Archaeology in Eighteenth-Century Rome*. Milan: Jaca Book, 2011.
Cooper, Tarnya. "Forgetting Rome and the Voice of Piranesi's 'Speaking Ruins.'" In *The Art of Forgetting*, edited by Adrian Forty and Susanne Küchler, 107–125. Oxford: Berg, 2001.
Dal Co, Francesco, ed. *10 immagini per Venezia: Raimund Abraham, Carlo Aymonino, Peter Eisenmann, John Hejduk, Bernhard Hoesli, Rafael Moneo, Valeriano Pastor, Gianugo Polesello, Aldo Rossi, Luciano Semerani. Mostra dei progetti per Cannaregio ovest; Venezia, 1 aprile–30 aprile 1980*. Venice: Officina Edizioni, 1980.
De Luca, V. A. "De Quincey's Icons of Apocalypse: Some Romantic Analogues." In *Thomas De Quincey: Bicentenary Studies*, edited by Robert Lance Snyder, 20–34. Norman: University of Oklahoma Press, 1985.
De Meyer, Dirk, Bart Verschaffel, and Pieter-Jan Cierkens, eds. *Aspects of Piranesi: Essays on History, Criticism and Invention*. Ghent: A&S/books, 2015.

De Quincey, Thomas. *The Confessions of an English Opium Eater*. Edited by David Masson. Vol. 3. *The Collected Writings of Thomas De Quincey*. Edinburgh: Adam and Charles Black, 1890.

Debord, Guy, and Asger Jorn. *Mémoires: structures portantes d'Asger Jorn*. New York: Wittenborn and Company, 1959.

Delbeke, Maarten. "Piranesi's Parere and the Beauty of Architecture." In *Aspects of Piranesi: Essays on History, Criticism and Invention*, edited by Dirk De Meyer, Bart Verschaffel, and Pieter-Jan Cierkens, 55–70. Ghent: A&S/books, 2015.

Delbeke, Maarten. "Roma Interrotta: The Urbs That Is Not a Capital." *Incontri. Rivista Europea di Studi Italiani* 26, no. 2 (2011): 37–49.

Deleuze, Gilles. *Cinema I: The Movement-Image*. Translated by Hugh Tomlinson and Robert Galeta. London: Bloomsbury, 2018.

Demachy, Robert. "The Straight and the Modern Print." *Camera Work*, no. 18 (1907): 358–359.

Devillers, Christian. "L'Indian Institute of Management ad Ahmedabad 1962–1974 di Louis I. Kahn." *Casabella* 571 (1990): 36–58.

Di Carlo, Tina. "The Construction of an Exhibition within Architecture Culture: Deconstructivist Architecture, The Museum of Modern Art, 1988." PhD, Oslo School of Architecture and Design, 2016.

Duboy, Philippe. "Ch. E. Jeanneret à La Bibliotèhque Nationale Paris 1915." *Architecture-Mouvement-Continuité* 49 (Numéro spécial Le Corbusier) (September 1979): 9–12.

Dupond, Grégoire, and Factum Arte. *Carceri d'invenzione di G. Battista Piranesi*. Booklet and DVD. Madrid: Julio Soto impresores/ Factum Arte, 2010.

Eck, Caroline van. "Architectural History without Words: Piranesi's Representation of Rome, Anachronism and Historical Experience." In *Aspects of Piranesi: Essays on History, Criticism and Invention*, edited by Dirk De Meyer, Bart Verschaffel, and Pieter-Jan Cierkens, 85–117. Ghent: A&S/books, 2015.

Eisenman, Peter. "Cannaregio (Three Texts for Venice)." In *Cities of Artificial Excavation: The Work of Peter Eisenman, 1978–1988*, edited by Jean-François Bédard, 46–53. New York: Rizzoli International, 1994.

Eisenman, Peter. "Piranesi and the City." In *Piranesi as Designer*, edited by Sarah E. Lawrence, 301–305. New York: Cooper-Hewitt, National Design Museum, Smithsonian Institution, 2007.

Eisenman, Peter. "The Graves of Modernism." In *Eisenman Inside Out: Selected Writings, 1963–1988*, 106–110. New Haven, CT: Yale University Press, 2004.

Eisenman, Peter. "The House of the Dead as the City of Survival." In *Aldo Rossi in America: 1976 to 1979*, 4–15. New York: Institute for Achitecture and Urban Studies, 1979.

Eisenman, Peter. "The Wicked Critic." In *Written into the Void: Selected Writings 1990–2004*, 151–159. New Haven, CT: Yale University Press, 2007.

Eisenman, Peter. "Written into the Void." In *Written into the Void: Selected Writings 1990–2000*, 79–86. New Haven, CT: Yale University Press, 2007.

Eisenstein, Sergei. "A Dialectic Approach to Film Form." In *Film Form: Essays in Film Theory*, translated by Jay Leyda, 45–63. San Diego: Harcourt, 1977.

Eisenstein, Sergei. *Beyond the Stars: The Memoirs of Sergei Eisenstein*. Edited by Richard Taylor. Translated by William Powell. Calcutta: Seagull Books, 1995.

Eisenstein, Sergei. "Form and Content: Practice." In *Film Sense*, 169–170. San Diego: Harcourt Brace & Company, 1947.

Eisenstein, Sergei. "Piranesi, Or the Fluidity of Forms." Translated by Roberta Reeder. *Oppositions* 11 (1977): 83–110.

Fasolo, Vincenzo. "Il Campomarzio di G. B. Piranesi." *Quaderni dell'Istituto di Storia dell'Architettura* 15 (1956): 1–14.

Fay, Elizabeth. "Hallucinogesis: Thomas De Quincey's Mind Trips." *Studies in Romanticism* 49, no. 2 (2010): 293–312.

Ferneyhough, Brian. "Carceri d'Invenzione" (1986). In *Collected Writings*, edited by James Boros and Richard Toop, 131–138. Amsterdam: Harwood Academic Publishers, 1995.

Feuerstein, Günther. "Function, Provocation." In *The Situationists and the City*, edited by Tom McDonough, 133–137. London: Verso, 2009.

Ficacci, Luigi. "Gabriele Basilico traduce Piranesi vedutista." In *Le arti di Piranesi: architetto, incisore, antiquario, vedutista, designer*, 205–281. Venice: Marsilio, 2010.

Focillon, Henri. *Giovanni-Battista Piranesi 1720–1778*. Paris: Librairie Renouard—Henri Laurens, 1918.
Focillon, Henri. *Giovanni-Battista Piranesi: Essai de catalogue raisonné de son oeuvre*. Paris: Librairie Renouard—Henri Laurens, 1918.
Focillon, Henri. *The Life of Forms in Art*. Translated by Charles Beecher Hogan and George Kubler. New York: Zone Books, 1992.
Foucault, Michel. *Discipline and Punish: The Birth of the Prison*. Translated by Alan Sheridan. London: Penguin Books, 1991.
Freud, Sigmund. *Civilization and Its Discontents*. Translated by James Strachey. New York: W. W. Norton, 1961.
Freud, Sigmund. *Dream Psychology: Psychoanalysis for Beginners*. New York: James A. McCann Company, 1921.
Freud, Sigmund. *The Interpretation of Dreams (1900)*. Translated by James Strachey. Vol. 4. *The Standard Edition of the Complete Psychological Works of Sigmund Freud*. London: Vintage Books, 2001.
Freud, Sigmund. "The 'Uncanny.'" In *Art and Literature*, translated by James Strachey, 14:339–376. The Pelican Freud Library. London: Penguin Books, 1985.
Frohne, H. W. "The Brooklyn Plaza and the Projected Brooklyn Central Library." *Architectural Record* 23, no. 2 (February 1908): 98–110.
Gautier, Théophile. "The Club of Assassins." In *Hashish, Wine, Opium: Charles Baudelaire, Théophile Gautier*, translated by Maurice Stang, 19–54. Richmond: Alma Classics, 2009.
Gautier, Théophile. *Travels in Spain*. Translated by Frederick C. de Sumichrast. Boston: Little, Brown and Co, 1912.
Gehler, Fred, and Ulrich Kasten. *Fritz Lang: Die Stimme von Metropolis*. Berlin: Henschel Verlag, 1990.
Geiser, Reto. *Giedion and America: Repositioning the History of Modern Architecture*. Zurich: Gta Verlag, 2018.
Giedion, Sigfried. *Architecture and the Phenomena of Transition: The Three Space Conceptions in Architecture*. Cambridge, MA: Harvard University Press, 1971.
Giedion, Sigfried. *Space, Time and Architecture: The Growth of a New Tradition*. Cambridge, MA: Harvard University Press, 1941.
Giesecke, Albert. *Giovanni Battista Piranesi*. Leipzig: Verlag von Klinkhardt und Biermann, 1911.
Gleizes, Albert, and Jean Metzinger. *Cubism*. London: T. Fisher Unwin, 1913. https://catalog.hathitrust.org/Record/000349963.
Gleizes, Albert, and Jean Metzinger. *Du "Cubisme."* Paris: Eugène Figuière, 1912.
Goethe, Johann Wolfgang von. *Goethe's Boyhood*. Translated by Wilhelm Wagner. Cambridge: The University Press, 1894.
Gombrich, Ernst H. *Art and Illusion: A Study in the Psychology of Pictorial Illusion*. London: Phaidon Press, 1960.
Gorkom, Joost van. "The Dialectic of the City." In *Thing Theory and Urban Objects in Rome*, edited by J. G. Wallis De Vries and K. Wuytack, 5:197–206. Eindhoven: Technische Universiteit Eindhoven, 2013.
Granli, Ola. *Omöjliga Rum*. Oslo: OCCAS/Oslo School of Architecture and Design, 2017.
Grau, Cristina. *Borges y la arquitectura*. Madrid: Ediciones Cátedra, 1989.
Grave, Johannes. *Der "Ideale Kunstkörper": Johann Wolfgang Goethe als Sammler von Druckgraphiken und Zeichningen*. Göttingen: Vandenhoeck & Ruprecht, 2006.
Graves, Michael. "Roman Interventions." *Architectural Design* 49, no. 3–4 (1979): 4–5.
Harnoncourt, René d', ed. *Timeless Aspects of Modern Art*. New York: Museum of Modern Art, 1949.
Hays, K. Michael. "Introduction to Manfredo Tafuri 'Toward a Critique of Architectural Ideology.'" In *Architecture Theory since 1968*, 1–5. Cambridge, MA: MIT Press, 1998.
Hind, Arthur M. *Giovanni Battista Piranesi: A Critical Study with a List of His Published Works and Detailed Catalogues of the Prisons and the Views of Rome*. London: Holland Press, 1968.
Hind, Arthur M. "Giovanni Battista Piranesi and His 'Carceri.'" *Burlington Magazine* 19, no. 98 (May 1911): 81–91.
Hirst, Paul. "Foucault and Architecture." *AA Files* 26 (1993): 52–60.
Hitchcock, Henry-Russell. *Modern Architecture: Romanticism and Reintegration*. New York: Da Capo Press, 1993.
Hitchcock, Henry-Russell, and Philip Johnson. *The International Style: Architecture Since 1922*. New York: W. W. Norton, 1995.

Holl, Steven. *Steven Holl*. Basel: Birkhäuser, 1993.
Hollander, Anne. *Moving Pictures*. Alfred A. Knopf: New York, 1989.
Hughes, Randolph. "Vers la contrée du rêve: Balzac, Gautier et Baudelaire, disciples de De Quincey." *Mercure de France* 8 (1939): 545–593.
Hugnet, Georges. "In the Light of Surrealism." In *Fantastic Art, Dada, Surrealism*, edited by Alfred H. Barr, 2nd ed., 35–52. New York: Museum of Modern Art, 1936. www.moma.org/calendar/exhibitions/2823?locale=ja.
Hugo, Victor. *Les contemplations*. 1856.
Huxley, Aldous. *Prisons*. London: Trianon Press, 1949.
Huyssen, Andreas. "Authentic Ruins: Products of Modernity." In *Ruins of Modernity*, edited by Julia Hell and Andreas Schönle, 17–28. Durham, NC: Duke University Press, 2010.
Iseli, Markus. *Thomas De Quincey and the Cognitive Unconscious*. Basingstoke: Palgrave Macmillan, 2015.
Ivins, William M. "Piranesi and Le Carceri d'Invenzione." *Print Collector's Quarterly* 5, no. 2 (April 1915).
Jacobs, Steven. "Eisenstein's Piranesi and Cinematic Space." In *Aspects of Piranesi: Essays on History, Criticism and Invention*, edited by Dirk De Meyer, Bart Verschaffel, and Pieter-Jan Cierkens, 142–159. Ghent: A&S/books, 2015.
Jamieson, Paul F. "Musset, de Quincey, and Piranesi." *Modern Language Notes* 72, no. 2 (1956): 105–108.
Jencks, Charles. *The Language of Post-Modern Architecture*. Fourth revised enlarged edition. London: Academy Editions, 1984.
Jencks, Charles. "Towards Radical Eclecticism." In *The Presence of the Past: First International Exhibition of Architecture. La Biennale di Venezia 1980*, edited by Gabriella Borsano, 30–37. Edizioni La Biennale di Venezia, 1980.
Johnson, Philip, and Mark Wigley. *Deconstructivist Architecture*. New York: Museum of Modern Art, 1988.
Jong, Sigrid de. "Piranesi and Primitivism: Origin as Invention." In *Aspects of Piranesi: Essays on History, Criticism and Invention*, edited by Dirk De Meyer, Bart Verschaffel, and Pieter-Jan Cierkens, 70–93. Ghent: A&S/books, 2015.
Jung, Carl Gustav. *Individual Dream Symbolism in Relation to Alchemy*. Translated by R. F. C. Hull. Princeton: Princeton University Press, 2010.
Jung, Carl Gustav. *Letters*. Edited by Gerhard Adler and Aniela Jaffé. Translated by R. F. C. Hull. Vol. 1: 1906–1950. Bollingen Series. Princeton: Princeton University Press, 2014.
Jung, Carl Gustav. "Picasso." In *The Spirit in Man, Art, and Literature*, translated by R. F. C. Hull. Princeton: Princeton University Press, 1971.
Jung, Carl Gustav. *The Archetypes and the Collective Unconscious*. Translated by R. F. C. Hull. Bollingen Series. Princeton: Princeton University Press, 1990.
Kantor, Sybil Gordon. *Alfred H. Barr Jr. and the Intellectual Origins of the Museum of Modern Art*. Cambridge, MA: MIT Press, 2002.
Kantor-Kazovsky, Lola. *Piranesi as Interpreter of Roman Architecture and the Origins of His Intellectual World*. Florence: Leo S. Olschki, 2006.
Keller, Luzius. *Piranèse et les romantiques français: le mythe des escaliers en spirale*. Paris: Librairie José Corti, 1966.
Kirk, Terry. "Piranesi's Poetic Licence: His Influence on Modern Italian Architecture." In *The Serpent and the Stylus: Essays on G. B. Piranesi*, edited by Mario Bevilacqua, Heather Hyde Minor, and Fabio Barry, 239–274. Ann Arbor: University of Michigan Press, 2006.
Koolhaas, Rem. "Bigness, or the Problem of Large." In *S, M, L, XL*, 494–517. New York: Monacelli Press, 1995.
Koolhaas, Rem. "Exodus." In *S, M, L, XL*, 2–19. New York: Monacelli Press, 1995.
Koolhaas, Rem. "Fieldtrip, (A)A Memoir." In *S, M, L, XL*, 570–578. New York: Monacelli Press, 1995.
Koolhaas, Rem. "The Generic City." In *S, M, L, XL*, 1238–1264. New York: Monacelli Press, 1995.
Koolhaas, Rem. "What Ever Happened to Urbanism." In *S, M, L, XL*, 958–71. New York: Monacelli Press, 1995.
Koolhaas, Rem, and OMA. "Hyperbuilding." *El Croquis*, no. 131–132 (2006): 60–69.
Koolhaas, Rem, and OMA. "Two Libraries for Jussieu." *El Croquis*, no. 79 (1996): 124–141.
Koolhaas, Rem, and Robert Somol. "Being O.M.U.'s Ghostwriter: Rem Koolhaas in

Conversation with Robert Somol." In *Reckoning with Colin Rowe: Ten Architects Take Position*, edited by Emmanuel Petit, 86–97. New York: Routledge, Taylor & Francis Group, 2015.

Koolhaas, Rem, Simon Brown, and John Link. "The Hyperbuilding." In *Content*, 420–421. Köln: Taschen, 2004.

Krawinkel, Günter, Wolfgang-M. Pax, and Katrin Sello. *Inventionen: Piranesi und Architekturphantasien in der Gegenwart*. Hannover: Kunstverein Hannover and Deutscher Werkbund Niedersachsen und Bremen, 1982.

Kubler, George. *The Shape of Time: Remarks on the History of Things*. New Haven, CT: Yale University Press, 1962.

Kupfer, Alexander. *Piranesis "Carceri": Enge und Unendlichkeit in den Gefängnissen der Phantasie*. Stuttgart: Belser Verlag, 1992.

Landgraf, Svante. "Drömmar av sten: Mot en posthumanistisk estetik i Sam J. Lundwalls Fängelsestaden." *Tidskrift för litteraturvetenskap* 49, no. 1 (2019): 41–50.

Lawrence, Amanda Reeser. *James Stirling: Revisionary Modernist*. New Haven, CT: Yale University Press, 2012.

Le Corbusier. *Towards a New Architecture*. Translated by Frederick Etchells. Mansfield Centre, CT: Martino Publishing, 2014.

Leach, Andrew. *Manfredo Tafuri: Choosing History*. Ghent: A & S Books, 2007.

Legrand, Jacques Guillaume. "Notice historique sur la vie et les ouvrages de J. B. Piranesi architecte, peintre et graveur. Manuscript (Paris, Bibliothèque Nationale Ms. Nouv. Acq. Fr. 5968) Transcribed and published in Erouart, Gilbert, and Monique Mosser, 'A propos de la "Notice historique sur la vie et les ouvrages de J.-B. Piranesi": Origine et fortune d'une biographie.'" In *Piranèse et les Français*, edited by Georges Brunel, 213–252. Rome: Edizioni dell'Elefante, 1978.

Lending, Mari. "Historisk Røntgen: Arkitekturfremstillinger i W. G. Sebalds 'Austerlitz.'" *Vinduet*, no. 1 (2010): 92–101.

Lerup, Lars. *The Continuous City: Fourteen Essays on Architecture and Urbanization*. Zurich: Park Books, 2017.

Lowry, Glenn D. "Giacometti." In *MOMA Highlights*, 153. New York: Museum of Modern Art, 2004.

Lucan, Jacques. *Composition, Non-Composition: Architecture and Theory in the Nineteenth and Twentieth Centuries*. Lausanne: EPFL Press, 2012.

Lundwall, Sam J. *Fängelsestaden: en roman*. Stockholm: Norstedt, 1978.

Mariani, Ginevra, and Giovanna Scaloni. "Il Campo Marzio dell'Antica Roma." In *Giambattista Piranesi: matrici incise 1761–1765*, edited by Ginevra Mariani, 243–331. Rome: Editalia/Istituto Centrale per la Grafica, 2017.

Marletta, Angelo. *Il Campo Marzio dell'antica Roma: Giovanni Battista Piranesi e l'arte del contemperare*. Rome: Ermes, 2016.

Mayor, A. Hyatt. *Giovanni Battista Piranesi*. New York: H. Bittner and Company, 1952.

McCarter, Robert. *Steven Holl*. London: Phaidon Press, 2015.

Michajlovskij, Semën, and Nikolaj Molok. "Piranesi in URSS." In *Piranesi Prima e Dopo. Italia-Russia XVIII-XXI Secolo*, edited by Federica Rossi, 127–138. Moscow: Antiga Edizioni, 2016.

Miller, J. Hillis. *The Disappearance of God: Five Nineteenth-Century Writers*. Urbana and Chicago: University of Illinois Press, 2000.

Minor, Heather Hyde. *Piranesi's Lost Words*. University Park: Pennsylvania State University Press, 2015.

Minor, Heather Hyde, and Carolyn Yerkes. *Piranesi Unbound*. Princeton: Princeton University Press, 2020.

Moholy-Nagy, László. *Painting, Photography, Film*. London: Lund Humphries, 1969.

Moholy-Nagy, László. *The New Vision: From Material to Architecture*. Translated by D. M. Hoffmann. New York: Brewer, Warren & Putnam, 1930.

Moos, Stanislaus von, and Arthur Rüegg. *Le Corbusier Before Le Corbusier: Applied Arts, Architecture, Interiors, Painting, and Photography, 1907–1922*. New Haven, CT: Yale University Press, 2002.

Naginski, Erika. "Romanticism's Piranesi." In *The Built Surface: Architecture and the Pictorial Arts from Antiquity to the Enlightenment*, edited by Christy Anderson and Karen Koehler, 1:237–259. Aldershot: Ashgate, 2002.

Neumann, Dietrich. *Film Architecture: Set Designs from Metropolis to Blade Runner*. Munich: Prestel, 1999.

Newhall, Beaumont. *The History of Photography from 1839 to the Present*. New York: Museum of Modern Art, 1982.
Nodier, Charles. "Piranèse: contes psychologiques: à propos de la monomanie réflective." In *Oeuvres complètes*, XI:167–204. Geneva: Slatkine Reprints, 1998.
Ockman, Joan. "Venice and New York." *Casabella: International Architectural Review*, no. 619–620 (1995): 57–71.
OMA. CCTV *New Site Construction & Development Program. Extended Preliminary Design.* EPD *Landscape Report*. OMA, 2004.
Pavanello, Giuseppe, Michele De Lucchi, and Adam Lowe. *Le arti di Piranesi: architetto, incisore, antiquario, vedutista, designer*. Venice: Marsilio, 2010.
Payne, Alina A. "Rudolf Wittkower and Architectural Principles in the Age of Modernism." *Journal of the Society of Architectural Historians* 53 (1994): 322–342.
Pennell, Joseph. *Etchers and Etching*. New York: Macmillan, 1919.
Pérez-Gómez, Alberto, and Louise Pelletier. *Architectural Representation and the Perspective Hinge*. Cambridge, MA: MIT Press, 1997.
Perry, Curtis. "Piranesi's Prison: Thomas De Quincey and the Failure of Autobiography." *Studies in English Literature, 1500-1900* 33, no. 4 (1993): 809–824.
Pevsner, Nikolaus. *A History of Building Types*. Princeton: Princeton University Press, 1976.
Pimlott, Mark. *Without and Within: Essays on the Territory and the Interior*. Rotterdam: Episode Publishers, 2007.
Pinto, John A. *City of the Soul: Rome and the Romantics*. Hanover: University Press of New England, 2016.
Pinto, John A. *Speaking Ruins: Piranesi, Architects, and Antiquity in Eighteenth-Century Rome*. Ann Arbor, MI: University of Michigan Press, 2012.
Piranesi, Giovanni Battista. "Opinions on Architecture: A Dialogue." In *Observations on the Letter of Monsieur Mariette*, translated by Caroline Beamish and David Britt, 102–114. Los Angeles: Getty Research Institite, 2002.
Polo, Alejandro Zaera, and Rem Koolhaas. "Finding Freedom: Conversations with Rem Koolhaas." *El Croquis*, no. 53 (1992): 6–31.
Poulet, Georges. *Trois essais de mythologie romantiques*. Paris: Librairie José Corti, 1966.
Proudfit, Charles L. "Thomas De Quincey and Sigmund Freud: Sons, Fathers, Dreamers—Precursors of Psychoanalytical Developmental Psychology." In *Thomas De Quincey: Bicentenary Studies*, edited by Robert Lance Snyder, 88–108. Norman: University of Oklahoma Press, 1985.
Proust, Marcel. *Remembrance of Things Past*. Translated by C. K. Scott Moncrieff. Vol. 1. New York: Henry Holt and Company, 1922.
Proust, Marcel. *Sur la lecture [Translator's Preface to John Ruskin's Sesame and Lilies]*. Vol. 401. Québec: La Bibliothèque électronique du Québec, n.d.
Reed, Marcia. "Reading Piranesi: The Architecture of the Book." In *The Art of Exaggeration: Piranesi's Perspectives on Rome*, edited by Eunice D. Howe, 22–31. Los Angeles: Fisher Gallery, University of Southern California, 1995.
Robison, Andrew. *Piranesi: Early Architectural Fantasies: A Catalogue Raisonné of the Etchings*. Chicago: University of Chicago Press, 1986.
Romera Rozas, Ricardo. *L'univers humoristique de Jorge Luis Borges et Adolfo Bioy Casares*. Paris: L'Harmattan, 1995.
Ropars-Wuilleumier, Marie-Claire. "The Function of Metaphor in Eisenstein's 'October.'" Translated by Mary Christopher Baseheart. *Film Criticism* 2, no. 2/3 (1978): 10–34.
Rosand, David. *Drawing Acts: Studies in Graphic Expression and Representation*. New York: Cambridge University Press, 2002.
Rosenfeld, Myra Nan. "Picturesque to Sublime: Piranesi's Stylistic and Technical Development from 1740 to 1761." In *The Serpent and the Stylus: Essays on G. B. Piranesi*, edited by Mario Bevilacqua, Heather Hyde Minor, and Fabio Barry, 55–91. Ann Arbor, MI: University of Michigan Press, 2006.
Rosenthal, Norman. "Giovanni Battista Piranesi and the Recurring Prisons of Art." In *Carceri d'invenzione di G. Battista Piranesi*, 10–19. Madrid: Julio Soto impresores/Factum Arte, 2010.
Rossi, Aldo. *The Architecture of the City*. Cambridge, MA: MIT Press, 1982.
Sadler, Simon. *The Situationist City*. Cambridge, MA: MIT Press, 1998.
Salmon, André. "La jeune peinture française (1912)." In *André Salmon on French modern art*,

translated by Beth S. Gersh-Nešić, 27–91. New York: Cambridge University Press, 2005.
Samuel, Arthur. *Piranesi*. London: B. T. Batsford, 1910.
Sartogo, Piero, Costantino Dardi, Antoine Grumbach, James Stirling, Paolo Portoghesi, Romaldo Giurgola, Robert Venturi, et al. *Roma Interrotta: Twelve Interventions on the Nolli's Plan of Rome*. Johan & Levi Editore, 2014.
Scaloni, Giovanna. "Carceri." In *Giambattista Piranesi: matrici incise 1743-1753*, edited by Ginevra Mariani, 52–69. Rome: Mazzotta/ Istituto Nazionale per la Grafica, 2010.
Scott, Jonathan. *Piranesi*. London: Academy Editions, 1975.
Scully, Vincent. "Louis I. Kahn and the Ruins of Rome." In *Modern Architecture and Other Essays*. Princeton: Princeton University Press, 2003.
Scully, Vincent. *Modern Architecture: The Architecture of Democracy*. New York: George Braziller, 1961.
Scully, Vincent. "Modern Architecture: Towards a Redefinition of Style." *Perspecta* 4 (1957): 4–11.
Scully, Vincent. *Louis I. Kahn*. New York: George Braziller, 1962.
Sebald, W. G. *Austerlitz*. Translated by Anthea Bell, 2002.
Seghers, Pierre. *Piranesi*. Translated by Ian Higgins. London: Forest Books, 1993.
Sekler, Patricia May. "Notes on Old and Modern Drawings: Giovanni Battista Piranesi's Carceri Etchings and Related Drawings." *Art Quarterly* 25 (1962): 331–363.
Shaw, George Bernard. "Bernard Shaw's Appreciation of Coburn." *Camera Work*, no. 15 (1906): 313–315.
Small, Irene. "Piranesi's Shape of Time." *Image [&] Narrative*, no. 18 (2007). www.image-andnarrative.be/inarchive/thinking_pictures/small.htm.
Soffici, Ardengo. *Cubismo e oltre*. Florence: Libreria della Voce, 1913.
Stapleton, Laurence. *The Elected Circle: Studies in the Art of Prose*. Princeton: Princeton University Press, 1973.
Steinberg, Leo. *Leonardo's Incessant Last Supper*. New York: Zone Books, 2001.
Stemshorn, Max. "Zur Piranesi-Rezeption in der Architekturavantgarde." In *Vision Piranesi*, edited by Max Stemshorn and Susanne Grötz, 85–104. Stadthaus Ulm/Hemsbach: Druckhaus Beltz, 2002.
Stewart, Susan. *Crimes of Writing: Problems in the Containment of Representation*. Durham: Duke University Press Books, 1994.
Stieglitz, Alfred. *Camera Work: The Complete Illustrations 1903–1917*. Cologne: Taschen, 1997.
Stieglitz, Alfred, Sarah Greenough, and Juan Hamilton. *Alfred Stieglitz: Photographs and Writings*. Washington, DC: National Gallery of Art, 1983.
Stierli, Martino. *Montage and the Metropolis: Architecture, Modernity, and the Representation of Space*. New Haven, CT: Yale University Press, 2018.
Sturgis, Russell. *The Etchings of Piranesi*. New York: Frederick Keppel & Co., 1900.
Szacka, Léa-Catherine. "Città Analoga: Aldo Rossi's Visual Theory on Display." In *Terms of Appropriation: Modern Architecture and Global Exchange*, edited by Amanda Reeser Lawrence and Ana Miljački, 263–277. London: Routledge, 2017.
Szacka, Léa-Catherine. "Debates on Display at the 1976 Venice Biennale." In *Place and Displacement: Exhibiting Architecture*, edited by Thordis Arrhenius, Mari Lending, Wallis Miller, and Jérémie Michael McGowan, 97–112. Zurich: Lars Müller Publishers, 2014.
Szacka, Léa-Catherine. *Exhibiting the Postmodern*. Venice: Marsilio, 2016.
Tafuri, Manfredo. *Architecture and Utopia: Design and Capitalist Development*. Cambridge, MA: MIT Press, 1976.
Tafuri, Manfredo. "L'architettura come 'utopia negativa.'" *Angelus Novus*, no. 20 (January 1971): 89–127.
Tafuri, Manfredo. "Per una critica dell'ideologia architettonica." *Contropiano* 1 (1969): 31–79.
Tafuri, Manfredo. "The Historicity of the Avant-Garde: Piranesi and Eisenstein." In *The Sphere and the Labyrinth: Avant-Gardes and Architecture from Piranesi to the 1970s*, 55–64. Cambridge, MA: MIT Press, 1987.
Tafuri, Manfredo. "'The Wicked Architect': G. B. Piranesi, Heterotopia, and the Voyage." In *The Sphere and the Labyrinth: Avant-Gardes and Architecture from Piranesi to the 1970s*, 20–64. Cambridge, MA: MIT Press, 1987.

Tafuri, Manfredo. *Theories and History of Architecture*. London: Granada, 1980.
Tafuri, Manfredo. "Toward a Critique of Architectural Ideology." In *Architecture Theory since 1968*, edited by K. Michael Hays, translated by Stephen Sartarelli, 2–35. Cambridge, MA: MIT Press, 1998.
Thompson, Christopher Warwick. *Victor Hugo and the Graphic Arts (1820–1833)*. Geneva: Librairie Droz, 1970.
Tournikiotis, Panayotis. *The Historiography of Modern Architecture*. Cambridge, MA: MIT Press, 1999.
Tschudi, Victor Plahte. "Goethe in the Hall and His Journeys in Printed Rome." *Architectural Histories* 3, no. 1 (2015): Art. 21. www.doi.org/10.5334/ah.cx.
Tschudi, Victor Plahte. "Recollecting Prints: Remembrance and Reproduction in Goethe's Italian Journey." In *From Site to Sight: The Transformation of Place in Art and Literature*, edited by Victor Plahte Tschudi and Turid Karlsen Seim, 139–163. Rome: Scienze e Lettere, 2013.
Umland, Anne, Adrian Sudhalter, Scott Gerson, and Museum of Modern Art. *Dada in the Collection of the Museum of Modern Art*. New York: Museum of Modern Art, 2008.
Venturi, Robert. *Complexity and Contradiction in Architecture*. New York: Museum of Modern Art, 1966.
Venturi, Robert, Bruce Adams, and Denise Scott Brown. "Mass Communication on the People Freeway: Or Piranesi Is Too Easy." *Perspecta* 12 (1969): 49–56.
Very, Françoise, and Manfredo Tafuri. "The Culture Markets." *Casabella: International Architectural Review*, no. 619–620 (1995): 36–45.
Vidler, Anthony. *The Architectural Uncanny: Essays in the Modern Unhomely*. Cambridge, MA: MIT Press, 1992.
Vogt-Göknil, Ulya. *Giovanni Battista Piranesi: Carceri*. Zürich: Origo Verlag, 1958.
Wallis de Vries, Gijs. *Archescape: On the Tracks of Piranesi*. Amsterdam: Thousand & One Publishers, 2014.
Weaver, Thomas. "Civitas Interruptus." In *Postmodernism: Style and Subversion, 1970–1990*, 126–131. London: Victoria and Albert Museum, 2011.
Wendort, Richard. "Piranesi's Double Ruin." *Eighteenth-Century Studies* 34, no. 2 (2001): 161–180.
Wilde, Oscar. *Intentions*. London: Methuen, 1908.
Wilton-Ely, John. *Giovanni Battista Piranesi: The Complete Etchings*. Vol. 1 and 2. San Francisco: Wofsy, 1994.
Wilton-Ely, John. *Piranesi as Architect and Designer*. New Haven, CT: Yale University Press, 1993.
Wilton-Ely, John. *The Mind and Art of Giovanni Battista Piranesi*. London: Thames and Hudson, 1978.
Wilton-Ely, John. "Utopia or Megalopolis? The 'Ichnographia' of Piranesi's 'Campus Martius' Reconsidered." In *Piranesi tra Venezia e l'Europa*, edited by Alessandro Bettagno, 293–304. Florence: Leo S. Olschki, 1983.
Winckelmann, Johann Joachim. *History of the Art of Antiquity*. Translated by Harry Francis Mallgrave. Los Angeles: Getty Research Institite, 2006.
Wittkower, Rudolf. "Piranesi's 'Parere su l'architettura.'" *Journal of the Warburg Institute* 2, no. 2 (October 1938): 147–158.
Wölfflin, Heinrich. *Renaissance and Baroque*. London: Collins, 1984.
Woodworth, W. J. "Piranesi, the Rembrandt of Architecture." *Brush and Pencil* 10, no. 5 (1902): 276–284.
Wright, Willard Huntington. *Modern Painting: Its Tendency and Meaning*. New York: John Lane Company, 1915.
Wurman, Richard Saul, ed. *What Will Be Has Always Been: The Words of Louis I. Kahn*. New York: Access Press and Rizzoli, 1986.
Yourcenar, Marguerite. "The Dark Brain of Piranesi." In *The Dark Brain of Piranesi and Other Essays*, translated by Richard Howard (in collaboration with the author), 88–128. Henley-on-Thames: Aidan Ellis, 1985.
Zayas, Marius de. "Photography and Artistic-Photography." *Camera Work*, no. 42/43 (1913): 709–710.

Copyright holders and sources are listed below. Every effort has been made to trace copyright holders and to obtain permission for the use of copyright material.

Metropolitan Museum of Art, New York. Harris Brisbane Dick Fund, 1937 *pp. 24, 94, 120, 122, 129, 152, 164–165, 178–179*
Minneapolis Institute of Art *pp. 26, 33, 83, 91, 95, 153 (foldout)*
Yale University Art Gallery *pp. 27, 43,*
Statens Museum for Kunst, Photo/Jakob Skou-Hansen. *pp. 39, 40, 58–60, 81, 99, 278–279*
Freud Museum London *p. 42*
© Getty Images *pp. 44–45*
Bollingen Foundation Collection. Manuscript Division, Library of Congress. © Getty Images *p. 47*
Princeton University Press, republished with permission, conveyed through Copyright Clearance Center, Inc. © 2021 *pp. 50–51*
Courtesy of the Jorge Luis Borges International Foundation *p. 56*
Metropolitan Museum of Art, New York. Rogers Fund *pp. 76–77*
Metropolitan Museum of Art, New York. Alfred Stieglitz Collection, 1949. © 2019 Metropolitan Museum of Art/Art Resource/ Scala, Florence *pp. 80, 85*
Philadelphia Museum of Art. Gift of the estate of Paul Strand. © 2019 Philadelphia Museum of Art/Art Resource/Scala, Florence *pp. 86–87*
© 2019 Museum of Modern Art, New York/ Scala, Florence. Gift of the artist *p. 82*; Gift of Lincoln Kirstein *p. 88;* Abby Aldrich Rockefeller Fund *p. 110;* Gift of Peter H. Deitsch *p. 123*; Lillie P. Bliss Collection *p. 130*; Acquired through the Lillie P. Bliss Bequest *p. 131*; Gift of Patricia Phelps de Cisneros, Takeo Ohbayashi Purchase Fund, and Susan de Menil Purchase Fund *pp. 218–219*
© 2019 Museum of Modern Art Library, New York/Scala, Florence *pp. 90, 105, 109, 114, 167*
Henie Onstad Collection, Henie Onstad Kunstsenter, Norway. Photographer Øystein Thorvaldsen *p. 102*
© 2019 Museum of Modern Art Archives, New York/Scala, Florence *pp. 107, 116, 117, 119, 126–127, 128, 133*
Detroit Institute of Arts *p. 111*
© Lucasfilm Ltd. LLC *p. 138*
Biblioteca Digital Luso-Brasileira *p. 139*
Courtesy of BFI National Archive *p. 140*
Harvard Art Museums *p. 140*
© 1937 Disney *p. 141*
Courtesy of Factum Arte and Grégoire Dupond *p. 144*
Alma Ata © 2019 Album/Scala, Florence *p. 149*
© Mosfilm Cinema Concern, 1927 *p. 150*
© 2019 Photo Art Resource/Scala, Florence/ John Bigelow Taylor *p. 154–155*
Photograph by Victor Plahte Tschudi *p. 162*
Le Corbusier © FLC/BONO, Oslo, 2021 *pp. 169, 170–171*
© NC Department of Agriculture *p. 181*
© 2006 Ron Sterling *p. 182*
Photograph by Nicholas Coates, 2014 *p. 184*
National Gallery of Art, Washington DC Gift of Frank Anderson Trapp *p. 185*
Harvard University Houghton Library *pp. 188, 288*
University of Pennsylvania, Marshall D. Meyers Collection, Architectural Archive *p. 193*
University of Pennsylvania and Pennsylvania Historical and Museum Commission, Louis I. Kahn Collection *p. 194*
© Eredi Aldo Rossi, courtesy of Fondazione Aldo Rossi *p. 195*
MAXXI Collezione Architettura,
inv. no. 061667 *p. 197 (foldout)*
inv. no. 20042 *p. 198*
inv. no. 061731 *p. 199*
New York Public Library Digital Collection *p. 205*
Cooper Hewitt Collection. The John Jay Ide Collection; 1977–52–77 *p. 207*
Courtesy of Eisenman Architects *p. 210*
Courtesy of Steven Holl Architects *pp. 214–215*
© OMA *pp. 220, 221–223 (foldouts), 226, 232–233, 262–263*
Research project on Piranesi's *Campo Marzio* developed for the exhibition *The Piranesi Variations* for the 2012 Architecture Venice Biennale. Project team: Pier Vittorio Aureli and Martino Tattara with Julia Tournaire, Tijn van de Vijdeven, Sara Usai *p. 229*
National Museum, Stockholm, inv. no. NMH 228/1963. Photograph: Erik Cornelius/ Nationalmuseum, Stockholm *pp. 236–238*

Page numbers in italic indicate illustrations.

overleaf Giovanni Battista Piranesi, *View of the Remains of the Forum of Nerva*, from *Vedute di Roma*, 1770.

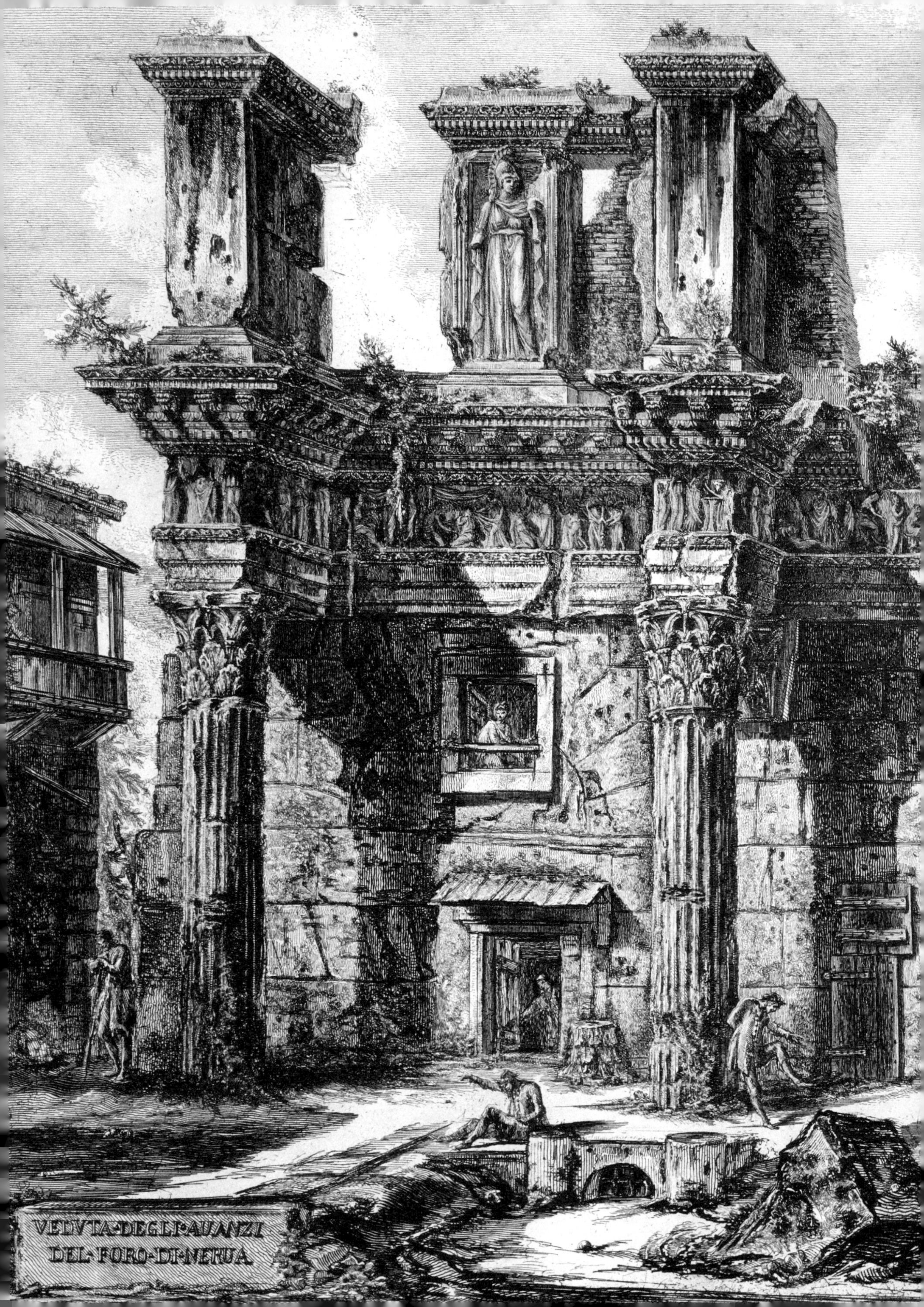
VEDVTA·DEGLI·AVANZI
DEL·FORO·DI·NERVA

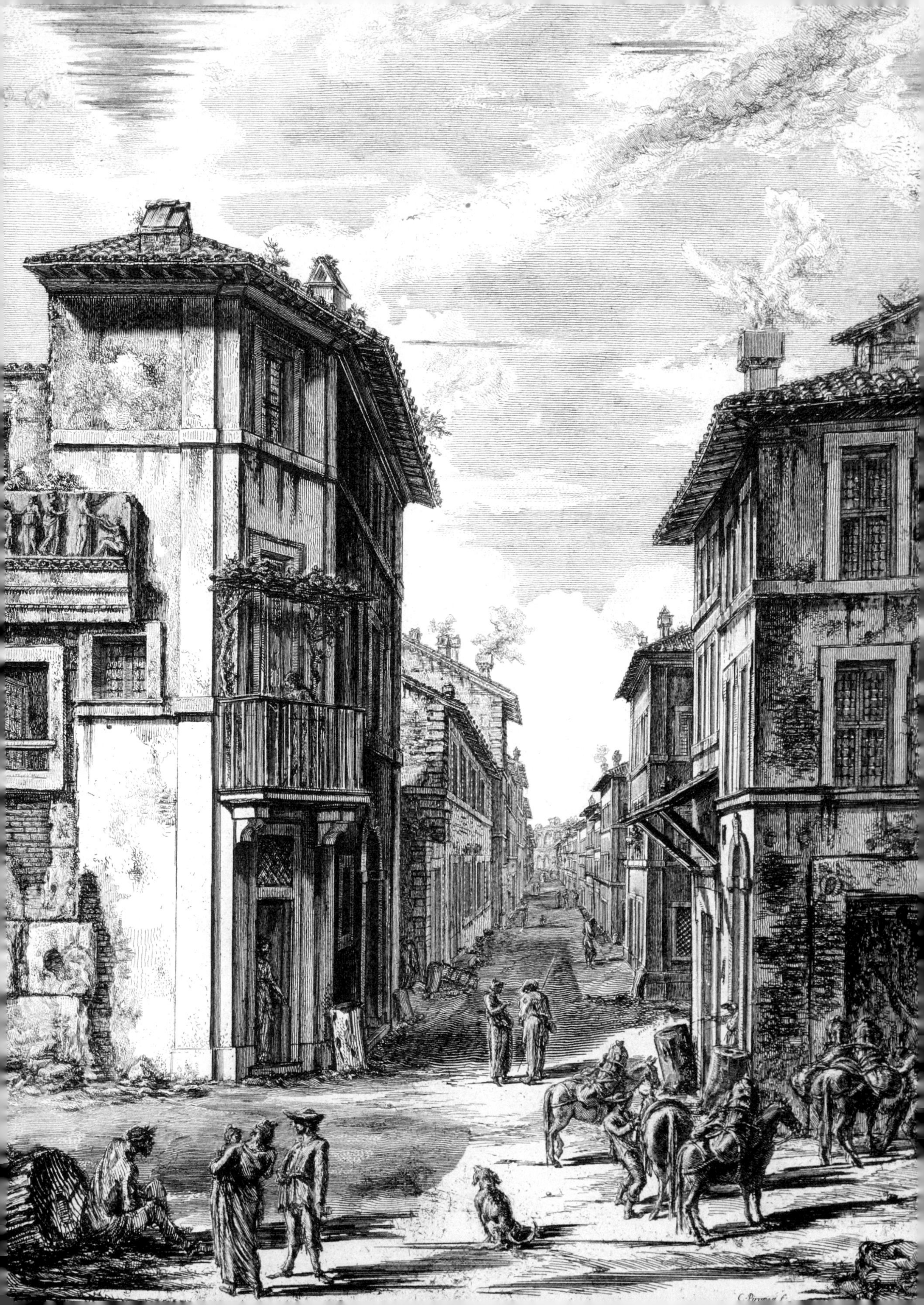
C. Piranesi f.

One day in Rome in 1996 I spent the entire inheritance from my grandfather on three prints by Giovanni Battista Piranesi. Since that day, the ambition to justify that purchase with a book has never left me. However, the idea, and indeed confidence, to couple Piranesi and the modern age matured twenty years later, while teaching at the Oslo School of Architecture and Design. In the fall of 2017, I conducted a master's course on Piranesi and the modern age that outlined many of the themes developed in this book. I am greatly indebted to the students on this course for the insights they shared and the discoveries they made. I am particularly grateful to Ola Granli, who ploughed the canon of modern literature, sorting out and cataloguing the lion's share of a vast amount of references, and to Nicholas Coates; without Nick's skills and steadfast manner, I doubt whether this book would have had any illustrations at all. I also cannot thank enough the staff at the AHO library. No book or article was too remote or too obscure for them to hunt down. I thank them too for their patience in dealing with an accumulation of overdue loans that would have earned me a prison sentence anywhere else.

This project has led to a collaboration with the National Museum of Norway and I am grateful to Karin Hindsbo and Stina Högkvist, who saw the potential for an exhibition in the material presented in this book, and to Wenche Volle and Rikke Lundgreen, for realizing with me the exhibition *Piranesi and the Modern* in 2022. I am also grateful for discussions with Maarten Delbeke, Caroline van Eck, Peter Eisenman, Adrian Forty, Steven Holl, Rem Koolhaas, and Bernard Tschumi. The contributions of John Pinto, Heather Hyde Minor, Angelo Marletta, Talitha van Dijk, Eivind Buene, Erik Langdalen, and Caroline Ugelstad have also been valuable. A heartfelt thanks to Karin Gundersen, Camilla Plahte, and Virginia Krasniansky, who helped me find my way in texts in French and Spanish.

I think with gratitude of my editor Thomas Weaver, who always believed in the book and enthusiastically and efficiently saw it through production. My gratitude also goes to three anonymous reviewers, for their valuable comments, and to my friends and colleagues Mari Hvattum and Mari Lending, who read parts of the manuscript and who never fail to inspire. The text was improved immensely by the precise, thoughtful interventions of Pamela Johnston. A warm thanks to Mathias Clottu for creating a beautiful book from a mere draft, lifting its design to a level I never could have imagined.

I am indebted to the Oslo School of Architecture and Design for generously supporting the publication of this book. Financial support was also given by the HERA-funded project PriArc (*Printing the Past. Architecture, Print Culture, and Uses of the Past in Modern Europe*).

Piranesi and the Modern Age
Victor Plahte Tschudi

The MIT Press would like to thank the anonymous peer reviewers who provided comments on drafts of this book. The generous work of academic experts is essential for establishing the authority and quality of our publications. We acknowledge with gratitude the contributions of these otherwise uncredited readers.

Edited by Thomas Weaver
Designed by Studio Mathias Clottu

Printed and bound in Germany

Library of Congress Cataloging-in-Publication Data is available.
ISBN 978-0-262-04717-3

10 9 8 7 6 5 4 3 2 1

Tab V